PageMaker Menus

To display a menu, place the mouse pointer on the menu name and press the left mouse button. To execute a command from the displayed menu, click on the command name.

File

- New... ^N
- Open... ^O
- Close

- Save ^S
- Save as...
- Revert
- Export...

- Place... ^D

- Links... Sh^D
- Book...
- Preferences...

- Page setup...
- Print... ^P

- Exit ^Q

Edit

- Undo ^Z

- Cut ^X
- Copy ^C
- Paste ^V
- Clear Del
- Multiple paste...
- Select all ^A

- Paste link
- Paste special...
- Insert object...

- Edit story ^E
- Edit original

Utilities

- Aldus Additions ▶

- Find... ^8
- Find next Sh^9
- Change... ^9
- Spelling... ^L

- Index entry... ^;
- Show index...
- Create index...
- Create TOC...

Layout

- View ▶

- Guides and rulers ▶
- Column guides...

- Go to page... ^G
- Insert pages...
- Remove pages...

- ✓Display master items
- Copy master guides

- Autoflow

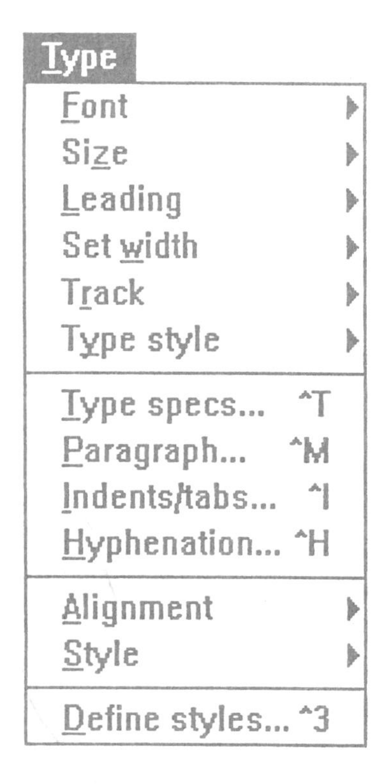

An Introduction to Desktop Publishing Using PageMaker®

version 5 for Windows®

Bruce Presley
William Freitas

First Edition published 1994

First Edition, Windows version

ISBN 1-879233-17-7 (softcover)
ISBN 1-879233-18-5 (hardcover)

Printed in the United States of America

All orders including educational, Canadian, foreign, FPO, and APO addresses may be placed by contacting:

Lawrenceville Press, Inc.
P.O. Box 704
Pennington, NJ 08534-0704
(609) 737-1148
FAX: (609) 737-8564

This text is available in both hardcover and softcover editions.

16 15 14 13 12 11 10 9 8 7 6 5 4 3 2 1

Table of Contents

Chapter One: An Introduction To Publishing & Computers

Chapter Two: Introducing PageMaker

Chapter Three: **Working with Text & Graphics**

Chapter Four: The Story Editor & Writing for DTP

Chapter Five: Elements of Good Design

Chapter Six: Brochures & Newsletters

Chapter Seven: Advertisements, Awards, & Invitations

T

Chapter Eight: Long Publications

Chapter Nine: Color & Graphics

T

Chapter Ten: *Advanced Topics & Tables*

Chapter Eleven: *Preparing Publications for Commercial Printing*

T

Appendix A: *The Windows Environment*

Appendix B: *PostScript Character Set & Font Samples*

T

Preface

We believe the best way to introduce students to desktop publishing is with an introductory course that gives them considerable "hands-on" computer experience using PageMaker. The objectives of such a course are not only to teach the PageMaker software, but more importantly to teach the basics of good design and page layout. *An Introduction to Desktop Publishing Using PageMaker* accomplishes both objectives by integrating the discussion of design concepts with the descriptions of how to use PageMaker. The emphasis of this text is on the concepts of desktop publishing and problem solving so that students learn how the techniques of good design and layout can be applied to a wide range of problems. Written to be used either in a one or two term course, the text assumes no previous computer experience.

Designs and Features

FORMAT

Each chapter contains numerous examples and diagrams printed in a two color format to help students visualize new concepts. Important command are listed on the first page of each chapter and PageMaker menus are displayed in the margins for easy reference.

OBJECTIVES

An outline of the significant topics that should be emphasized is presented at the beginning of each chapter.

HISTORY OF PUBLISHING AND COMPUTING

Before learning to use PageMaker, Chapter One introduces students to the histories of publishing and computing as well as the vocabulary needed to understand the concepts presented in later chapters.

CONCEPTS OF APPLICATION

Each new desktop publishing concept begins with an introductory section that describes the concept and its application. In this way, students are taught the purpose of the application as well as design and layout considerations without being overly concerned with software specifics. If the student then goes on to use another desktop publishing package, he or she will fully understand the general concepts behind each application.

HANDS-ON PRACTICE

As each new concept is presented, it is first discussed, and then followed by a hands-on Practice which requires the student to test newly learned skills on the computer. Many of the Practices ask students to use files that are included on the Master Diskette. Practice sections also serve as excellent reference guides to review PageMaker commands.

P

CHAPTER SUMMARY At the end of each chapter is a synopsis that briefly discusses the concepts covered in the chapter.

VOCABULARY A vocabulary section which defines the new terms used is given at the end of each chapter.

REVIEW PROBLEMS Numerous Review problems are presented that are keyed to each section of the chapter, providing immediate reinforcement of new concepts. Answers to all Review problems are included in the *Teacher's Resource Package* described below.

EXERCISES Each of the desktop publishing chapters includes a set of exercises of varying difficulty, making them appropriate for students with a wide range of abilities. Answers to all exercises are included in the *Teacher's Resource Package* described below.

COMMERCIAL PRODUCTION The final chapter presents the techniques required to produce commercially printed publications, including creating files for imagesetter output and working with service bureaus.

APPENDICES Summaries of PageMaker and Windows commands, the Windows character set, and examples of several PostScript typefaces are presented in appendices at the end of the text for easy reference.

Teacher's Resource Package

When used with this text, the Lawrenceville Press Teacher's Resource Package provides all the additional material required to offer students an excellent introductory desktop publishing course. These materials, along with the text, place a strong emphasis on developing student design and problem-solving skills. The Package divides each of the chapters in the text into a series of lessons which contain the following features:

- **OBJECTIVES** – A brief listing of the important skills and topics for that lesson is given.
- **ASSIGNMENTS** - Reading and problem assignments are suggested for each lesson.
- **DISCUSSION TOPICS** - Additional material is provided which supplements the text and can be used in leading classroom discussions. Often this includes explanations of more advanced commands or concepts not covered in the text.
- **TRANSPARENCY MASTERS** - Many lessons contain transparency masters which often present diagrams of the different PageMaker screens.

P

- **WORKSHEETS** - Included in each lesson is a worksheet containing problems which are meant to be completed on the computer. These problems supplement those in the text, giving students additional reinforcement of the concepts they have just learned. Many of the worksheets make use of the data files included on the Master Diskette described below.

- **QUIZ** - Each lesson contains a short quiz which tests recently learned skills.

- **MASTER DISKETTES** - Master Diskettes that contain files to be used in conjunction with text problems and worksheets are included in the Teacher's Resource Package. These files are especially helpful in allowing students to work with large amounts of data without first having to enter it into the computer. Student diskettes can be easily made by following the included directions. 10-packs of prepared student diskettes are also available.

In addition to the material in the lessons, the following features are found at the end of each chapter:

- **TESTS** - Two sets of comprehensive end of chapter tests are provided as well as mid-term and final examinations. A full set of answers and a grading key are also included. The tests are included in PageMaker files on the Master Diskettes so that you may edit them.

- **ANSWERS** - Complete answers are provided for the Review and Exercise problems presented in the text. Where appropriate, answer files have been included on the Master Diskettes.

As an added feature, the above material is contained in a 3-ring binder. This not only enables pages to be removed for easy duplication but also for the insertion of additional teacher notes.

Acknowledgments

The authors would like to thank the following people whose talents contributed to the production of this text.

Most of the design discussions in this text have been written by Elaine Malfas, the newest member of our development staff. The information on Windows as well as the technical proofreading has been done by Beth Brown. To both of our colleagues we are indebted.

Rachel Stern designed the imaginative cover and created the page format. We very much appreciate her efforts and willingness to work under tight deadlines.

Thanks are due Courier Printing, Inc., especially Bob Valentine and Rick Dunn who supervised the printing of this text.

The success of this and many of our other texts is due to the efforts of Heidi Crane, Vice President of Marketing at Lawrenceville Press. She has developed the promotional material which has been so well received by instructors around the world, and coordinated the comprehensive customer survey which led to many of the refinements in this edition. Michael Porter and Joseph Dupree are responsible for the efficient service Lawrenceville Press offers in fulfilling orders.

For their help with the PageMaker software we wish to thank Freda Cook and Ellen Wixted at the Aldus Corporation. For her quick assistance with a myriad of technical questions we are indebted to Gail Brenchley at Aldus technical support.

A note of appreciation is due our colleague Patricia Whelan who has helped test this text in her classes, and has offered valuable suggestions on ways in which it could be improved.

Finally, we would like to thank our students, for whom and with whom this text was written. Their candid evaluation of each lesson and their refusal to accept anything less than perfect clarity in explanation have been the driving forces behind the creation of *An Introduction to Desktop Publishing Using PageMaker*.

About the Authors

Bruce W. Presley, a graduate of Yale University, taught computer science and physics at The Lawrenceville School in Lawrenceville, New Jersey for twenty-four years where he served as the director of the Karl Corby Computer and Mathematics Center. Mr. Presley was a member of the founding committee of the Advanced Placement Computer Science examination and served as a consultant to the College Entrance Examination Board. Presently Mr. Presley, author of more than twenty computer textbooks, is president of Lawrenceville Press and teaches computing applications in Boca Raton, Florida.

William R. Freitas, a graduate in computer science of Rutgers University, is director of development at Lawrenceville Press where he has co-authored more than a dozen programming and applications texts as well as a number of Teacher's Resource Packages. Mr. Freitas currently teaches computing applications and desktop publishing in Boca Raton, Florida.

Chapter One:
The History of Publishing & Computers

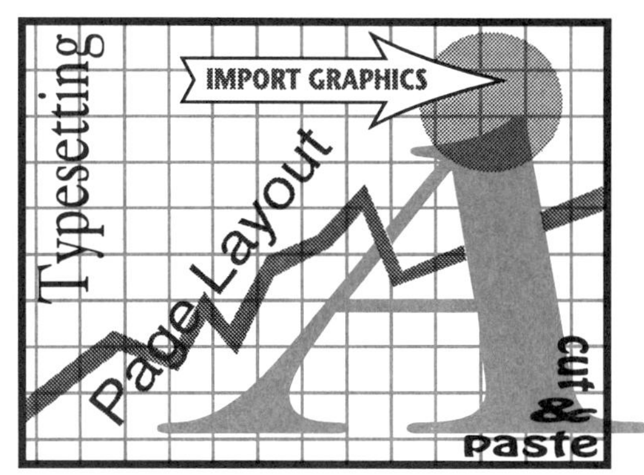

Objectives

1

After completing this chapter you will be able to:

1. Understand the historical developments of writing and publishing.
2. Discuss the printing process.
3. Understand what a computer is.
4. Discuss the history of computers.
5. Name the components of a modern computer system.
6. Understand the advantages of using a computer in publishing.
7. Define the terms "software" and "hardware," and list several different types of applications software.

1

This text is about publishing: its history and how the computer can be employed in the publishing process. We will use a popular computer program named PageMaker® to teach you how to create professional looking documents.

There are three reasons for learning how to use a computer. The first and most important is to develop problem-solving skills. This is done by learning how to analyze a problem carefully, developing a step-by-step solution, and then using the computer as a tool to produce a solution. In publishing, the "problem" is how to communicate information. You will learn how to identify the purpose of a publication, and how to best express it to the desired audience.

A second reason for learning about computers is to become acquainted with their capabilities and limitations. When applied to publishing we will learn what problems the computer can and cannot solve. We will also discover how it is human creativity and not the computer that determines how effective a publication is.

Finally, using a computer can be fun! The intellectual challenge of controlling a computer is not only rewarding but also an invaluable skill. The techniques you will learn can be applied to a wide variety of careers from working on a newspaper to publishing the latest scientific discoveries.

1.1 The Development of Writing

Man has long used pictures and drawings to communicate ideas. Aboriginal petroglyphs found in Australia date back to 80,000 B.C. Cave paintings in Spain tell us a story from 20,000 B.C. About 3000 B.C. the Egyptians invented a special form of writing using pictures called *hieroglyphics* which means "sacred writings," because much of the writing was produced by priests. Writing made it possible for the Egyptians to keep track of an enormous amount of information, enabling them to take on large projects such as building the pyramids, huge tombs in which the Pharaohs were buried:

Hieroglyphics were used to communicate complex ideas

Some 500 years later, the Egyptians are credited with creating the first form of paper. Called *papyrus*, these rough sheets were manufactured from reeds that were cut into strips, soaked in water, pressed together, and then dried in the sun. To accompany the new writing surface the Egyptians developed a form of writing (hieratic) that is similar to cursive or script. Earlier writing was pressed into moist clay or wax tablets with a sharpened stick or *stylus*, or carved into stone blocks with a hammer and chisel. The first papyrus book is believed to be *The Book of the Dead*, prepared in approximately 1500 B.C.

Complete alphabets for writing are thought to have been developed as early as 1600 B.C. and brought to Greece by Phoenician traders around 1100 B.C. Over the years, the Greeks modified the alphabet, adding vowels. Examples of Greek writing can be found on pottery, jewelry, and carved into stone columns. Books at that time were hand written; so many were produced that a library was established in Athens in 540 B.C. Around 350 B.C. the Greek city-states adopted a standardized alphabet containing 24 letters which the Romans later modified. By 100 B.C., slaves and scribes were producing books in such large quantities that more libraries were required, and copyright laws proposed. By this time, published scrolls (books) included the works of many well known ancient authors including Euclid (*Elements*), Homer (*Iliad* and *Odyssey*), and the philosophical works of Plato and Aristotle. Around 150 A.D. scrolls were replaced by folded paper to produce books such as the Bible, but because of the manual work involved, such books were very expensive. Due to the expense, books were usually owned by the wealthy who could read while the majority of people were illiterate.

1.2 The History of Printing

In the earliest days, books were hand lettered by scribes who used quill pens or hair brushes dipped in ink or paint. To "mass produce" a book, a reader would dictate from an original copy to a room full of scribes. Since books were valuable, libraries were often the target of aggressors or thiefs. It was soon realized that one way to destroy a civilization was to burn its books, a deplorable practice that has continued into the twentieth century. In 48 A.D. the Romans invaded Alexandria in Egypt and destroyed its libraries. Hundreds of years later the vast libraries of Alexandria would again be sacked. During the Middle Ages many important manuscripts, including the works of the ancient authors and Christian theologians, were saved by monks who hid them in churches or monasteries. It was during this time, beginning around the year 400, that the monks became the keepers of such books, and copied them by hand, often adding *illuminations*—large, illustrated letters:

Books were "illuminated" by adding elaborately illustrated letters

In order to produce a greater number of copies, mechanical devices were invented that allowed an entire page to be printed at a time. This required some skill, as all the letters for the page were cut in reverse from slabs of wood (and sometimes stone, or other materials such as clay). The slabs were inked, and then pressed against paper. This technique was mostly used for 1 or 2 page documents, but in 868 an entire book of Buddhist scripture was printed in this way.

Creating the wooden slabs needed to print was a time consuming and error-prone process. Additionally, it was impossible to make changes to a document after the wood had been cut. By 1034, the Chinese developed a process of printing with ***movable type*** where individual letters were cut in reverse out of blocks of baked clay. The printer could then assemble different pages by placing the blocks in proper order into a frame. When the page was complete, the frame was loaded into a press, inked, and pressed onto paper. The concept of moveable type allowed pages to be created faster and changes to be made, increasing the productivity of the printer. However, the clay blocks were fragile and by 1221 had been replaced by blocks of wood. By 1390 bronze blocks were being used in Korea. The metal type produced cleaner printed letters because it was smoother and had no grain such as wood possesses. In the 1400s the Chinese were working with copper type for the same reasons. During this time, many other advances in printing technology were being made in Asia, including the development of new inks and different methods for manufacturing paper.

1.3 The Gutenberg Printing Press

Around 1450, Johannes Gutenberg invented a printing press in Germany specially designed to use moveable type. His metal type blocks consisted of over 300 letters and symbols, and in 1455 he printed a Bible, which is believed to be the first complete book printed with movable type. In 1460, Albrecht Pfister modified the frames used to hold the type to allow for the inclusion of wood block drawings. In that year he produced the first book which included movable type and wood block drawings on the same page. Printing was a rapidly expanding industry, and paper mills were established throughout Europe to supply the needs of printers.

Although the *Gutenberg press* allowed for the faster creation of books, most books in the fifteenth century were still created by scribes handwriting each page. Additionally, the bindings and covers used for those early books were extremely large and heavy, requiring the books to be supported by a lectern while read. Because books remained expensive, they continued to be owned primarily by the rich, the church, and certain colleges. This soon changed in the early sixteenth century with the creation of publishing companies which produced smaller, more affordable books.

1.4 Aldus Manutius, Publisher

The company which produces PageMaker is named for the Venetian Aldus Manutius, a fifteenth century printer and entrepreneur who created one of the most important European publishing companies, the Aldine Press. One of his goals was to make Greek literature available to a large number of people and he believed that the best way to do this was to produce small, lightweight books which could be sold at reasonable prices to the growing middle class.

To produce smaller books, it was necessary to use smaller letters, but still maintain legibility. Together with the artist Francesco Griffo da Bologna, Aldus developed a typeface that was compact and imitated the calligraphy used on official documents. This was the precursor of today's italic letters. Besides publishing the first edition of Dante's *Divine Comedy*, Aldus also published many texts of Greek literature: the epics of Homer, the histories of Herodotus and Thucydides, the tragedies of Sophocles, and the treatises of Plato and Aristotle.

The new books from the Aldine Press were an immediate success. As the middle class grew throughout Europe, Aldine began to publish for different countries and languages. Other companies soon followed, and books became available to a very wide audience. By 1662, a royal census found that there were more than 60 publishers in London alone, creating not only books, but also newsletters, newspapers, pamphlets, and monographs (scholarly articles). In the seventeenth and eighteenth centuries such philosophers and political writers as John Locke, Voltaire, Benjamin Franklin, Thomas Paine, and Thomas Jefferson would use the awesome power of the printing press to spread their messages. The result would be both changes in European society and the birth of American democracy.

1

1.5 Paperback Publishing

Before the invention of the paperback book in the early nineteenth century, books were relatively expensive costing a common laborer about a week's wages. Literature for the masses began in England in 1827 with the establishment of the Society for the Diffusion of Useful Knowledge whose purpose was to promote economic and social change through widespread literacy and compulsory education, a movement which quickly gained acceptance in the United States. Magazines and newspapers won widespread popularity at this time as an increasing number of people learned to read. Technological improvements in the production of paper, mechanical typesetting, and high-speed presses made possible the large scale printing of inexpensive publications. In America reprints of popular British authors such as Charles Dickens gained wide audiences as the price of a book dropped from one dollar for a hardcover to ten cents for a paperback. Many Civil War soldiers carried paperbacks in their knapsacks reading them when the opportunity arose. These inexpensive books were a popular form of nineteenth century entertainment much as movies and television are today.

1.6 The Power of the Press

The wide distribution of inexpensive books had a profound impact on European society. For the first time printed information was to become readily available to large numbers of people allowing them to learn to read. The wide availability of the Bible and related theological works is credited by many historians as a factor in causing the religious unrest of the sixteenth and seventeenth centuries. Also, the works of such major scientists as Copernicus and Galileo were made readily available. Their revolutionary findings that the earth moved around the sun conflicted with scientific beliefs of the time.

Heads of state viewed publishing in political terms, sensing the powerful influence that the printed word could have in fostering dissent and revolution. Censorship became widespread in the hope that controlling what people could read would also control what they thought. The guarantee of freedom of the press in the American constitution was given as a protection against such political control of publishing.

It is today widely accepted that the world changes rapidly when information flows freely and is easily accessible, and that is exactly what happened in the sixteenth century. We live in a similar time now where electronic information flowing freely over phone lines, computer networks, and through satellites around the world is revolutionizing the way our society is structured.

1.7 Modern Printing

Over the years many improvements were made to Gutenberg's original press. First steam and then electricity would be used to power the presses. Instead of printing on single sheets of paper, large rolls were employed, increasing the speed at which a press could operate. Advances in chemistry brought about new inks, in a variety of colors. In 1846 a rotary press which used round plates instead of flat type was created with a capability of printing 2,000 newspapers an hour.

Advances were also made in the way that movable type was used. Automatic composition machines were created that allowed lines of type to be entered on a keyboard, instead of setting them by hand. Later, full pages could be made by casting them in hot metal. In the 1960s type setting machines were developed which use lasers to expose photographic plates, a process that remains in wide use.

Today, most large printing is done using the *offset lithography* method. In this technique, oil based ink is applied to specially prepared metal plates. The ink adheres only to the portions of the plate that represent the text or graphics to be printed. The plates carry the ink onto a rubber "blanket" roller which is then pressed against a sheet of moving paper:

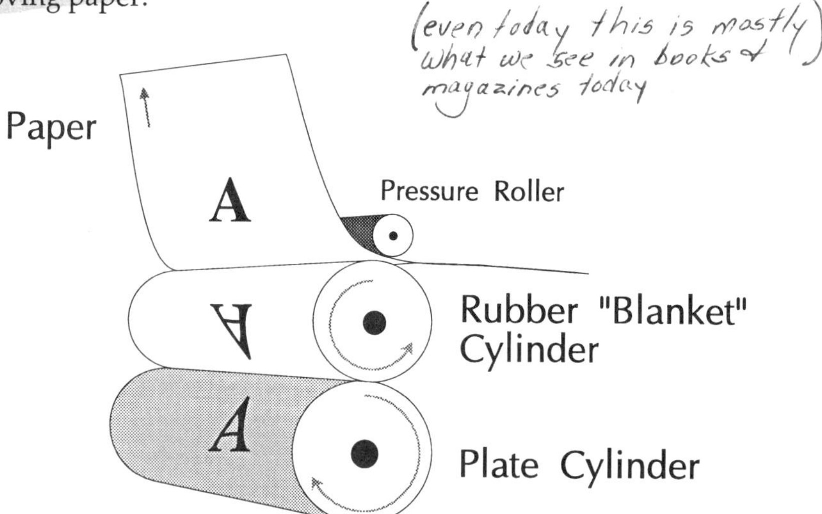

The offset lithography method of printing

On many larger offset presses the paper is supplied in large rolls called *webs* instead of single sheets which increases the speed at which the press can run. Some presses are capable of printing on both sides of the paper at the same time. The paper is wide, often several feet across, which allows the press to print many pages at a time. After the ink has dried, the large sheets are folded to place the pages in proper order.

Modern offset presses can be fast and large. Typical is the Harris model M1000A, which can print 2 colors at a time on both sides of the paper. The press is capable of printing over 31,000 *signatures* per hour, with each signature containing thirty-two 8.5" by 11" pages. As the sheets leave the press they are air dried, cut to size, and then automatically folded. This press, which was used to print this book, is over 80 feet long and 10 feet wide, and costs approximately $4,000,000.

1.8 Desktop Publishing

One of the most exciting technological advances in publishing has been the recent invention of desktop publishing. For the purpose of this text, the term *desktop publishing* (DTP) is defined as using a personal computer to produce professional-looking documents. Using PageMaker software you will learn how to use DTP to arrange text and graphics to produce a wide variety of documents. These documents, or *publications*, can be newsletters, advertisements, newspapers, technical manuals, or a wide variety of other printed materials.

Previous to the invention of DTP software each page of a publication was usually prepared by pasting (often using molten wax) different pieces of text and graphics on to a piece of cardboard. The completed "paste-up" was then photographed and a printing plate made from the photographic negative. The problem with this process is that making changes is difficult. For example, to change a word the text must be typeset again and then pasted on the board. Changing a graphic is equally cumbersome.

A problem often encountered with manual layout is that the wax holding text or graphics would dry and harden, allowing type or graphics to slip or fall off the board. In desktop publishing all the text and graphics are in electronic form and easily manipulated on the computer screen. Changes are made quickly using the computer's keyboard and mouse. Rather than ending with a paste-up on a board, DTP produces a document in electronic form allowing it to be stored on disk. The advantages of this approach will become increasingly obvious as you learn PageMaker.

Before desktop publishing existed, creating a document such as an advertising brochure often involved many people:

- ✔ A writer to create the text of the brochure.
- ✔ An artist to produce the graphics.
- ✔ A typesetter to print the text.
- ✔ A layout person to combine the text and illustrations into the completed brochure.

Now a single person can perform all of these tasks using a computer. Changes can be made to a document in much the same way as changes are made to text using a word processor. Illustrations and text can be added or deleted, changed in size, or the whole layout redone—all on a computer screen.

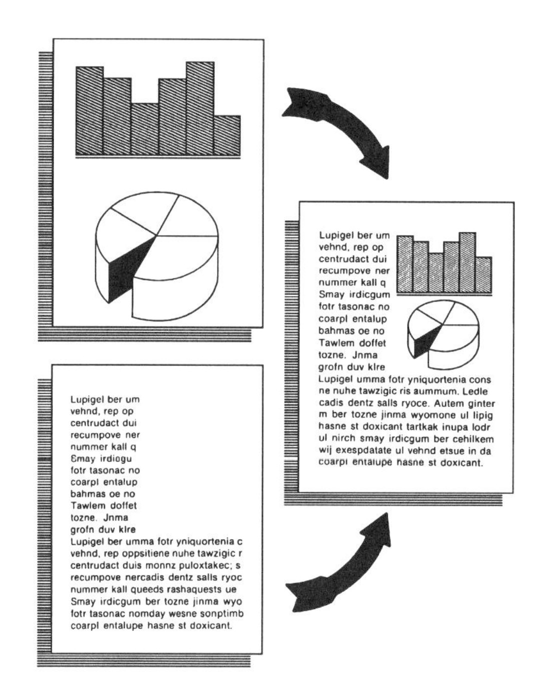

DTP software combines graphics and text into one file

By performing the layout of a document on the computer screen instead of producing a manual paste-up, different layouts can be created and printed until the desired combination is found. Once completed, the final version can be printed and the document saved on disk so that it can be edited or reprinted at any later time.

1.9 Laser and Dot Matrix Printers

The final step for most desktop published documents is to print them. The least expensive printer is called an impact printer. Like a typewriter, impact printers require that an inked ribbon be pressed against paper to produce an image. The most common impact printer is the *dot matrix* which prints characters as a series of small dots. Because the characters are made up of dots, dot matrix print can appear jagged, especially on curved letters:

The quick brown fox jumped.

This is an example of magnified dot matrix print

Examining the print closely shows how the dots are used to create a character:

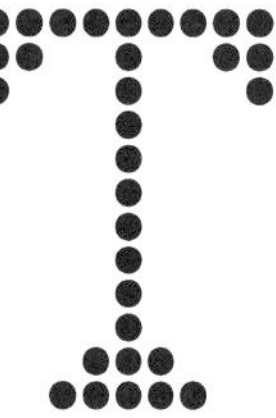

Dot-matrix printer characters are composed of groups of small dots

Because they are not precise, dot matrix printers are not good at printing graphics, and their output often appears sloppy. They are also slow, often taking many minutes to print a single page.

An important advance in making desktop publishing possible was the creation of a low-cost, dependable *laser printer*. A laser printer uses a beam of light to draw each character on the page, employing a process similar to a photocopier. This allows the characters to be fully formed, eliminating the use of dots. A close examination of a character produced by a laser printer illustrates this:

T

A character produced by a laser printer is smoother

Laser printers are also able to produce graphics such as pictures and diagrams with the same level of clarity.

1.10 Scanners

Another hardware device which is useful to desktop publishers is the *scanner* which "reads" an image from a page and converts it into an electronic format. In this way a scanner works like a copy machine, except that the copy is made in a computer-readable format. In fact, most scanners look like a small copy machine, with a glass plate and cover. However, special scanners exist which are smaller and hand-held. Other scanners are specifically designed to scan photographic slides or three-dimensional objects.

The use of scanners in DTP raises many ethical and legal questions. Most art and photographs are copyrighted, and it is illegal to make scanned copies for use in other publications. Different groups are attempting to clarify the laws about what can and cannot be scanned, but a good practice to follow is never to scan and reuse art without the artist's permission. However, there are several companies who publish books of images specifically for legal scanning.

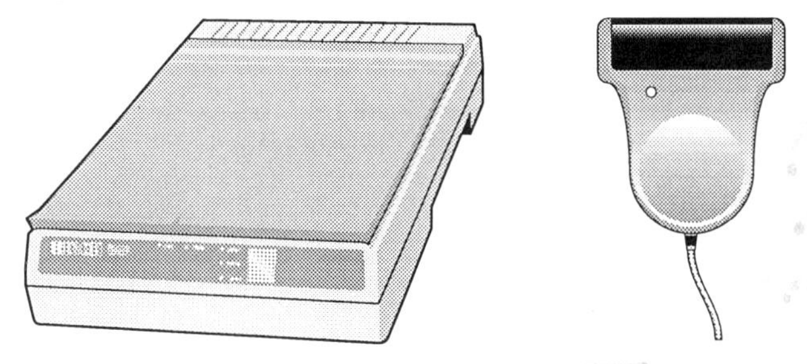

Two different scanner types — flatbed (left) and hand-held

The process of publishing has changed dramatically with the introduction of computers. In the next section we discuss the history of how these computers have evolved.

1.11 Calculating Machines

As early civilizations began to develop, they created both written languages and number systems. Simple numeric calculations were carried out on a device known as an abacus which uses sliding beads mounted on a frame. In 1642 the French philosopher and mathematician Blaise Pascal invented the Pascaline, one of the first mechanical calculators containing a complicated set of gears capable of performing addition:

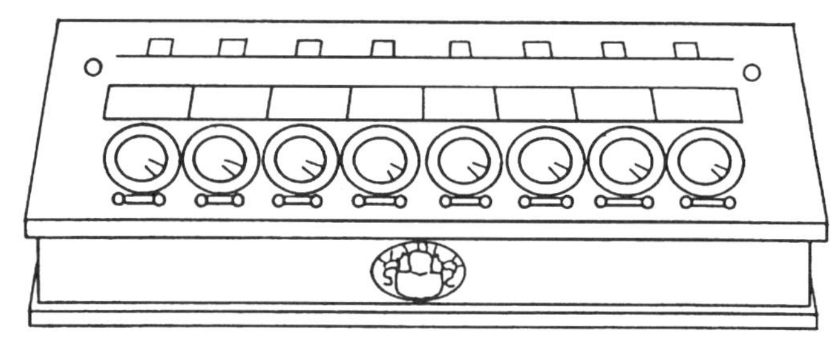

The Pascaline, an early mechanical calculating device

Later attempts at mechanical calculators by Charles Babbage and others were equally cumbersome and usually unreliable since their many gears would easily jam. It was the introduction of electronic methods of performing calculations that began the computer revolution of the mid-twentieth century. These electronic machines, which had evolved from the earlier mechanical calculators, had the benefit of containing few if any mechanical parts thereby greatly increasing their speed and reliability.

1.12 What is a Computer?

A *computer* is an electronic machine that accepts information called *data*, processes it according to specific instructions, and provides the results as new information. It can store and move large quantities of data at very high speed and even though it cannot think, it can make simple comparisons. For example, a computer can determine which of two numbers is larger or which of two names comes first alphabetically and then act upon that information. Although the computer can help to solve a wide variety of problems, it is merely a machine and cannot solve problems on its own. It must be provided with instructions in the form of a computer program.

A *program* is a list of instructions written in a special language that the computer understands. It tells the computer which operations to perform and in what sequence to perform them. In this text we will use a program named PageMaker.

1.13 ENIAC, the First True Computer

In June 1943, John Mauchly and J. Prosper Eckert began work on the Electronic Numerical Integration and Calculator, or ENIAC. It was originally a secret military project which began during World War II to calculate the trajectory of artillery shells. Built at the University of Pennsylvania, it was not finished until 1946, after the war had ended. But the great effort put into the ENIAC was not wasted. In one of its first demonstrations it was given a problem that would have taken a team of mathematicians three days to solve. It solved the problem in twenty seconds.

ENIAC occupied 1,500 square feet, which is the same area taken up by the average three bedroom house, and weighed over 30 tons. It contained over 17,000 vacuum tubes, which were the same kind used in radio sets. Because the tubes consumed huge amounts of electricity the computer produced a tremendous amount of heat and required special fans to cool the room where it was installed. Most importantly, because it was able to make decisions, it was the first true computer.

Because it could make decisions, ENIAC was the first true computer

ENIAC had two major weaknesses. First, it was difficult to change its instructions to allow the computer to solve different problems. It had originally been designed only to compute artillery trajectory tables, but when it needed to work on another problem it could take up to three days of wire pulling, replugging, and switch-flipping to change instructions. Second, because the tubes it contained were constantly burning out, the ENIAC was unreliable.

Grace Murray Hopper, a Commodore in the Navy, was the first person to apply the term *debug* to the computer. While working on a computer program, a moth flew into the circuitry, causing an electrical short which halted the computer. While removing the dead moth, she said that the program would be running again after the computer had been "debugged." Today, the process of removing errors from programs is still called debugging.

1.14 The Transistor

It was the invention of the transistor that made smaller and less expensive computers possible, with increased calculating speeds of up to 10,000 calculations per second. Although the size of the computers shrank, they were still large and expensive. In the early 1960's, IBM, using ideas it had learned while working on projects for the military, introduced the first medium-sized computer named the model 650. It was still expensive, but it was capable of handling the flood of paper work produced by many government agencies and businesses. Such organizations provided a ready market for the 650, making it popular in spite of its cost.

These new computers also saw a change in the way data was stored. The earliest computers used *punch cards* which are cards punched with holes to store data. These were replaced by magnetic tape and high speed reel-to-reel tape machines. Using magnetic tape gave computers the ability to read (input) and write (output) data quickly and reliably.

1.15 The Microprocessor

The most important advance to occur in the early 1970s was the invention of the microprocessor, an entire *Central Processing Unit* (CPU) on a single chip. The CPU electronically controls the functions of the computer. In 1970, Marcian Hoff, an engineer at Intel Corporation, designed the first of these chips. As a result, in 1975 the ALTAIR microcomputer was born. In 1977, working out of a garage, Stephen Wozniak and Steven Jobs designed and built the first Apple computer. Microcomputers were now inexpensive and therefore available to many people. Because of these advances almost anyone could own a machine that had more computing power and was faster and more reliable than the ENIAC or its descendants. As a comparison, if the cost of a sports car had dropped as quickly as that of a computer, a new Porsche would now cost about one dollar.

1.16 How Computers Work

All computers process information, or more generally, *data*. This data may be in the form of numbers, words, pictures, or symbols. In order for it to process data, a computer must carry out four specific activities:

1. Input data
2. Store data while it is being processed
3. Process data according to specific instructions
4. Output the results in the form of new data

Using the PageMaker program is a good example of this process. Data is input in the form of text and graphics which are then converted into electronic form and stored. As you give instructions to PageMaker using the keyboard or mouse the stored data is processed. For example, you might ask for a graphic to appear at the top of a page with text below it. These instructions require the computer's CPU to perform a large number of instructions. The output, which is the page, is displayed on the screen and sent to a disk for storage or a printer for a printed copy.

1.17 The Components of a Computer

Computers contain four major components. Each component performs one of the four tasks we have described:

1. Input Device: a device from which the computer can accept data. A keyboard, disk drive, and scanner are examples of input devices.
2. Memory: an area inside the computer where data can be stored electronically.
3. Central Processing Unit (CPU): processes data and controls the flow of data between the computer's other units. It is here that the computer makes decisions.
4. Output Device: a device that displays or stores processed data. Monitors and printers are the most common visual output devices while disks drives are the most common storage output devices.

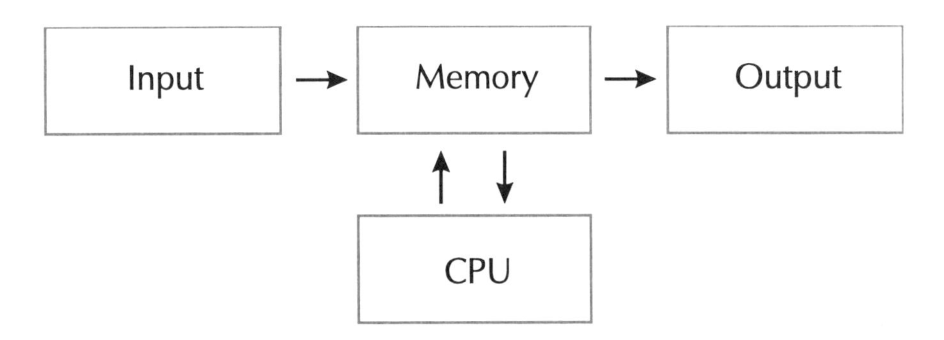

1.18 Memory — ROM and RAM

Most computers have two types of memory contained on chips, ROM and RAM. Read Only Memory or ROM contains the most basic operating instructions for the computer. It is made a permanent part of the computer and cannot be changed. The instructions in ROM enable the computer to complete simple jobs such as placing a character on the screen or checking the keyboard to see if a key has been pressed.

Random Access Memory or RAM is temporary memory where data and instructions can be stored. Data stored here can be changed or erased. When the computer is first turned on this part of memory is empty and when turned off, any data it stores is lost. Because RAM storage is temporary, computers use disks as auxiliary memory storage. Before turning the computer off, the data stored in RAM can be saved on a disk so that it can be used again at a later time. Desktop publishing and graphics applications normally require more RAM than simpler jobs such as word processing.

When data is stored in a computer's memory it is stored by an electric circuit which has one of two states OFF or ON. Therefore, a system was developed that uses only two numbers 0 and 1: 0 representing OFF and 1 representing ON. This number system, which uses only two digits, is called the *binary* (base 2) system. Each 0 and 1 in the binary code is called a *bit* (BInary digiT) and these bits are grouped into 8 bit units called *bytes*. Each byte stores a character which can be one letter of the alphabet. The size of a computer's RAM is usually measured in *megabytes* which is millions of bytes. For example, a computer with 4 megabytes of RAM can store 4 million bytes of data.

1.19 Hardware and Software

A computer requires both *hardware* and *software* to make it work. Hardware refers to the physical parts that make up a computer system and include keyboards, printers, memory, CPU's, monitors, disk drives, etc. Software describes the instructions or the program that is given the computer. Some software is made a permanent part of most computers, so that the tasks a computer must always be ready to perform can be carried out easily. Other software is entered into the computer only when a specific task is required.

1.20 Applications Software

One of the most useful ways in which a computer can be used is to run commercially produced *applications software*. This is software written by professional programmers to perform specific applications or tasks. In this text we will use an applications program called PageMaker to perform desktop publishing tasks. There are three other common applications: word processing, data base, and spreadsheet.

Word processing allows you to enter text from the keyboard into the computer and then manipulate it electronically. With word processors, it is possible to insert and delete text, correct mistakes, move text and perform numerous other functions all on the computer screen. The text can then be printed. The text in a desktop published document is often first prepared using word processing software.

Data bases store and manipulate large quantities of data using the computer. For example, a data base can store the names, addresses, grades, and extra-curricular activities for all of the students in a school. It is possible to add, delete, or change data and produce printed reports using the data base. Desktop published documents such as catalogs and product specification sheets often use the data in data bases.

Spreadsheets primarily store numeric data which can then be used in calculations. For example, teachers often use a spreadsheet to store grades and calculate student averages. The primary advantage of a computerized spreadsheet is its ability to quickly redo the calculations should the data it stores be changed. Many times tables of figures or charts used in documents come from spreadsheet programs.

One factor shared by all applications is their ability to store data on disk in a *file*. A file is simply a collection of data stored on a disk in a form the computer can read. Unlike the computer's RAM memory, data placed in a file is not erased when the computer's power is turned off. This way, the applications program can access the information again and again. We will use disk files to store PageMaker documents.

Besides the programs discussed above there are numerous other applications programs available. There are programs that can be used by musicians to produce musical scores and then play them on a synthesizer, programs that assist an architect in designing a building, programs that produce the special effects graphics that you see in the movies and on television, and much more. Of special interest to desktop publishers are graphics programs. These are programs such as CorelDraw, Adobe Illustrator, and Aldus Freehand which allow professional-looking graphics to be created by non-artists. Most of these programs include libraries of *clip art*, drawings already created by professional artists that can be modified or used as is by the desktop publisher.

As we progress in this text the usefulness of applications software will become increasingly obvious. With computers becoming more widely used, applications software is being written to assist people in almost every profession. Learning to use PageMaker will give you an idea of how the computer and applications software can be applied to help solve many types of problems.

Chapter Summary

Modern printing and publishing is the result of centuries of developments which took place around the world. Thousands of years ago people used pictures to express ideas. This evolved into the hieroglyphics used by the Egyptians in 3,000 B.C. This style of writing was modified into a more formal alphabet by the Greeks and Romans, starting in about 1,100 B.C. By 350 B.C., the Greeks had a standardized 24 letter alphabet which is similar to our own today.

The earliest messages were painted on cave walls. Later, letters were pressed into clay or wax tablets, or carved into stone. Around 2,500 B.C. the Egyptians developed a form of paper called papyrus on which they wrote using vegetable- and mineral-derived inks. The process of hand writing documents continued for a thousand years.

To speed the production of printed documents, printing presses were developed. These used plates of wood, stone, and other materials which were dipped into ink and then pressed against paper. As early as 1,034 A.D. the Chinese developed the process of printing with movable type, which greatly increased the amount of work that could be done on a single press. Around 1,450, Johann Gutenberg invented a printing press specially designed to use moveable metal type. With this, he printed a Bible in 1455, which is believed to be the first book printed with movable type. As the years went by, steam and then electric power were applied, increasing the speed of printing presses dramatically. Moveable type was set by hand until the creation of automatic composition machines.

Today's printing presses are capable of printing thousands of pages a minute, and in multiple colors. The development of web fed offset presses allows multiple pages to be printed on both sides of the paper at once. Inexpensive personal computers and desktop publishing software allow almost anyone to become a publisher.

Mechanical calculating machines were often unreliable. Electrical machines which used vacuum tubes were capable of performing thousands of calculations a minute, but were also unreliable which led to the development of the transistor and integrated circuit. Computers based on these devices were smaller, faster, more reliable, and less expensive than before.

All computers have several parts in common: (1) an input device which allows data and commands to be entered, (2) some way of storing commands and data, (3) a Central Processing Unit (CPU) which controls the processing, and (4) some way of returning the processed information in the form of output. In general, a computer is a machine which accepts information, processes it according to some specific instructions called a program, and then returns new information as output.

Today's microcomputer makes use of a CPU on a chip. Computers store both data and instructions in memory at the same time. Memory comes in two forms, RAM chips which can be erased and used over, and ROM chips, which are permanent. Keyboards and disk drives are used to input data. Monitors and printers are used to output data. Because the contents of RAM are lost when the computer's power is turned off, disks are used to store data.

Software (programs) is written to allow the computer to perform tasks such as word processing and creating graphics. Desktop publishing uses computer software to combine text (usually created in a word processor) with graphics (usually produced by a graphics program). Today's powerful software allows a single person to do the jobs of many different specialists. Publishing is made easier by the development of affordable hardware devices such as laser printers for precise printing and scanners capturing graphics not originally produced on the computer.

Vocabulary

Applications software - Software designed to perform specific applications or tasks.

Bit - Binary digit, a single 0 or 1 in a binary (base 2) number.

Byte - Standard unit of storage in a computer, a group of 8 bits.

Clip art - Collections of drawings created by professional artists that can be modified or used as is by desktop publishers.

Computer - is an electronic machine that accepts information, processes it according to specific instructions, and provides the results as new information.

CPU - Central Processing Unit, the device which electronically controls the functions of the computer.

Data - Information either entered into or produced by the computer.

Debug - Removing errors from programs.

Desktop Publishing - Using a computer to combine text and graphics into professional looking documents.

Dot matrix printer - Prints characters as a series of small dots.

File - Collection of data stored on a disk that the computer can read.

Gutenberg press - Printing press invented in Germany around 1450 by Johannes Gutenberg that was specially designed to use moveable type.

Hardware - Physical devices which make up the computer and its peripherals.

Hieroglyphics - Egyptian form of writing using pictures also called "sacred writing."

Illuminations - Large, ornately illustrated letters typical in hand lettered books produced by monks.

Input - Data used by the computer.

Keyboard - Device resembling a typewriter used for inputting data into a computer.

Laser Printer - Output device which uses a laser to draw characters and graphics on the page.

Megabyte (MB) - One million bytes.

Memory - Electronic storage used by the computer. See RAM or ROM.

Microprocessor - CPU on a single chip.

Monitor - Television-like device used to display computer output.

Movable type - Important advancement in printing where individual letters were cut in reverse out of blocks of baked clay, wood, or metal and assembled into frames.

Offset lithography - Common printing technique where oil based ink is applied to specially prepared metal plates that carry the ink onto a rubber roller which is then pressed against a sheet of moving paper.

Output - Data produced by a computer program.

Papyrus - Rough sheets of Egyptian paper manufactured from reeds that were cut into strips, soaked in water, pressed together, and then dried in the sun.

PC - Personal Computer, a small computer employing a microprocessor.

Peripheral - Secondary hardware device connected to a computer such as a printer, monitor or disk drive.

Program - Series of instructions written in a special language directing the computer to perform certain tasks. Also called software.

Punch card - Cards punched with holes used to store data.

Publication - Any printed document prepared using desktop publishing.

RAM - Random Access Memory, memory which the computer can both read from and write to.

ROM - Read Only Memory, memory from which the computer can read only.

Scanner - Input device that copies printed graphic into a computer file.

Signature - A number of pages printed together on a single sheet of paper which is then folded to place the pages in correct order.

Software - Computer programs.

Stylus - Early writing instrument, usually a sharpened stick, used for creating impressions in moist clay or wax tablets.

Web - Large rolls of paper used in modern printing presses.

Reviews

Sections 1.1 — 1.5

1. When was the first alphabet believed to have been developed?
   1600 BC pg 2, 1100 B.C pg. 2 & 15, 350 B.C. pg. 2 & 15
2. How were books mass produced before the invention of printing?
   a reader would dictate from an original copy to a roomful of scribes.
3. Briefly describe how the earliest printing was produced.
   Printing presses were developed, using plates of wood, stone, & other materials which were dipped into ink & then pressed against paper.
4. What is moveable type and how was it used to produce printed pages?
   Individual letters were cut in reverse out of blocks of baked clay, wood, bronze, then copper & placed into a frame, loaded into a press, inked & pressed onto paper.
5. Why did governments attempt to impose censorship on printed materials?
   Heads of state viewed publishing in political terms sensing the powerful influence that the printed word could have in fostering dissent & revolution -- controlling what people read would also control what they thought.
6. What contribution did Aldus Manutius make to the field of publishing?
   He made Greek literature available to a large number of people by producing small, lightweight books which could be sold at reasonable prices to the growing middle class. Paperbacks
7. Why was the invention of the paperback in the nineteenth century important?
   These inexpensive books were a popular form of nineteenth century entertainment much as movies & television are today.

Sections 1.6 — 1.9

8. Briefly explain how printing is done using offset lithography.
   Oil based ink is applied to specially prepared metal plates. The ink adheres only to the portions of the plate that represent the text or graphics to be printed. The plates carry the ink onto a rubber "blanket" roller which is then pressed against a sheet of moving paper.
9. How were most publications produced before the introduction of desktop publishing?
   Each page of a publication was usually prepared by pasting (often using molten wax) different pieces of text & graphics onto a piece of cardboard. The "paste-up" was then photographed & a printing plate made from the photographic negative.
10. How does the output produced by a laser printer compare with that produced by a dot-matrix printer? Dot matrix printers are not good at printing graphics, & their output often appears sloppy. Laser printers produce both text & graphics with great clarity.
11. Explain how a scanner could be used when producing a desk-top publishing document.
    It "reads" an image from a page & converts it into an electronic format.

Sections 1.10 — 1.19

12. What were the major weaknesses of the ENIAC?
    It was difficult to change its instructions, the tubes it contained were constantly burning out, causing it to be unreliable.
13. How did the invention of the transistor improve computers?
    It made smaller & less expensive computers possible, with increased calculating speeds of up to 10,000 calculations per second

14. Explain what debugging is?
    The process of removing errors from programs.
15. What is a CPU and what function does it serve?
    The Central Processing Unit of a computer proceses data + controls the flow of data between the computer's other units. It is where the computer makes decisions.
16. Explain the difference between ROM and RAM.
    Rom is Read Only memory, is permanent + contains the most basic operating instructions for the computer. Ram is Random Access Memory - temporary memory where data + instructions can be stored.
17. Explain the difference between hardware and software.
    Hardware refers to the physical parts that make up a computer system, keyboards, printers, memory, CPU, monitor, disk drive, etc. Software is the instructions or program that is given to the computer.
18. List three types of applications software and explain what each can do.
    Word processing - enter text from the keyboard into the computer + then manipulate it electronically. Data bases store + manipulate large quantities of data using the computer. Spreadsheets primarily store numeric data which can then be used in calcutations.
19. Explain what a computer file is and what it can store.
    A collection of data stored on a disk in a form the computer can read

Chapter Two:
Introducing PageMaker

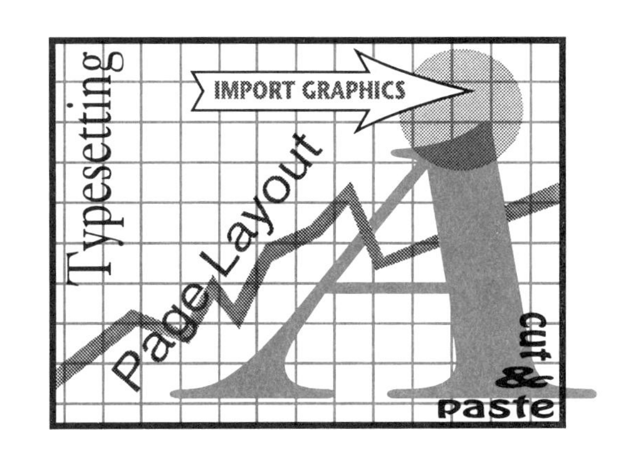

File - New

Layout - View

Edit - Undo

File - Save

File - Print

File - Close

File - Exit

Objectives

After completing this chapter you will be able to:

1. Start the computer and run PageMaker.
2. Use the mouse to select commands from menus.
3. Select different tools from the Toolbox.
4. Use different views.
5. Use the keyboard to enter and edit text in a publication.
6. Undo and redo edits with the Undo command.
7. Select and modify text blocks.
8. Save and print a publication.
9. Close the current publication and exit PageMaker.

2

PageMaker, although sophisticated, is simply a computer program. PageMaker requires another program called DOS to run, and a second program called Windows® to handle its printing, screen displays, and other elements. In this chapter you will learn how to start DOS and Windows, run the PageMaker program, and create a new publication. Text will then be entered and edited, and the publication saved and printed.

2.1 How to Use this Text

Throughout this text new commands and procedures are introduced in a two-step process. First, the command or procedure is discussed. You will be told what the command does and how to apply it, but will not use the computer at this time. Second, the discussion is followed by a section titled *Practice*. Each Practice leads you through a step by step example of how to use the command on the computer. You should actually perform the steps given in a Practice using PageMaker. Practices also serve as reviews of the steps required to perform specific tasks. Because the discussion sections explain the details of what is to be demonstrated, you should read them carefully before proceeding to the Practice. When performing a Practice, do each step in order as directed. Also, do not skip any Practices because they are related—skipping one may mean that you do not get the correct results at the end of the next.

2.2 Using Disks

You will most likely use disks to save the files that you create. It is important to handle the disks carefully because they store large quantities of data in a magnetic format that is vulnerable to dirt and heat. Observing the following rules will help to insure that your disks give you trouble free service:

1. Keep disks away from electrical and magnetic devices such as computer monitors, television sets, stereos, and any type of magnet.
2. Make sure that your disks are not exposed to either extreme cold or heat. Being made of plastic they are sensitive to temperature.

3. Be careful not to allow dust, dirt, or moisture to penetrate the disk by keeping it in a safe place when not in use.
4. Never touch the disk's magnetic surface because this can damage it, destroying valuable data.
5. Do not bend or crimp the disk and never place paper clips on it.

It is important to treat all your computer equipment with care. Do not eat, and especially do not drink around the computer.

2.3 The Mouse

Computers running PageMaker are normally equipped with an input device called a *mouse* which is used to perform a variety of different tasks:

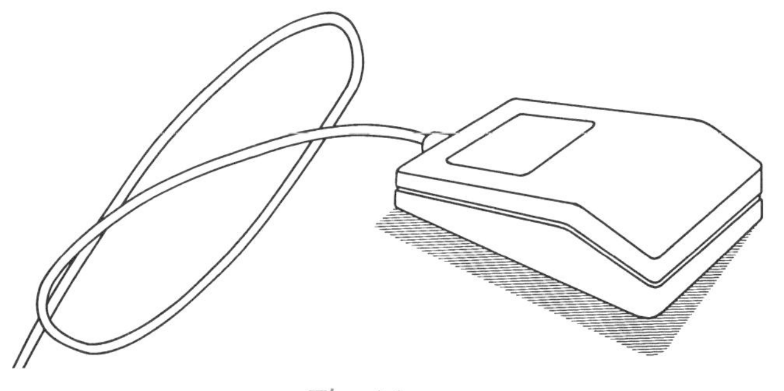

The Mouse

Before proceeding, you need to learn four important words that are used to describe the actions of the mouse.

Pointing:

The most basic use of the mouse is for pointing at different objects on the computer screen. When the mouse is in use an arrow called the *mouse pointer* is displayed on the screen:

The mouse pointer

Moving the mouse causes the pointer to move on the screen; slide the mouse to the left on the table and the pointer moves to the left on the screen, slide the mouse to the right and the pointer moves to the right.

By moving the mouse, it is possible to place the pointer on different objects on the screen, which is called *pointing*. In this text, when we say to point to an object, we mean to place the mouse pointer on it on the screen.

Clicking:

When the pointer is pointing to an object, it is possible to select that object by pressing the left button on the mouse and releasing it. This type of selection is called *clicking*, and has different effects on different objects. When we say to select or click on an item, we mean to move the pointer to it, and then press and release the left mouse button. (If your mouse has two or more buttons, be sure to click with the left button only.)

Double-Clicking:

A special form of clicking is the *double-click*. As the name implies, double-clicking requires that the mouse pointer be placed on an object and the left button pressed twice in rapid succession. Double-clicking an object has different effects with different objects.

Dragging:

The last mouse technique is called *dragging*. To drag an object, first place the pointer on it. Then press and hold down the left mouse button while moving the mouse. In most cases this will move the selected object with the pointer. When we say to drag an object, we mean to place the mouse pointer on it, press and hold the left button, and move the mouse. When the object is in the desired location, release the mouse button.

Getting Started on the Computer

You are now ready to start using the computer. This chapter takes a "hands on" the computer approach to introduce basic skills. You will learn how to start the computer, enter the date and time, and run the PageMaker program. Simple *text* (characters, words, and phrases) will be entered into a publication to demonstrate how it may be edited, printed, and saved.

2.4 Starting DOS and Windows

Before using PageMaker, it is first necessary to load the disk operating system (*DOS*)—programs that the computer needs in order to run. The process of transferring DOS from disk to computer memory is called *booting*, and you may be asked to enter the current date and time. When the computer is ready for you to enter a command it displays the *DOS prompt*, usually a C> or C:\>.

PageMaker also requires the Windows program in order to run. From the DOS prompt, it is possible to start Windows by typing `WIN` and pressing the Enter key. After a few seconds the screen will clear and Windows loads, displaying its own screen. Once you have Windows started, you should see the Aldus group icon:

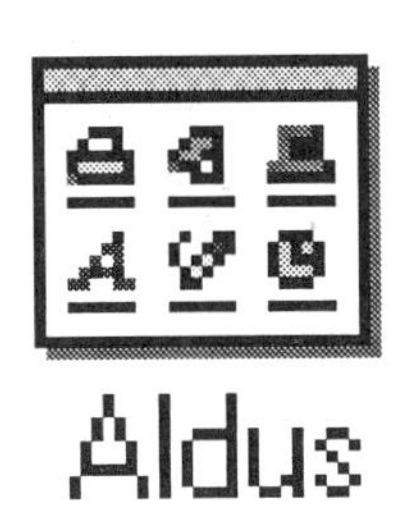

Double-clicking on this icon displays the Aldus window:

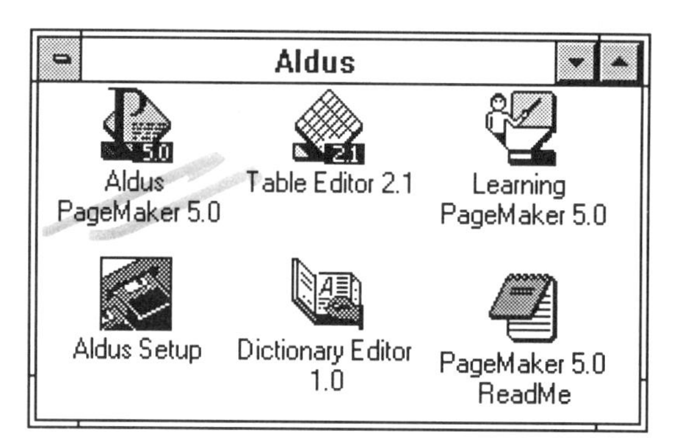

Double-clicking on the Aldus PageMaker 5.0 icon starts PageMaker which displays an opening copyright screen.

Practice 1

In this Practice, you will start DOS and Windows, and run the PageMaker program. (If you are using a network these instructions will be slightly different. See your instructor for complete details on how to run PageMaker on your system.)

1) *TURN ON BOTH THE COMPUTER AND MONITOR*

Locate the power switch on both devices and turn them on. In a few seconds the computer will beep and boot DOS. Enter the time and date if you are asked to:

```
Current date is Tue  1-1-1980
Enter new date (mm-dd-yy):
```
<Date may be different>

Type today's date using the form *mm-dd-yy* and then press the key marked `Enter`. (Note that on some computers this key is marked Return, or with the symbol ↵.) The computer will not accept an invalid date. If you make a mistake entering the date, just start over again.

```
Current time is 0:05:17.29a
Enter new time:
```
<Time may be different>

Enter the current time using the form *hh:mm* and then press the `Enter` key. The computer will not accept an invalid time. If you make a mistake entering the time, just start over.

2) *START WINDOWS*

After DOS has booted, the computer displays the DOS prompt, usually `C>` or `C:\>`. This means that DOS is ready to accept a command from you. To start Windows, type `WIN` and press the Enter key. Windows will take several seconds to load.

3) *START THE PAGEMAKER PROGRAM*

After Windows has loaded, you should see a display similar to the one shown in Section 2.4 above. If the Aldus group is shown, double-click on it using the mouse. Locate the Aldus PageMaker 5.0 icon and double-click on it. Because it is a very large program, it may take some time for PageMaker to start. PageMaker will load and display a copyright screen similar to:

After several seconds the copyright notice will be removed and the PageMaker screen shown.

2.5 Menus

At the top of the PageMaker screen is the *Menu bar*. Each word in the bar represents a menu from which different commands may be chosen:

File Edit Utilities Layout Type Element Window Help

The Menu bar contains menus used to access different commands

Clicking on the menu name with the mouse displays the available commands for that menu. For example, clicking on File displays the File menu:

File	
New...	^N
Open...	^O
Close	
Save	^S
Save as...	
Revert	
Export...	
Place...	^D
Links...	Sh^D
Book...	
Preferences...	
Page setup...	
Print...	^P
Exit	^Q

The File menu contains commands which affect files

Clicking on a command in the displayed menu executes that command. Clicking anywhere on the screen except the menu cancels the selection without executing any command.

Commands and menus may also be selected with the keyboard. Note that one letter in each of the menu names is underlined. Pressing the `Alt` key and the underlined letter at the same time displays the commands on that menu. For example, holding down the `Alt` key while pressing `F` displays the File menu. In this text we denote this sequence of keystrokes as `Alt+F`, meaning to hold down the `Alt` key and press `F` at the same time. Each command on the menu also has an underlined letter. Pressing that letter when the menu is displayed executes the command. Pressing `Alt+F A` would execute the Save as command from the File menu. Pressing Escape before a command is selected removes the menu from the screen.

A special command is located at the far right of the Menu bar; Help (`Alt+H`). Help provides information about PageMaker commands and techniques. The best place to start is by selecting the Using PageMaker Help command which displays a new window with instructions on how to use the Help system:

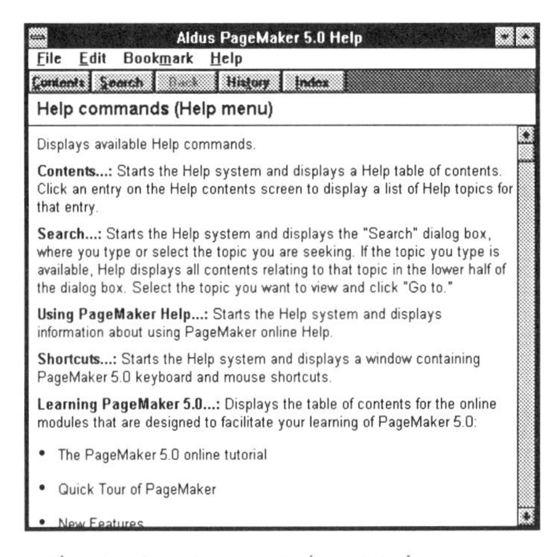

The Using PageMaker Help screen

To leave Help, select the Exit command from the Help window's File menu.

2.6 Dialog Boxes

Many commands listed in menus are followed by three dots (. . .) which indicate that this command has a *dialog box*. The New and Open commands in the File menu shown in the previous section are examples. The purpose of a dialog box is to allow you to supply information that PageMaker needs to execute the command. Below is an example dialog box:

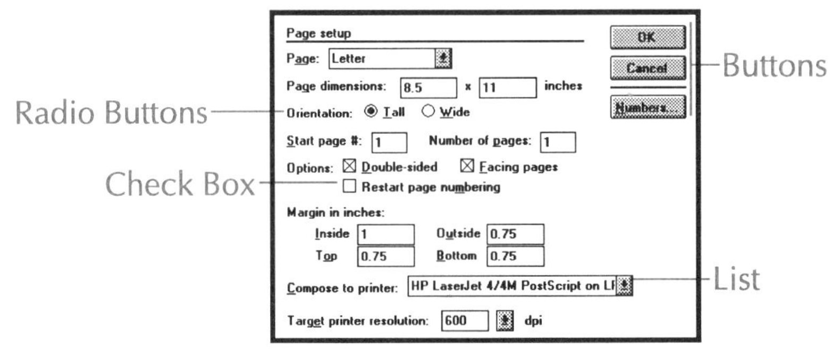

The Page Setup dialog box

Different options may be selected from a dialog by clicking on them with the mouse, or holding down the `Alt` key and pressing the underlined letter. If you display a dialog box by mistake, pressing the `Esc` key or selecting Cancel will remove it.

There are several different types of items which may be found in a dialog box, but most dialog boxes have certain similarities. For example, most will include OK and Cancel options:

Most dialog boxes have at least these two buttons

Because they resemble push buttons, these options are called *buttons*, and may be selected by clicking on them.

Another option is the *list*:

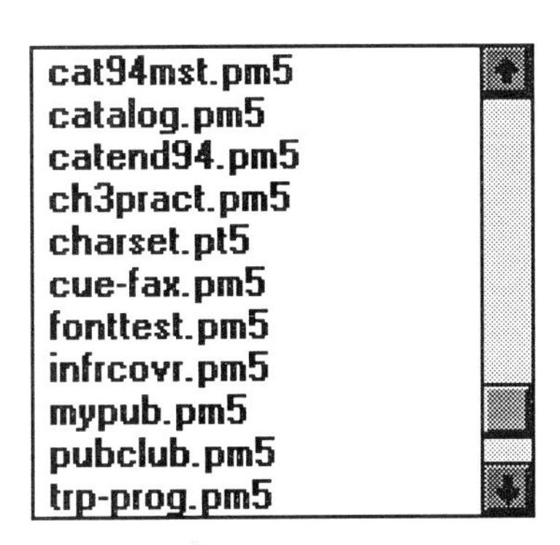

A scrollable list—note the scroll arrows

Lists are scrollable, and may contain more information than currently displayed. Click on the scroll arrows to the right of the list to show other items. An item is selected from a list by clicking on it, which highlights it.

There are two other common elements, the *radio button* and the *check box*:

Open:
◉ Original ○ Copy

Type style: ☐ Normal ☒ Bold ☒ Italic ☐ Underline

Left: Radio buttons (Original is selected)
Right: Check boxes (Bold and Italic are selected)

These options are selected by clicking on them or pressing `Alt` and the underlined letter. When radio buttons are used, only one option may be selected. With check boxes, any number of the listed options may be selected at the same time.

When a dialog box is first displayed, certain *default* options are already selected, usually the most common options for that command. There are also default buttons which are indicated by a heavy outline:

A default button (Print) is indicated by a heavy outline

The default button may be selected by pressing Enter.

2.7 The PageMaker Screen

Before producing a publication you should be familiar with the PageMaker screen:

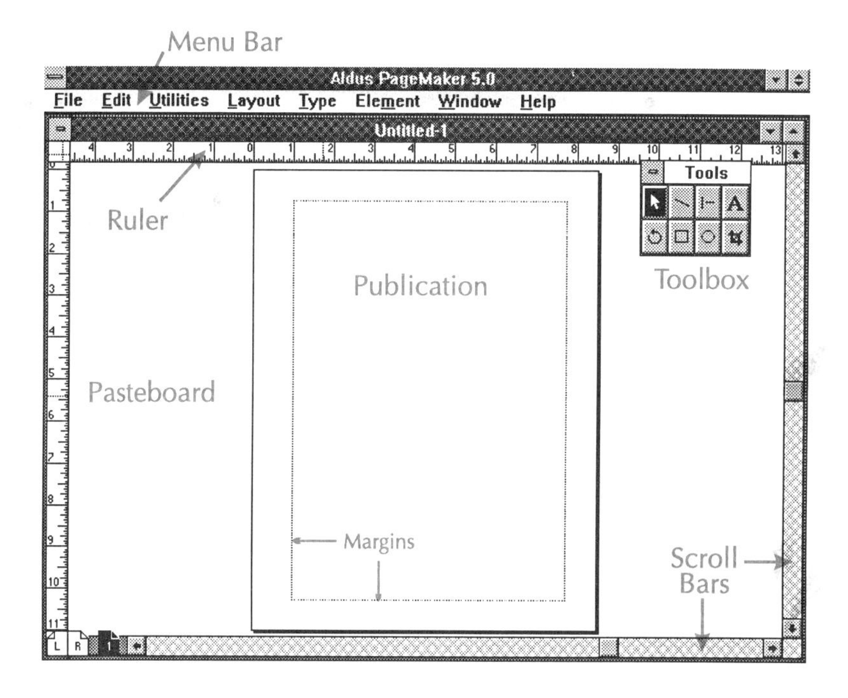

The PageMaker Screen

This screen has several important parts which are described below:

Menu Bar - All of PageMaker's commands can be accessed through these drop-down menus. To display a menu, click on the menu's name with the mouse, or hold down the `Alt` key and press its underlined letter (for example, `Alt+F` for the File menu).

Rulers - The Rulers are used to measure distances within the publication. As you move the mouse pointer, small dashed lines can be seen on the Rulers, indicating the position of the mouse.

Pasteboard - An area around the actual publication where currently unused text or graphics may be stored until needed.

Publication - The actual page being created. Text and graphics placed here will be printed. The dashed lines indicate the margins (top, bottom, left, and right).

Toolbox - As mentioned previously, the mouse can be used to perform different tasks in PageMaker. Each of these tasks has a specific "tool" associated with it which is shown in this box. The tools are described in more detail in the next section.

Scroll bars and arrows - It is possible to view different parts of the publication by clicking on the scroll bars and arrows.

Practice 2

In this Practice, you will use the File menu and a dialog box to create a new PageMaker publication.

1) *CREATE A NEW PAGEMAKER PUBLICATION*

a. Using the mouse, click on the word File in the Menu bar. The File menu is displayed.
b. Click on the New command in the File menu. The Page setup dialog box is shown. This dialog box has several options which will be described in future chapters, including page size and margins.
c. Click on the OK button to create a new publication using these settings. A new, empty publication is shown on the Pasteboard. Take a few seconds to locate and identify each of the following items: Menu bar, Ruler, Scroll bars, Scroll arrows, Pasteboard, Toolbox, publication, and margin lines.

2.8 The Toolbox

The Toolbox allows you to select the actions that the mouse will perform:

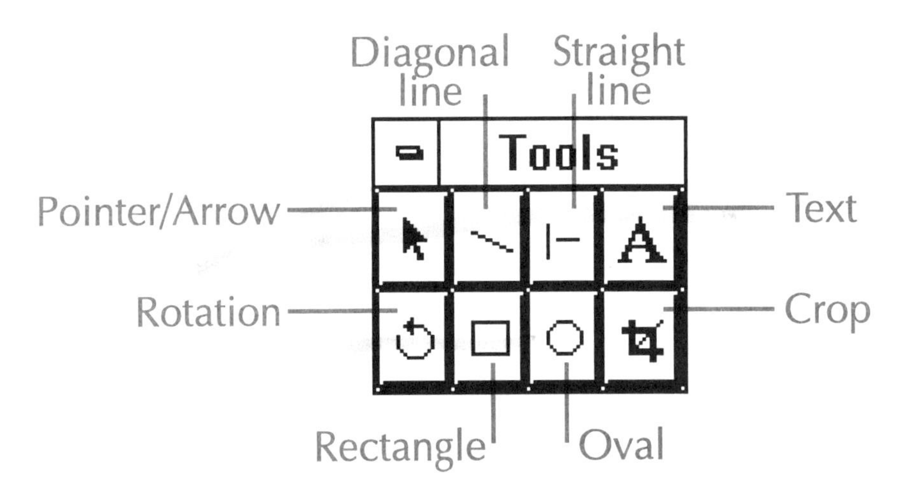

Pointer / Arrow - Used to select blocks of text and graphics, and for any operation that requires menus, dialog boxes, etc. Sometimes called the arrow tool, arrow pointer, or selection tool.

Diagonal line - Draws lines at different angles.

Straight line - Draws lines which are only vertical, horizontal, or at 45 degree angles.
Text - Inserts and edits text, and selects blocks of characters.
Rotation - Rotates text and graphics.
Rectangle - Draws squares and rectangles.
Oval - Draws ovals, circles, and ellipses.
Crop - Crops (trims) and edits graphics.

When selected, each tool changes the shape of the pointer to act as a reminder as to which tool is in use. As we introduce each tool we will describe both its actions and its pointer shape.

2.9 Entering Text

PageMaker publications are composed primarily of two separate items: text and graphics. We will start with *text,* which is any combination of letters, words, and symbols that can be entered from the keyboard. Text is placed in a PageMaker publication in one of two ways; it may be entered directly by typing onto the publication page, or it may be *imported* from another source, usually a word processing program. We will start by entering some text from the keyboard.

Before entering text, the Text tool must be selected from the Toolbox. When a tool is selected, its icon is highlighted in the Toolbox:

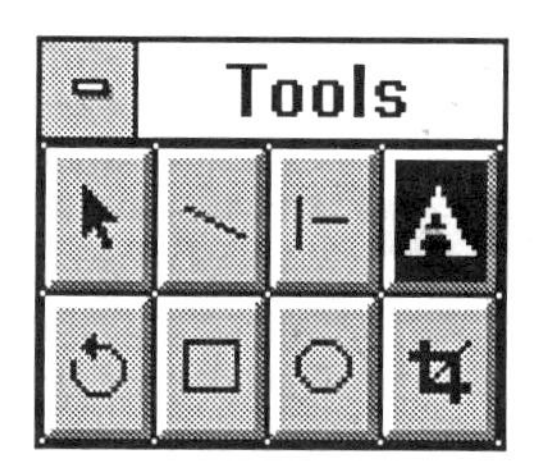

The selected tool is highlighted, in this case the Text tool

When the Text tool is selected, the mouse pointer changes shape to what is called the *I-Beam* or Text pointer:

The I-Beam or Text pointer

This pointer can be used to select text, or indicate where typed text is to be inserted. Clicking on the publication with this pointer creates an *insertion point* where text may be typed. The insertion point is shown on the screen as a blinking vertical line, and is sometimes referred to as the *cursor*.

2

2.10 Viewing the PageMaker Screen

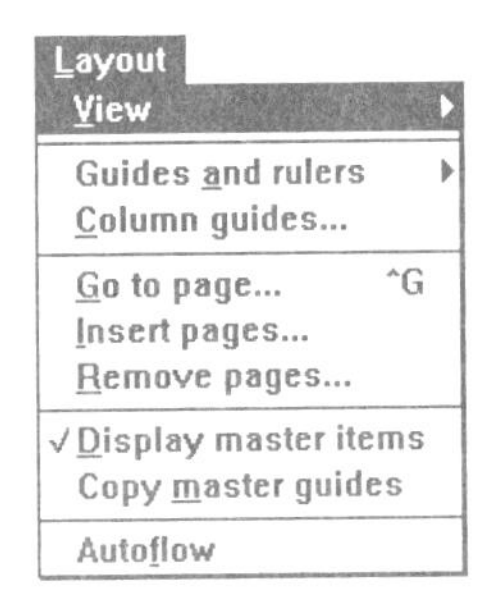

There are many different ways to view the PageMaker screen and the operation that you are performing will determine which view is most useful. The different views are selected using the View command from the Layout menu, which displays a *submenu*, a small list of options from which you may choose only one:

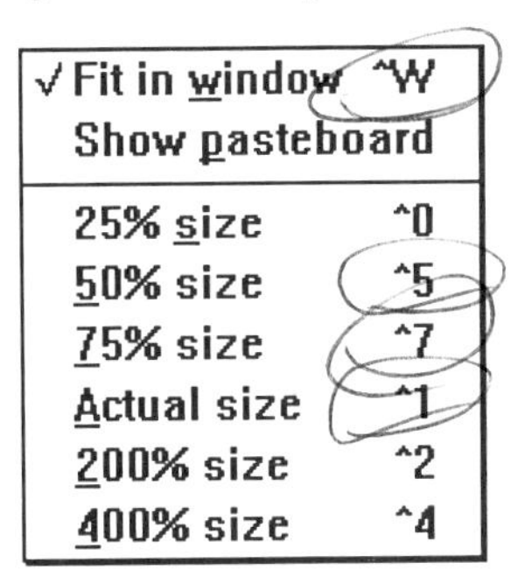

The View command's submenu—note the Ctrl key shortcuts for quickly changing views

Note the keyboard shortcuts in this menu which may be used in place of selecting a command with the mouse. Holding down the `Ctrl` (Control) key and pressing 5 (written as `^5` in menus and `Ctrl+5` in this text) displays the current publication in 50% size, which means that all elements on the page are displayed at 50% of their actual size. Pressing `Ctrl+1` selects Actual size, which is 100%.

The starting view is Fit in window which places the entire publication page on the screen. This view is useful for determining how the different pieces of a page relate to one another. However, in order to fit the entire page on the screen, the text is reduced to small, often unreadable letters. This is called *greeking* or greek text:

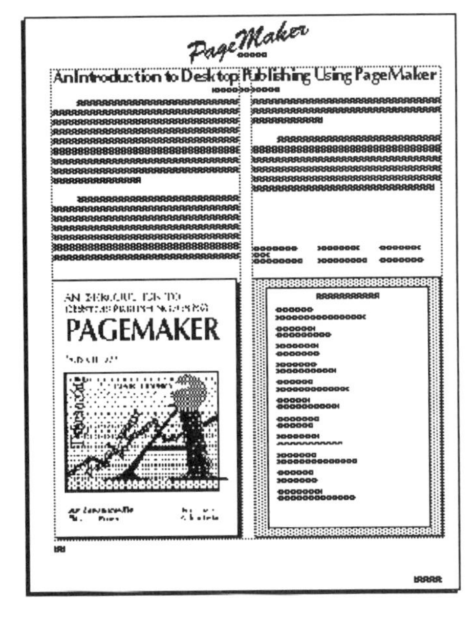

Text is greeked (unreadable) in some views

Using a closer view, such as Actual size (100%) provides more detail about a smaller area of the publication. This view and 75% size are good for entering and editing text:

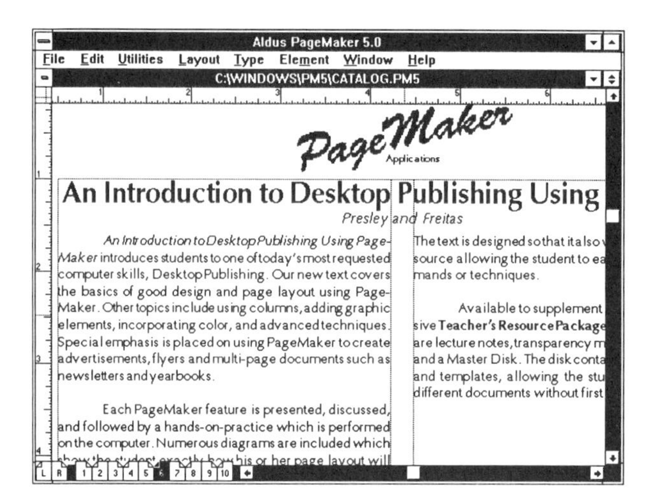

Actual size is really 100%

"Zoomed" views such as 200% and 400% size show an even smaller part of the current page at 2- and 4-times their actual size. These views are good for placing graphics, working with very small type, and making very precise changes:

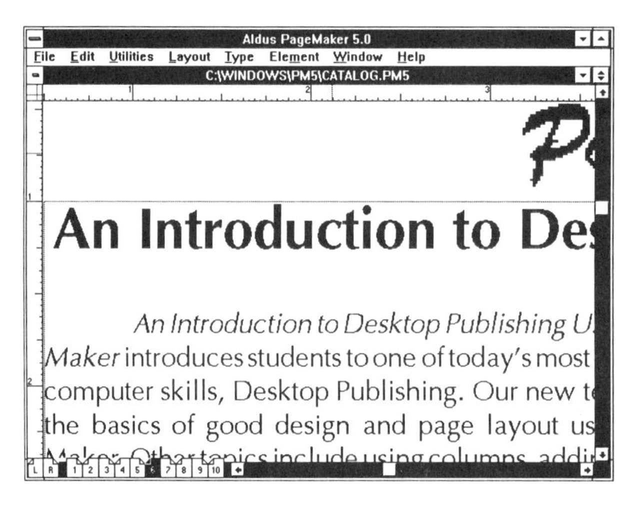

A typical 200% size view

2.11 The Keyboard

Before proceeding, you need to take time to familiarize yourself with some of the keys needed to enter and edit text, some of which have special features.

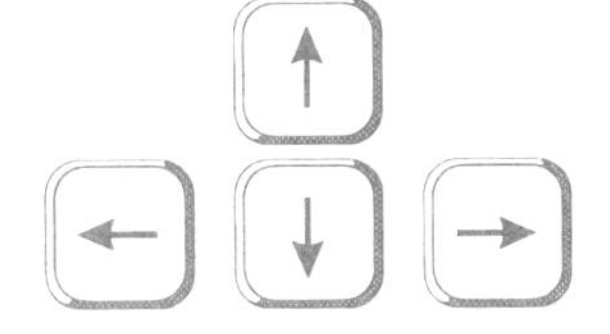

When the Text tool is selected, a small blinking line called the insertion point is shown on the screen. The insertion point can be moved around the screen, without erasing or entering text, using the arrow keys which are marked with arrows (up, down, left, and right).

To move the insertion point down one line press the key marked with a down-arrow. Similarly, to move the insertion point up, left, or right, use the keys marked with the appropriate arrows. Each of these keys is a *repeat key*, meaning that it will continue moving the insertion point as long as it is held down. The arrow keys can only move the insertion point where text has already been typed.

Esc (sometimes marked Escape) is used to terminate (escape from) the computer's current operation. The specific effect that pressing the Escape key will have depends on the operation that is being performed. For example, pressing Escape when a dialog box is displayed removes the dialog box without executing the command.

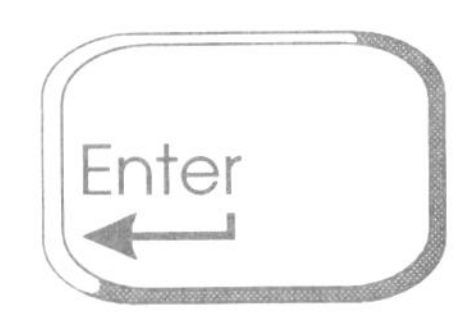

Enter (sometimes marked Return or with the symbol ↵) is used to end a paragraph or to terminate any line which does not reach the right side of the page. When Enter is pressed the insertion point moves to the next line. Enter also instructs PageMaker to accept a highlighted menu command, list choice, or selected dialog box options.

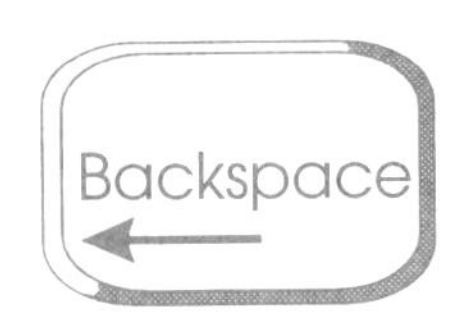

Pressing the Backspace key (sometimes marked only with a ←) deletes the character to the left of the insertion point and moves the insertion point one space to the left. Do not confuse Backspace with the left-arrow key. Both move the insertion point one character to the left; Backspace erases characters as it moves, while left-arrow does not.

The Delete key (also marked Del) is also used to erase a character. Pressing Delete erases the character directly to the right of the insertion point. When a character is deleted any characters to its right are automatically moved over to close the gap previously occupied by the deleted character.

To insert text the insertion point is first placed where the new material is to appear using the arrow keys and then the new material typed. PageMaker automatically inserts the characters you type at the current insertion point position. Any text following the insertion is moved to the right to accommodate the new material. Deleting and inserting are powerful text editing features that allow almost any type of change to be made to a document.

Practice 3

In this Practice you will enter some text into the new publication created in Practice 2. If the Toolbox is not shown on your screen, select the Tool palette command from the Window menu to display it.

1) PRACTICE SELECTING TOOLS FROM THE TOOLBOX

a. The current tool should be the arrow pointer. Move the pointer to the Toolbox and select any tool by clicking on it. Note how the selected tool is now highlighted in the Toolbox.

b. Move the pointer away from the Toolbox and onto the Pasteboard. The pointer changes to different shapes for different tools.
c. Select several other tools and move the pointer onto the Pasteboard, noting its shape. Notice that whenever the pointer is in the Toolbox that it has the arrow shape.

2) SELECT THE TEXT TOOL FROM THE TOOLBOX

Move the pointer to the Text tool in the Toolbox (A). Click the mouse button once to select the Text tool. Move the pointer off the Toolbox onto the Pasteboard. The shape of the mouse pointer changes to the I-Beam (text) pointer.

3) CREATE AN INSERTION POINT

With the Text tool still selected, place the pointer over the publication page, within the margin lines. Click the mouse button once. An insertion point is created, as indicated by the blinking vertical line near the left margin line. Make certain that your insertion point is inside the publication, not on the pasteboard.

4) SWITCH TO ACTUAL VIEW

a. Click on Layout in the Menu bar. The Layout menu is displayed.
b. In the Layout menu, select the View command. A submenu of different views is shown.
c. In the submenu, select the Actual size command. The screen zooms in on the insertion point. (If your insertion point is not visible, use the scroll bars and arrows to locate it.)

5) ENTER SOME TEXT AT THE INSERTION POINT

Type:

```
This is some test text!
```

Use the Shift key to generate the capital "T" and the exclamation point. Note how the text is inserted into the publication at the position of the insertion point. While text is being entered, the I-Beam pointer is hidden so that it does not interfere with your view of the screen.

6) CHANGE VIEWS USING KEYBOARD SHORTCUTS

a. From the Layout menu, select the View command. The submenu is displayed.
b. From the View submenu, select the 200% size command. Note how the text in enlarged on the screen, but only a small part of the screen is shown.
c. Press `Ctrl+W` to select the Fit in window command using a keyboard shortcut. Note how the text is greeked.
d. Press `Ctrl+1` to select the Actual size command and return to the original view.

2.12 Editing Text

Once text has been entered it will almost always need to be edited. PageMaker has several different ways of editing previously entered text.

2

The easiest way to make corrections as you type is with the arrow, Delete, and Backspace keys. When the insertion point is visible on the current line, the Delete and Backspace keys can be used to erase single characters, and new material can be inserted at the position of the insertion point.

The mouse can be used to change the position of the insertion point. For example, clicking the Text pointer over a line of already typed text creates an insertion point at that position. Any text typed will be inserted at the position of the insertion point.

The mouse can also be used to select words or sections of text in two ways. Selected text is shown on the screen as white letters on a black background and is called *highlighted*:

This text is highlighted. This text is not.

Highlighted text is shown as reversed on the screen

Clicking the mouse once places an insertion point at the current pointer location. Clicking twice (double-click) on a word highlights that entire word. Clicking three times (triple-click) highlights an entire paragraph.

The second way to highlight text using the mouse is to drag the Text pointer over it. That is, with the Text tool selected, holding down the mouse button and moving the I-Beam pointer over a section of text highlights it.

Once highlighted, any number of editing and formatting commands can be applied to the selected text. One of the most common is to delete the highlighted text. This can be accomplished by pressing the Delete key, which deletes all the highlighted text from the publication. Text can also be replaced. Typing new text replaces any highlighted text. This is a useful technique but can cause accidental erasures if you are not careful. In the next Practice we will demonstrate all of these techniques.

2.13 The Undo Command

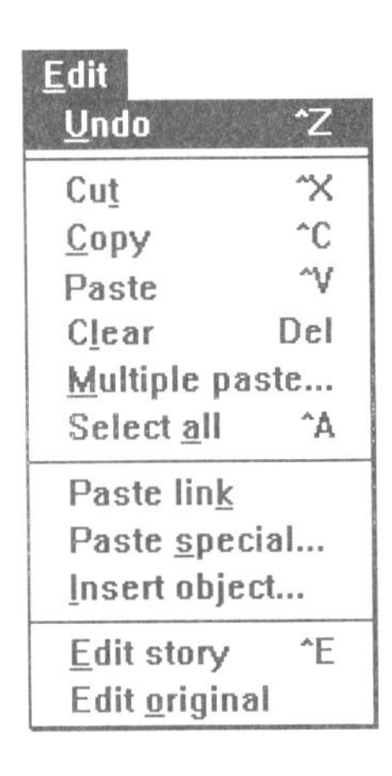

At times you will make an edit or execute a command only to find that you have made a mistake. For example, you may delete a block of characters by mistake. PageMaker supplies a way to negate the effects of the last action performed with the Undo command from the Edit menu (`Ctrl+Z` or `Alt+Backspace`). Executing Undo reverses the effect of the previously executed command.

Undo only works for the command just executed, and it is not possible to undo the effect of the second or third previous command. However, you can Redo a command by executing Undo immediately again. That is, the second Undo, "undoes" the effects of the first Undo, and the edited text is restored.

The Undo command listed in the Edit menus changes based on the operation you have just completed. For example, if you have just edited some text the Undo command will be listed as "Undo edit." If you had moved a graphic the command would say "Undo move."

Practice 4

In this Practice you will edit the text entered in Practice 3 using the mouse and keyboard.

1) *ERASE THE EXCLAMATION POINT USING THE BACKSPACE KEY*

The insertion point (blinking vertical line) should be visible at the end of the sentence. Press the Backspace key once. The exclamation point is erased and the insertion point moved one character to the left.

2) *INSERT NEW TEXT*

a. Type a period. The period is inserted at the position of the insertion point.
b. Move the mouse. Note that the I-Beam pointer is again shown.

3) *UNDO AND REDO THE LAST EDIT*

a. From the Edit menu, select the Undo edit command. The period entered in step 2 is removed, and the exclamation point is restored.
b. Display the Edit menu (`Alt+E`). Note that the command now reads "Redo edit" instead of Undo edit.
c. Select the Redo edit command. The exclamation point is replaced by the period.

4) *HIGHLIGHT TEXT*

a. Place the I-Beam pointer on the word "some".
b. Click the mouse once. An insertion point is placed at the location of the I-Beam. Any characters typed now would be inserted into the publication at the position of the insertion point.
c. With the pointer still on "some" double-click. The entire word is highlighted including the space after the "e".
d. With the pointer anywhere on the sentence, triple-click. The entire sentence is highlighted. If this were a paragraph with many lines, all lines in the paragraph would be highlighted.
e. Click anywhere within the line. The highlight is removed and the insertion point again shown.
f. Press and hold down the mouse button. While holding the button down, drag the mouse several characters to the left, and then to the right. A highlight is created as the mouse is moved over characters. Release the button.

5) *REPLACE HIGHLIGHTED TEXT*

a. Place the pointer on the word "some" and double-click. The word and the following space are highlighted.
b. Type "my" and a space. The highlighted text is replaced, and the sentence should now read:

```
This is my test text.
```

6) MOVE THE INSERTION POINT USING THE ARROW KEYS AND INSERT TEXT

a. Press the left-arrow key several times. The insertion point moves to the left. Note that characters are not erased, highlighted, or affected in any way.
b. Press the right-arrow key several times. The insertion point moves, but characters are unaffected. If this were a paragraph with more than one line, the up- and down-arrow keys could also be used to move from line to line.
c. Using the arrow keys, place the insertion point directly before the first "t" in "test".
d. Type the word "important" and a space. The word is inserted, and the sentence now reads:

```
This is my important test text.
```

2.14 Text Blocks

All text in a PageMaker publication is stored in *text blocks*. A text block can consist of a single letter, or an entire page with many paragraphs. Blocks are selected and manipulated using the arrow pointer. Each text block is marked with horizontal lines at its top and bottom:

An Introduction to Desktop Publishing Using PageMaker introduces students to one of today's most requested computer skills, Desktop Publishing. Our new text covers the basics of good design and page layout using PageMaker. Other topics include using columns, adding graphic elements, incorporating color, and advanced techniques. Special emphasis is placed on using PageMaker to create advertisements, flyers and multi-page documents such as newsletters and yearbooks.

Each PageMaker feature is presented, discussed, and followed by a hands-on-practice which is performed on the computer. Numerous diagrams are included which show the student exactly how his or her page layout will look when produced by PageMaker. Completing each chapter are a variety of exercises of varying difficulty

These lines have square *handles* at each corner which allow text blocks to be manipulated in a variety of ways. By dragging a handle with the mouse, the block can be compressed or expanded, changing the look of the text:

An Introduction to Desktop Publishing Using PageMaker introduces students to one of today's most requested computer skills, Desktop Publishing. Our new text covers the basics of good design and page layout using PageMaker. Other topics include using columns, adding graphic elements, incorporating color, and advanced techniques. Special emphasis is placed on using PageMaker to create advertisements, flyers and multi-page documents such as newsletters

An Introduction to Desktop Publishing Using PageMaker introduces students to one of today's most requested computer skills, Desktop Publishing. Our new text covers the basics of good design and page layout using PageMaker. Other topics include using columns, adding graphic elements, incorporating color, and advanced techniques. Special emphasis is placed on using PageMaker to create advertisements, flyers and multi-page documents such as newsletters and yearbooks.

Each PageMaker feature is presented, discussed, and followed by a hands-on-practice which is performed on the computer. Numerous diagrams are included which show the student exactly how his or her page layout will look when produced by PageMaker. Completing each chapter are a variety of exercises of varying difficulty

Windowshade handles are shown in the middle of each text block line. These are used to indicate the status of the text block:

Empty windowshade handles indicate the beginning or ending of a block. A triangular arrow (▼), which will only be shown in the bottom handle, means that this text block contains more text which is not currently being shown. This could be the result of an editing operation or changing the size of the block. There are also other symbols which may appear in a windowshade handle.

Practice 5

In this Practice you will select and modify the text block created in Practices 3 and 4.

1) SELECT THE ARROW TOOL FROM THE TOOLBOX

a. Move the pointer to the Toolbox and click on the arrow tool, selecting it. The Arrow tool is highlighted in the Toolbox.
b. Move the pointer off the Toolbox. The pointer shape is an arrow.

2) SELECT THE TEXT BLOCK

Using the arrow pointer, click on one of the words in the sentence. The text block is selected, and the handles appear. Because of the current view (100%), only part of the text block may be shown.

3) USE A DIFFERENT VIEW TO SEE THE TEXT BLOCK

a. From the Layout menu, select the View command and choose 75% size. Note how the block runs from the left margin to the right. The two windowshade handles and four text block handles are also visible. Because this block is shown in its entirety, the windowshade handles are empty.
b. Click once on the right horizontal scroll arrow at the bottom of the screen. The view moves (scrolls) to the right. Click once on the left horizontal scroll arrow at the bottom of the screen. The view scrolls to the left.
c. Click once on the bottom vertical scroll arrow to scroll down. Click once on the top vertical scroll arrow to scroll up.

4) MODIFY THE TEXT BLOCK

a. Position the pointer on the lower-right handle of the text block.
b. Press and hold down the mouse button. the pointer changes to a double-headed arrow (↘) and PageMaker shows a temporary outline of the text block.
c. Drag the handle down several lines and to the left so that the right side of the block is over the "m" in the word "important".
d. Release the mouse button. The text block is resized, and the text within it is changed:

2

e. Zoom in to Actual size by pressing `Ctrl+1`.

5) SHRINK AND EXPAND THE TEXT BLOCK

a. Place the pointer on the lower windowshade handle.
b. Drag the handle up, until the bottom of the text block is on the word "important".
c. Release the mouse button. The lower windowshade handle now shows a red triangular arrow, indicating that this block contains more text which is not currently being shown:

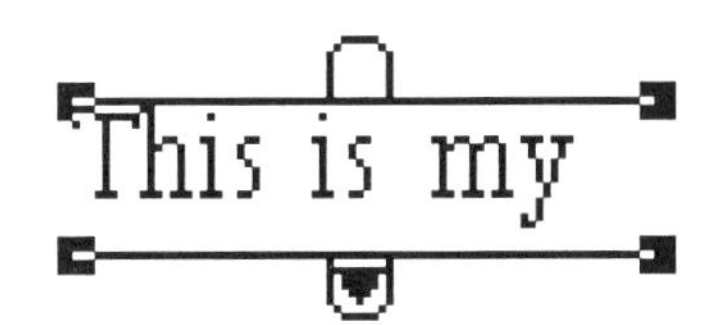

d. Again "grab" the bottom windowshade handle with the mouse and drag down, almost to the bottom of the screen.
e. Release the mouse button. The text block is expanded to include all of the text, but no more.

6) MOVE THE BLOCK

a. Place the pointer anywhere in the text block and hold down the mouse button. The cursor changes to a four-headed arrow:

b. Without releasing the button, drag the text block around the screen. Note how the entire text block is moved.
c. Position the block anywhere in the publication and release the mouse button. The text block is placed at the current position.

2.15 Saving Publications on Disk

Saving publications on disk is an important part of using PageMaker. Because the computer's memory can only store information while the power is on, any data in memory is lost when the computer is turned off. However, if a copy of the publication is saved on disk before the power is shut off, the publication can later be retrieved from the disk and loaded into memory. Unfinished publications, as well as those that might need future editing or re-printing should always be saved.

Another important reason for saving publications is to prevent their accidental loss. A momentary power interruption can wipe everything out of the computer's memory. Even accidentally bumping the power cord can sometimes cause the memory to be cleared. It is therefore a good practice, especially when working on long publications, to save the publication repeatedly. Then should a power failure occur, the publication can be restored from the disk at the point where it was last saved. It is also important to save a publication on disk before you attempt to print it because a problem involving the printer could cause the publication to be lost if it has not previously been saved.

When a publication is saved a copy of what is currently stored in the computer's memory is placed on the disk. It is important to realize that the computer also retains the publication in memory so that there are now two copies, one in memory and one on the disk. The copy in memory is erased when the computer is turned off, but the copy on the disk is permanent and can be recovered at any time.

Publications stored on disk are called *files*, and files must be given names by which they can be identified. This name can be up to 8 characters long but may only contain letters and numbers. Special symbols such as spaces, question marks, and periods may not be used. Examples of valid file names are BROCHURE, CHAPTER5, and 2PAGEAD. It is important to give a file a name that describes what it contains. For example, a file containing a résumé for Suzy Lee is better named SUZYLEE or SUZYLRES rather than just RESUME. When a new file is first saved, PageMaker asks you to supply a name for it. PageMaker automatically adds the extension .PM5 to all publication names to distinguish them from files produced by other applications.

Publications are saved by selecting the Save command from the File menu:

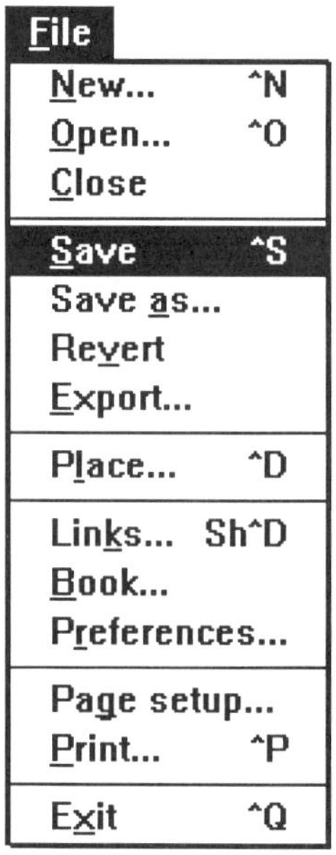

```
File
 New...        ^N
 Open...       ^O
 Close
 ----------------
 Save          ^S
 Save as...
 Revert
 Export...
 ----------------
 Place...      ^D
 ----------------
 Links...    Sh^D
 Book...
 Preferences...
 ----------------
 Page setup...
 Print...      ^P
 ----------------
 Exit          ^Q
```

This command can be executed with the keystrokes `Alt+F S`, or using the shortcut `Ctrl+S`. If this is the first time the file has been saved, PageMaker displays a dialog box. You must then type the file's name and press the Enter key:

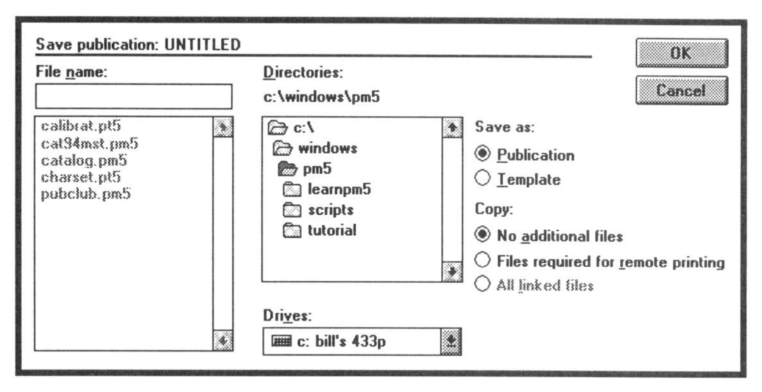

The Save dialog box

A copy of the publication in the computer's memory is then placed on the disk, using that name.

It is important to realize that any editing changes made to a previously saved file are not stored on the disk unless the file is again saved. It is also important to realize that saving an edited publication replaces the file on the disk, erasing the original version.

2.16 Printing a Publication

Printing involves sending a copy of a publication in the computer's memory to the printer. First, make sure that your computer is connected to a printer. Then check that the printer is turned on, is "on line," and, for dot matrix printers, that the paper is positioned at the top of a page. Before printing, the publication should be saved on disk so that, should an error occur and the publication be erased from the computer's memory, it can be restored from the disk.

The current publication can be printed by selecting the Print command from the File menu (`Ctrl+P`). The Print dialog box is then displayed, which allows you to specify a number of different options, including which pages and how many copies to print:

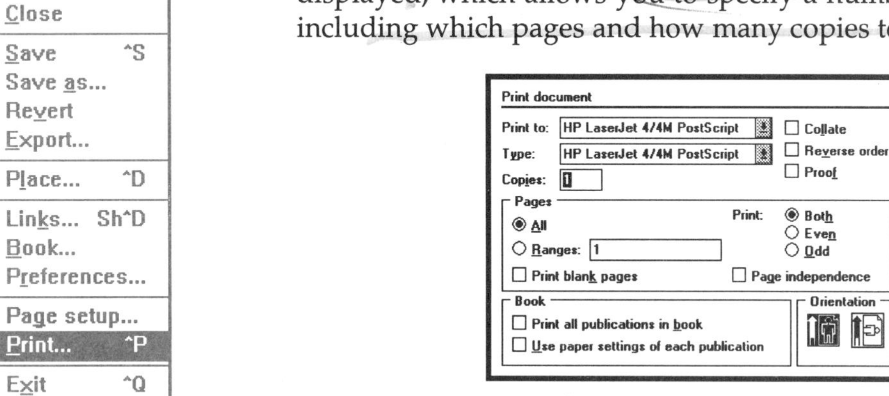

The Print command's dialog box

Because the default values are most normally used, simply clicking on the Print button starts the printing. If more than one copy of the publication is to be printed, the number required can be typed in the Copies box before selecting Print. It is possible to interrupt the printing by pressing the Escape key.

Practice 6

In this Practice you will save and print the publication created in the previous Practices.

1) *SAVE THE PUBLICATION USING THE NAME MYPUB*

a. From the File menu, select the Save command. The Save publication dialog box is shown.
b. Type MYPUB in the File name box and press the Enter key to select OK. PageMaker adds the proper extension (.PM5) and saves the publication using the name MYPUB.PM5. When the dialog box is removed, note that the MYPUB.PM5 is displayed at the top of the publication window.

2) *PRINT THE PUBLICATION*

a. Check to make certain that your computer is connected to a printer, and that the printer is turned on and has paper.
b. From the File menu, select the Print command. The Print document dialog box is shown.
c. Verify that the number of Copies is 1 and that All is selected as the Pages option.
d. Select Print to print the publication. PageMaker displays a message telling you that the publication is being printed. In a few moments the printing should be complete and the document is printed. Note that more complex publications can take many minutes per page to print.

2.17 Closing the Publication and Exiting PageMaker

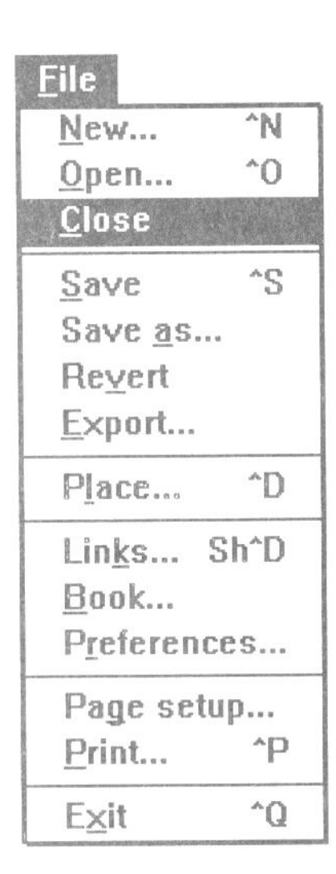

After you are through working with a publication it should be closed using the Close command from the File menu. This ensures that it will be safely stored on the disk. If you have created a new publication or made changes to an existing publication and not saved it, you will be prompted before closing:

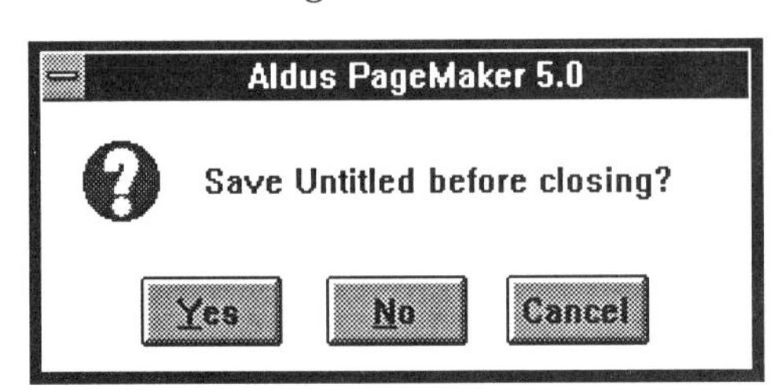

This warning appears if you attempt to close a publication which has not been saved

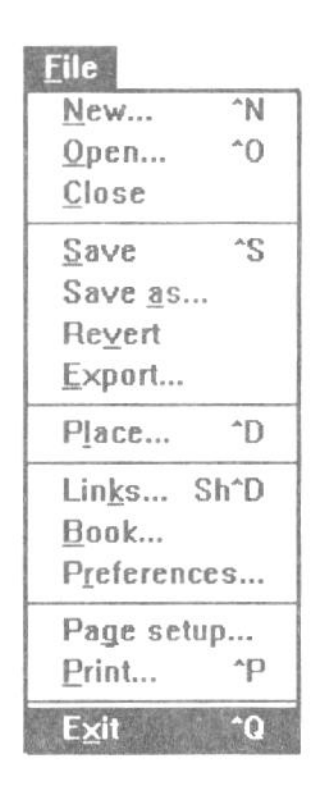

If you wish to discard the changes, select No. If you do not wish to close the publication, select Cancel. To save the changes and then close the publication select Yes.

It is important to exit PageMaker when you are done using it. Never just turn the computer off or walk away from it because doing so could damage the files on the disk. Always select the Exit command from the File menu (`Ctrl+Q`) when you are through. If you are through using Windows, you should exit that as well (with the Exit command from the File menu, or with the shortcut `Alt+F4`).

Practice 7

In this Practice you will close the current publication and exit PageMaker. Windows will be closed and the computer returned to the DOS prompt.

1) *CLOSE MYPUB*

From the File menu, select the Close command. The publication is closed and the publication window is removed. Note: if you have made any changes to the publication you will be prompted here to save them. Select Yes.

2) *EXIT PAGEMAKER*

From the File menu, select the Exit command. The PageMaker program is terminated, and the Windows screen is again shown. From this screen it is possible to restart PageMaker by double-clicking on the Aldus PageMaker 5.0 icon as described in Practice 1.

3) *EXIT WINDOWS*

From the Windows File menu, select the Exit command to exit Windows. Windows displays a warning:

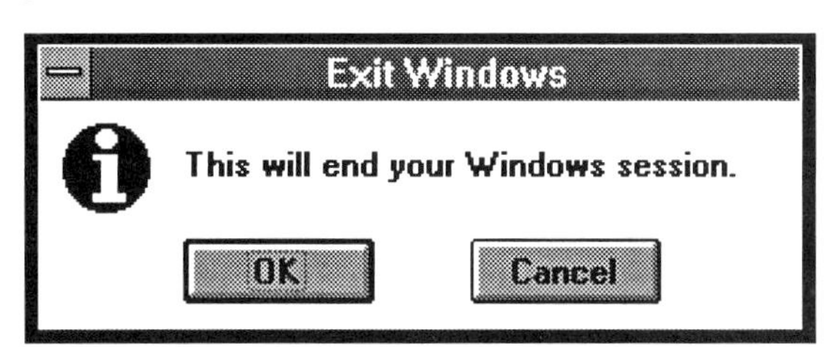

Click on OK. The Windows screen is removed and you are returned to the DOS prompt. Only at this point can the computer be safely turned off. It is possible to restart Windows from this point by typing `WIN` as described in Practice 1.

Chapter Summary

PageMaker is a powerful desktop publishing program which allows text and graphics to be combined in a variety of different ways to create professional looking publications. Both DOS and Windows must be loaded before PageMaker can be run.

PageMaker and Windows require the use of a mouse to select different objects on the screen. The mouse can be used to point (place the mouse on an object), click (place the pointer on an object and press the mouse button), double-click (click twice in rapid succession), and drag (point to an object, hold down the mouse button and move the pointer). A triple-click is used to highlight an entire paragraph with the Text tool.

Like all Windows programs, the PageMaker screen has several different parts. The menu bar at the top of the screen contains lists of commands which can be accessed either by using the `Alt` key or clicking on the menu name with the mouse. Commands in menus can be executed by typing the highlighted letter or clicking on them. Many commands have dialog boxes which contain different options that can be selected using the keyboard or mouse.

Another important part of the PageMaker screen is the Toolbox. Here, different tools are selected which allow text to be entered and modified, graphics to be drawn, and other actions taken. The currently selected tool is highlighted in the box, and most tools change the shape of the mouse pointer. For example, the commonly used Text tool changes the shape of the mouse pointer to an I-Beam.

Once PageMaker has been started, a new publication may be created using the New command from the File menu. A dialog box allows the margins and other options to be selected for this publication. Once these have been specified, the empty publication is displayed on the screen.

PageMaker has a comprehensive Help system that is accessible through the Help command and includes information, examples, and tutorials. The Using PageMaker Help command describes how to use the Help system to find answers to specific questions that you might have.

With a page visible, text can be typed into the publication using the Text tool. Changes to the text itself can be made by inserting, deleting and replacing. The mouse is used to select the text to be modified, and to create insertion points where new text is entered. Text is contained within a text block, which can be stretched and modified using the Pointer tool.

2

Publications should be saved frequently to avoid loss due to power failures. Saved publications may also be recalled at a later date for editing. Once saved, a publication may be printed. When work on a publication is complete, the publication should be closed, and when all work in PageMaker is complete it should be exited. All of the commands necessary to perform these tasks are found in the File menu.

Some commands have keyboard shortcuts, most involving the `Ctrl` (Control) key. For example, pressing `Ctrl+S` is a shortcut for the executing the Save command from the File menu, and saves the current publication on disk. It is best to use the menu commands until you are familiar with the shortcuts.

Vocabulary

Booting - Starting the computer and loading DOS.

Button - Option on a dialog box which may be selected by clicking on it.

Check box - Dialog box option used to select one or more options from a related group of options.

Clicking - Pressing the mouse button.

Cursor - Blinking vertical line shown on the screen which indicates where text will be inserted. (Also called Insertion point.)

Default - A command or option that is initially selected and used if no other command or option is chosen.

Desktop Publishing - Using a computer to combine text and graphics in different ways to produce a professional looking printed publication.

Dialog Box - An area on the screen where PageMaker displays messages and information, and accepts data from the keyboard.

DOS (Disk Operating System) - The most basic programs that the computer needs in order to run.

DOS prompt - Screen message displayed by DOS which lets you know that it is ready to receive a typed command.

Double-clicking - Pressing the mouse button twice in rapid succession.

Dragging - Moving the mouse while holding down the mouse button.

File - A collection of data stored electronically on disk.

Greeking - Small, often unreadable letters produced by certain views.

Handle - Corner of text block used to adjust size of block.

Highlighting - Selecting text which is shown as reversed (white on black) on the screen.

I-Beam pointer - Text tool pointer used when entering or editing text.

Import - Bring a file produced by another application, usually a word processor, into PageMaker.

Insertion Point - Blinking vertical line shown on the screen which indicates where text will be inserted. (Also called cursor.)

List - Dialog box option used to select from a scrollable list of items.

Menu - List of available commands from which a command may be chosen using the keyboard or mouse.

Menu Bar - List of available menus shown at top of the screen.

Mouse - Hardware device used to select items on screen.

Mouse Pointer - Image on screen produced by moving the mouse.

Pasteboard - An area around the publication where unused text or graphics may be stored until needed.

Pointing - Placing the mouse pointer on an object on screen.

Publication - Related text and graphics stored together in a PageMaker file.

Radio button - Dialog box option used to select one option from a related group of options.

Rulers - Screen rulers at top and left of screen used to measure distances within the publication and indicate current mouse position.

Scroll Arrow - Arrows on scroll bars for displaying different parts of a publication.

Scroll Bar - Bars to right and below publication which can be used to display different parts of the publication.

Submenu - List of options produced by a menu from which you may select.

Text - Any combination of letters, numbers, and symbols that may be entered from the keyboard.

Text Block - Group of contiguous text in a PageMaker publication. Text blocks may be stretched, shrunk, moved, etc.

Toolbox - Area on the PageMaker screen from which different tools may be selected.

Windows - Graphical interface for DOS which PageMaker needs to run.

Windowshade handle - handle in middle of text block used to adjust length of block and indicate links between blocks.

Reviews

Sections 2.1 — 2.6

1. Briefly explain what pointing and clicking are.
   Pointing is placing the mouse pointer on an object on the screen & clicking is pressing & releasing the left mouse button (selects that object)
2. How is an object dragged on the computer screen?
   Place mouse pointer on object, hold down left mouse button & move the mouse.
3. What is meant by booting?
   The process of transferring DOS from disk to to computer memory (if necessary). Otherwise just turn on computer.
4. Describe the process of starting PageMaker beginning from the DOS prompt.
   Type WIN & press Enter to load Windows, Double Click on Aldus Group Icon, Double Click on Aldus Pagemaker 5.0 icon.
5. a) What is a menu? A list of different commands that may be chosen
   b) Where are menu names found? Menu Bar at top of screen
   c) How may a menu be displayed? Click on menu Name
   d) Give two ways in which a command may be chosen from a menu.
   Click on the command or use keyboard & press Alt plus the underlined letter of the command at the same time
6. What is a dialog box and what is one used for?
   A box displayed after selecting a menu item followed by ... & allows you to supply additional information PageMaker needs to execute the command.
7. How is a button selected from a dialog box?
   Click on the button
8. If a list contains more information than is currently displayed, how may the hidden information be displayed?
   Click on scroll arrows to the right of the list
9. Explain the difference between a Radio button and a Check box.
   When radio buttons are used, only one option may be selected. With check boxes any number of the listed options may be selected at the same time.

Sections 2.7 — 2.11

10. Explain what the Pasteboard is and what it is used for.
    An area around the actual publication where currently unused text or graphics may be stored until needed.
11. What is the Toolbox? How is a tool selected from it?
    A Box with different pictures in it which represent different tasks that can be performed with the mouse. Click on desired tool with mouse to select.
12. Explain the two different ways in which text may be entered into a PageMaker publication. Directly by typing onto the publication page + Imported from another source, usually a word processing program
13. What is an insertion point and how is one created?
    A blinking vertical line (cursor) indicating where text may be typed. Select the text tool, then click on the publication.
14. a) Why does PageMaker have different views? To view how the entire pg. looks on screen, or to view a specific smaller portion of publication up close.
    b) How are views changed? Choose Layout, View, then 25% size, etc. or Shortcut Keys or Zoom tool
    c) What is Actual Size view? How much of a PageMaker page is displayed in Actual Size view? 100% view. - all elements of page shown at 100% of size. Only a small portion.
15. What is the difference between moving the insertion point using the cursor keys or the Delete key? Using cursor keys does not change text = Using delete key deletes each character to the right of the cursor

Sections 2.12 — 2.16

16. a) What is the effect of executing the Undo command? Reverses the effect of the previously executed command
    b) What will occur if Undo is executed two times in sequence? "Undoes" the effects of the first Undo, + the edited text is restored.
17. a) Explain how a text block is selected. Click on the arrow tool, then click on one of the words in the sentence (or ¶, page, etc) + it will be selected.
    b) How is a selected block indicated on the screen? Selected text is indicated by horizontal lines at it's top + bottom, with square handles at each corner.
    c) What may be done to the text block once selected? Once selected, text can be moved, compressed or expanded.
18. How can a text block be expanded?
    By dragging a handle with the mouse.
19. a) What is indicated by an empty windowshade handle? Block is shown in its entirety.
    b) What is indicated by a windowshade handle containing a triangle arrow? This block contains more text which is not currently being shown.
20. Why is it important to save a publication on disk before printing it?
    The publication can later be retrieved from the disk + loaded into memory for re-printing and/or editing.
21. When a publication is saved on disk what happens to the copy stored in the computer's memory? Any data in memory is lost when the computer is turned off.
22. What is a file and why must it be given a name? A file is a publication (or letter, report, etc.) stored on a disk (or hard drive). It must be given a name in order to be identified so that it can be retrieved for reviewing, editing and/or printing.
23. What should be considered in naming a file?
    Give a file a name that describes what it contains, using up to 8 characters containing only letters + numbers. NO SPECIAL SYMBOLS SUCH AS SPACES, QUESTION MARKS + PERIODS ARE ALLOWED.
24. If a file is saved on disk and then subsequently edited what must be done to retain the edits? The file must be saved again, which erases the original version + replaces it with the edited version.
25. Explain the steps required to print a document. Check to make certain computer is connected to a printer + that it is on + has paper. Select the Print command from the File menu. Verify desired # of copies + that All selected at the Print document Dialog box. Select Print.
26. a) What happens when the Close command is executed? The publication is closed + the publication window is removed.
    b) When should you execute the Close command? After you are through working with a publication, it should be closed using the close command from the file menu.
27. Describe the steps necessary to close an open publication and return to the DOS prompt. Select Close from File menu. (If you have made any changes, you will be prompted here to save them. Select Yes)
    From File menu, select Exit.
    From Windows File menu, select Exit. Click on OK (This will end your Windows session)
    Windows screen is removed + you are returned to DOS prompt.

2

Exercises

1. California Sunshine produces gourmet beverages in six flavors made from natural fruit juices. They are in the process of expanding their product line to include three new flavors—cherry, apple, and tangerine. A press release is being prepared to announce the new flavors. Follow the steps below to create and format the release.

   a) Create a new PageMaker file and enter the following in a new text block. Select a view of 75% to allow you to see the entire text block as it is entered:

      California Sunshine, producers of natural fruit juices, today announced the release of three delicious new flavors: cherry, apple, and tangerine. Only the finest cherries from Oregon will be used to produce our new Cheery Cherry Cooler. Apples from Washington will be specially selected from that state's finest orchards and blended to concoct Sweet Apple Refresher. From the sunny valleys of southern California native tangerines will be peeled by hand and slow processed to produce a tart but lively Tasty Tangerine juice. All three new flavors will be available later this month in select retail outlets.

   b) Switch to Fit in Window view. Select the story and resize the text block so that it is a tall, thin column that runs from the top margin to the bottom.

   c) Save the publication naming it CSPRESS.

   d) Print a copy of CSPRESS.

   e) Resize the text block so that is runs from the left margin to the right margin. Move the story to the center of the page.

   f) Tangerines are currently in short supply so California Sunshine has decided to postpone the release of their Tasty Tangerine juice. Switch views and edit the article to remove all references to tangerines. Your publication should be similar to:

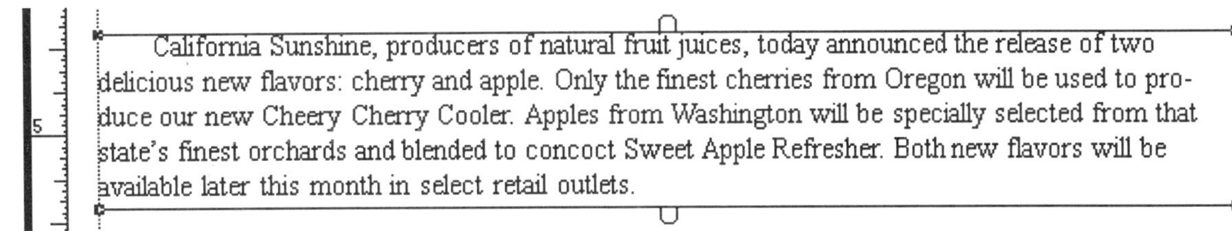

   g) Save the edited publication and print a copy.

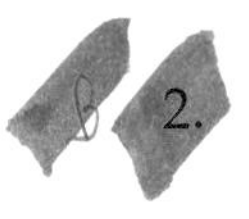

2. The Aztec Café, a local Mexican restaurant, is planning an advertising brochure that will include articles about the café. Follow the steps below to create and format one of the stories for the brochure.

   a) Create a new PageMaker file and enter the following in a new text block. Select a view of 75% to allow you to see the entire text block as it is entered:

   ```
      The Aztec Cafe is planning an addition to its
   facilities that will include a new dining room seating
   120 customers. The dining room will be named the
   Acapulco Room and decorated in a native Mexican motif.
   This beautiful room will be used primarily for private
   parties, banquets, weddings, and organizational
   meetings.
   ```

   b) Select the story and resize the text block so that it fits across the left half of the page.

   c) Save the publication naming it ACBROCH.

   d) Print a copy of the publication.

   e) Highlight the word "The" in "The Aztec Cafe" and delete it. Aztec has decided to make its new room smaller. Change the seating capacity from 120 to 80.

   f) Move the story to the bottom of the page. Your publication should be similar to:

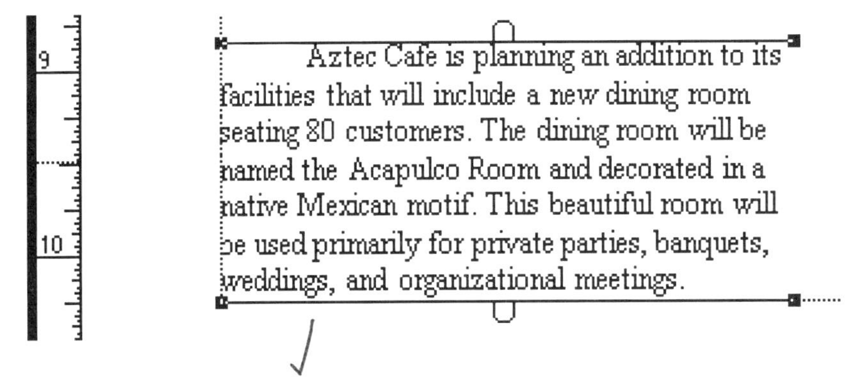

   g) Save the modified ACBROCH and print a copy.

3. Aztec Café has just raised its prices and needs a new menu. Follow the steps below to create and format the menu.

   a) Create a new PageMaker file and select 75% view. Enter the text below spaced approximately as shown. Press the Tab key once between the food names and prices and leave a blank line between items:

```
Aztec Cafe

The finest Mexican food in all of Dade County

Hot tamales    $3.50

Beef fajitas   $9.95

Chicken fajitas     $8.95

Shrimp fajitas $11.95

Beef tacos (3) $5.95

Chicken tacos (3)   $4.95

Taco salad     $6.95
```

b) Save the publication naming it ACMENU.

c) Print a copy of ACMENU.

d) Aztec's owner has decided that some prices are too high. Reduce the price of each of the fajitas by $1.00.

e) Add a new item to the menu before the tacos:

```
Mexican Fiesta platter   $14.95
```

Your publication should be similar to:

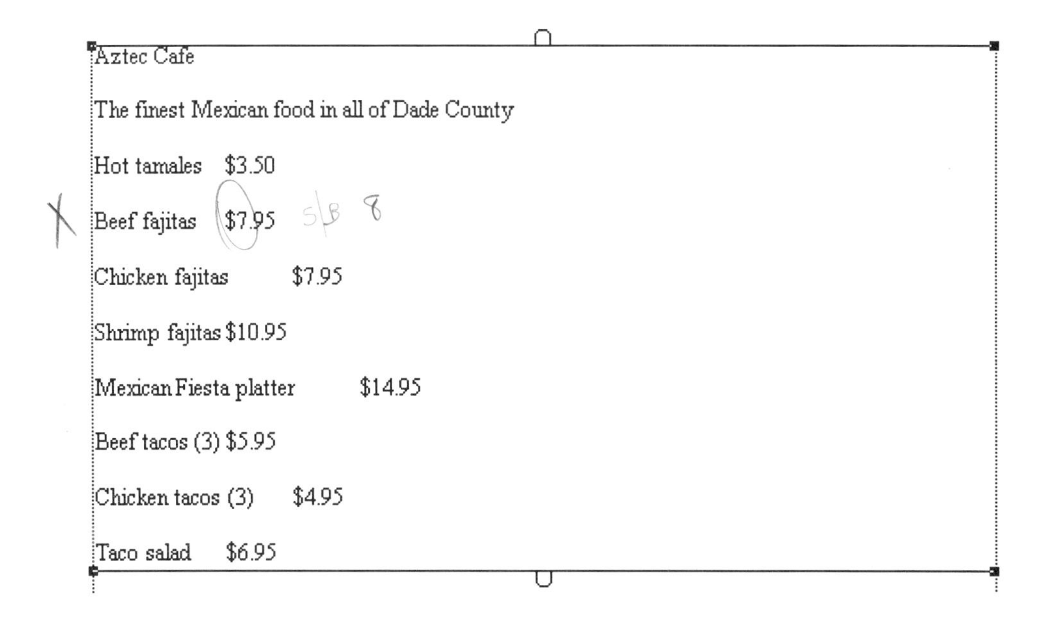

Aztec Cafe

The finest Mexican food in all of Dade County

Hot tamales $3.50

Beef fajitas $7.95

Chicken fajitas $7.95

Shrimp fajitas $10.95

Mexican Fiesta platter $14.95

Beef tacos (3) $5.95

Chicken tacos (3) $4.95

Taco salad $6.95

f) Save the modified ACMENU and print a copy.

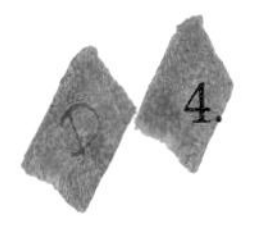

4. Deborah Debit has asked you to produce her résumé using PageMaker. Follow the steps below to create the résumé so that it is similar to:

```
Deborah N. Debit
1117 East Hathaway Drive
Newtown, FL 33445
407/555-6970

OBJECTIVE
A leadership position in the financial affairs
department of a publishing company.

WORK EXPERIENCE
1991 - present
Bennett Chemical Industries, Newtown, FL: Accountant.
Manage all accounts payable/receivable using a
computerized system which includes spreadsheet and
other accounting software.

1990 - 1991
Dr. Roger Calculate, College Circle, FL: Research
Assistant. Prepared case studies for new accounting
textbook.

EDUCATION
1987 - 1991
BS Accounting: State University, College Circle, FL.
Departmental Honors in Business and Finance.
Chairperson, Future Accountants of America. College
Circle Community Service Award.

1983 - 1987
High School Diploma: Newtown High School, Newtown, FL.
Senior Class President. Member, Small Business Club.

REFERENCES
Available from:
Students' Career Placement Office
State University
College Circle, FL 32306
```

a) Create a new text block and enter the data shown above.

b) Save the file naming it DDRESUME.

c) Print a copy of DDRESUME.

Chapter Three:
Working with Text & Graphics

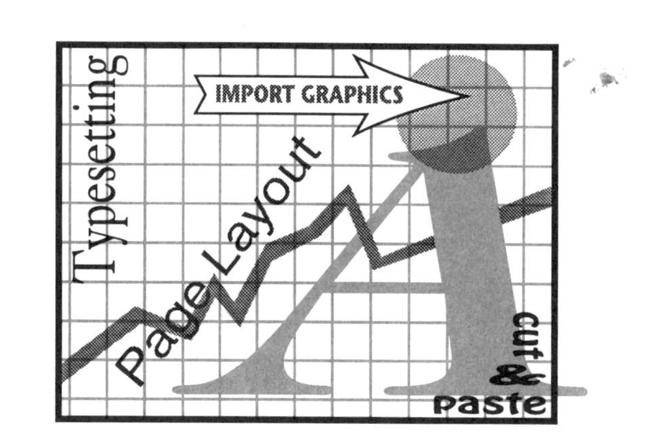

File - Place

File - Open

Type - Font, Size, Style

Type - Type specs

Type - Alignment

Edit - Select all

Edit - Cut, Copy, Paste

Element - Line

Element - Fill

Objectives

3

After completing this chapter you will be able to:

1. Import text using the Place command.
2. Open existing files and make modifications.
3. Change typefaces.
4. Create superscripts and subscripts.
5. Apply different alignments to text blocks.
6. Change the flow of linked text blocks.
7. Use the Clipboard to cut and paste information.
8. Create and edit PageMaker graphics.
9. Import and modify graphics.

3

Desktop publishing has previously been defined as combining text and graphics to create a single document, or *publication*. A publication can be a newsletter, magazine, advertisement, newspaper, book, business card, technical manual, etc. In the last chapter you entered text into a new publication and learned that PageMaker has some tools for the creation of simple graphics. However, the majority of the text and graphics that appear in desktop-published documents are not created in PageMaker. The text is usually created in a separate word processing package such as Word, WordPerfect, or Microsoft Works. Graphics are created using other programs such as Corel Draw, Adobe Illustrator, or PC Paintbrush. In this chapter you will learn how the individual text and graphic files are *imported* into PageMaker using the Place command. This chapter also covers the ways in which text can be formatted, and how text blocks are linked to form *stories*.

3.1 Of Filters and Importing

Each word processor program creates files which are unique to that program. In other words, a file created by Word cannot be read by WordPerfect, and vice versa. It would be inconvenient if we required different versions of PageMaker to import text from each different word processor. Instead, PageMaker utilizes *filters* which allow it to translate different word processing files into a format which it can understand.

Filters are created when PageMaker is originally installed. If the correct filter is not available, you will not be able to import files for that specific word processor. Filters can be added and deleted later using the Aldus Setup program. Full instructions for using Aldus Setup are found in the PageMaker manuals from Aldus.

This text assumes the existence of two common filters; *ASCII text* for plain, unformatted files and *Microsoft Word* for longer, formatted files. Your PageMaker should already have these filters installed. If not, see your instructor or check the PageMaker manuals for instructions on how to install these filters.

3.2 Importing Text

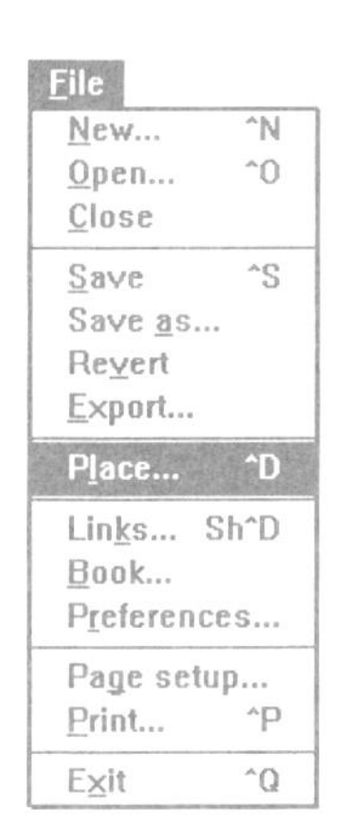

The Place command from the File menu (Ctrl+D) is used to import text and graphics. When selected, PageMaker displays a list of importable files from which you may choose:

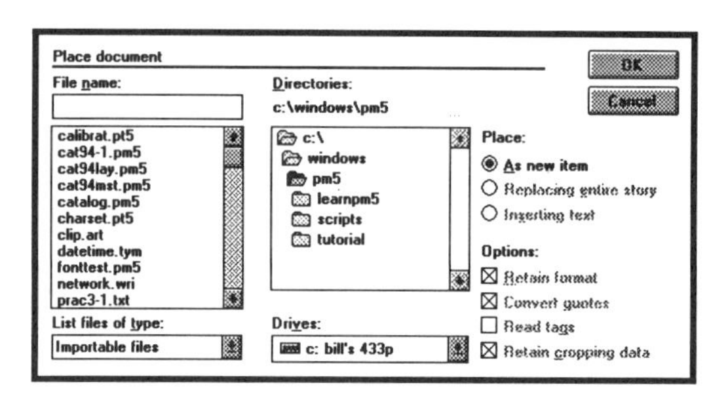

The Place document dialog box

The file to be imported is selected from the list and OK clicked. ASCII text files (normally indicated by the file name extension .TXT) require that certain options be selected:

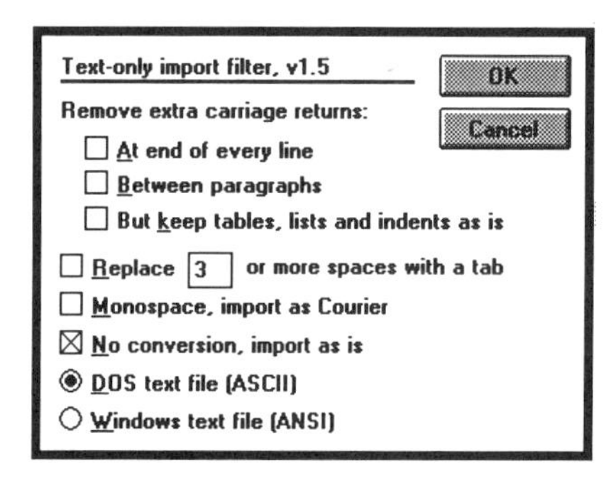

Some filters have dialog boxes

Normally the defaults are correct and the file may be imported by clicking on OK.

At this point the filter is applied to translate the file into a form that PageMaker can understand. After the translation is complete, the pointer changes to the *loaded Text* shape, indicating that text is ready to be placed:

The loaded Text pointer

Clicking a loaded Text pointer causes the imported text to be placed in the publication, starting at the current position of the pointer. Depending on the amount of text to be placed, and the size of the publication, this could result in more than one text block being created.

3

Practice 1

In this Practice you will import a small text file and place it into a new publication. Both DOS and Windows will be loaded, then PageMaker started.

1) START WINDOWS AND PAGEMAKER

a. Following the instructions given in Chapter Two, turn on the computer.
b. Type `WIN` to start Windows.
c. Locate the Aldus PageMaker 5.0 icon and double-click on it to start PageMaker.

2) CREATE A NEW PUBLICATION

a. From the File menu, select the New command. The Page setup dialog box is shown.
b. Verify that the Page option is Letter, Orientation is Tall, and that your printer is listed as the Compose to printer.
c. Select OK to accept the options and create a new publication.
d. Using the Layout menu's View command, switch to 75% size.
e. Use the scroll bars and arrows to position the window so that the upper-left corner of the publication is showing.

3) IMPORT A WORD PROCESSING FILE

a. From the File menu, select the Place command. The Place document dialog box is shown.
b. Locate the file named PRAC-3.TXT in the files list. If the file name is not immediately visible, click on the up and down scroll arrows next to the list to display more file names.
c. Click on PRAC-3.TXT. PageMaker copies that file name to the File name line above the list.
d. Click on OK. The Text-only import filter dialog box is displayed.
e. Select OK to accept the default options. PageMaker removes the box and displays the publication screen. The translation operation can take a few seconds, especially with long files. After the file is processed, the pointer is changed to the loaded text shape.

4) PLACE THE IMPORTED FILE

a. Place the loaded Text pointer at the upper-left corner of the document, at the intersection of the left and top margin lines:

b. Being careful not to move the mouse from this position, click the button. The text is placed, with the text block running from the left margin to the right margin. Your publication should be similar to:

The Place command from the File menu (Ctrl+D) is used to import text and graphics. When selected, PageMaker displays a list of importable files from which you may choose.

Placed text may consist of several or just one text block. This is dependent on two things; the amount of text placed, and the size of the text block. However, text blocks are not permanent. Several smaller text blocks may be combined into a single, large block, or a lengthy text block may be broken into a group of smaller ones.

This is the start of the next block. In the next Practice, you will divide this one block into several others, and then combine them all back into one large block. You will need to recall several skills from the last chapter where text blocks were manipulated by changing their widths and lengths.

PageMaker refers to a group of related text as a "story." Therefore, this entire imported document is one story. A story may consist of one text block, or many linked text blocks. A PageMaker document may contain a single story or many different ones.

5) SAVE THE FILE ON DISK

a. From the File menu, select the Save command. The Save publication dialog box is displayed.
b. Type the file name `CH3PRACT` and select OK. The publication with the imported text is saved on disk using the name CH3PRACT.PM5.

6) CLOSE THE FILE

From the File menu, select the Close command. The file is closed and the publication removed from the screen. Do not exit PageMaker. In the next Practice this file will be opened and modified.

3.3 Opening Files

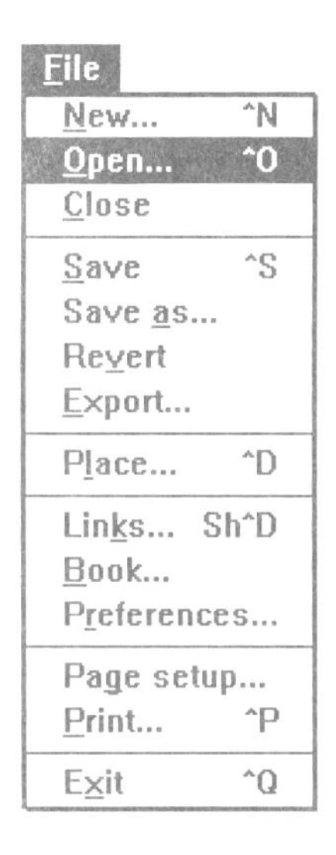

Files that have been saved can be loaded back into PageMaker and edited or modified. Before a previously saved file may be edited it must first be transferred from the disk to the computer's memory. This is accomplished by selecting the Open command from the File menu (`Ctrl+O`). A list of previously saved file names is displayed:

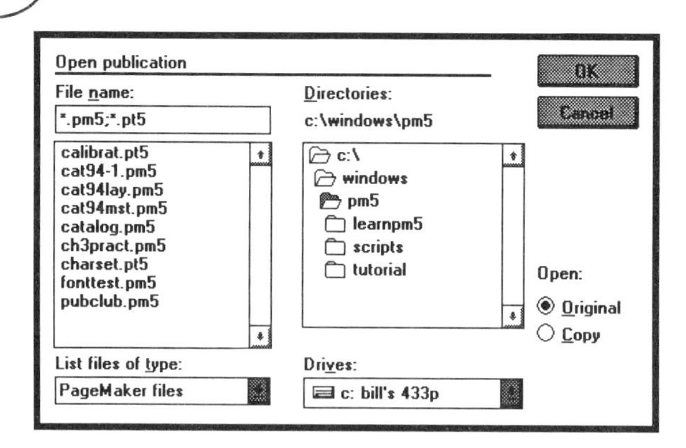

The Open publication dialog box—different files may be listed

The name of the file to be opened is highlighted in the files list. If the file name is not immediately visible, the up and down arrow buttons next to the list can be used to scroll the list to display more file names. Once the file's name has been highlighted, selecting OK transfers a copy of the file to the computer's memory and screen where it may then be edited. Note that you may see different files in this dialog box depending on what has been saved on your disk.

Practice 2

In this Practice you will open the CH3PRACT.PM5 file created in Practice 1. Boot the computer and start Windows and PageMaker if you have not already done so.

1) EXECUTE THE OPEN COMMAND

From the File menu, select the Open command. The Open publication dialog box is displayed.

2) SELECT THE FILE TO BE OPENED

Click on the file named CH3PRACT.PM5 in the files list. If the file name is not immediately visible, click on the up and down arrows next to the list until it is.

3) OPEN THE FILE

With CH3PRACT.PM5 highlighted, select OK to open the file. A copy of the file is loaded into the computer's memory and displayed on the screen.

3.4 Fonts and Typefaces

A *font* or *typeface* is a family of letters drawn in a specific style. For example, the word "fonts" in the heading to this section looks different than the same word in the first sentence. That is because each is printed in a different typeface.

There are literally thousands of typefaces, each with its own "personality." However, typefaces can generally be grouped into two categories, *serif* and *sans serif*. Serifs are the small lines found at the tops and bottoms of letters. Part decoration, the serifs help draw the reader's eye from letter to letter:

Serif **The** No Serif (Sans Serif) **The**

Probably the most common serif typeface is named Times (or Times Roman, Times New Roman, or Tms Rmn):

Times Roman

Times Roman, a serif font. Note the serifs at the top and bottom of each letter

This typeface was originally designed for use with the *London Times* newspaper in the 1930's. Because it can be used in small spaces, like the column of a newspaper, it remains popular today.

The most popular sans serif (meaning without serifs) typeface is named Helvetica, or just Helv for short:

Helvetica

The ubiquitous Helvetica, a sans serif font, can be found on everything from street signs to soup cans

Sans serif faces tend to be easier to read in short lines, and for that reason Helvetica is used in titles, on signs and labels, or anywhere the length of the line is small. Compare the letters "i", "e", and "a" in the Times font to Helvetica and you will see that, although the basic shapes are the same, each letter is really very different.

There is a third group of typefaces called fancy or *decorative*. These fonts are used for special purposes, such as wedding invitations or advertisements, and include symbols and picture-like elements called *dingbats*:

Fette Fraktur MACHINE *Nuptial Script* Tekton

✎☆✢✍✉✤❀❂✲★✸ ✄ ☎

Examples of four decorative fonts and dingbats

Zapf Chancery is a good example of a decorative font. Symbol, Zapf Dingbats, and WingDings are dingbat fonts.

Typefaces also have different styles. **Bold** is a darker or heavier version. *Italic* (or oblique) is slanted and slightly cursive. ***Bold Italic*** is a combination of both:

Times Roman (plain)
Times Bold
Times Italic
Times Bold Italic

Technically the word *typeface* refers to the entire family of styles, such as Times shown above. *Font* refers to a specific style of a typeface, such as Times Bold. PageMaker uses both words interchangeably.

One of the major advances made by PageMaker is that it shows the font on the screen as it will be printed. That is, letters in a bold italic serif face appear bold and italic with serifs on the screen. While this sounds logical, it takes a great deal of computing power to perform, and was noticeably absent from early word processors. This ability is referred to as WYSIWYG ("whizzy wig"), and stands for What You See Is What You Get.

3.5 Type Size

Letters can also be made different sizes. In typesetting, letter size is measured vertically in *points*, each of which is 1/72 of an inch. *Body copy*, the text that makes up the majority of a publication, is most commonly found in sizes from 6 to 14 points. Headlines, titles, and other attention getting lines appear in 16 to 72 points. Of course, any size may be used depending on the message to be expressed. An important newspaper headline such as "War Declared" would probably be printed at several hundred points. Here are several common sizes, all shown in Helvetica:

8 point: The Quick, brown fox...
10 point: The Quick, brown fox...
11 point: The Quick, brown fox...
12 point: The Quick, brown fox...
14 point: The Quick, brown fox...
18 point: The Quick, brown fox...

As you saw in Chapter Two, small type is often greeked, or shown in unreadable characters on the screen. Very large type is stretched or *vectored* to fit the space:

This is stretched/vectored Helvetica.
This is stretched/vectored Times.

The choice of size and typeface can be difficult because it is important that the way the message is presented does not interfere with the message itself. The different options and considerations for size and typeface are covered in more detail in Chapter Five.

3.6 Selecting Fonts, Sizes, and Styles

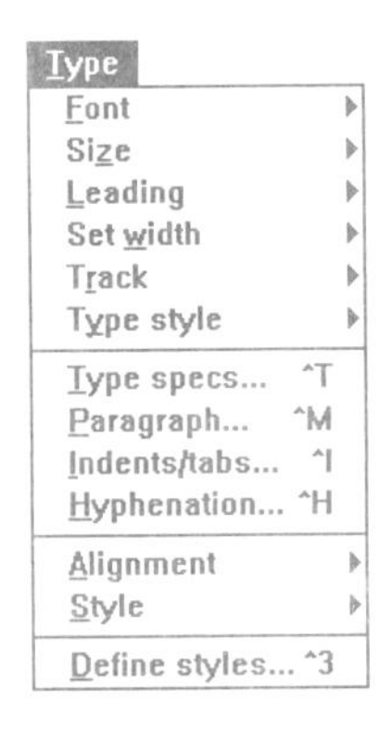

Options for type are selected from the Type menu. Before using these commands, the text to be changed must first be highlighted. This can be done a number of different ways, using the mouse or keyboard as described in the previous chapter. Several of the commands in the Type menu have triangular arrows pointing to the right following the command's name. This indicates that the command contains a *submenu*, a list of options from which you may choose only one. When a command with a submenu is selected, the submenu is displayed next to the menu. The View command discussed in the last chapter had a submenu.

The Font command allows the typeface to be selected from a submenu. Available typefaces vary from printer to printer, and shown below are the Font submenus for two common printers, a Hewlett-Packard LaserJet printer and a PostScript printer:

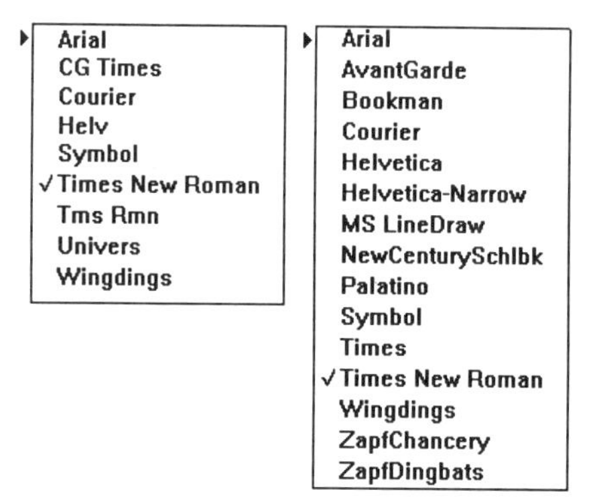

Font submenus for HP LaserJet and PostScript printers

The check mark indicates the current font of the highlighted text. If no text is highlighted, the check mark indicates the *default* font—the font which will be used automatically for any new text.

The Size command changes the size of the highlighted text, in points. PageMaker will list the available sizes on a submenu and show the current size with a check mark:

Other...
6
8
9
10
11
✓12
14
18
24
30
36
48
60
72

The Size submenu—different fonts may be available in different sizes

The available sizes on this submenu differ from font to font, and from printer to printer. Some fonts are available in sizes from 1 to several hundred points. When this is the case, the Other option can be used to specify a size which is not displayed on the list.

Different styles are selected using the Type style command's submenu. The checked style is the style of the highlighted text:

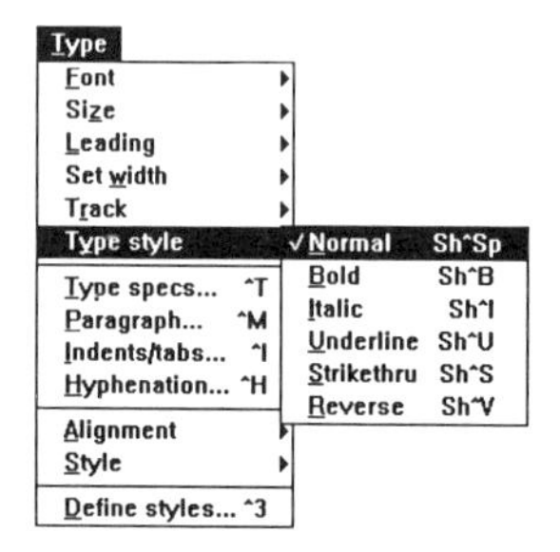

3

In addition to bold, italic, and underline, PageMaker allows fonts to be printed in several other styles. Strikethrough draws a line through the middle of the characters and is most often used for legal documents. Reverse prints white letters on a dark background and will be used later in the text. Normal removes any style options previously set.

There are a few things to remember when using Style commands. The first is that the command only affects the highlighted text. Second, to apply a style such as bold italic actually takes two commands—one to set bold and a second to set italic. This is where the keyboard shortcuts come in handy. You will note in the menu above that the shortcuts for styles contain a third abbreviation, Sh. This refers to the Shift key, and means that applying a type style using a keyboard shortcut requires three keys to be pressed at the same time. For example, the shortcut for Bold, Sh^B, means to hold down the Shift, Control, and B keys together. To remove all styles, select Normal by pressing Shift, Control, and the Space Bar.

Practice 3

In this Practice you will change fonts, sizes, and styles for the text imported in Practice 1. Start Windows and PageMaker if you have not already done so, and open the CH3PRACT.PM5 publication created in the first Practice.

Note: Different printers have different fonts. We will specify and show PostScript fonts in this Practice, and for the remainder of this text.

1) *ZOOM TO 75% SIZE AND DISPLAY THE FIRST PARAGRAPH*

a. If it is not already, display the publication at 75% size.
b. Use the scroll bars and arrows to display the first paragraph on screen.

2) *HIGHLIGHT THE FIRST PARAGRAPH*

a. Select the Text tool from the Toolbox. The pointer changes to the I-Beam shape.
b. Place the pointer anywhere in the first paragraph and triple-click. The entire first paragraph is highlighted.

3) *SET THE TEXT SIZE TO 18 POINTS*

a. From the Type menu, select the Size command. The submenu appears to the right of the menu.
b. Click on 18 in the submenu to select it. (Note: if 18 is not available in your submenu, select 'Other' and enter 18.) PageMaker changes the size of the highlighted text to 18 points and reformats the publication:

The Place command from the File menu (Ctrl+D) is used to import text and graphics. When selected, PageMaker displays a list of importable files from which you may choose.

Placed text may consist of several or just one text block. This is dependent on two things; the amount of text placed, and the size of the text block. However, text blocks are not permanent. Several smaller text blocks may be combined into a single, large block, or a lengthy text block may be broken into a group of smaller ones.

4) MAKE SOME TEXT BOLD

a. Locate the word "dependent" in the second sentence of the second paragraph.
b. Place the pointer on the word and double-click. "dependent" is highlighted.
c. From the Type menu, select the Type style command. The submenu is displayed.
d. Select Bold from the submenu. PageMaker makes the highlighted text bold.

5) UNDERLINE A SENTENCE USING THE KEYBOARD SHORTCUT

a. Place the pointer on the "H" in "However", which begins the next sentence.
b. Drag the mouse across the entire sentence, until the pointer is just beyond the period after "permanent."
c. Use the keyboard shortcut `Shift+Ctrl+U` to underline the highlighted text .

6) CHANGE THE FONT USING THE KEYBOARD

a. Triple click on the second paragraph to highlight it.
b. Press `Alt+T` to display the Type menu.
c. Press `F` to execute the Font command.
d. Using the arrow keys, highlight Helvetica in the list of fonts. (If Helvetica is unavailable, look for Arial or Gill Sans.)
e. Press Enter. The new font is applied and the paragraph reformatted on screen. Click to remove the highlight. Compare the letter shapes in this paragraph to the previous one. Your publication should be similar to:

> The Place command from the File menu (Ctrl+D) is used to import text and graphics. When selected, PageMaker displays a list of importable files from which you may choose.
>
> Placed text may consist of several or just one text block. This is **dependent** on two things; the amount of text placed, and the size of the text block. <u>However, text blocks are not permanent.</u> Several smaller text blocks may be combined into a single, large block, or a lengthy text block may be broken into a group of smaller ones.
>
> This is the start of the next block. In the next Practice, you will divide this one block into several others, and then combine them all back into one large block. You will need to recall several skills from the last chapter where text blocks were manipulated by changing their widths and lengths.
>
> PageMaker refers to a group of related text as a "story." Therefore, this entire imported document is one story. A story may consist of one text block, or many linked text blocks. A PageMaker document may contain a single story or many different ones.

7) SAVE THE MODIFIED PUBLICATION ON DISK

From the File menu, select the Save command. The modified publication is saved on disk, replacing the old version.

3.7 The Type Specs Command

Changing the typeface, size, and style can be a time consuming process. For example, to change some text to bold italic 14 point Courier is a five step process: highlight the text, select the font, select the size, select bold, select italic. PageMaker offers a quick way to set multiple type options using the Type specs command (`Ctrl+T`).

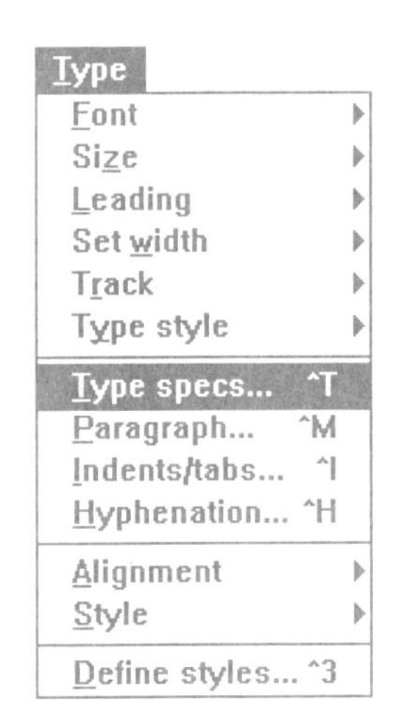

The Type specifications dialog box gives access to all of the type options with one command:

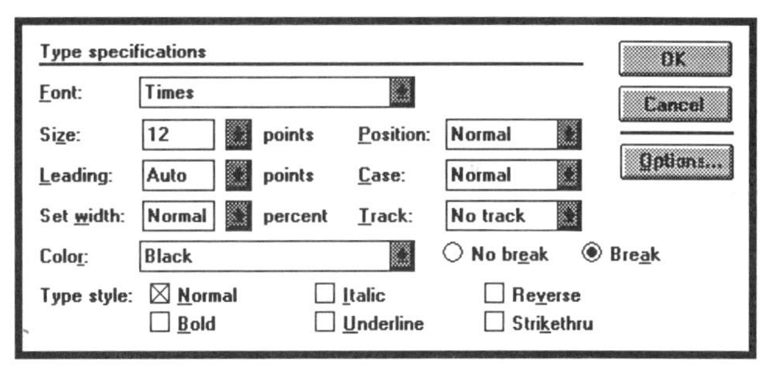

The Type specifications (specs) dialog box can be used to set multiple type options at the same time

This dialog box contains a special form of list called *a collapsible list*. Rather than have a very large dialog box with all of the possible options listed, options such as Font have a collapsible list from which the desired font may be chosen. Next to the current font name is a button which resembles a down scroll arrow:

The down-arrow next to the Font option indicates a collapsible list

Clicking on this button displays a scrollable list of possible options:

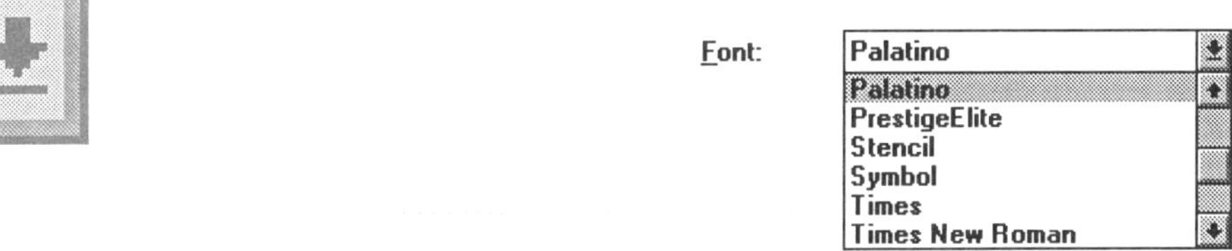

Clicking on the arrow displays the list

The desired font (or size, etc.) may be selected from this list by clicking on it. Clicking on the arrow again removes ("collapses") the list without changing the current value. Once all of the desired options have been selected, selecting OK applies them all in one step. Like the options described above, the Type specs command only affects the highlighted text.

3.8 Subscripts and Superscripts

Many times a publication must contain a *superscript* or *subscript*. A superscript is a section of text which is raised slightly above the current line while a subscript is printed slightly below the current line. In both cases, the text size is smaller than the rest of the line. Superscripts and subscripts are most often used to indicate footnotes or other reference material in research papers or in mathematical and scientific formulas. For example:

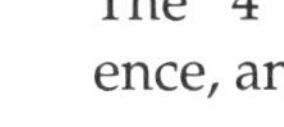  

Dr. Sulfuric[4] proved that the formula for water is H_2O.

The "4" after Dr. Sulfuric is a superscript representing a footnote reference, and the "2" in H2O is a subscript. It is possible to have more than one character in a superscript or subscript. The following line has the word "super" as a superscript and the word "sub" as a subscript:

This is a ^{super}script and this is a $_{sub}$script.

Both superscripts and subscripts are created using the Position option from the Type specs dialog box:

Position: Normal
Normal
Superscript
Subscript

Like all text formats, the text to be formatted must be highlighted before the command is executed.

3

Practice 4

In this Practice you will change fonts and styles using the Type specs command, and create superscripts and subscripts. Start Windows and PageMaker if you have not already done so, and open the CH3PRACT.PM5 publication created in the first Practice.

1) *INSERT A LINE OF TEXT AT THE BOTTOM OF THE CURRENT TEXT BLOCK*

a. Select the Text tool from the Toolbox.
b. Place the I-Beam pointer directly after the last character in the story, the period after "different ones."
c. Click to create an insertion point. The blinking vertical line should appear directly after the period.
d. Press the Enter key twice to insert a blank line.
e. Type the following line:

```
This is a superscript and this is a subscript.
```

Your text block should be similar to:

The Place command from the File menu (Ctrl+D) is used to import text and graphics. When selected, PageMaker displays a list of importable files from which you may choose.

Placed text may consist of several or just one text block. This is **dependent** on two things; the amount of text placed, and the size of the text block. However, text blocks are not permanent. Several smaller text blocks may be combined into a single, large block, or a lengthy text block may be broken into a group of smaller ones.

This is the start of the next block. In the next Practice, you will divide this one block into several others, and then combine them all back into one large block. You will need to recall several skills from the last chapter where text blocks were manipulated by changing their widths and lengths.

PageMaker refers to a group of related text as a "story." Therefore, this entire imported document is one story. A story may consist of one text block, or many linked text blocks. A Page-Maker document may contain a single story or many different ones.

This is a superscript and this is a subscript.

2) CREATE A SUPERSCRIPT

a. Switch to Actual size. If necessary, scroll so that the new line is visible.
b. The text to be formatted must first be highlighted. Drag the pointer over the letters "super" in superscript, highlighting them.
c. From the Type menu, select the Type specs command. The Type specs dialog box is shown.
d. Click on the down arrow next to Position to display the list of position options.
e. Click on Superscript. The list is removed and Position is set to Superscript.
f. Select OK to apply the superscript. The highlighted text is made a superscript as displayed on the screen. Note that the text is both raised slightly and made smaller by this one command.

3) CREATE A SUBSCRIPT

a. Drag the pointer over the letters "sub" in subscript, highlighting them.
b. Press `Ctrl+T` to execute the Type specs command.
c. Click on the down arrow next to Position to display the list of position options.
d. Select Subscript.
e. Select OK to apply the subscript. The highlighted text is made a subscript. Your screen should be similar to:

This is a ^{super}script and this is a $_{sub}$script.

4) APPLY SEVERAL STYLES USING THE TYPE SPECS COMMAND

a. Scroll to the top of the publication. Triple click on the first paragraph, highlighting it.
b. Execute the Type specs command. Note that the current options for this text (i.e., font, size, etc.) are shown.
c. For the Type style, select Bold and Italic.
d. Select OK. The highlighted text is made both bold and italic with this one command.
e. Drag the pointer from the first character in the document to the last, highlighting the entire publication.
f. Execute the Type specs command. Note that options such as Font, Size, and Position are blank. This is because the highlighted text contains more than one option for each.
g. Select Times for the Font, 12 for the Size, and Normal for the Type style.
h. Select OK. All of the text is changed to normal (plain) 12 point Times.
i. Click anywhere in the text to remove the highlight. Note that, because we did not modify the Position option, the superscript and subscript were unchanged.

5) SAVE THE MODIFIED PUBLICATION ON DISK

From the File menu, select the Save command (`Ctrl+S`). The modified publication is saved on disk.

3.9 Paragraph Alignments

PageMaker provides five ways to align text in a paragraph relative to the margins: Left, Centered, Right, Justify, and Force justify. These formats are selected by choosing the desired option from the Alignment submenu:

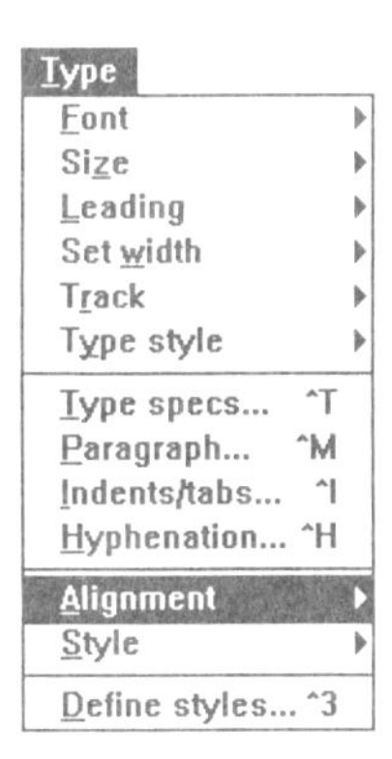

✓Align left	Sh^L
Align center	Sh^C
Align right	Sh^R
Justify	Sh^J
Force justify	Sh^F

The Alignment command's submenu

Left alignment (Shift+Ctrl+L), the default, means that each line begins at the left margin. The resulting right margin is jagged. This is the format produced by a typewriter and is most often used in drafts, letters, or research papers.

Center (Shift+Ctrl+C) is the alignment most often used for headings and titles. It involves positioning a line so that it is equidistant from the left and right margins. PageMaker automatically calculates the proper position of the line and then centers it.

Right alignment (Shift+Ctrl+R) is the opposite of left alignment: each line extends to the right margin while the left margin is jagged.

Justified (Shift+Ctrl+J) creates straight paragraph borders at both margins. To justify a paragraph, PageMaker automatically increases the space between words to fill up each line. As a result the rightmost word in each line is pushed over to the right margin. Justified formats are common in newspapers and books; this textbook for example.

Force justify (Shift+Ctrl+F) forces a line which would not normally reach the right margin to run from margin to margin. It can be used for titles and special effects.

Selecting an alignment option affects only the paragraph that the insertion point is in. Multiple paragraphs may be formatted by highlighting first, and then applying the formatting option. When an alignment is selected, the paragraph is reformatted on the screen, showing the new alignment. Examples of each of the alignments are shown below:

This paragraph is **left aligned**, the default alignment. Notice how the length of each line is different. The effect of a left aligned paragraph is that the right side appears jagged. This format is often called *ragged right* for this reason.

This paragraph is **centered**. Notice that each of the lines is placed halfway between the margins. Centered text is most often used for titles.

3

This paragraph is **right aligned**. Each of the lines reaches the right margin. The effect of a right aligned paragraph is that the left margin is jagged.

This paragraph is **justified**. Each of the lines is extended to reach the right margin. The effect of justifying a paragraph is that the borders on each margin appear straight. Note the increased spacing between some words that is used to extend the lines to the right margin.

This paragraph is **force justified**. All lines reach the right margin, even those which would not normally because of their short line length.

Practice 5

In this Practice you will set and change paragraph Alignments. Start Windows and PageMaker if you have not already done so, and open the CH3PRACT.PM5 publication.

1) PLACE THE INSERTION POINT IN THE FIRST PARAGRAPH

a. Switch to 75% size and scroll so that the entire story is visible.
b. Select the Text tool if it is not already. Click the mouse anywhere in the first paragraph to place the insertion point.

2) RIGHT ALIGN THE FIRST PARAGRAPH

a. From the Type menu, select the Alignment command. The current alignment, Align left, is indicated with a check mark on the submenu.
b. Select Align right from the submenu. The paragraph containing the insertion point is right aligned as shown on the screen.

3) JUSTIFY TWO PARAGRAPHS USING A KEYBOARD SHORTCUT

a. Place the pointer anywhere near the end of the second paragraph. Drag the pointer so that some text is highlighted in both of the second and third paragraphs. Note that it is not necessary to highlight the entire paragraph. If one character in a paragraph is highlighted, the entire paragraph will be affected by the Alignment command.
b. Press `Shift+Ctrl+J` to select Justify. The two paragraphs are justified as shown on the screen.

4) CENTER THE NEXT PARAGRAPH

a. Place the insertion point in the fourth paragraph, "PageMaker refers to...".
b. From the Type menu, select the Alignment command and choose Align center.

5) FORCE JUSTIFY THE LAST PARAGRAPH

a. Place the insertion point in the last paragraph, the superscript created in Practice 4.
b. Execute the Alignment command and choose Force justify. Note the extra space between words needed to justify the line.

c. Save the modified file on disk. Your publication (in 75% view) should be similar to:

The Place command from the File menu (Ctrl+D) is used to import text and graphics. When selected, PageMaker displays a list of importable files from which you may choose.

Placed text may consist of several or just one text block. This is dependent on two things; the amount of text placed, and the size of the text block. However, text blocks are not permanent. Several smaller text blocks may be combined into a single, large block, or a lengthy text block may be broken into a group of smaller ones.

This is the start of the next block. In the next Practice, you will divide this one block into several others, and then combine them all back into one large block. You will need to recall several skills from the last chapter where text blocks were manipulated by changing their widths and lengths.

PageMaker refers to a group of related text as a "story." Therefore, this entire imported document is one story. A story may consist of one text block, or many linked text blocks. A PageMaker document may contain a single story or many different ones.

This is a ^{super}script and this is a $_{sub}$script.

Your superscript and subscript may be greeked

3.10 Stories

PageMaker refers to a group of related text as a *story*. Therefore, the entire document imported in Practice 1 is considered to be one story. A story may consist of one text block, or many *linked* text blocks. A PageMaker publication may contain a single story or several different ones. This is one of PageMaker's strengths; in a multi-story publication one story could have been produced by Microsoft Word, another by WordPerfect, etc. Once imported, it makes no difference how the original text (or graphic) was produced because it is now part of the PageMaker publication.

3.11 Flowing Text from Block to Block

In the last chapter a text block was edited by dragging its handles. When a text block contains more text than is currently being shown, its lower windowshade handle displays a triangle (▼):

This is the first paragraph in a short story.

This is the second paragraph in the same story. This paragraph has two sentences.

→

This is the first paragraph in a short story.

The block on the left is made smaller by dragging one of the handles upward—note the triangle in the bottom windowshade handle indicating that more text exists in this block

Clicking on that triangle changes the pointer into the loaded text shape, the same as when the Place command is used:

This is the first paragraph in a short story.

Clicking on the triangle changes the pointer to the loaded text shape

Clicking the loaded pointer will then create a new text block which contains the text that was not visible in the first block. The newly created block is linked to the original one, and the text is said to be *threaded*. The bottom windowshade handle of the first block and the top windowshade handle of the second block display plus signs (+) indicating that a link exists between them:

This is the first paragraph in a short story.

This is the second paragraph in the same story. This paragraph has two sentences.

Clicking the loaded Text pointer creates a new text block—note the plus signs in the handles indicating that the blocks are threaded

This link, or thread, allows changes to one block to affect another. For example, if the size of the first block is increased, text will be taken from the second block to fill the first. This is called *flowing*, and allows many changes to be made to a publication without having to edit each text block:

This is the first paragraph in a short story.

This is the second paragraph

in the same story. This paragraph has two sentences.

Changes to the first block cause text to flow from the second

This process may be continued by creating another text block, and then another, and so on. The group of linked blocks is still considered to be one story, no matter how many blocks are created:

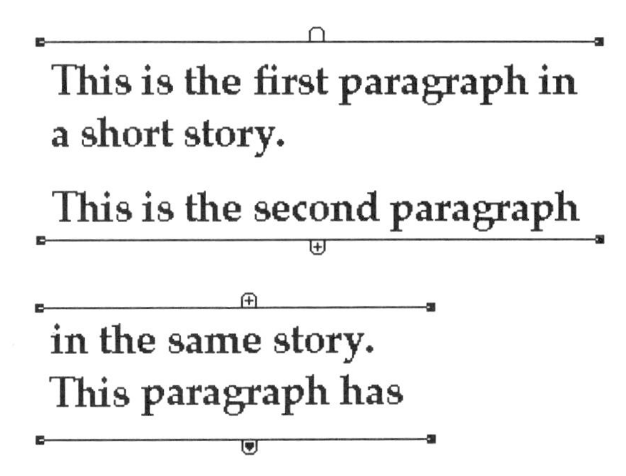

The second block may be edited, and a third block created, and so on

Practice 6

In this Practice you will split the current story into several text blocks. Start PageMaker if you have not already done so, and open the CH3PRACT.PM5 publication.

1) USE THE POINTER TOOL TO SELECT THE STORY

a. Select the Pointer tool from the Toolbox.
b. Click anywhere on the current story to select it. The text block handles are shown.

2) REDUCE THE SIZE OF THE TEXT BLOCK

a. Drag the lower-right text block handle straight up until the bottom of the block is on the first sentence of the third paragraph ("This is the start...").
b. Release the mouse. The text block is resized. Because the block contains more text than is currently shown, the lower windowshade handle shows a down triangle (▼).

3) LOAD THE POINTER

Click once on the downward triangle in the windowshade handle. The pointer changes to the loaded text shape.

4) CREATE A NEW TEXT BLOCK

a. Place the loaded pointer on the left margin line, several lines below the current text block.
b. Click the mouse. A new text block is created which contains the rest of the text from the current story:

The Place command from the File menu (Ctrl+D) is used to import text and graphics. When selected, PageMaker displays a list of importable files from which you may choose.

Placed text may consist of several or just one text block. This is dependent on two things; the amount of text placed, and the size of the text block. However, text blocks are not permanent. Several smaller text blocks may be combined into a single, large block, or a lengthy text block may be broken into a group of smaller ones.

This is the start of the next block. In the next Practice, you will divide this one block into several others, and then combine them all back into one large block. You will need to recall several skills from the last chapter where text blocks were manipulated by changing their widths and lengths.

PageMaker refers to a group of related text as a "story." Therefore, this entire imported document is one story. A story may consist of one text block, or many linked text blocks. A PageMaker document may contain a single story or many different ones.

This is a ^{super}script and this is a $_{sub}$script.

Note the plus sign in the top windowshade handle of the new block. This indicates that there is a link to the previous block.

c. Click on the top (first) text block. The plus sign in the bottom windowshade handle indicates the link to the next block.

5) CHANGE THE SIZE OF THE FIRST BLOCK

a. Grab a lower text block handle on the first block and drag straight down several lines. Text from the second block flows into the first:

The Place command from the File menu (Ctrl+D) is used to import text and graphics. When selected, PageMaker displays a list of importable files from which you may choose.

Placed text may consist of several or just one text block. This is dependent on two things; the amount of text placed, and the size of the text block. However, text blocks are not permanent. Several smaller text blocks may be combined into a single, large block, or a lengthy text block may be broken into a group of smaller ones.

This is the start of the next block. In the next Practice, you will divide this one block into several others, and then combine them all back into one large block. You will need to recall several skills from the last chapter where text blocks were manipulated by changing their widths and lengths.

PageMaker refers to a group of related text as a "story." Therefore, this entire imported document is one story. A story may consist of one text block, or many linked text blocks. A PageMaker document may contain a single story or many different ones.

This is a ^{super}script and this is a $_{sub}$script.

b. Save the modified publication on disk.

3.12 Consolidating Text Blocks

It is sometimes necessary to consolidate linked text blocks into fewer, larger blocks. To do this, simply drag the bottom of the text block to be removed up until it meets the top:

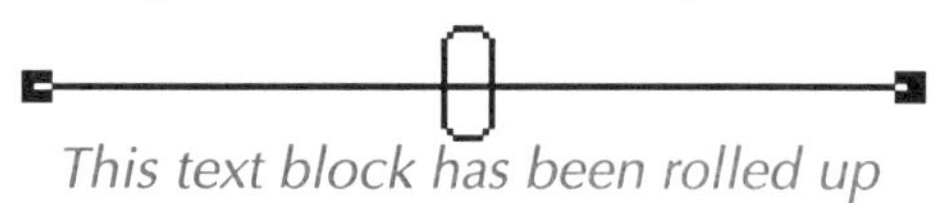

This text block has been rolled up

PageMaker will then remove the closed block. The text from the "rolled up" block is then available in the previous block, which can be stretched to reveal it.

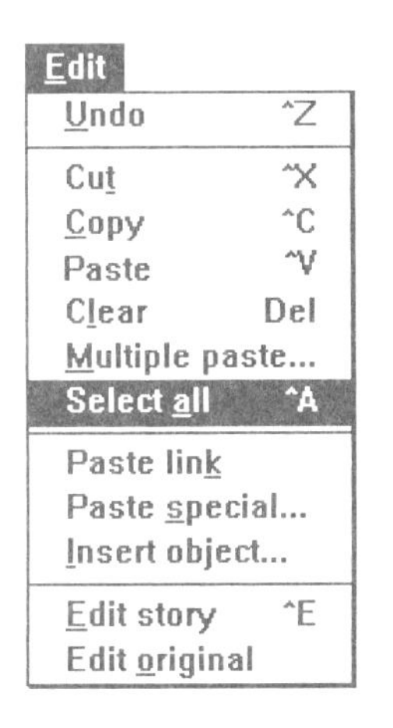

It is important to close the block completely, otherwise PageMaker will continue to flow text to it. One way to check if the block has been removed is with the Select all command from the Edit menu (`Ctrl+A`). If the block still exists, Select all will display its handles.

Many beginning desktop publishers are tempted to create separate text blocks for each item in a publication: the headline in its own block, the first paragraph in its own block, etc. This can cause a publication to become more complex and difficult to work with. Whenever possible, keep related material in one text block. This chapter in your textbook, for example, consists primarily of one large, multi-page block which makes it easier to edit and update, minimizes questions about text flow, and makes applying formatting options faster.

Aztec Café
The Best Mexican Food in Dade County!
Appetizers
Grilled Shrimp with Salsa Verde $5.95
Poquitos de Pollo $4.95
Black Bean soup $2.95
Nachos Machismos $6.95

Aztec Café
The Best Mexican Food in Dade County!
Appetizers
Grilled Shrimp with Salsa Verde $5.95
Poquitos de Pollo $4.95
Black Bean soup $2.95
Nachos Machismos $6.95

One continuous block (shown on left) is better than many (right)

Practice 7

In this Practice you will close the block created in Practice 6. Start PageMaker if you have not already done so, and open the CH3PRACT.PM5 publication.

1) *CLOSE THE BOTTOM TEXT BLOCK*

a. Click on the second block, selecting it.
b. Using the Pointer tool, drag the bottom handle of the second text block up until it touches the top handle.
c. Click anywhere on the page to remove the handles.
d. From the Edit menu, execute the Select all command. If handles appear for the second text block, repeat steps (a) and (b) until the block is properly closed.

2) *RESTORE THE FIRST BLOCK*

a. Click on the top text block if it is not already selected. The bottom handle again shows a downward triangle, indicating that this block has more text than is currently displayed.
b. Drag the bottom handle of the text block down to the bottom of the screen and release the mouse. The text from the rolled up text block flows back into the first.

3) *SAVE THE MODIFIED PUBLICATION ON DISK AND EXIT PAGEMAKER*

a. Use the Save command to save the modified publication on disk.

3.13 Copying and Pasting Blocks of Text

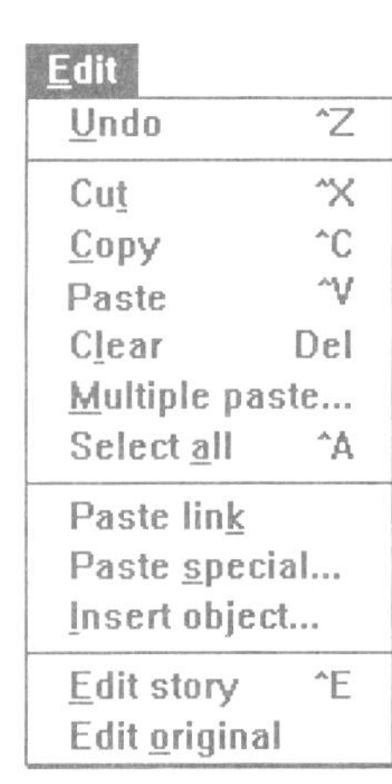

There are times when the same text should be repeated in a publication. Rather than typing or importing the text multiple times, it is possible to use PageMaker's Edit menu to Copy (Ctrl+C) a highlighted block of text and then Paste (Ctrl+V) it in a new location. The copied text can be as small as a single character or word or as large as a group of pages, but it must be highlighted first.

When Paste is executed, the block is inserted at the cursor position. Text currently stored in that location is moved down to make room for the new block.

Whenever text is Copied, PageMaker places it in a special area of memory called the *Clipboard*. The Clipboard can only store one block of text at a time, so the next Copy replaces the contents of the Clipboard with the new text.

Copying a block of text is a four step process:

1. Using any of the techniques described in the last chapter, highlight the text to be copied.
2. Execute the Copy command from the Edit menu (Ctrl+C). The highlighted text is copied to the Clipboard.
3. Place the cursor at the location for the copy.
4. Execute the Paste command from the Edit menu (Ctrl+V) which inserts the contents of the Clipboard (the previously copied text) into the publication at the current cursor position.

3.14 Moving a Block of Text with Cut

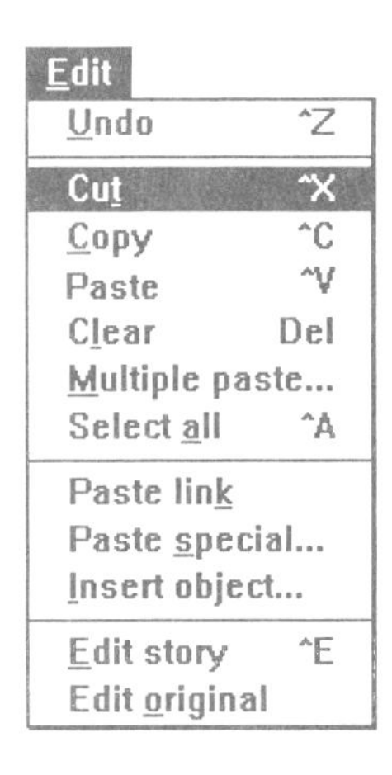

One of the most powerful editing tools is the ability to move a block of text from one area of a publication to another. For example, a sentence can be moved from one paragraph and placed in another, or a paragraph moved from one page to another. PageMaker closes the space that formerly held the moved text and opens new space to receive it, rearranging the rest of the publication to accommodate the change.

Moving a block is a four step process very similar to that for copying a block. The exception is that, after highlighting the text, the Cut command is executed instead of Copy. This places the highlighted text on the Clipboard and then deletes it from the publication.

Moving a block of text is a four step process:

1. Using any of the techniques described in the last chapter, highlight the text to be copied.

2. Execute the Cut command from the Edit menu (`Ctrl+X`). The highlighted text is copied to the Clipboard and deleted from the publication.
3. Place the cursor at the new location for the text.
4. Execute the Paste command from the Edit menu (`Ctrl+V`) which inserts the contents of the Clipboard (the previously cut text) at the current cursor position.

Cutting is the best way to move text between stories, even when those stories are not linked. For example, a publication may have two separate (non-linked) stories in two different text blocks. To move text from one block to the other, simply highlight the text in the first block, and Cut it. Place the cursor at the desired position in the second block and execute Paste. This moves the text from the first text block to the second.

This technique can also be used if you have created too many stories and wish to consolidate them. Two non-linked stories can be combined by moving the entire first story into the second story's block: Simply highlight the entire story before executing Cut and then Paste the material into the second block.

Practice 8

This Practice demonstrates the use of block move and copy. A block consisting of a sentence will be copied, and an entire paragraph moved. Start PageMaker and open CH3PRACT.PM5 if you have not already done so.

1) HIGHLIGHT THE BLOCK TO BE COPIED

a. Select the Text tool and place the cursor at the beginning of the sentence which begins "The Place command from...", the first sentence in the publication.
b. Drag the mouse to the right to highlight the sentence, making sure to include the period at the end of the sentence in the block.

2) COPY AND PASTE THE HIGHLIGHTED BLOCK

a. From the Edit menu, select Copy. A copy of the text is placed on the Clipboard.
b. Place the cursor before the "T" that begins the sentence "This is dependent on..." in the second paragraph.
c. From the Edit menu, select the Paste command. The sentence is inserted in the paragraph at the cursor position.

3) HIGHLIGHT THE BLOCK TO BE CUT

a. You will rearrange the story by moving the fourth paragraph to the beginning of the document. Place the pointer anywhere in the fourth paragraph which begins "PageMaker refers to...". Triple-click to highlight the entire paragraph.
b. We also want to move the blank line below the paragraph. Hold down the Shift key and press the down arrow key to extend the highlight to include the blank line directly below.

3

4) MOVE THE HIGHLIGHTED BLOCK WITH CUT AND PASTE

a. From the Edit menu, select the Cut command. The highlighted block is removed from the publication and placed on the Clipboard. Text below flows up to fill the space.
b. Position the cursor at the very beginning of the publication (`Ctrl+PgUp`).
c. Paste the block using the shortcut `Ctrl+V`. The paragraph is inserted at the top of the publication.
d. Save the modified publication.

Check - The sentence about the Place command should be copied into the third paragraph and the "PageMaker refers to..." paragraph moved to the very beginning of the document:

PageMaker refers to a group of related text as a "story." Therefore, this entire imported document is one story. A story may consist of one text block, or many linked text blocks. A PageMaker document may contain a single story or many different ones.

The Place command from the File menu (Ctrl+D) is used to import text and graphics. When selected, PageMaker displays a list of importable files from which you may choose.

Placed text may consist of several or just one text block. The Place command from the File menu (Ctrl+D) is used to import text and graphics. This is dependent on two things; the amount of text placed, and the size of the text block. However, text blocks are not permanent. Several smaller text blocks may be combined into a single, large block, or a lengthy text block may be broken into a group of smaller ones.

This is the start of the next block. In the next Practice, you will divide this one block into several others, and then combine them all back into one large block. You will need to recall several skills from the last chapter where text blocks were manipulated by changing their widths and lengths.

This is a ^{super}script and this is a $_{sub}$script.

3.15 Creating PageMaker Graphics

We have said that desktop publishing involves both text and graphics. PageMaker can generate rudimentary graphics using four tools from the Toolbox: the Rectangle tool, the Oval tool, the Diagonal line tool, and the Straight line tool. All of the tools are used similarly:

1. Select the desired graphics tool. The pointer changes to cross-hairs.
2. Place the pointer at the starting position for the graphic. Hold down the mouse button and drag. The graphic is created.

In all cases PageMaker shows an outline of the graphic as it is being created. Releasing the mouse places the graphic on the page.

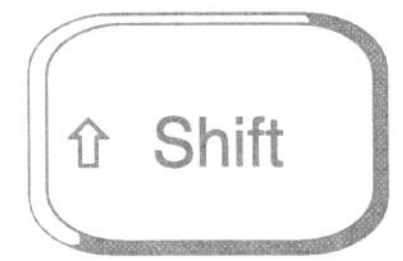

When creating graphics, holding down the Shift key acts to constrain the drawing to a "perfect" shape. For example, holding down the Shift key while creating a rectangle forces the rectangle to be a square. Other uses of the constrain key are described below.

Rectangle Tool	☐	Useful for creating outlines or emphasizing text, the Rectangle tool draws rectangular boxes. Holding down the Shift key while dragging creates a perfect square.
Oval Tool	○	Creates ovals or, with the Shift key depressed, circles.
Diagonal Line	⟍	Draws lines at any angle. Holding down Shift constrains the line to 45 degree angles.
Straight Line	|—	Creates lines at 45 degree angles only. The Shift key has no effect on this tool.

3

Practice 9

In this Practice you will add some PageMaker graphics to the file used in the last Practice. Start PageMaker and open CH3PRACT.PM5 if you have not already done so.

1) DRAW A RECTANGLE

a. Scroll down so that the blank space below the story is shown.
b. Select the Rectangle tool. The pointer changes to cross-hairs.
c. Using the Ruler, place the pointer at the left edge of the page, near the 5" vertical, 1" horizontal mark.
d. Press the mouse button and drag down and to the right, until the pointer is near the 6" vertical, 2.5" horizontal mark. Release the button and the rectangle is drawn:

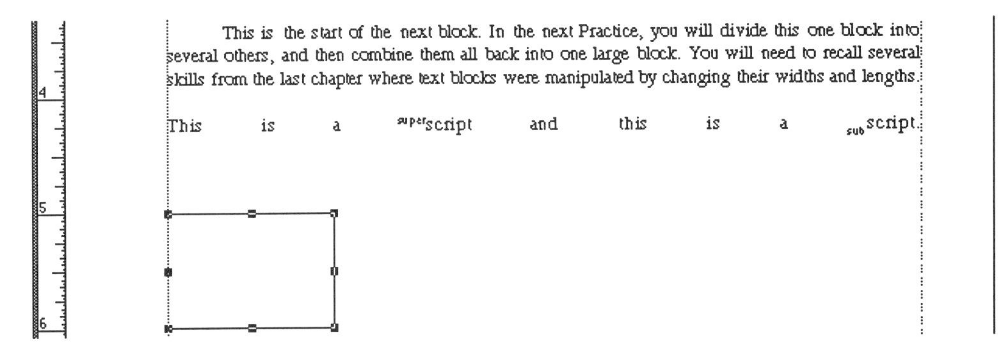

e. Note the handles around the graphic. Select the Pointer tool to remove the handles.

2) DRAW AN OVAL

a. Select the Oval tool.
b. Using the Ruler, place the pointer at the 5" vertical, 4" horizontal mark.
c. Press the mouse button and drag down and to right, until the pointer is near the 6" vertical, 6" horizontal mark.
d. Select the Pointer tool. Your graphics should be similar to:

3) DRAW A DIAGONAL LINE

a. Select the Diagonal line tool.
b. Using the Ruler, place the pointer at the 5" vertical, 6.5" horizontal mark.
c. Press the mouse button and drag down and to right, until the pointer is on the blue vertical margin line.
d. Select the Pointer tool. Your graphics should be similar to:

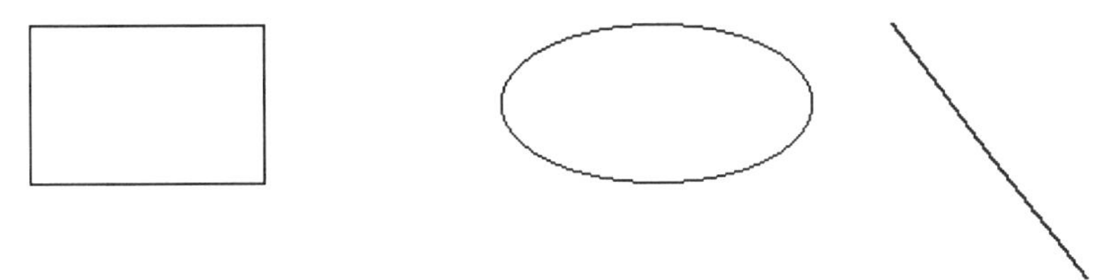

e. Save the document.

3.16 Editing and Changing PageMaker Graphics

PageMaker graphics can be edited by dragging their handles, just like text blocks. Clicking on a previously drawn graphic with the Pointer tool displays its handles. Holding down the Shift key while dragging a handle forces the graphic to a perfect shape as described in the previous section.

To move a graphic, click on any part of the graphic *except* a handle and drag to the new position. When a graphic is selected (handles are shown), it can be deleted by executing the Cut command from the Edit menu, or by pressing the Delete key.

3.17 Fills and Line Widths

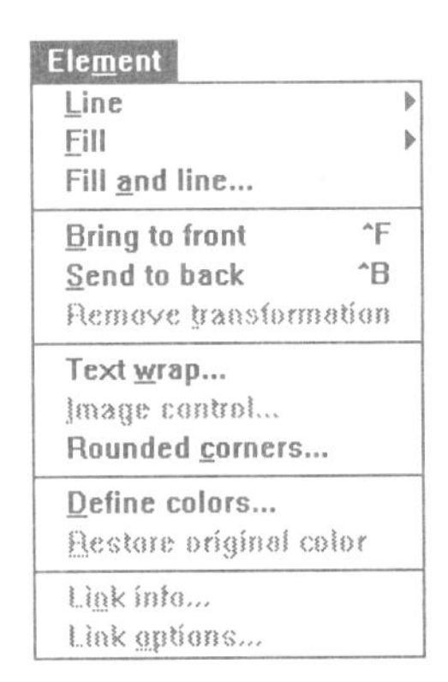

PageMaker can apply a variety of different formats to graphics. Graphics may be empty (hollow) as in the last Practice or filled with different shades. Lines, including the outlines of rectangles and ovals, may be thin or thick and appear in many different patterns.

The graphic to be edited must be selected first with the Pointer tool so that handles are shown. Different fills and line widths and styles are then selected using the Fill and Line commands from the Element menu:

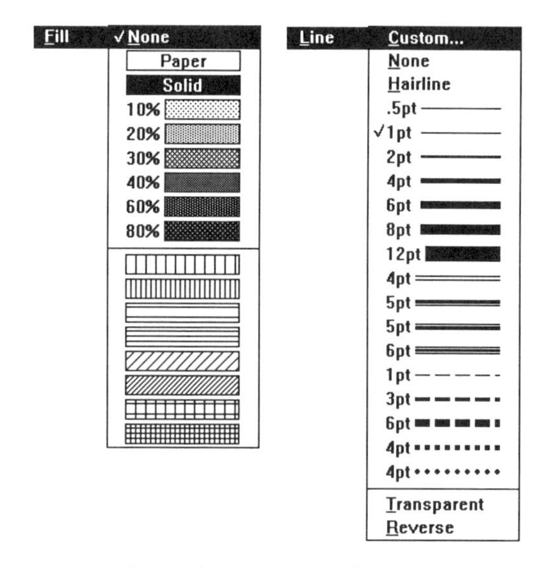

The Fill and Line submenus

Practice 10

In this Practice you will modify the PageMaker graphics created in the last Practice. Start PageMaker and open CH3PRACT.PM5 if you have not already done so.

1) *STRETCH THE RECTANGLE*

a. If not already, select the Pointer tool in the Toolbox.
b. Place the pointer over one of the lines in the rectangle drawn in the last Practice. Click the mouse. The rectangle is selected and handles are shown. (If your rectangle is not selected, reposition the pointer and try again.)
c. Place the pointer on the handle in the lower-right corner of the rectangle. Drag the handle down and to the right, making the rectangle wider and taller.
d. Release the mouse. The rectangle is modified.

2) *TURN THE RECTANGLE INTO A PERFECT SQUARE*

a. The rectangle should still be selected from the last step. Place the pointer over the lower-right handle.
b. Drag the handle slightly. With the mouse button still held down, press the Shift key. The shape changes from a rectangle to a perfect square.
c. Keeping the Shift key held down, drag the mouse around. The shape always remains a perfect square. Using the Rulers as guides, drag the pointer to the 6" vertical, 2" horizontal mark. Your graphics should be similar to:

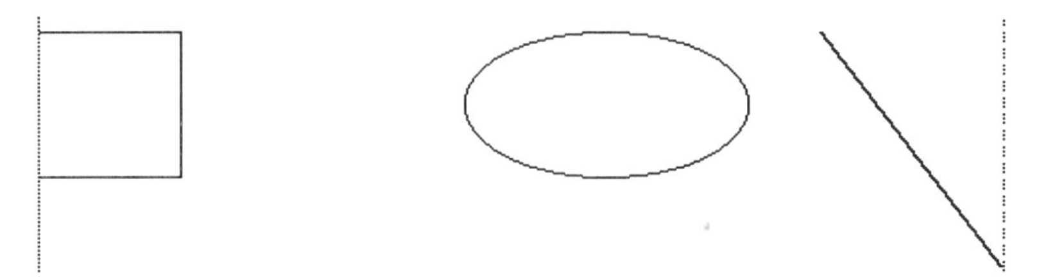

3

3) *CHANGE THE FILL OF THE OVAL*

a. Click on the oval graphic to select it. Handles are shown.
b. From the Element menu, select the Fill command. A submenu of different fills is shown with the current value indicated with a check mark.
c. From the submenu, select 10%. The oval is filled with a 10% grey.
d. Using the Fill command, experiment with several different fills, including some of the hatch (checkerboard) fills at the bottom of the submenu.
e. Fill the oval with 40% grey.

4) *DRAG THE OVAL TO A NEW POSITION*

a. Place the pointer anywhere in the oval graphic and hold down the mouse button. The pointer shape changes to a 4-headed arrow.
b. Drag the oval to the left about half an inch and release the button. The oval is moved:

5) *CHANGE THE LINE OPTIONS FOR THE DIAGONAL LINE*

a. Click on the diagonal line graphic, selecting it.
b. In the Element menu, select the Line command to display a submenu of line options. The current line width is 1pt (1 point) as indicated by the check mark.
c. Select 12pt from the submenu. The line is now 12 points and is shown much heavier on the screen.
d. Using the Line command, experiment with several different line types, including some of the dashed and dotted lines at the bottom of the submenu.
e. Make the line 8 points wide and solid. Your graphics should be similar to:

f. Save the document, with modified graphics.

3.18 Importing and Sizing Graphics

PageMaker's graphics tools, while useful, are rudimentary. For this reason, it is possible to import graphics from other programs, similar to the way text is imported from word processor files. There are many different types of graphics and graphic programs, and these will be discussed in more detail in Chapter Nine.

To import a graphic, select the Place command from the File menu which displays the Place dialog box. Simply select the desired graphic from the list of file names, scrolling first as necessary. The graphic is then loaded, and the pointer shape changes to the *loaded graphic* shape.

There are a number of different loaded graphic pointer shapes, but the two most common are:

Common loaded graphic pointer shapes

Clicking places the graphic at the current pointer position.

Placed graphics can be selected by clicking on them with the pointer, which displays handles. Graphics can be resized by dragging one of the handles, and moved by dragging anywhere *except* a handle.

A special stretching technique is to hold down the Shift key while dragging a handle. This changes the size of the graphic, but makes the change proportional—the width will change as much as the height. This is why holding down the Shift while stretching turned the rectangle into a square in the last Practice. This technique, called *magic stretching*, is normally used when changing the size of an imported graphic so that the graphic is not distorted.

Practice 11

In this Practice you will import and modify a graphic. Start PageMaker and open CH3PRACT.PM5 if you have not already done so.

1) IMPORT A GRAPHIC

a. From the File menu, select the Place command. The Place file dialog box is shown.
b. Locate the file named PHOTO.WMF in the files list. If the file name is not immediately visible, click on the scroll arrows next to the list to display more file names.
c. Click on PHOTO.WMF. PageMaker copies that file name to the File name line.
d. Select OK. The graphic file is processed, and the pointer shape is changed.
e. Using the Rulers as guides, place the pointer at the 7" vertical, 3" horizontal mark and click. The graphic is placed. Zoom out to view the screen:

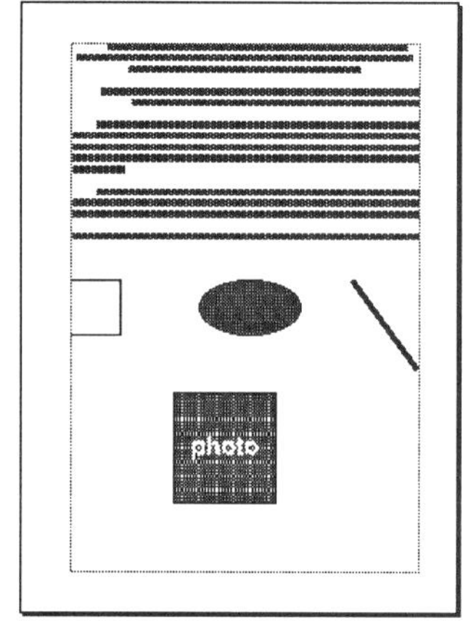

This graphic is simply a grey box marked "photo." We will use this graphic as a placeholder to represent where a real photograph would go in a finished document.

2) CHANGE THE SIZE OF THE GRAPHIC

a. Handles should be shown around the graphic. If not, select the graphic using the pointer.
b. Drag the bottom, middle handle down, making the rectangle taller.
c. Drag the left middle handle to the left, making the graphic wider.

3) DRAG THE GRAPHIC TO A NEW POSITION

a. Place the pointer anywhere in the graphic and hold down the mouse button until the pointer shape changes to a 4-headed arrow.
b. Drag the graphic down and to the left so that the bottom of the graphic is at the lower-left corner of the page, at the intersection of the margin lines. Release the button to place the graphic:

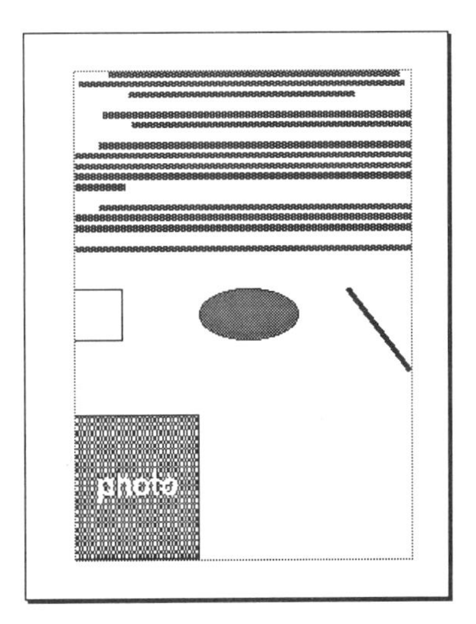

4) PROPORTIONALLY STRETCH THE GRAPHIC

a. Place the pointer on the upper-right corner handle of the graphic.
b. Press and hold down the Shift key. With the Shift key held down, drag the handle slowly up and to the right. As the width of the graphic increases so does its height. This is different than in step 2 above where the height and width were changed independently.
c. Release the mouse button and then the Shift key. After a magic stretch it is important to release the mouse button before the Shift key in order to keep the stretch proportional.

5) SAVE AND PRINT THE DOCUMENT

a. Save the modified document.
b. From the File menu, select the Print command and click on Print. The document is printed. Note how the inclusion of graphics affects the amount of time it takes to print your document—more graphics means longer print time.
c. From the File menu, select Exit to exit PageMaker and return to Windows.
d. If you wish to exit Windows, select the Exit command from the Windows File menu.

Chapter Summary

The majority of the text in a desktop published document is created in a separate word processing program. PageMaker can import (read and translate) a word processing file using the Place command. Each word processor produces different files, so PageMaker employs special programs called filters to translate the files into a form that it can read. Some filters produce a dialog box where translation options may be selected.

Previously saved files may be viewed using the Open command. Once opened, a publication can be edited, formatted, printed, and then saved again.

There are a variety of different formats that may be applied to text. It is important to remember that text formats are only applied to the highlighted portion of the text. One of the most important formats is the typeface or font—how the different letters and symbols are shaped. Fonts also have styles such as bold, italic, and underline.

There are three major families of fonts: serif, sans (without) serif, and decorative. Serif fonts have small lines at the tops and bottoms of the letters which improve readability at small sizes. Sans serif fonts do not have these lines and are better used for small amounts of text in larger sizes. Decorative fonts are used in special situations like a wedding invitation and include dingbats—fonts made up of pictures or symbols.

Fonts are measured in points, and each point is 1/72nd of an inch. Body copy, which is the text that makes up the majority of a publication, is most commonly found in sizes from 6 to 14 points. Headlines, titles, and other attention getting text often appears in 16 to 72 points or larger.

The font, size, and style for highlighted text can be set using separate commands in the Type menu. All three of these options can be changed at once with the Type specs command, also in the Type menu. Type specs also has the option of creating superscripts and subscripts.

PageMaker provides five ways to align a paragraph relative to the publication's margins: Left, Centered, Right, Justify, and Force justify. These formats are selected using the Alignment command in the Type menu. To apply one of these formats the cursor must be in the paragraph before the command is executed, but it is not necessary to highlight the entire paragraph.

A group of related text is called a story, and a publication may contain a single story or several different ones. A story may consist of one text block, or many text blocks that are linked together. When text

3

blocks are linked, also called threaded, text will flow from one to the next as the sizes of the blocks change.

The windowshade handles show the link status of a block. A plus sign in the handle means that another block comes before (plus sign in top handle) or after (plus sign in bottom handle) this block. An empty handle means that no other blocks are linked in that direction. A red triangle in the bottom windowshade handle means that this block contains more text that is not currently displayed. This text can be made visible by either increasing the size of the current block, or clicking on the triangle to create a new block.

New text blocks can be created by clicking on the triangle in the windowshade handle (as described above). This loads the pointer with the undisplayed text, and the pointer changes shape. To create a new block, click the loaded Text pointer. A linked block can be consolidated by dragging the bottom handle up to meet its top handle. The text in this block then flows back into the previous block, which may need to be lengthened to display its new contents.

Text may be duplicated using the Copy and Paste commands. Executing Copy places the highlighted text on the Clipboard, an area in the computer's memory. The Cut command moves the highlighted text to the Clipboard, deleting it from its original position. Selecting Paste inserts a copy of the clipboard's contents at the current cursor position. When Pasting, note that the cursor may be in the same text block or another, so it is possible to copy and move text between blocks in this way.

PageMaker has a number of graphics tools in the Toolbox including rectangle, oval, and different lines. Holding down the Shift key when creating a graphic makes the shape perfect: a rectangle becomes a square, an oval a circle, and lines are kept perfectly horizontal or vertical. Different line sizes and styles are available in the Element menu, as well as a variety of fills for ovals and rectangles.

PageMaker can also import graphics produced by a number of different drawing programs. Graphics can then be placed, moved, and sized using handles like a text block. A special form of stretch called the magic stretch is usually used with imported graphics. To magic stretch, hold down the Shift key while dragging a handle. The causes the graphic to be resized proportionally, avoiding distortion.

Vocabulary

ASCII text file - Plain, unformatted word processing file identified by a file name ending in .TXT. Also called a text file.

Body copy / Body text - The text that makes up the majority of a publication.

Bold - Darker, thicker, or heavier version of a typeface. Also a text formatting option.

Centered - Paragraph option where lines are placed equidistant from the margins.

Clipboard - Area of memory where Copied and Cut items are stored temporarily.

Collapsible list - Dialog box option where a list of choices may be displayed by clicking on an arrow next to the option.

Decorative - Group of typefaces used for special purposes such as wedding invitations or advertisements. Zapf Chancery is an example of a decorative typeface.

Default font - Font which will be used automatically for any new text. Indicated by a check mark on the Font submenu.

Dingbats - Typefaces consisting of symbols and picture-like elements. Zapf Dingbats is an example of a dingbat typeface.

Filter - Special software that allows PageMaker to translate different word processing and graphics files into a format that it can place in a publication.

Flow / Flowing text - Moving text from one linked text block to another.

Font - A family of characters (letters, numbers, symbols) drawn in a specific style. Also called typeface.

Greeked - Text displayed on the screen as small, unreadable characters.

Importing - Bringing word processing and graphics files created by other programs into PageMaker using the Place command.

Italic - Slanted and slightly cursive version of a typeface. Also called oblique. A text formatting option.

Justified - Paragraph option where each line is extended to reach the right margin by increasing the space between words.

Linked - A group of text blocks where text can flow between blocks.

Loaded graphic pointer - During a Place command, the pointer changes shape to indicate that a graphic is ready to be placed in the publication.

Loaded Text pointer - During a Place command, the pointer changes shape to indicate that text is ready to be placed in the publication.

Magic stretch - Holding down the Shift key while resizing a graphic, which causes the graphic to be stretched proportionally.

Point - Measurement for type size, 1/72 of an inch.

Publication - Text and graphics stored together in a PageMaker file.

Ragged right - Name for left aligned text.

Sans Serif - Category of typeface without serifs (small lines at the tops and bottoms of letters). Helvetica and Arial are examples of sans serif typefaces.

Serif - Category of typeface where small lines are found at the tops and bottoms of letters. (Serif is also the name of the lines themselves.) Times New Roman is an example of a serif typeface.

Story - A group of related text in a publication.

Stretch - To resize a graphic by dragging one of its handles.

Submenu - List of options displayed when a command is selected from which you may select one.

Subscript - Type option where character(s) are printed slightly below the current line in a smaller size than the rest of the line.

Superscript - Type option where character(s) are printed slightly above the current line in a smaller size than the rest of the line.

Text file - See ASCII text file.

Threaded / Threaded text - A text block linked to other text blocks.

Typeface - A family of characters (letters, numbers, symbols) drawn in a specific style. Also called a font.

Vectored - PageMaker method for displaying type in large sizes on the screen. Also called stretched.

Reviews

Sections 3.1 — 3.5

1. What is a filter used for in PageMaker?
2. Outline the steps required to place an importable file into a PageMaker document.
3. Explain the steps required to open a previously saved PageMaker file.
4. What is a font? Why are there many different fonts?
5. What is the difference between serif and sans serif typefaces?
6. What is meant by the term WYSIWYG?
7. What factors should be considered when selecting a size for type in a publication?

Sections 3.6 — 3.12

8. Outline the steps required to format a sentence of text as Helvetica, Bold, 24 points.
9. Explain how the formatting in Review 8 could be applied using only the Type specs command.
10. How can the superscript and subscript be created in the sentence:

    Superscript is ^{up} and subscript is $_{down}$

11. Explain how to center the first paragraph of text in a document and justify the second paragraph.
12. What is indicated by a lower windowshade handle which displays:

    a) A triangle?
    b) A plus sign?
    c) Nothing? (Is empty.)

13. If a text block is too large to fit an area, explain how it may be shortened and the additional text moved to a new location. Click on red triangle in lower windowshade handle. Pointer changes to loaded text shape. Click loaded pointer to create a new text block

14. How can the text in two linked blocks be combined into a single block? Grab a lower text block handle on first block & drag down over second block. Text in 2nd block flows back into 1st block. Or close bottom text block "roll up" (Edit, Select all to make sure block is closed)

3

Sections 3.13 — 3.18

15. Outline the steps required to copy a line of text from the first paragraph of a document to the last paragraph. Highlight line. Select Edit, copy. Position cursor in last ¶ where you want line to be copied. Select Edit, Paste.

16. What is the difference between copying and moving a block of text? Copy copies the text & leaves original in its place. Moving moves the text & deletes it from original place.

17. Explain how to draw a box around a block of text. Select rectangle tool. Position around text.

18. a) What is the difference between using the Diagonal Line and Straight Line tools?
    b) What is the pointer shape for each of these tools? Diagonal draws lines at any angle. Straight line at 45 degrees angles only. +

19. a) How can a previously drawn graphic be selected? Click on it w/ pointer tool.
    b) How is a selected graphic indicated? With handles.

20. Once a rectangle has been drawn, how can its shape be changed? Place pointer on handle & click & drag

21. How can an oval drawn at the top of a document be moved to the middle of the page? Place pointer anywhere in graphic (except on handles) & click & drag

22. Outline the steps required to draw a perfect square and fill it with a pattern of horizontal lines. Select rectangle tool. Click & drag while holding down shift key. Release mouse button before Shft key. Select Element, Fill, [illegible]

23. How can the width of a line be changed from 1 point to 6 point? Select line, select 6 pt

24. Explain how to import a graphic. File, Place, select graphic. Click on loaded graphic pointer.

25. How may an imported graphic be moved? Place pointer in the graphic, click & drag.

Exercises

1. In Exercise 1 of Chapter Two you created a press release named CSPRESS. Open CSPRESS and follow the steps below to edit and format it to appear similar to the following (text blocks are shown as guides):

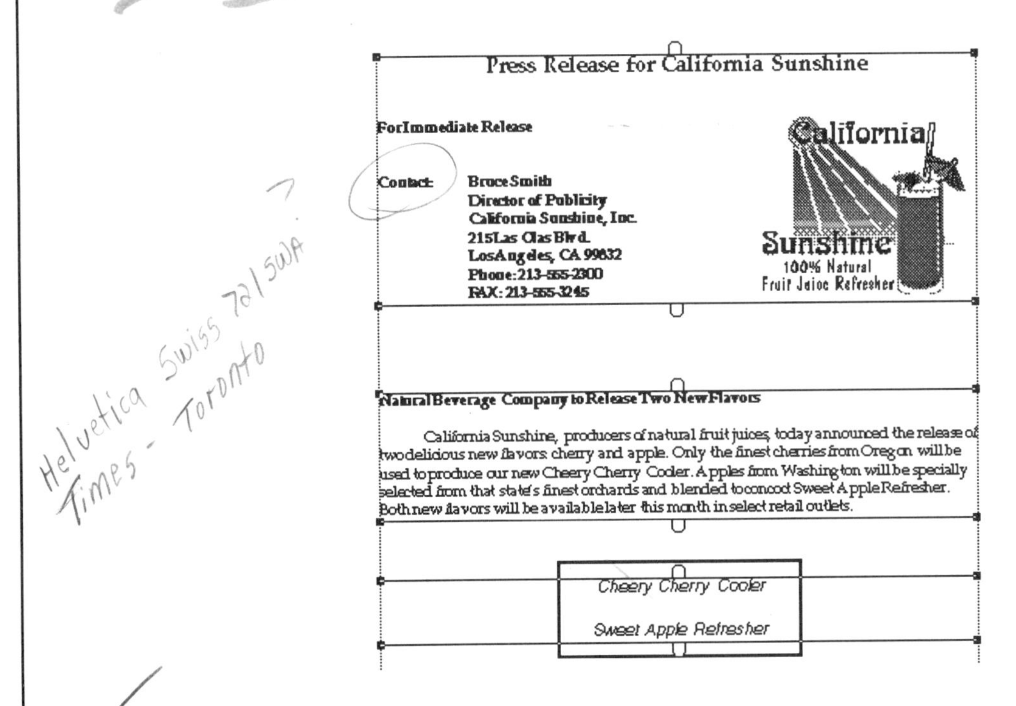

Press Release for California Sunshine

For Immediate Release

Contact: **Bruce Smith**
Director of Publicity
California Sunshine, Inc.
215 Las Olas Blvd.
Los Angeles, CA 99832
Phone: 213-555-2300
FAX: 213-555-3245

Natural Beverage Company to Release Two New Flavors

California Sunshine, producers of natural fruit juices, today announced the release of two delicious new flavors: cherry and apple. Only the finest cherries from Oregon will be used to produce our new Cheery Cherry Cooler. Apples from Washington will be specially selected from that state's finest orchards and blended to concoct Sweet Apple Refresher. Both new flavors will be available later this month in select retail outlets.

Cheery Cherry Cooler

Sweet Apple Refresher

a) In a new text block at the top of the publication enter the "Press Release..." heading and contact information as shown. Use your name as the person to contact. One tab is used to indent the name, and two tabs for the address and other information.

b) Format the "Press Release..." heading as Palatino, 18 points, Bold, and Centered. "For Immediate Release," the name, address, phone, and fax numbers are Palatino, 14 points, and Bold.

c) Add the title "Natural Beverage Company to Release Two New Flavors" and a blank line to the top of the original text block. Format the entire block as Palatino, 12 points, and make the title Bold.

d) In a new text block list the new flavors with a blank line between as shown. Format the list as Helvetica, 14 points, Italic, and Centered.

e) Draw a 2 point rectangle around the flavors list.

f) Place the California Sunshine logo CALIFSUN.WMF in the upper-right corner. Using the Shift key, proportionally stretch the logo so that it is about the same height as the release and contact information.

g) Save and then print a copy of CSPRESS.

2. You are going to expand the Aztec Café brochure created in Exercise 2 of Chapter Two. Open ACBROCH and follow the steps below to edit and format the publication so that it is similar to:

Hot New Happenings at Aztec Cafe

Beautiful New Dining Room To Open Soon

Aztec Cafe is planning an addition to its facilities that will include a new dining room seating 120 customers. The dining room will be named the Acapulco Room and decorated in a native Mexican motif. This beautiful room will be used primarily for private parties, banquets, weddings, and organizational meetings.

a) Create a new text block near the top of the page and enter the title as shown. Format the title as Avant-Garde, 24, Bold, Italic, and Centered.

b) Draw a rectangle around the title using the 4 point dashed line.

c) Move the original text block from the bottom of the page. Resize the block so that it runs from margin to margin.

d) At the beginning of the text block, add the "Beautiful New Dining Room ..." subtitle and a blank line. Format the subtitle as Helvetica, 12, Underline and the body text as Times New Roman, 12, Normal.

e) Save and then print a copy of ACBROCH.

You will now add a second story and a logo to the brochure:

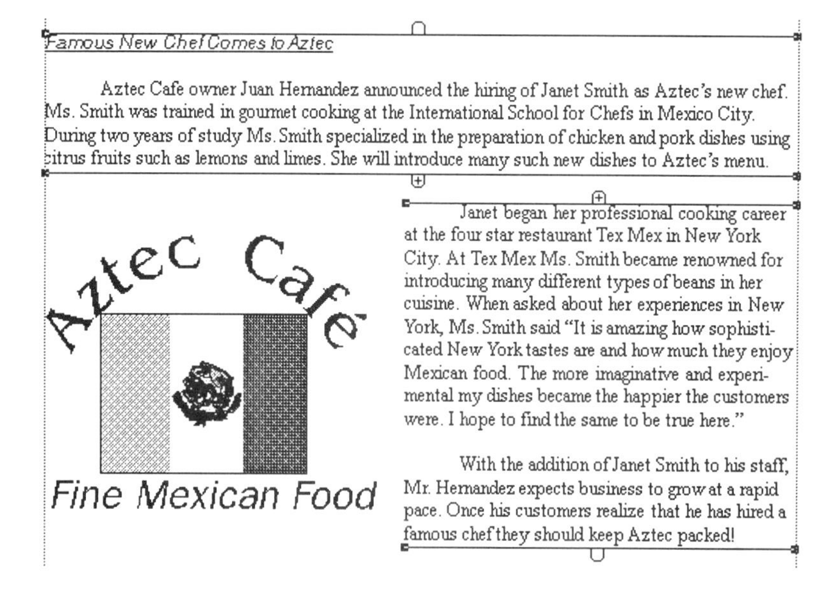
Famous New Chef Comes to Aztec

Aztec Cafe owner Juan Hernandez announced the hiring of Janet Smith as Aztec's new chef. Ms. Smith was trained in gourmet cooking at the International School for Chefs in Mexico City. During two years of study Ms. Smith specialized in the preparation of chicken and pork dishes using citrus fruits such as lemons and limes. She will introduce many such new dishes to Aztec's menu.

Janet began her professional cooking career at the four star restaurant Tex Mex in New York City. At Tex Mex Ms. Smith became renowned for introducing many different types of beans in her cuisine. When asked about her experiences in New York, Ms. Smith said "It is amazing how sophisticated New York tastes are and how much they enjoy Mexican food. The more imaginative and experimental my dishes became the happier the customers were. I hope to find the same to be true here."

With the addition of Janet Smith to his staff, Mr. Hernandez expects business to grow at a rapid pace. Once his customers realize that he has hired a famous chef they should keep Aztec packed!

f) Place the CHEF.TXT file below the current text in a separate story. Move the top of the new story near the 3" vertical mark. Format the subtitle and body text in this story as you did in step (d).

3

g) Reduce the size of the text block so that it ends after "new dishes to Aztec's menu." Create a new block with the linked material and reduce its width as shown.

h) Place Aztec's logo AZTECAFE.WMF to the left of the new block as shown.

i) Save and then print a copy of ACBROCH.

3. In Chapter Two Exercise 3 you created a menu for Aztec Café. Open ACMENU and follow the steps below to edit and format it to appear similar to:

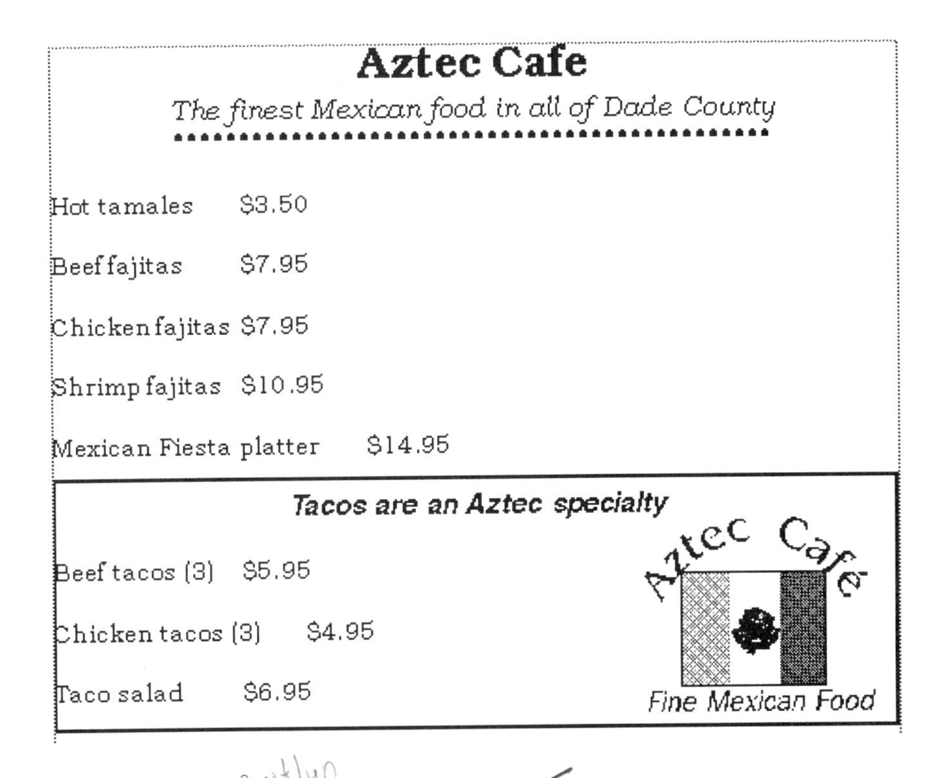

a) Format all the text as Bookman, 14 point.

b) Make the Aztec Cafe title 24 point, Bold, and Centered.

c) Format "The finest..." as 16 point, Italic, and Centered.

d) Delete the blank line between "Aztec cafe" and "The finest..." Add a blank line between "The finest..." and "Hot tamales...". Draw a 4 point straight dotted line below "The first...".

e) Insert the subtitle "Tacos are an Aztec specialty" and a blank line above the taco items. Format the subtitle as Helvetica, 16 points, Bold, Italic, and Centered.

f) Create a 2 point box around the subtitle and the taco items.

g) Place and size the Aztec Café logo AZTECAFE.WMF as shown.

h) Save ACMENU and print a copy.

4. In Exercise 4 of Chapter 2 you produced a resume for Deborah Debit. Open DDRESUME and follow the steps below to edit and format it to appear similar to the following:

Deborah N. Debit
1117 East Hathaway Drive
Newtown, FL 33445
407/555-6970

OBJECTIVE
A leadership position in the financial affairs department of a publishing company.

WORK EXPERIENCE
1991 - present
Bennett Chemical Industries, Newtown, FL: Accountant. Manage all accounts payable/receivable using a computerized system which includes spreadsheet and other accounting software.

1990 - 1991
Dr. Roger Calculate, College Circle, FL: Research Assistant. Prepared case studies for new accounting textbook.

EDUCATION
1987 - 1991
BS Accounting: State University, College Circle, FL. Departmental Honors in Business and Finance. Chairperson, Future Accountants of America. College Circle Community Service Award.

a) Make all the text Helvetica, 12 points.

b) Center the heading containing Deborah's name, address, and phone number. Format it as 14 point, Bold.

c) Format each of the section subheadings as Italic. Draw a 2 point line above each subheading.

d) Save DDRESUME and then print a copy.

Chapter Four:
The Story Editor & Writing for Desktop Publishing

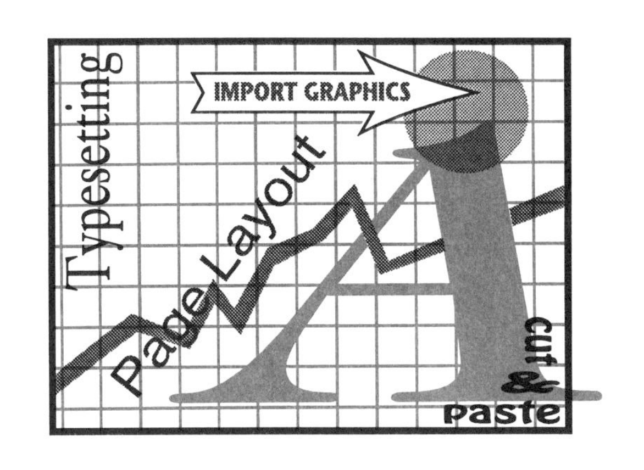

Edit - Edit story

Story - Display ¶

Edit - Edit layout

Utilities - Spelling

Utilities - Find

Utilities - Change

Objectives

4

After completing this chapter you will be able to:

1. Use PageMaker's Story Editor to enter and edit stories.
2. Use Story Editor commands to find, change, and spell check text.
3. Identify and understand the four elements of effective writing:
   - Clarity
   - Accuracy
   - Brevity
   - Organization
4. Understand how the audience and message for that audience affects the writing in a document.
5. Understand and utilize four stages of a process to follow when writing:
   - Pre-writing
   - Drafting
   - Revising
   - Editing

4

We should begin by answering the question "Why have a chapter on writing in a desktop publishing textbook?" The answer is simple. The rest of this text deals with design considerations—how to make publications look good so that they effectively convey your desired message to its intended audience. However, even the best of designs will not help if your message is not expressed clearly.

Because the words that make up your message are at least half of the equation to producing successful desktop published documents, it is important to take time to consider the process of writing. This chapter introduces a technique called *process writing* which is used to break any writing task down into a series of steps which can be easily followed. Additionally, the use of PageMaker's built-in word processor will make writing easier and less tedious than using pen and paper or a typewriter.

Even if you have had considerable writing experience, you should still cover Sections 4.1 through 4.11 which describe how to use PageMaker's Story Editor. This material is also important for those who will be editing someone else's writing.

4.1 PageMaker's Story Editor

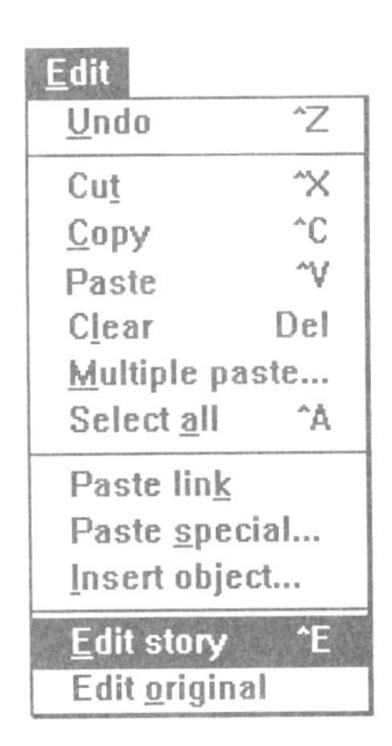

Built into PageMaker is a mini-word processor called the *Story Editor*. It has some advantages and disadvantages compared to full, "stand alone" word processing packages such as Microsoft Word and WordPerfect. The advantages to the Story Editor are that it is built-in to PageMaker, and is quick to learn and use. The disadvantages are that it lacks certain high-end features such as a thesaurus and grammar checker, although it does contain a spelling checker.

The Story Editor is the best way to enter new text of any length into a PageMaker publication. It can also be used to edit and spell check stories (files) that have already been imported into PageMaker. Using the Story Editor differs from entering text on the PageMaker screen as you did in the last chapter because the Story Editor does not show certain formatting features such as different typefaces and sizes. Because of this, it is able to operate quickly, and is designed to allow you to concentrate on what is being written, not how it looks. If you are entering more than a few lines of text, or making considerable editing changes, you should use the Story Editor.

4.2 Starting the Story Editor

To start the Story Editor select the Edit Story command from the Edit menu (`Ctrl+E`), which brings up the Story Editor window:

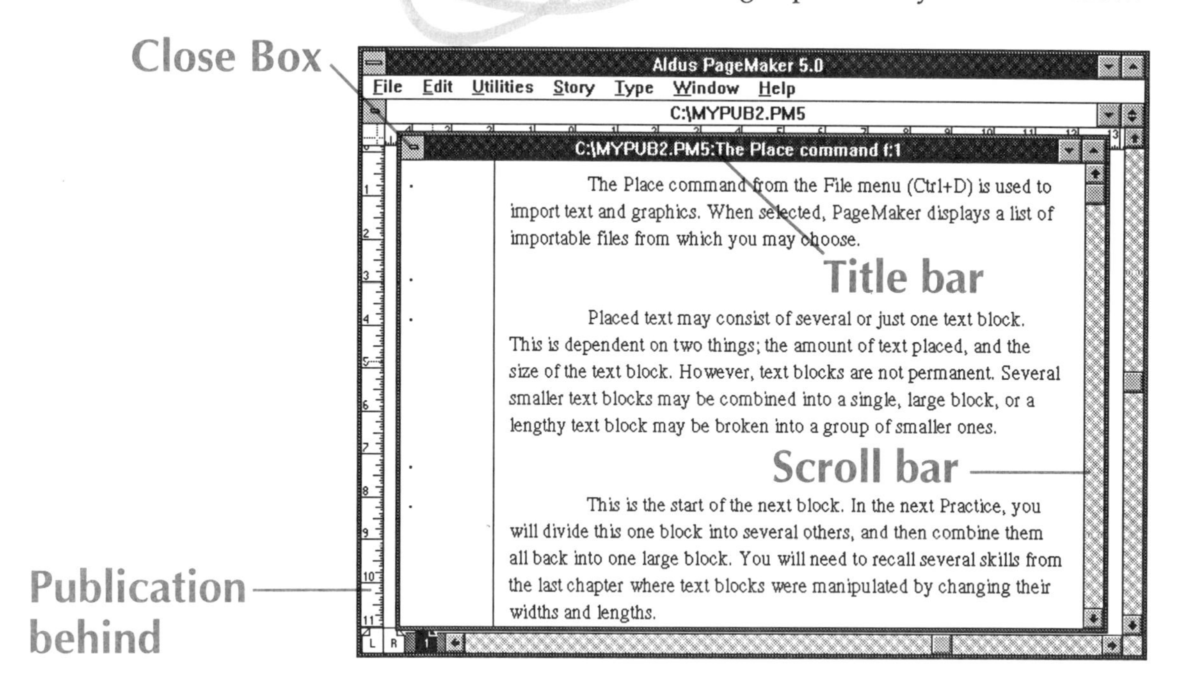

The Story Editor window

The Edit Story command has different effects based on the location of the pointer. If the I-Beam pointer is in a story when the command is executed, or a text block is selected with the pointer tool, the Story Editor window is shown with that story loaded. The first few characters in the story are shown as the title at the top of the window. If a tool other than the Text tool is highlighted, or no text block is selected, an empty window ("Untitled") is shown.

Practice 1

In this Practice you will start PageMaker, create a new publication, and place a previously created story. The story will then be opened in the Story Editor.

1) START PAGEMAKER AND CREATE A NEW PUBLICATION

a. Following the directions given in Chapter Two, turn on the computer, start Windows, and run PageMaker.
b. From the File menu, select the New command. The Page setup dialog box is shown.
c. Make certain that the Page option is Letter, Orientation is Tall, and that your printer is listed as the Compose to printer. Click on OK to create the new publication.

2) *IMPORT A WORD PROCESSING FILE*

a. From the File menu, select the Place command. The Place file dialog box is shown.
b. Locate the file named PRAC-4.TXT in the files list. If the file name is not immediately visible, use the scroll arrows next to the list to display more file names.
c. Click on PRAC-4.TXT. PageMaker copies that file name to the File name line.
d. Select OK. The Text-only import filter dialog box is displayed.
e. Select OK to accept the default import options. PageMaker removes the box and displays the publication screen. The translation operation can take a few seconds, especially with long files. After the file is processed, the pointer is changed to the loaded text shape.
f. Place the pointer in the upper-left corner of the publication and click to place the story. Handles around the text block indicate that it is selected.

3) *ENTER THE STORY EDITOR*

a. From the Edit menu, select the Edit Story command. The Story Editor window is shown. Because a text block was selected when the command was executed, the story is displayed and ready to be edited. Note the publication window behind the Story Editor window.
b. Locate the Story Editor title bar, cursor, scroll bar, and close box. The mark at the bottom of the screen is the end of story marker. The cursor may not be moved beyond this marker, but text may be inserted in front of it.

4.3 The Story Editor and the Keyboard

As stated above, the Story Editor is a mini-word processor where text may be entered, deleted, and edited, and then spell checked. Before proceeding, it is important to take time to familiarize yourself with some of the keys needed to do word processing in the Story Editor.

When the Story Editor window is first opened, a thin blinking vertical line called the insertion point or *cursor* appears in the upper-left corner. All of the techniques for manipulating text that you practiced in the last chapter are applicable to the Story Editor—text can be highlighted by dragging over it, new text inserted, characters, words, and sentences deleted, and so on. Because the Story Editor is often used to enter large portion of text, many people do not like to remove their hands from the keyboard to use the mouse. For this reason, we will describe how the keyboard alone can be used to perform editing operations in this section. (You are free to use either the mouse or keyboard.) Additionally, many of the techniques described here work when there is an insertion point displayed in a story on the main PageMaker screen (the *layout*).

The cursor can be moved around the screen, without erasing or entering text, using the cursor control keys which are marked with arrows (up, down, left, and right). To move the cursor down one line press the key marked with a down-arrow. Similarly, to move the cursor up, left or right, use the keys marked with the appropriate arrows:

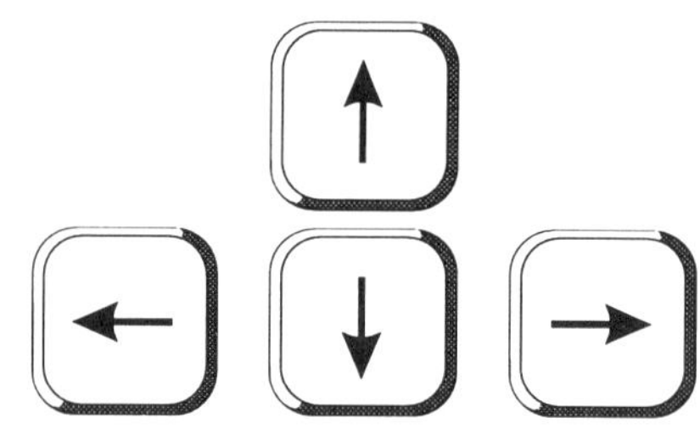

The cursor control or "arrow" keys

Each of these keys is a *repeat key*, meaning that it will continue moving the cursor as long as it is held down. The arrow keys can only move the cursor where text has already been typed. If you attempt to move the cursor to an area of the screen which does not contain any text, past the end of story marker, the computer beeps and the cursor does not move.

The actions of the cursor control keys can be modified by holding down another key at the same time as the arrow key is pressed. Holding down the Control key and pressing the left arrow key at the same time (`Ctrl+Left arrow`) moves the cursor not one character to the left but one word to the left. Similarly, `Ctrl+Right arrow` moves the cursor one word to the right. `Ctrl+Up arrow` moves the cursor to the beginning of the previous paragraph, and `Ctrl+Down arrow` moves to the beginning of the next paragraph. When the cursor is inside a paragraph, pressing `Ctrl+Up arrow` moves to the first character in that paragraph.

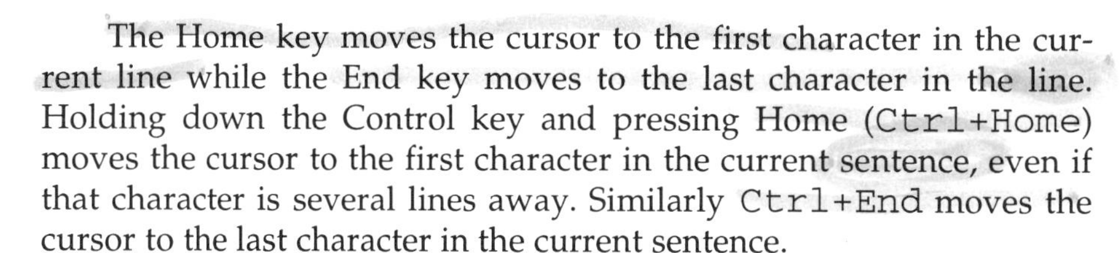

The Home key moves the cursor to the first character in the current line while the End key moves to the last character in the line. Holding down the Control key and pressing Home (`Ctrl+Home`) moves the cursor to the first character in the current sentence, even if that character is several lines away. Similarly `Ctrl+End` moves the cursor to the last character in the current sentence.

The PgUp and PgDn keys (sometimes marked Page Up and Page Down) also move the cursor. PgUp moves the cursor up 1 screen and PgDn moves down 1 screen. Holding down Control and pressing PgUp (`Ctrl+PgUp`) moves the cursor to the first character in the story. Similarly `Ctrl+PgDn` moves to the last character in the story.

To insert text the cursor is first placed where the new material is to appear using the cursor control keys and then the new material typed. PageMaker automatically inserts the characters you type at the current cursor position. Any text following the insertion is moved to the right to accommodate the inserted material. Deleting and inserting are powerful text editing features that allow almost any type of change to be made to a story.

Several other important Story Editor keys are described on the next page.

The Del key (also marked Delete) is used to erase characters that have been highlighted. When characters are deleted any characters to their right are automatically moved over to close the gap made by the deleted characters.

Esc is used to terminate (escape from) the computer's current operation. The specific effect that pressing the Escape key will have depends on the operation being performed.

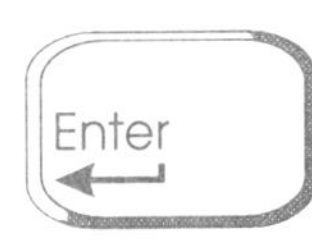

In the Story Editor the Enter key is used to end a paragraph or to terminate any line which does not reach the right side of the screen (such as a list or table). When Enter is pressed the cursor moves on to the next line. It is important to press Enter at the end of a paragraph only.

Pressing the Backspace key deletes the character to the left of the cursor and moves the cursor one space to the left. Do not confuse Backspace with the left-arrow key. Both move the cursor one character to the left, but Backspace erases characters as it moves, while left-arrow does not.

4.4 Highlighting in the Story Editor

As you saw in the last chapter it is possible to highlight text with the mouse by dragging the I-Beam pointer over it, or by double- and triple-clicking the pointer on a word. Several keyboard techniques also exist for highlighting text. While used primarily in the Story Editor window, most of these techniques also work in the regular publication view.

Highlighting with the keyboard requires that the Shift key be held down while a cursor control key is pressed. For example, holding down the Shift key and pressing left arrow (`Shift+Left arrow`) highlights one character to the left of the cursor. `Shift+Right arrow` highlights one character to the right. `Shift+Up arrow` and `Shift+Down arrow` highlight to the previous or next line. `Shift+Home` creates a highlight from the current character to the first character in the current line, while `Shift+End` highlights to the last character in the current line. `Shift+PgUp` highlights up one screen, and `Shift+PgDn` highlights down.

Different highlights can be created by pressing three keys at the same time: Shift, Control, and a cursor control key. `Shift+Control+Left arrow` highlights from the current position to the beginning of the current word. `Shift+Control+Left arrow` again extends the highlight to the next word to the left. `Shift+Control+Right arrow` does the same thing to the right but includes the space after each word. `Shift+Control+Up arrow` and `Shift+Control+Down arrow` highlight to the beginning or end of the current paragraph. `Shift+Control+Home` highlights from the current character to the beginning of the sentence, while Shift+Control+End highlights to the end. Shift+Control+PgUp and Shift+Control+PgDn highlight to the beginning or end of the story.

The actions of the cursor control keys are listed in the following table:

Key	Action
←, →	Moves one character left/right
↑, ↓	Moves one line up/down
Home, End	Moves to beginning/end of current line
PgUp, PgDn	Moves up/down one screen
Ctrl+←, →	Moves one word left/right
Ctrl+↑, ↓	Moves to beginning/end of paragraph
Ctrl+Home, End	Moves to beginning/end of sentence
Ctrl+PgUp, PgDn	Moves to beginning/end of story
Shift+←, →	Highlights one character left/right
Shift+↑, ↓	Highlights one line up/down
Shift+Home, End	Highlights to beginning/end of current line
Shift+PgUp, PgDn	Highlights up/down one screen
Shift+Ctrl+←, →	Highlights one word left/right
Shift+Ctrl+↑, ↓	Highlights to beginning/end of paragraph
Shift+Ctrl+Home, End	Highlights to beginning/end of sentence
Shift+Ctrl+PgUp, PgDn	Highlights to beginning/end of story

Practice 2

In this Practice you will edit a story by adding text to it using the Story Editor. Start PageMaker and open the current story in the Story Editor window if you have not already done so.

1) *INSERT TEXT*

Make sure that the cursor is at the beginning of the story. Type This is the Story Editor and press Enter. Note how the existing text moves as new characters are inserted.

2) *HIGHLIGHT TEXT USING THE KEYBOARD*

a. Using the left-arrow key, move the cursor back so that it is directly to the left of the "E" in Editor.
b. Hold down the Shift key and press the right-arrow key (Shift+Right arrow). The "E" is highlighted.
c. Continue to press Shift+Right arrow until the entire word "Editor" is highlighted.

4

3) EXPAND AND CONTRACT THE HIGHLIGHT

a. Press `Shift+Down arrow`. The highlight is extended to the next line.
b. Press `Shift+Down arrow` several more times. Note how the highlight is expanded with each keypress.
c. Press `Shift+Up arrow`. The highlight is reduced by a line.

4) REMOVE THE HIGHLIGHT

Press any arrow key (without Shift). The highlight is removed.

5) CREATE SEVERAL MORE HIGHLIGHTS

a. Press `Ctrl+Pg Dn`. The cursor is moved to end of the story.
b. Press `Ctrl+Pg Up` to move the cursor to the beginning of the story.
c. Press `Ctrl+Shift+End`. A highlight is created from the cursor position to the end of the current line.
d. Press `Ctrl+Shift+Pg Dn` to highlight the entire story.

6) REMOVE THE HIGHLIGHT AND SAVE THE PUBLICATION

a. Click the mouse anywhere in the story. The highlight is removed.
b. From the File menu, select the Save command.
c. Type the name `CH4PRACT` and select OK.

4.5 Showing Invisible Characters

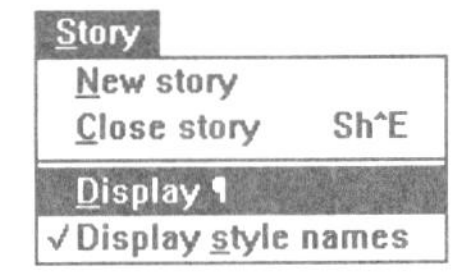

The Display ¶ command from the Story menu allows normally invisible characters such as tabs and spaces to be shown on the screen. This is helpful when editing because it makes it easier to include all the desired characters in a highlighted block. PageMaker uses the following symbols to represent characters:

Symbol	Meaning
· (raised dot)	Space bar pressed
¶	Enter key pressed
→	Tab key pressed

These symbols are shown on the screen as an aid in formatting and do not appear when the publication is printed. To remove these symbols, select Display ¶ again. The characters remain in the file, only the symbols are no longer displayed. It is a good practice to always use Display ¶ when formatting or editing text in the Story Editor.

4.6 Formatting in the Story Editor

Formatting options may be applied in the Story Editor, but not all will be shown on the screen. For example, type styles such as bold and italic are shown in the Story Editor. Fonts and sizes are not shown; the Story Editor only uses one font in one size to display all text.

The same formatting procedures must be followed whether in the Story Editor or the layout. First, highlight the text to be formatted. Then select the desired formatting commands from the Type menu. Only the highlighted text will be affected.

4.7 Returning to the Layout

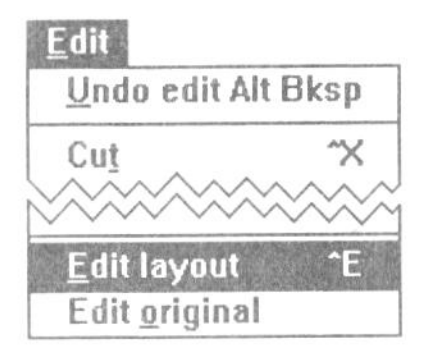

To return to the actual publication (the WYSIWYG *layout*), select the Edit Layout command from the Edit menu (`Ctrl+E`). This is an example of PageMaker's *smart menus*—commands that change to fit the operation you are performing. When viewing the layout the command reads Edit story, and in the Story Editor it reads Edit layout.

Practice 3

In this Practice you will format text in the Story Editor. The Display ¶ command, which makes editing and formatting easier, will be used. Start PageMaker and open CH4PRACT. Select the story and switch to the Story Editor if you have not already done so.

1) SHOW INVISIBLE CHARACTERS

From the story menu, select the Display ¶ command. Note the tabs, spaces, and Enters in this story.

2) HIGHLIGHT THE TEXT TO BE FORMATTED

Place the pointer over the first sentence, which begins "This is the...". Triple-click to highlight the entire paragraph.

3) BOLD THE HIGHLIGHTED TEXT

a. From the Type menu, select the Type Style command. A submenu is displayed.
b. In the submenu, select Bold. The highlighted text is made bold on the screen.

4) CHANGE THE SIZE OF THE HIGHLIGHTED TEXT

a. From the Type menu, select the Size command to display its submenu.
b. In the submenu, select 48 to make the text 48 points. Note that the size of the text does not change in the Story Editor:

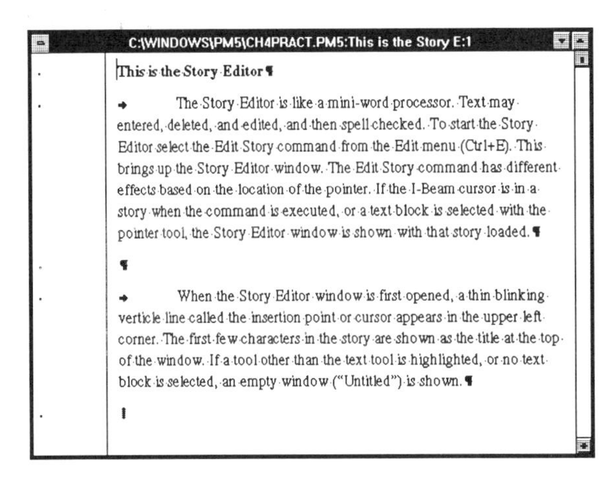

5) *RETURN TO THE LAYOUT*

a. From the Edit menu, select the Edit layout command. The publication is shown in full layout view and all formatting options are shown.

b. Switch to 75% view. Your screen should be similar to:

This is the Story Editor

The Story Editor is like a mini-word processor. Text may entered, deleted, and edited, and then spell checked. To start the Story Editor select the Edit Story command from the Edit menu (Ctrl+E). This brings up the Story Editor window. The Edit Story command has different effects based on the location of the pointer. If the I-Beam cursor is in a story when the command is executed, or a text block is selected with the pointer tool, the Story Editor window is shown with that story loaded.

c. Save the modified publication.

4.8 Check Spelling

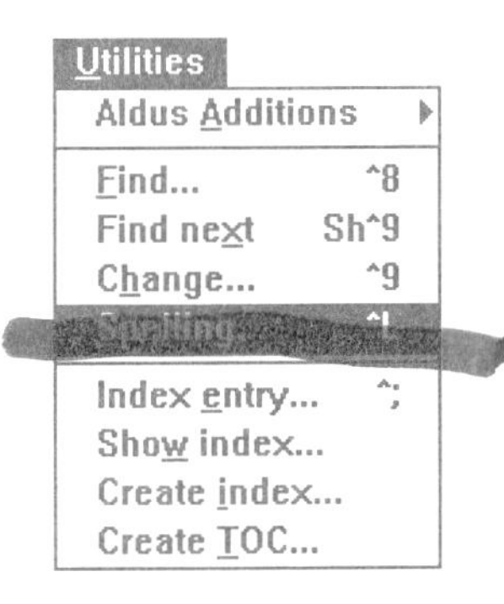

One of the most useful features of the Story Editor is the ability to have PageMaker check the spelling of the words in a publication. This is accomplished by selecting the Spelling command from the Utilities menu (Ctrl+L). When this command is executed, PageMaker starts at the current cursor position and compares each word in the publication to a dictionary file.

Words not found in the dictionary are displayed in a dialog box where you have the option of typing a correction or having PageMaker produce a list of suggested spellings from which you may select:

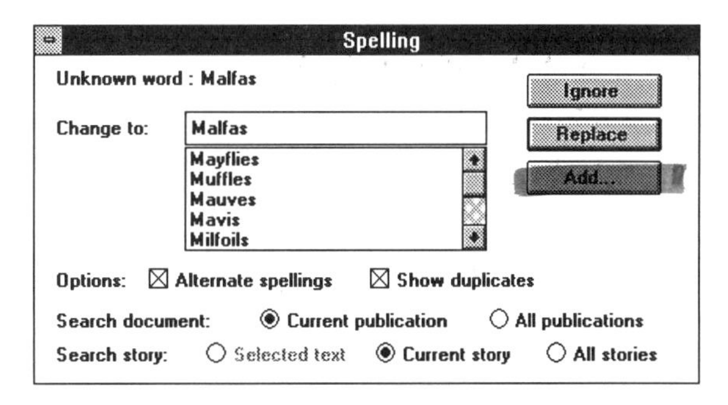

The Spelling command's dialog box

Because the dictionary file cannot contain every word in the English language, it is possible that Spelling may come across a word that it does not have in its dictionary. When this happens you have two options. If the word is spelled correctly you can tell PageMaker to Ignore it and proceed to the next misspelled word. If the word is one that you will use often in your writing, such as your name, you can Add the word to its dictionary. Once added, such words are no longer considered misspelled when they appear in a publication.

Practice 4

In this Practice you will check the spelling of a story in the Story Editor. Start PageMaker and open CH4PRACT. Select the story and switch to the Story Editor if you have not already done so.

1) PLACE THE CURSOR

PageMaker starts its spelling check from the current cursor position. Press `Crtl+PgUp` to move the cursor to the very top of the story.

2) CHECK THE SPELLING

a. From the Utilities menu, select the Spelling command. The Spelling dialog box is shown.
b. Select Start to begin the spell check. PageMaker finds a word that is not in its dictionary.
c. The unknown word "Ctrl+E" is spelled correctly so select Ignore to continue.
d. The next unknown word is "verticle." Note the list of suggested spellings. Click on the correct spelling, "vertical," to display it on the Change to line.
e. Select Replace. PageMaker replaces the unknown word with the selected word and continues the spell check.
f. No more spelling errors are found and "Spelling check complete" is displayed in the dialog box.

3) RETURN TO THE LAYOUT

a. Remove the Spelling dialog box by double-clicking on its Close box in the upper-left corner.
b. Close the Story Editor by double-clicking on its Close box in the upper-left corner. The Layout is again displayed.
c. Save the modified file. Note how the misspelled word has been corrected in the publication:

This is the Story Editor

The Story Editor is like a mini-word processor. Text may entered, deleted, and edited, and then spell checked. To start the Story Editor select the Edit Story command from the Edit menu (Ctrl+E). This brings up the Story Editor window. The Edit Story command has different effects based on the location of the pointer. If the I-Beam cursor is in a story when the command is executed, or a text block is selected with the pointer tool, the Story Editor window is shown with that story loaded.

When the Story Editor window is first opened, a thin blinking vertical line called the insertion point or cursor appears in the upper left corner. The first few characters in the story are shown as the title at the top of the window. If a tool other than the text tool is highlighted, or no text block is selected, an empty window ("Untitled") is shown.

4.9 Searching for Text with Find

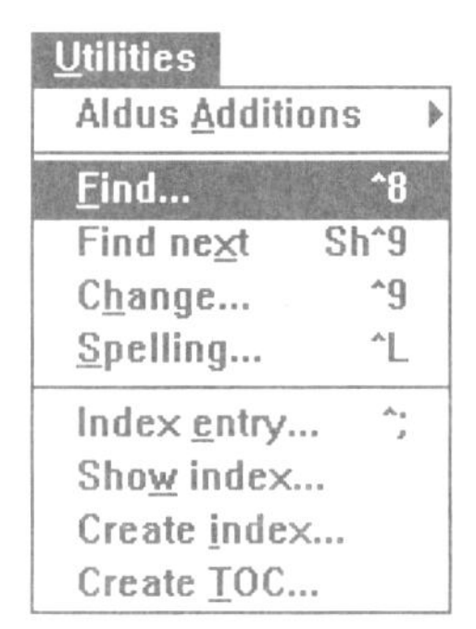

The Find command from the Utilities menu (Ctrl+8) scans a publication looking for a particular combination of letters. This may be a single letter, a word, or a phrase and is entered as the Find what option in the dialog box:

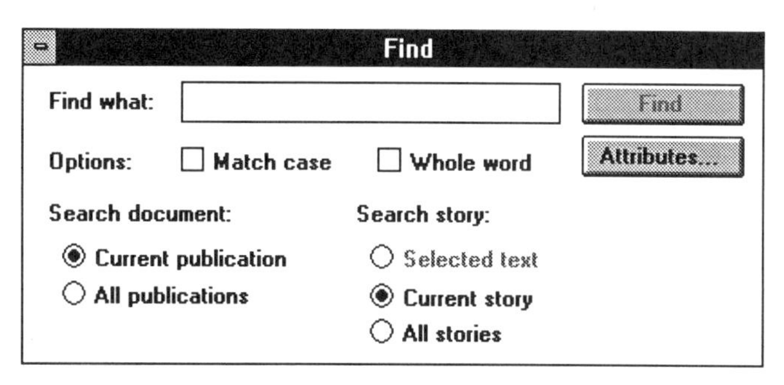

The Find command's dialog box

Starting from the current cursor position, PageMaker moves through the current story looking for a sequence of letters that matches the Find what text. If a match is found the scanning stops, allowing the document to be read or edited. The search can also be repeated by clicking on the Find next button until all occurrences of the Find what text have been found. Find is useful when trying to locate a specific word or passage in a large publication.

Note that Find begins its search at the current cursor position. To search the entire story the cursor should first be moved to the beginning of the story (Ctrl+Home) before executing Find. When starting a new Find, any old Find what text is automatically removed from the dialog box when the new text is typed.

Find has a number of different options. Normally, PageMaker ignores case differences (i.e., uppercase and lowercase) during a search. If the Find what text is Dog PageMaker will find dog, Dog, DOG, etc. Selecting the Match case option tells PageMaker to find only text with the same capitalization as the Find what text. For example, a Match case find for CAT will not find Cat or cat.

It is important to realize that a match is also considered to be found when the Find what text is located within another word. For example, specifying the will not only find "the" but also they, theory, another, etc. Such false finds can be eliminated by using the Whole word option which locates only those occurrences of the Find what text that are not part of another word.

PageMaker normally searches only the currently displayed story. To check all of the stories in the current publication, select All stories.

4.10 Replacing Text with Change

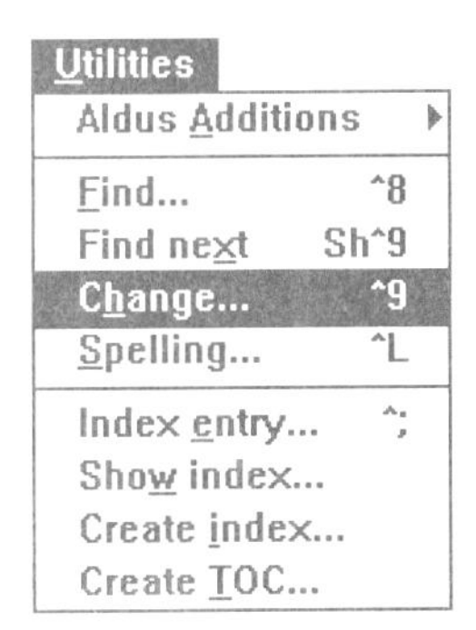

The Change command from the Utilities menu (`Ctrl+9`) locates text in a publication, just as the Find command does, but then replaces it with another piece of text that you supply. This makes it easy to create different versions of the same publication that have some specified differences. For example, PageMaker could be used to create an advertisement for an upcoming football game against Ivy University. After printing the letter, the Change command could be used to change each occurrence of "Ivy University" to "Trenton State" and then to "New Brunswick College" and so on. Thus all the flyers needed could be easily created without having to type each one separately; the master flyer is typed once and the name of the school changed using Change:

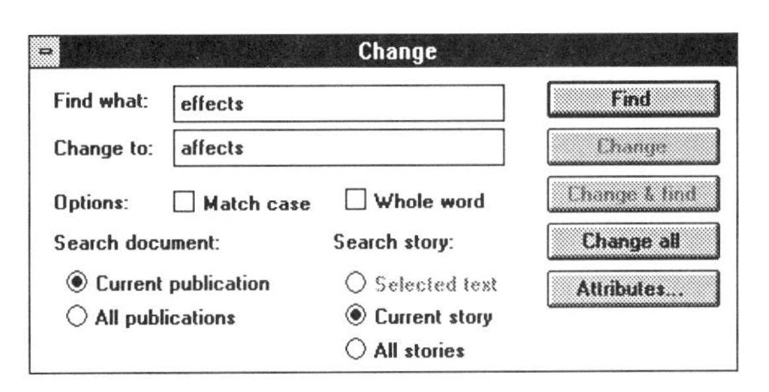

The Change command's dialog box

The Change command can be dangerous. If the Find what text is not clearly defined unwanted replacements may be made. For example, a Find what text of `the` will not only affect every occurrence of "the", but also any word that contains the, such as they, theory, another, etc. One way to avoid unwanted replacements is to define the Find what text very carefully. Another way is to use the Match case and Whole word options as described in the previous section.

Like the Find command, Change starts its search from the current cursor position and can be made to replace only uppercase and lowercase matches. Change also has the option of replacing all occurrences with the new text (Change all), or one at a time (Find, Change), prompting you to verify that each change should be made. It is usually advisable to verify each replacement before it is made, thereby avoiding unwanted changes.

4.11 New Stories in the Story Editor

If you execute the Edit Story command without having an existing story selected, PageMaker will create a new, empty story named Untitled. You may then enter new text, format, and edit it. Selecting Edit Layout changes the pointer to loaded text shape and clicking places the new story.

When To Use the Story Editor

- When editing or entering a large amount of text
- When you need to see the position of invisible characters such as tabs, spaces, or Enters
- When spell checking
- When using Find or Change

Practice 5

In this Practice you will use the Find and Change commands to search for and replace pieces of text. Start PageMaker and open CH4PRACT. Select the story and switch to the Story Editor if you have not already done so.

1) *PLACE THE CURSOR*

PageMaker starts its search from the current cursor position. Press `Crtl+PgUp` to move the cursor to the very top of the story.

2) *FIND A WORD*

a. From the Utilities menu, select the Find command. The Find dialog box is shown.
b. Type `edit` as the Find what text.
c. Select Find to begin the search. PageMaker locates the text in the word "Editor" in the first line.
d. Select Find next to locate the next occurrence of edit. "Editor" is found in the first paragraph.
e. Select Find next several more times. The words "Editor", "edited", and "edit" are found.
f. Continue to select Find next until all occurrences of the Find what text have been located and PageMaker displays the message:

g. Select OK to remove the message.

3) *FIND USING OPTIONS*

a. The Find dialog box should still be displayed. Select the Whole word option by clicking on it.
b. Select Find. Because the cursor is located near the end of the story, PageMaker asks:

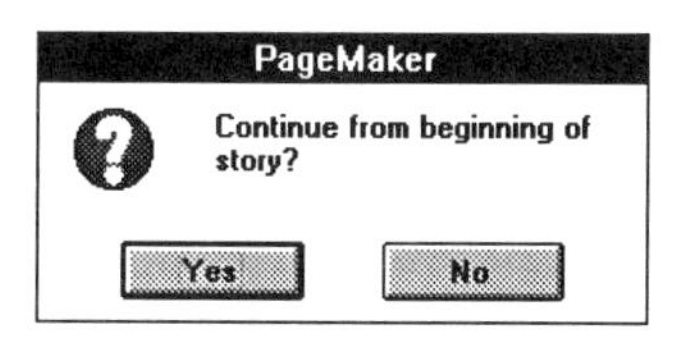

d. Select Yes. PageMaker skips the words "Editor" and "edited" and finds just "edit".

e. Continue to select Find next until all occurrences of edit have been found and PageMaker displays the Search complete message. Select OK to remove the message.
f. Remove the Find dialog box by double-clicking on its Close box in the upper-left corner.

4) REPLACE TEXT

a. Press Ctrl+PgUp to move the cursor to the beginning of the story.
b. From the Utilities menu, select the Change command. The Change dialog box is shown.
c. Type cursor as the Find what text, replacing any existing text.
d. Type insertion point as the Change to text.
e. Select Find. PageMaker locates the text near the end of the first paragraph.
f. Select Change. The highlighted word is changed.
g. Select Find next. The next occurrence of "cursor" is located. Select Change.
h. Select Find next. There are no more "cursors" in the file and PageMaker displays Search complete.
i. Select OK to remove the message. Close the Change dialog box by double-clicking on its Close box in the upper-left corner.

5) REPLACE ALL

a. Press Ctrl+PgUp to move the cursor to the beginning of the story.
b. Press Ctrl+9 to execute the Change command.
c. Type insertion point as the Find what text, and cursor as the Change to text.
d. Select Change all. PageMaker locates all occurrences of "insertion point" and changes them to "cursor".
e. Close the Change dialog box by double-clicking on its Close box. Check the story; do any "insertion points" remain? Your Story Editor screen should be similar to:

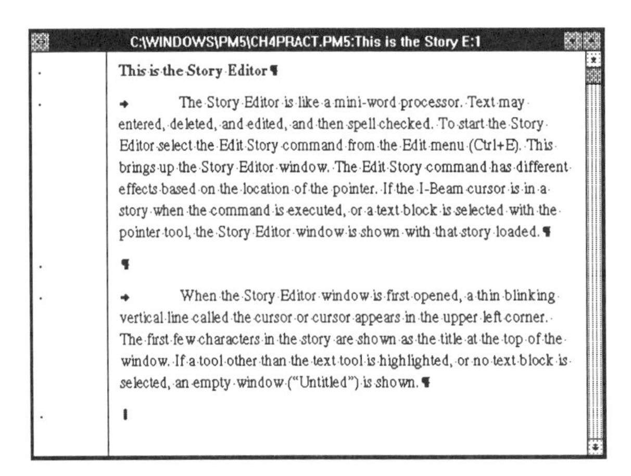

6) CREATE A NEW STORY

a. From the Edit menu, select Edit Layout to return to the layout.
b. Click anywhere in the white space. Nothing should be selected.
c. Press Ctrl+E to execute the Edit story command. A new, empty story is shown.
d. Type: This is my new story.
e. From the Edit menu, select Edit layout. The layout is shown and the pointer is the loaded Text shape.
f. Click below the current text to place the new story. The new story is shown with handles placed:

This is the Story Editor

The Story Editor is like a mini-word processor. Text may entered, deleted, and edited, and then spell checked. To start the Story Editor select the Edit Story command from the Edit menu (Ctrl+E). This brings up the Story Editor window. The Edit Story command has different effects based on the location of the pointer. If the I-Beam cursor is in a story when the command is executed, or a text block is selected with the pointer tool, the Story Editor window is shown with that story loaded.

When the Story Editor window is first opened, a thin blinking vertical line called the cursor or cursor appears in the upper left corner. The first few characters in the story are shown as the title at the top of the window. If a tool other than the text tool is highlighted, or no text block is selected, an empty window ("Untitled") is shown.

This is my new story.

g. Save and close the modified file.

4.12 Effective Writing

This chapter discusses four of the most important elements of effective writing. Even in this age of technology, when we can communicate using a variety of sophisticated equipment, the ability to write clear, effective publications remains essential. For example, using the telephone is a fast and efficient way to communicate, but in business you will often need to follow a call with written confirmation of your discussion. Facsimile (fax) machines provide another popular way to exchange information, but they are useful only after you have written the message you wish to transmit. In this day and age, a message can travel with great speed, but the quality of that message still depends on your writing skills. Therefore, it is important to understand and use some essential qualities of good writing, including clarity, accuracy, brevity, and organization.

4.13 Clarity in Writing

Make your writing as clear as possible. Written communications which lack clarity confuse or frustrate the reader rather than deliver the message. You can enhance the clarity of your writing by using the following guidelines:

- ✔ Know your audience
- ✔ Know your subject
- ✔ Know your specific message
- ✔ Know your purpose

Know Your Audience

Any message has a good chance of being readily understood if the writer knows the subject thoroughly; however, the writer also needs to be aware of the intended reader. Everything you write will have an *audience*, the individual or group of people who will read what you have written. If you know the individual being addressed, ask yourself how to "speak" to him or her most successfully. If you are writing to a group of people, be aware of the group's shared characteristic which leads you to address them. Are they potential customers? Are they people who have just moved into your city or town? Are they people who have missed a payment on their monthly bill? Determine what common factor has brought these people together in a group. Why have they become the audience of the communication you are about to compose? If you know your audience, you can design your message to communicate more directly and effectively.

Know Your Subject

Be fully informed about the overall topic of your publication. If the purpose of a letter is to ask someone to attend a business meeting, get all the available information about the meeting before starting to write. If your information is limited, the message will be vague. For example, read the following paragraph from a memorandum written by a company president and sent to the staff:

> We will probably hold a meeting of the staff on the first, second, or third day of next month. I think we should get underway some time between 8 and 11 in the morning. As far as I can determine, the best location for the meeting would be the company conference room. On the other hand, one of the larger offices might meet our needs. I will decide later. Also, the agenda has not been set, but I assume that there will be some monthly reports, maybe some general announcements and personnel matters, along with some other stuff. Why don't you see if you can plan to join us?

The writer has provided the audience with very little useful information. When and where will the meeting be held? What will be discussed at the meeting? Is it important for the reader to attend?

If the writer had gathered facts about the meeting before writing the memorandum, the following passage might have been the result:

> I have scheduled a staff meeting from 9 to 10 AM on Monday, July 1st, in the company conference room. At present, the agenda includes reports on sales and investments, a discussion of deadlines, and a series of brief, general announcements. All managers are asked to attend.

NOTE: Reading your work aloud to yourself or a listener is an effective technique for examining what you have written. Reading enables you and the listener to "hear" the strengths and weaknesses of the document. You will catch awkward or wordy sentences, find hidden errors, and get a good sense of how effectively the writing has been organized.

4

Know Your Specific Message

From all the data gathered about a subject, select only the information needed for your specific message, which is the actual content of the letter, article, or other communication you are preparing to write. If the subject of a letter is a meeting to be held next week, the specific message might only include the time, and place, and a broad outline of the business to be discussed.

Know Your Purpose

Just as the writer's awareness of the audience, knowledge of the general subject, and ability to determine the precise content of a message help to make a written communication clearer for the audience, an understanding of the publication's intent is also important. Ask yourself *why* you are writing. What are the desired effect and response to the written communication? What is your purpose, to get someone to come to a meeting, to make customers aware of a new product so they will consider buying it, or to get sports fans to read your article? Ask, "Why am I writing," and keep the answer (the purpose) in mind. If you ignore your purpose, so will your audience.

These last three topics, subject, message, and purpose, can be broadly defined as your message. Therefore, when writing any document it is important to concentrate on two important points:

Know your audience
Know your message

Practice 7

1. You have been asked by the editor of your local newspaper to write an article on the town council's decision to save money by closing the city library on Mondays and Tuesdays. Identify each of the following for the article:

   audience people in that town
   subject Saving money
   specific message Saving money by closing Library on Mon. & Tues.
   purpose Inform town

2. The local Chevrolet dealer has received a specially modified Corvette which is to sell for $90,000. Because the dealer is a major newspaper advertiser, the editor wants you to write an article to publicize the car and the dealership. Identify each of the following for the article:

   audience local towns people
   subject Modified Corvette
   specific message Specifically Modified Corvette for $90,000
   purpose Sales

4.14 Accuracy in Writing

4

If you prepare for each writing task by knowing the audience and the message, your communications will be clear and much more accurate. Accuracy is another important aspect of effective writing.

Keep your writing as accurate as possible because a message which misleads or misinforms an audience is worse than no message at all. The accuracy of the message is enhanced by the use of precise, correct information.

Know your facts. When you collect data about a subject, make sure the information is correct. If what you know about a subject is reliable, then it follows that the information you select for a specific message will be accurate. In addition to making your message clearer, accuracy can save money and prevent frustration by avoiding errors and time consuming corrections later in the publishing process.

4.15 Brevity in Writing

In most cases you will need to keep your writing as brief as possible. Business executives, employees, and even faithful customers will most likely not be able or willing to spend a great deal of time reading what you have written. On the other hand, the length of each document you write will be determined, in part, by your purpose.

Assume that the audience for what you write is just as busy as you are and understand that time is important to everyone. In effect, when you send a written communication you are asking the recipient for the use of some of his or her time to read what you have written. If your communication drags on, or your reader gets lost in repetitious sentences and paragraphs, your message is buried and the audience will be lost.

After you complete the first draft of your message, and before you revise and edit, conduct a Brevity Check by asking yourself the following questions:

Brevity Check

Have I used extra words, phrases, or clauses?
Have I said things clearly and only once?
Have I wasted time and space by digressing?

This Brevity Check can work for a sentence, a paragraph, or even an entire publication; it helps to keep your writing as brief as possible. However, remember that a number of factors contribute to your publication's overall, final length, especially its purpose. If you are writing an advertisement, you may only need a paragraph or two. A semi-annual sales report or an elaborate new marketing plan written for the Board of Directors might require dozens of pages. Each writing task will have a corresponding length requirement; however, make your publication as short as possible.

4.16 Organization in Writing

Organization is important because it enables the audience to follow and understand your message without having to struggle. If you write a newsletter article in which you intend to discuss three points, the most logical, effective order in which to present them needs to be considered. Obviously, most of this "internal" organizing takes place in the body of the publication.

For example, if you intend to write an article explaining hiring procedures for job applicants, a paragraph might be devoted to each aspect of the process. If the steps include making the final decision, collecting letters of reference and other supporting documentation, and holding a preliminary interview, it would make sense to arrange the paragraphs in the order that the steps occur:

1. A preliminary interview
2. Collecting documentation
3. The final decision

In this case, the internal organization of the publication imitates the very process you are describing, and that makes it easier for your audience to follow the discussion.

Internal organization refers to the order in which you present the ideas or topics within a publication; external organization refers to the broader design or structure in which those ideas (topics) are presented.

4.17 The Writing Process

This section discusses an effective process to use when you are writing. The process, which consists of **Pre-writing, Drafting, Revising,** and **Editing,** can be used for any writing project but works particularly well when applied to most desktop published documents. Pre-writing provides for a period of preparation which begins before the writer starts to write, and Drafting is a period of initial composition which consists of the writer's first efforts to compose the required document. Revising encourages trial and experimentation so the writer can rephrase, rearrange, and restructure the first draft in search of the most effective prose possible. Editing promotes refinement so that writing and formatting errors can be corrected to produce the document's final draft. All of these steps are made with the use of a word processor, or PageMaker's Story Editor.

The Pre-Writing Stage

A project of any kind requires some planning, and a writing project is no exception. The Pre-writing stage provides an opportunity to think about the writing task. You can do some mental planning well ahead of the time that you sit down to start writing. Just as a quarterback might think through a series of plays while dressing for the game, or a musician might mentally play each note in a difficult piece of music while driving to the concert, writers need to take time to contemplate their work. Think about your general subject. Review the facts. Begin to formulate the ideas and organize the information that you want to use.

Use the Story Editor during the Pre-writing stage to create a new file and list information about the general subject. At first, do not worry about organization; simply record the facts and ideas in any order. Once you have listed everything that you can think of, arrange you notes under specific headings. Define your audience and the message that you wish to communicate.

From this organized list you can select just the information needed for the particular document you are preparing to draft. The Pre-writing exercise should always be printed so it can be referred to when starting to actually write the first draft of the communication.

The Drafting Stage

After having completed the Pre-writing stage by (mentally) planning the writing project, making random notes, and beginning to organize ideas, the next stage is to compose a first draft.

During the Drafting stage, the first draft of the communication is created. A "first draft" is exactly what the term suggests, the first version of the document. The first draft does not have to be perfect. In fact, you will have more success if you just keep writing; express your ideas, or "state your business," and worry about rearranging (Revising) and refining (Editing) the work later. Start the Drafting stage by using the preliminary plan developed as a Pre-writing exercise.

The Revising Stage

The Revising stage is an opportunity to change and improve the first draft. This is the time to add or delete information, examine the document's diction (wording), experiment with the structure of sentences and the order of paragraphs, and check the draft against notes made during the Pre-writing stage. This is a good time to read the document aloud, and change anything that is awkward or confusing. Keep your audience and message in mind, and strive to be clear, brief, and accurate.

The Editing Stage

The Revising stage results in a near-final version of the document. What remains of the writing process is a careful check for errors—the Editing stage.

The Editing stage begins after revisions have been made, and the final form of the document has been established. This stage provides the opportunity to check the writing for punctuation and grammar errors, use the spelling checker to find any spelling or typing errors, and read the work from beginning to end to assure that the appropriate level of language has been used.

The four-stage writing process can help you in a variety of ways. Pre-writing allows for brainstorming and collecting information; it helps you get organized. The Drafting stage is a time for you to compose freely, with "no risks" regarding content or errors. Revising allows for innovation and refinement of your writing, and the Editing stage provides the time to perfect the document and produce an error-free final draft. Admittedly, the importance and value of the entire process increases with the length and complexity of the writing task; however, the four-stage procedure remains an extremely useful writing tool for even a one-page document.

The Writing Process
Pre-writing
Drafting
Revising
Editing

Practice 8

1. In Practice 7 part 1 you identified the audience, subject, message, and purpose for an article on the town council's decision to close the city library on Mondays and Tuesdays. Open a PageMaker file and then use the Story Editor to write a brief article titled **Library To Close on Monday and Tuesday**. Use the following writing process in producing the article:

   a. Pre-writing: Make notes on the information needed to write the article including quotes from council members.
   b. Drafting: Complete a first draft of the article.
   c. Revising: Conduct a careful and thorough revision of the article. Include an accuracy and brevity check.
   d. Editing: Conduct a careful edit of the article.
   e. Place the story in the PageMaker layout.
   f. Save the file naming it Library.
   g. Print a copy of the story.

2. In Practice 7 part 2 you identified the audience, subject, message, and purpose for an article on the new Corvette at the local Chevrolet dealer. Open a PageMaker file and then the Story Editor and write a brief article titled **Flashy New 90K Corvette Arrives at Lawrenceville Chevrolet**. Use the following writing process in producing the article:

   a. Pre-writing: Make notes on the information needed to write the article including quotes from the Chevrolet dealer.
   b. Drafting: Complete a first draft of the article.
   c. Revising: Conduct a careful and thorough revision of the article. Include an accuracy and brevity check.
   d. Editing: Conduct a careful edit of the article.

e. Place the story in the PageMaker layout.
f. Save the file naming it Corvette.
g. Print a copy of the layout.

4

Chapter Summary

PageMaker has a built-in word processor called the Story Editor accessed by executing the Edit story command from the Edit menu. Advantages of the Story Editor are that it is built-in to PageMaker, and is easy to learn and use. The disadvantages are that it lacks some advanced features such as a thesaurus and grammar checker, although it does contain a spelling checker. However, the Story Editor is normally the best way to enter large amounts of new text into PageMaker, or perform complex edits on an existing publication.

Because the Story Editor is used to enter and edit text, this chapter presented a number of keyboard alternatives for highlighting and editing text. Holding down the Shift key while pressing an arrow extends the selection highlight in the direction of the arrow. The Home, End, PgUp, and PgDn keys moves the cursor around the document, and may be combined with the Ctrl key to move even further distances.

The Display ¶ command from the Story menu displays normally invisible characters such as tabs and spaces as special symbols:

Symbol	**Meaning**
· (raised dot)	Space bar pressed
¶	Enter key pressed
→	Tab key pressed

This is helpful when editing because it makes it easier to include all the desired characters in a highlighted block.

One of the most useful features of the Story Editor is the ability to check the spelling in a publication using the Spelling command in the Utilities menu. When executed, PageMaker starts at the current cursor position and compares each word in the publication to a dictionary file. Unknown words are selected and suggested spellings displayed. The Utilities menu also contains commands to Find and Change text.

This chapter also discusses four important elements of effective, written communications: clarity, accuracy, brevity, and organization. The clarity of writing is enhanced when the writer knows the audience and message of the publication. To know the audience, the writer must carefully consider the readers to whom the publication is addressed. To know the message, the writer needs to gather and become familiar with as much relevant information as possible (the subject), determines the exact content of the communication (the specific message), and carefully consider the reason the communication is being written by asking, "Why am I writing this document?" (the purpose).

4

Accuracy and Brevity are other requirements of effective communications. The recipients of a report, newsletter, or other publication should not be expected to waste time reading material which is wrong or could be more concise. Conducting a Brevity Check can help ensure that a publication is as concise as possible. The Check consists of asking at least three questions: Have I used extra words, phrases, or clauses? Have I said things clearly and only once? Have I wasted time and space by digressing? The Brevity Check can be applied to a sentence, paragraph, or an entire document.

This chapter discusses a four-stage process for writing which includes Pre-writing, Drafting, Revising, and Editing stages. The use of the computer makes each of these steps easier. It is important during each of the steps to keep the audience and message in mind.

The Pre-writing stage is used to think through and plan the writing project. This stage is the time to collect information, formulate ideas, and begin to organize the communication to be written.

The Drafting stage is the writer's opportunity to create a first draft (first version) of the planned document. This stage makes use of the information gathered during Pre-writing.

The Revising stage is used to examine the first draft, experiment with sentence and paragraph structure, consider diction (word choice), and work toward achieving a final draft of the document.

The Editing stage is a period of refinement. The writer makes final adjustments to the organization of the document, checks for grammar, punctuation, and spelling errors, and, ultimately, produces the final draft.

Vocabulary

Accuracy - The use of correct information in a publication.

Audience - The readers to whom or for whom a message (or publication) is intended.

Body - The main text in a publication.

Brevity - The preferred length of a publication: brief; short; concise.

Clarity - Making a publication easy to read and understand, as opposed to being vague or difficult to follow.

Document - Any written communication, including advertisements, letters, reports, business plans, newsletters, memoranda, etc.

Drafting Stage - The second writing process stage during which the writer creates a first draft (first version) of a communication.

Editing Stage - The fourth and last stage of the writing process during which the writer checks a publication for errors in grammar, punctuation, and spelling to produce a final draft.

First Draft - The first version of a written publication.

Layout - WYSIWYG view of a publication.

Message - The idea or ideas that the writer wants to communicate in a publication.

Organization - A publication's internal organization, meaning the order in which the contents of a communication are arranged.

Pre-writing Stage - The first writing process stage during which the writer mentally plans the writing project, begins to collect information, and makes the initial effort to organize the publication being prepared.

Purpose - The writer's primary reason for writing a particular publication or communication.

Repeat key - A key that acts as if it were continuously pressed as long as it is held down.

Revising Stage - The third writing process stage during which the writer experiments with sentence and paragraph structure, diction, and organization of the written publication.

Smart menus - Commands listed on menu change to fit the operation you are performing.

Specific Message - The particular contents of an advertisement, letter, memorandum, report, or other communication.

Story Editor - Word processor built-in to PageMaker.

Reviews

Sections 4.1 — 4.4

1. Explain what the Story Editor is used for.
2. Briefly outline the advantages and disadvantages of using the Story Editor compared to a full word processing program.
3. How is text entered into the Story Editor?
4. If the cursor is inside a paragraph, what is the quickest way to move it to the first character in that paragraph?
5. What is the Esc key used for?
6. What is the difference between using the Backspace key and the left-arrow key to move the cursor to the left?
7. Pressing `Shift+Up arrow` does what when the cursor is located in a paragraph?

Sections 4.5 — 4.11

8. Executing the Display ¶ command in the Story Editor does what?
9. What is shown in the Story Editor when fonts and sizes of type are changed?
10. Why is it useful not to have certain formatting options shown while editing?
11. How do you return to the layout from the Story Editor?
12. Explain what happens when the Spelling command is executed and a spelling error detected?
13. How and why would you add a word, such as a name, to the Spelling dictionary file?

4

14. Explain how to use the Find command to locate the name "Beth" in the Story Editor.
    select Find (Ctrl+8) from the Utilities menu -- Enter the name "Beth" at the Find What line of the Find dialog box (click on whole word too)
15. How could you keep the search in Practice 14 from finding the word "Bethlehem"?
    Use the whole word option
16. Explain how you could have PageMaker change each occurrence of the name Lawrenceville to Boca Raton. select Change (Ctrl+9) from the Utilities menu. Enter Lawrenceville at the Find what line + Enter Boca Raton at the Change to line of the Change dialog box.
17. What happens when you execute the Edit Story command without having an existing story selected? An empty window ("Untitled") is shown.

Sections 4.13 — 4.17

18. Why is it important to identify your audience before writing? If you know the individual(s) you are to address, you will be able to "speak" to him/her (them) more successfully.
19. Define the audience, subject, message, and purpose when writing an advertisement for:

    a) wedding dress Brides, wedding dress,
    b) wheel chair
    c) $200,000 Rolls Royce

20. What is meant by being accurate in your writing? What are the benefits of accurate writing? The use of precise, correct information. Will make your message clearer + save money + prevent frustration by avoiding errors + time consuming corrections later in the publishing process.
21. Why is it important to be as brief as possible in your writing?
    If your communication drags on, your message is buried + the audience is lost.
22. Explain the difference between internal and external organization.
    Internal organization refers to the order in which you present the ideas or topics within a publication; external org. refers to the broader design or structure in which those ideas (topics) are presented
23. Briefly describe and explain the four steps in the writing process.

    Pre-writing: Think through + plan the writing project. Collect information, formulate ideas, + begin to organize the communication.

    Drafting: Create a first draft (first version) of the planned document.

    Revising: Examine the first draft, experiment with sentence + ¶ structure, consider diction (word choice), + work toward achieving a final draft of the document.

    Editing: Make final adjustments to the organization of the document, check for grammar, punctuation + spelling errors, + produce the final draft.

Exercises

1. California Sunshine has decided that its press release modified in Chapter Three exercise 1 should contain information about its original six flavors. You will add this information using the Story Editor. Open CSPRESS and follow the steps below to edit and format it to appear similar to:

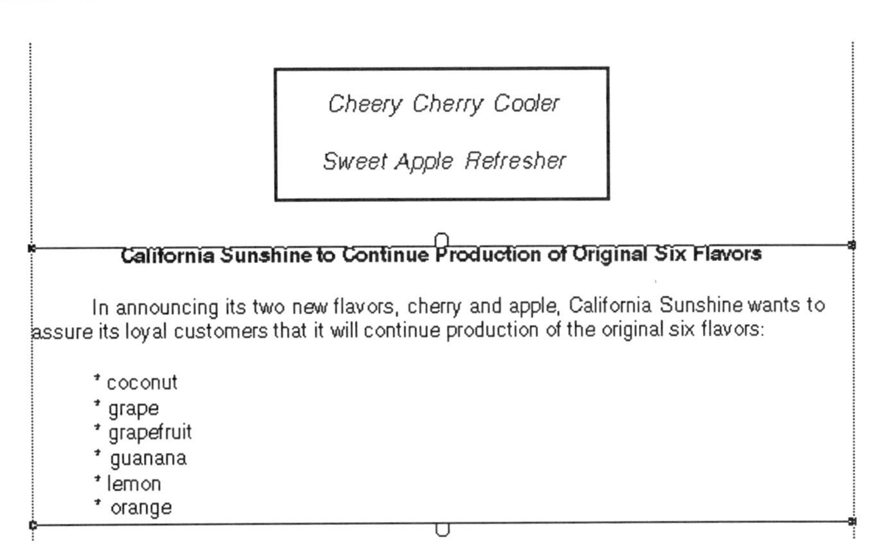

   a) Create a new text block by opening the Story Editor without selecting a block.

   b) Enter the following text into the Story Editor:

```
California Sunshine to Continue Production of Original
Six Flavors

   In announcing its two new flavors, cherry and apple,
California Sunshine wants to assure its loyal customers
that it will continue production of the original six
flavors:

   * coconut
   * grape
   * grapefruit
   * guanana
   * lemon
   * orange
```

   c) Format all the text as Helvetica, 12 points. Center the title and make it bold. Note that some formatting is not displayed in the Story Editor.

   d) Check the spelling using the Spelling command. Note that PageMaker's dictionary does not contain the word "guanana," which you should Ignore.

e) Return to the layout. Place the new story in the document as shown.

f) Save and then print a copy of CSPRESS.

2. Aztec Café owner Juan Hernandez has determined that the article about new chef Janet Smith needs additional text and errors corrected. Open ACBROCH modified in Chapter Three exercise 2 and follow the steps below to edit and format the publication so that it is similar to:

Aztec Cafe owner Juan Hernandez announced the hiring of Juanette Smith as Aztec's new chef. Ms. Smith was trained in gourmet cooking at the International Cuisine Academy in Mexico City. During two years of study Ms. Smith specialized in the preparation of chicken and pork dishes using citrus fruits such as lemons and limes. She will introduce many such new dishes to Aztec's menu. The new dishes will also include swordfish and salmon prepared in a fiery hot sauce.

Juanette began her professional cooking career at the four star restaurant *Tex Mex* in New York City. At *Tex Mex* Ms. Smith became renowned for introducing many different types of beans in her cuisine. When asked about her experiences in New York, Ms. Smith said "It is amazing how sophisticated New York tastes are and how much they enjoy Mexican food. The more imaginative and experimental my dishes became the happier the customers were."

With the addition of Juanette Smith to his staff, Mr. Hernandez expects business to grow at a rapid pace. Once his customers realize that he has hired a famous chef they should keep Aztec packed! It might be smart to make reservations for busy evenings now by calling 555-3241.

a) Load the story titled "Famous New Chef Comes to Aztec" into the Story Editor.

b) Change "International School for Chefs" to "International Cuisine Academy".

c) At the end of the paragraph that begins "Aztec Cafe owner..." add the sentence:

```
The new dishes will also include swordfish and salmon
prepared in a fiery hot sauce.
```

d) Mr. Hernandez believes that the sentence which begins "I hope to find..." might be offensive to local residents. Delete the sentence.

e) At the end of the paragraph that begins "With the addition of..." add the sentence:

```
It might be smart to make reservations for busy
evenings now by calling 555-3241.
```

f) Using the Find command, locate and then italicize all occurrences of the restaurant name Tex Mex.

g) Ms. Smith's first name is not Janet, buy Juanette. Use the Change command to make the appropriate name change through out the story.

4

h) Check the spelling of the story. Ignore any proper names.

i) Return to the layout and check that the changes have been made. Resize any text blocks that need it.

j) Save and print a copy of ACBROCH.

3. Deborah Debit needs to have some changes made to her résumé. Open DDRESUME and follow the steps below to edit and format it to appear similar to:

Deborah N. Debit
1117 East Hathaway Drive
Newtown, FL 33445
407/555-6970

OBJECTIVE
A leadership position in the management of a small to medium size company.

WORK EXPERIENCE
1991 - present
Bennett Chemical Industries, Newtown, FL: Accountant. Manage all accounts payable/receivable using a computerized system which includes spreadsheet and other accounting software.

1990 - 1991
Dr. Roger S. Calculate, College Circle, FL: Research Assistant. Prepared case studies for new accounting textbook. Edited and revised the financial sections of the text.

EDUCATION
1987 - 1991
BS Accounting: State University, College Circle, FL. Departmental Honors in Business and Finance. Chairperson, Future Accountants of America. College Circle Community Service Award.

1983 - 1987
High School Diploma: Newtown High School, Newtown, FL. Senior Class President. Member, Small Business Club.

REFERENCES
Available from:
Students' Career Placement Office
State University
College Circle, FL 32306
phone: 407-555-1392
fax: 407-555-2983

a) Load the résumé into the Story Editor.

b) Change the OBJECTIVE to:

```
A leadership position in the management of a small to
medium size company.
```

c) Add the following sentence to the WORK EXPERIENCE section after the sentence "Prepared case studies...".

```
Edited and revised the financial sections of the text.
```

d) Add the phone and fax numbers of the Student's Career Placement Office at the end of the `REFERENCES` section:

```
phone: 407-555-1392
fax: 407-555-2983
```

e) Use the Find command to locate Roger Calculate and add his middle initial, S.

f) Check the spelling of the résumé. Ignore any proper names.

g) Return to the layout and check the changes.

h) Save and print a copy of DDRESUME.

Chapter Five:
Elements of Good Design

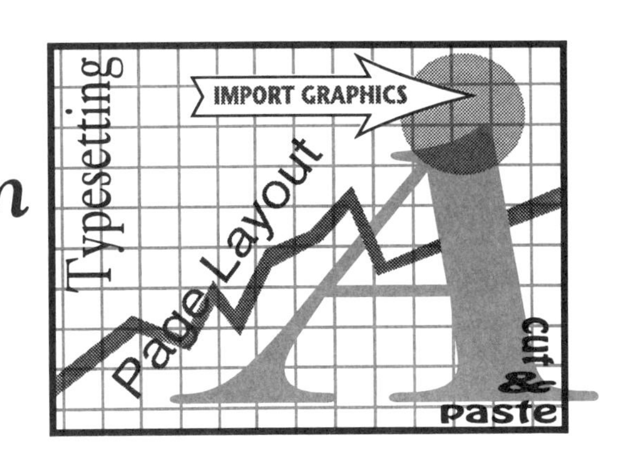

Appropriateness

Balance

Focus and Flow

Consistency

Purpose and Audience

File - Page setup

View - Guides and rulers

View - Column guides

Type - Leading

Objectives

5

After completing this chapter you will be able to:

1. Identify and discuss elements of good design.
2. Determine the purpose and audience of a publication.
3. Effectively plan the production of a publication.
4. Use the Master Pages in PageMaker.
5. Create and manipulate a grid with Ruler guides.
6. Use the Snap to guides command.
7. Create multiple columns on a grid.
8. Change margins in a publication.
9. Change the leading in text blocks.

5

This chapter provides an introduction to design. Specific tasks that are performed when designing a publication are covered, and specialized terms defined. We will learn that the design of a document should be determined by its purpose and audience.

Chapters Six, Seven, and Eight provide step-by-step instructions for creating brochures, newsletters, advertisements, and longer documents. Because a knowledge of design concepts and terminology is required, it is important to thoroughly understand the material in this chapter before proceeding to the next.

5.1 What is Document Design?

Document design is the creation of both the visual and physical presentation of a publication. The visual presentation is the *layout*—how the text and graphics are arranged on each page. The physical presentation is the *format*—how and what it is made of, such as the size of the finished product, the materials (paper and covers), and the type of binding.

This chapter introduces basic design elements and illustrates them using PageMaker's design tools. Be aware that professional designers sometimes disagree on the terms used for design concepts. Part of this confusion is caused by the merger of three different professional fields: printing, art (design), and computer technology. For clarity we have chosen to use the design terms employed by PageMaker.

5.2 Concepts of Document Design

It is important to realize that with document design there are no absolute rules, only guidelines. Each project is different, so while there are accepted guidelines that are usually employed to create a successful design, there are times when these guidelines are not the best design choice. Ideas that effectively communicate the desired message in one document might not be appropriate to the message in a different document.

The original design of a document goes through changes as the publication is refined (and obstacles encountered) so that a good design usually results only after considerable experimentation. The four basic design concepts are *appropriateness, balance, focus and flow,* and *consistency* and each should be kept in mind as a document is designed.

5

Appropriateness

Ask yourself if your design choices are appropriate for the document's content and audience. For example, a financial newspaper is not expected to look like a sales brochure. Readers get certain expectations about a document from its general design. Imagine, for example, a magazine about Beverly Hills. You would probably expect many color photographs, along with interviews and colorful advertisements, published on glossy paper. You would not expect it to be a black and white, four page newsletter printed on cheap paper. Beverly Hills is a glitzy place and a reader would expect a glitzy publication. You must first identify the audience (the reader) of the publication so that you can make the appropriate design decisions.

Not only should the overall design be suitable to the purpose and audience, but each element of the publication should also be appropriate. The typeface(s), graphics, and layout should be chosen while thinking about the purpose and audience. You should ask yourself questions. Does the type style fit the purpose and audience? Is it too big, small, bold, or fancy? Is the typeface readable? What is the overall feeling of the layout? Is it in keeping with the subject? Is it appropriate for the audience? Is the right story on the front page? Should there be more (or less) graphics?

Notice the differences in the two brochure covers below:

A well-defined audience and purpose helps determine appropriate elements for each design

The brochure on the left has the name of the country club in a modern, digital-style font, and the phrase "Facilities for All Occasions" in a blocky font. Both fonts are inappropriate to the image of a country

5

club. The brochure on the right has placed the country club name in a fancy font appropriate to a country club. The "Facilities..." phrase is less important than the country club name so it is in a simpler, plain font that does not compete with the title. The graphic of a golfer on the second brochure is much more appropriate than the car image on the other brochure.

Balance

Balance, as it applies to design, refers to the relative *weight* of each element in a publication. The thicker, darker, and larger an element is, the heavier it appears on a page. Likewise, the thinner, less dense, and smaller an element is, the lighter it appears. A large photograph is usually heavy, but as the contents of the picture get lighter in color or tone, the weight of the graphic appears lighter. For example, a picture of the night sky is heavier in visual weight than a picture of the beach during the daytime because it contains more dark areas. The placement of the elements on a page also influences the balance. A page with all of its graphical elements at the top of the page is unbalanced; it is top heavy.

It is important to make sure that a publication is balanced as a whole. Are there many graphics on the first three pages, and just text on the last five pages? That is not balanced. The first three pages will appear to be more important than the last five. More than likely those last pages will not be read. Some rearranging should be done.

Balance is tricky. If elements balance too well, the publication may become boring and the reader's interest decrease. For example, if every page of a newsletter has a headline at the top, one graphic in the center, and text throughout the rest, the document is balanced but has too many similar pages, and the separate elements tend to disappear. On reaching page three, the reader sees the page as one unit and not as separate stories and graphics. Small variations in layout can create a less static appearance and hold the reader's interest:

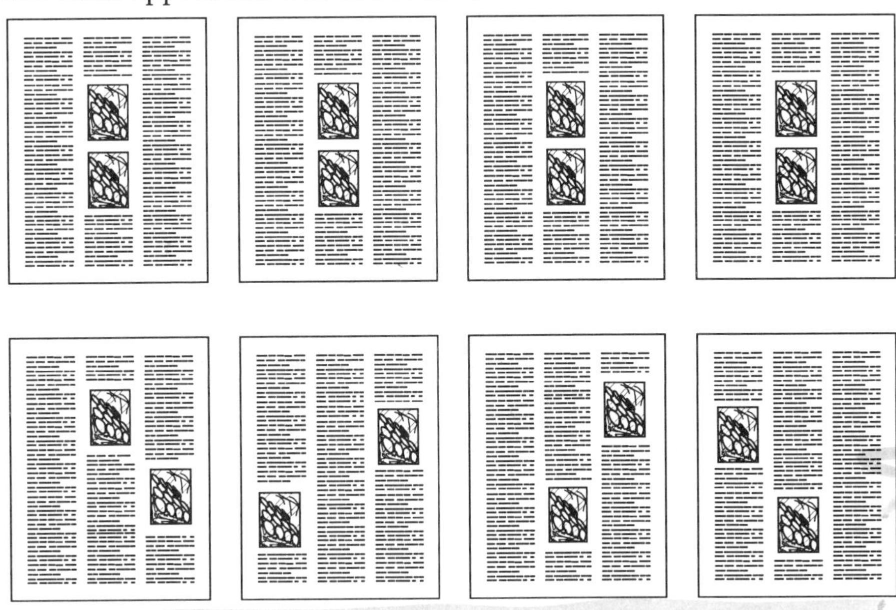

Varying graphic placement makes a document more interesting

When elements are too far off balance, the reader's eye either does not see them or else travels all over the page. If a page design is too busy with many heavy elements, then the reader can not distinguish between different levels of information. It is therefore important to balance the amount of large elements with small elements so that the reader can glance at the page and then zero in on specific areas of interest. This is called ***readability***—how easily the reader can understand the publication.

Problems with balance are often caused by graphics of the same size and weight, and poorly arranged text. Notice how each element on this page seems to have the same weight and is perfectly balanced:

photo

Lorem ipsum dolor sit amet, consectetue adipiscing elit, sed diam nonummy nibh euismod tincidunt ut lareet dolore magna aliquam erat lutpat. Ut wisi enim ad minim veniam, quis nostrud exerci tation ullamcorper suscipit lobotis nisl ut liquip ex eam commodo coneqat. Dui autem vel eum iriure dolor in hendrerit in vulp utate velit esse mol estie consequat, vel illum dolore eu feugiat nulla fac ilisis at vero eros et accumsan et iusto odio dignissim qui blandit praesent luptatum zzril de lenit augue duis dolore te feugait nulla facilisi. Ut wisi enim ad minim veniam, quis nos rexerci

tation ulla mcorper suscipit lobortis nisl ut ali quip ex commodo consequat.Duis autem vel eum iriure dolor in hendrerit in vulputate velit esse molestie consequat. obotis nisl ut liquip ex eam commodo coneqat. Dui autem vel eum iriure dolor in hendrerit in vulp utate velit esse mol estie consequat, vel illum dolore eu feugiat nulla fac ilisis at vero eros et accumsan et iusto odiisis at vero eros et accumsan et iusto odio dignissim qui blandit praesent luptatum zzril de lenit augue duis dolore te feugait nulla facilisi. Ut wisi enim ad minim veniam, quis nos rexerci tation feugiat nulla zzril lobotis ut.

photo

This page is completely balanced, confusing the reader about what is most important

To prevent reader boredom a design needs visual *tension*. Tension refers to the symmetry or asymmetry of the balanced design elements. Tension requires that text and illustrations work with each other to produce an interesting page:

ipsum dolor sit amet, consec tetuer adipis cing elit, sed diam non ummy nibh euis mod tincid unt. Ut laore et dolore magna aliqu am erat volutpat. Ut wisi enim ad minim veniam, quis no strud exerci tation ullam corper susc ipit lobo rtis nisl ut aliquip ex ea com modo cons equat. Duis autem vel eum iriure dolor in hen drerit in vul putate velit esse mo lestie con sequat, vel illum dolo re eu feugiat nulla facilisis at vero eros et accum san et iusto

odio dignissim qui blandit praesent luptatum zzril delenit augue duis dolore te feugait nulla facilisi. Lorem ipsum dolor sit amet, consectetuer adipiscing elit, sed diam nonummy nibh euismod tincidunt ut laoreet dolore magna aliquam erat volut.

Ut wisi enim ad minim veniam, quis nostrud exerci tation ullamcorper suscipit lobortis nisl ut ali quip ex ea co m modo consequat. Duis autem vel eum iriure dolor in hendrerit in vul putate velit esse molestie consequat, vel illum dolore eu feugiat nulla facilisis at vero eros et accum an et iusto odio dignissim qui blandit praesent luptatum zzril delenit augue duis dolore te feugait nulla facilisi. Nam liber tempor cum soluta nobis eleifend option congue nihil imperdiet doming id quod mazim placerat facer possi.

Lorem ipsum nsit dolor sit amet, con sectetuer adipiscing elit, sed diam nonum my nibh euismod tincidunt ut laoreet dolore magna ali quam erat volutpat. Ut wisi enim ad minim veniam, quis nostrud exerci tation ullamcorper suscipit lobortis nisl ut aliquip ex ea modo consequat.

Duis autem vel eum iriure dolor in he ndrerit in vulputate velit esse molestie consequat, vel illum dolore eu feugiat nulla facilisis at vero eros et accumsan et iusto odio dignissim qui blandit praesent luptatum zzril delenit augue duis dolore te feugait nulla facilisi. Lorem ipsum sitdolor sit amet, con sectetuer adipiscing elit, sed diam numm nibh euis mod tin cidunt ut laet dolore

This page is balanced asymmetrically, creating a tension that interests the reader

Here the text has been rearranged from two columns to three, eliminating the block symmetry of a two column format. On the original page the first illustration looms overhead and overshadows the text. Reducing the illustration's size and moving it into the text reduces the emphasis on the graphic. The second illustration has also been reduced and moved into the text. Instead of appearing like building blocks, the two design elements work together to create the appearance of movement, or tension.

Focus and Flow

The focus of a page is where the reader's eye goes when first looking at a page. The eye then flows, or travels, around the page in a path created by all the elements. This path is directed by the weight of each element and by the *white space* around and between the elements. White space is any blank area on a page. The shapes of the white spaces will influence the directions that the reader's eye travels around the page. Although white space areas are blank, they are just as important as text and graphics in determining focus and flow.

Focus is especially important in a one page document because they are usually only glanced at, and in that split-second the decision is made whether to read it or not. Capturing the interest of the reader requires a headline or graphic strong enough to catch their attention without overwhelming the other design elements:

This is the Headline

Lorem ipsum dolor sit amet, consectetuer adipisc ing elit, sed diam nonu mmy nibh euis mod tinc idunt ut laoreet dolore magna aliquam erat volutpat. Ut wisi enim ad minim veniam, quis nostrud exerci tation ullam corper suscipit lobo rtis nisl ut aliquip ex ea comm odo conse quat. Duis autem vel eum iriure dolor in hend rerit in vulputate velit esse mo lestie conseq uat, vel illum dolore eu feugiat nulla facilisis at vero eros et accumsan et iusto odio dignis

sim qui blandit praesent luptatum zzril delenit augue duis dolore te feugait nulla facilisi. Lorem ipsum dolor sit amet, con secte tuer adipisci ng elit, sed diam non mmy nibh e ismod tin cidunt ut laoreet dolore magna aliqu am erat volutpat. Ut wisi enim ad minim veniam, quis nostr ud exerci tation ullamc orper suscipit lobortis nisl ut aliquip ex ea comm odo co nsequat. Duis autem vel eum iriure dolor in hendrerit in vulputate velit esse molestie consequat, vel illum dolore eu

feugiat nulla facilisis at vero eros et accumsan et iusto odio dignissim qui blandit praesent luptatum zzril delenit augue duis dolore te feugait nulla facilisi. Nam liber tempor cum soluta nobis eleifend option congue nihil imperdiet doming id quod mazim placerat facer possim assum. Lorem ipsum dolor sit amet, consectetuer adipiscing elit, sed diam nonummy nibh euismod tincidunt ut laoreet dolore magna aliquam erat volutpat. Ut wisi

Illustration

On this page, the headline and illustration are of similar weight and placement, and compete for the reader's attention

In the document above, both the headline and the graphic are approximately the same weight, and their weight is much heavier than the uniform text. The reader's eye moves back and forth from the top of the page to the bottom without focusing on the text in between. This page lacks a visual focus. The problem is easily solved by making one simple change:

This is the Headline

Lorem ipsum dolor sit amet, consectetuer adipiscing elit, sed diam nonummy nibh euismod tincidunt ut laoreet dolore magna aliquam erat volutpat. Ut wisi enim ad minim veniam, quis nostrud exerci tation ullamcorper suscipit lobortis nisl ut aliquip ex ea commodo consequat. Duis autem vel eum iriure dolor in hendrerit in vulputate velit esse molestie consequat, vel illum dolore eu feugiat nulla facilisis at vero eros et accumsan et iusto odio dignissim qui blandit praesent luptatum zzril delenit augue duis dolore te feugait nulla facilisi. Lorem ipsum dolor sit amet, consectetuer adipiscing elit, sed diam nonummy nibh euismod tincidunt ut laoreet dolore magna aliquam erat volutpat. Ut wisi enim ad minim veniam, quis nostrud exerci tation ullamcorper suscipit lobortis nisl ut aliquip ex ea commodo consequat. Duis autem vel eum

amet, consectetuer adipiscing elit, sed diam nonummy nibh euismod tincidunt ut laoreet dolore magna aliquam erat volutpat. Ut wisi enim ad minim veniam, quis nostrud exerci tation ullamcorper suscipit lobortis nisl ut aliquip ex ea commodo consequat. Duis autem vel eum iriure dolor in hendrerit in vulputate velit esse molestie consequat, vel illum dolore eu feugiat nulla facilisis at vero eros et

um dolor sit amet, consectetuer adipiscing elit, sed diam nonummy nibh euismod tincidunt ut laoreet dolore magna aliquam erat volutpat. Ut wisi enim ad minim veniam, quis nostrud exerci tation ullamcorper suscipit lobortis nisl ut aliquip ex ea commodo consequat. Duis autem vel eum iriure dolor in hendrerit in vulputate velit esse molestie consequat, vel illum dolore eu feugiat nulla

Illustration

aliquam erat volutpat. Ut wisi enim ad minim veniam, quis nostrud exerci tation ullamcorper suscipit lobortis nisl ut aliquip ex ea commodo consequat. Duis autem vel eum iriure dolor in hendrerit

ut laoreet dolore magna aliquam erat volutpat. Ut wisi enim ad minim veniam, quis nostrud exerci tation ullamcorper suscipit lobortis nisl ut aliquip ex ea commodo consequat. Duis autem vel eum

The focus of this page is the headline, and the flow is towards the illustration

By reducing the size of the illustration and moving it into the text area, the competing weight and placement of the headline and illustration are eliminated. Now the headline is the focus of the page, and the photo and text have a dynamic, asymmetrical relationship that creates the desired tension. The tension causes the reader's eye to flow first to the headline and then through the text to the illustration. The tension creates a sense of movement that is essential to all good designs.

Consistency

Consistency can be thought of as the glue in a design; a document is held together by repetitious patterns in the layout. Repetition creates an expectancy for the reader. An example would be making the first letter of each story in a newsletter a large letter, as this book does at the beginning of each chapter. After the first few stories, the reader expects a large letter at the beginning of each story; in fact, the reader unconsciously uses it as a *visual cue* to find the next story. A visual cue is a pattern or object that the reader sees and identifies with an element. For example, each new section in this text starts with a line and a large heading. Another example of a visual cue is using a *dingbat* such as a star or a check mark at the end of each story to cue the reader that the story has ended. As long as there is the same dingbat at the end of each story, the reader knows when to stop looking for more to read. When a visual cue is used, it should be used everywhere that it is appropriate throughout the publication. Forgetting to make the first letter larger or leaving out an ending dingbat confuses the reader. Where is the big letter—did I miss the beginning of the story? There is no little diamond here... where is the end of the story?

There are many elements of a publication that improve with consistency. A logo can be used as a design element in a newsletter with smaller logos repeated at the top or bottom of each page. Special graphical elements like dingbats, reverse headlines (white letters on a black background), or *rules* (lines) can also cue the reader to special elements and create a continuity throughout the document:

Assorted rules and dingbats

The importance of consistency in the use of design elements increases with the length of a document. For a one page document, there are few similar elements, and therefore consistent visual cues are not needed. In a long document, such as a large newsletter, consistent visual cues help the reader keep a point of reference:

Aztec Café
Fine Mexican Food
Aztec Café NewS
Volume XII, Number 4
This is the Headline

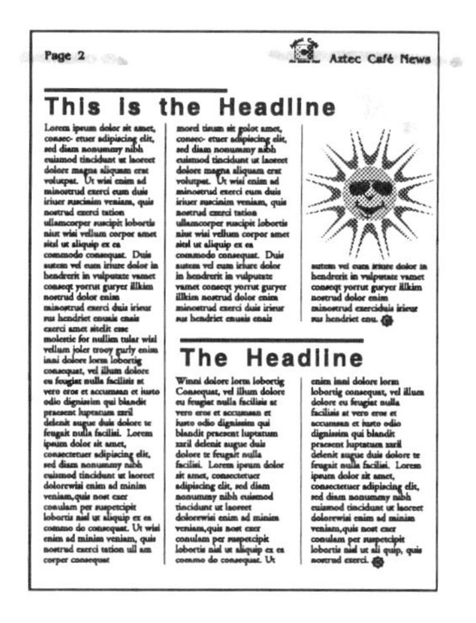
Page 2
Aztec Café News
This is the Headline
The Headline

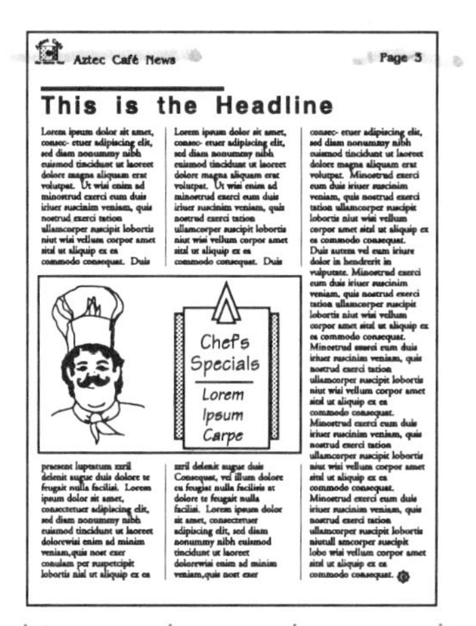
Aztec Café News
Page 3
This is the Headline

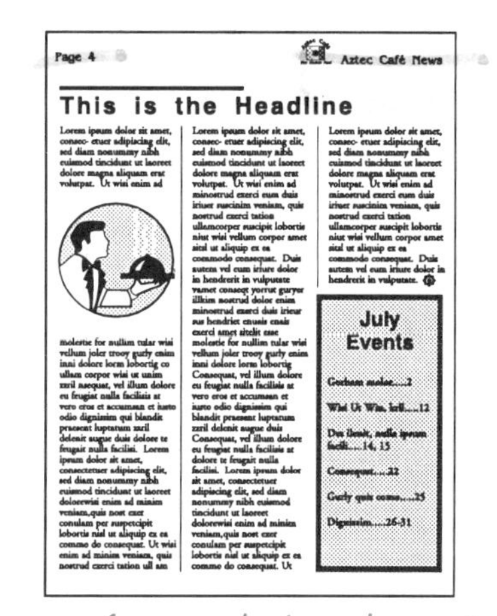
Page 4
Aztec Café News
This is the Headline
July Events

This sample newsletter makes use of many design elements

Each page of this Aztec Café newsletter has three columns with the graphics placed within or across the columns. Each headline has a thick rule directly above it signifying the start of a story and acting as a visual transition or separation between stories. A dingbat marks the end of each story. All of the inside pages include a *running header* that incorporates the title and logo of the café with the page number. *Running headers* and *running footers* are text and graphics that appear in the top or bottom margin (respectively) of each page of a document, although they are usually not found on the first page. Note that in this newsletter, the running header does not appear on the first page. It is common to have the page number in the header or footer, along with the chapter title or number, or the title of the publication.

Practice 1

In this Practice you will further examine the design of the Aztec Café newsletter above. Write your answers down on paper.

1) *DISCUSS THE APPROPRIATENESS*

This 4-page newsletter was written for the employees of the Aztec Café Mexican Restaurants, as a service to keep them informed of the company's status and to improve their quality of life.

5

a. With the purpose and audience in mind, which one of the following fonts would be most appropriate for the headlines in the Aztec Café newsletter:

1. **Headline** 2. Headline 3. HEADLINE

b. When would the other two fonts be appropriate as headlines? List one publication (either real or fictitious) for each font, and describe the purpose and audience of that publication.

2) *DISCUSS THE BALANCE*

Pages 1, 3, and 4 of the newsletter are all similar in that they each contain one story, with the headline at the top of the page and one or two graphics on the page.

a. Is this an ideal layout? Why or why not?
b. What are the differences between these three pages?

3) *DISCUSS THE CONSISTENCY*

a. List all of the elements in the Aztec Café newsletter that are used consistently as visual cues.
b. Where is the Aztec Café logo used in this newsletter? Does it appear consistently?

4) *DISCUSS THE FOCUS AND FLOW OF PAGE 2*

a. What is the focal point of page 2 (where does the reader's eye land first)?
b. List, in order, the elements of page 2 that the reader's eye flows past.

5.3 Planning a Publication

A successful publication is one that is thoroughly planned right from the beginning. Without sufficient planning time-consuming problems can be encountered with each aspect of the publication process. These problems can be avoided by following this or a similar sequence of steps when creating a publication:

With pencil and paper:
1. Determine the *purpose* and *audience* for the publication.
2. Draw *thumbnail* sketches of the preliminary layout.

Using PageMaker:
3. Create the *grid* (guidelines to help line up elements).
4. Create and place the masthead or title.
5. Place the graphics and text.
6. Print a copy and then review it carefully.
7. Make any changes necessary to the design.

Steps 6 and 7 are repeated until the desired effect is achieved.

In the following sections we will review these steps in detail.

5.4 Purpose, Audience, and Other Factors

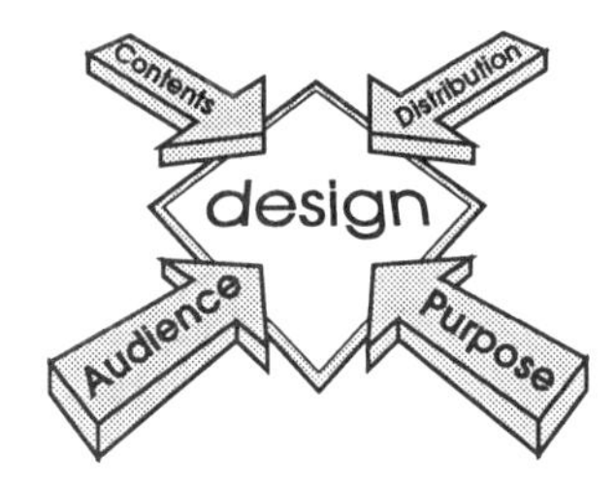

It is often tempting to plunge right into a project without first planning, but the best way to begin designing a publication is to sit down away from the computer and brainstorm using paper and pencil. By writing down ideas, you can plan more effectively thereby avoiding problems later in the production process.

The very first step is to define the purpose of the publication. Is it to attract new clients or customers? To keep present customers informed? To provide information to a group with a common interest? Clearly defining the purpose helps to make decisions about content, layout, and form.

Once the purpose is clarified, it is important to define who the audience of the publication is. Thoroughly analyzing the audience is important because it influences not only the form of the publication, but also the layout and the contents of the text and graphics. Two common audiences for brochures are current users of a product and potential customers. Common audiences for newsletters are users of a product, members of an organization, and subscribers who share a common interest.

Analyzing the audience for a publication requires that some specific characteristics about the audience be determined. How old are they? Where do they live? What are their common interests? What are their educational backgrounds? How does this information relate to the purpose of the publication. The answers to these and other questions are needed before the appropriate layout can be determined. For example, an elderly couple would probably not have an interest in a newsletter about triathlon strategies, or in an advertisement selling rock music posters. However, they should be kept in mind when producing a newsletter about retirement benefits or a brochure selling homes in sunny Arizona.

The next consideration is what the possible contents (amount of text and graphics) of the publication might be. An attempt should be made to try and determine the approximate number of pages needed to fit the contents including text and graphics.

Another factor to consider is the method of distributing the publication (mailed, placed in stacks or displays, or hand delivered). If a brochure or newsletter is distributed through a paid subscription it should be in a form that can be easily mailed. Good quality paper and a strong binding is needed to guarantee that such a publication will survive the mail. If the publication is internal (produced for a local audience such as a school or small company) the publication can be hand delivered which requires only cheap paper and binding.

5.5 Creating & Using Thumbnail Sketches

Thumbnail sketches are small pictures of pages drawn by hand that are similar to the Fit in window view in PageMaker. They should be used when designing a publication to help you see what a document will look like. In drawing the sketches it is best to start with small rectangles proportionately shaped to the size of one page of the publication, then sketch in where text and graphics will go:

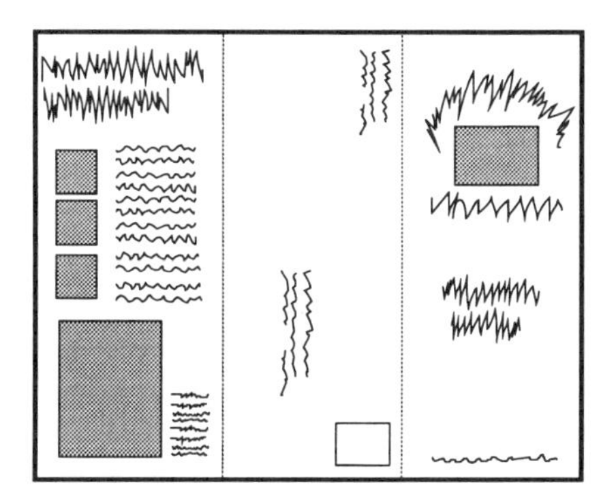
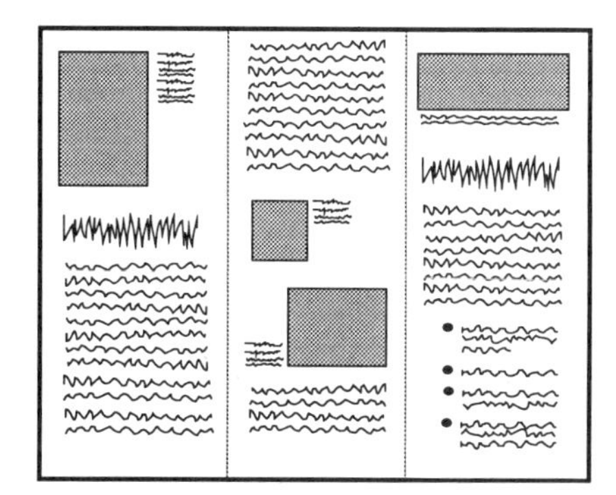

Thumbnails for a three fold brochure, about actual size

Shaded rectangles are drawn to represent graphics and squiggles are used to represent text. The squiggles are drawn larger and darker for the headlines. A thumbnail sketch gives an effect similar to squinting at a full size page which blurs the words and pictures, placing the emphasis on placement, not content. Thumbnail sketches usually go through several revisions before a workable layout is found.

Practice 2

In this Practice you will make some thumbnail sketches.

1) DRAW SOME BLANK THUMBNAILS

On a plain piece of paper, draw six rectangles, about 1.5" by 2" each. Draw some the long way (which is called landscape) and some the tall way (which is called portrait). Leave space between the sketches.

2) MAKE SKETCHES FOR A RÉSUMÉ

Using the blank thumbnails, make three different sketches for a résumé, including these sections:

Name, address, and phone number
Education section - one college
Experience section - three past jobs
Achievements section - three awards

As you make each new sketch, try to improve on the design of the last sketch.

3) MAKE SKETCHES FOR A PROMOTIONAL FLYER

Using the blank thumbnails, make three different sketches for a promotional flyer with these criteria:

Standard flyer, 8.5" by 11", printed on one side
One large graphic and one small graphic
Two paragraphs about the product
One list of features about the product
One title

As you make each sketch, try to improve on the design of the others you sketched.

5.6 Margins

An important design consideration is determining the size of a document's margins. The margins should set the document's text apart from everything else within the reader's view. Poorly designed margins can confuse or frustrate readers:

Lorem ipsum dolor sit amet, consectetuer adipiscing elit, sed diam nonummy nibh euismod tincidunt ut laoreet dolore magna aliquam erat volutpat. Ut wisi enim ad minim veniam, quis nostrud exerci tation ullamcorper suscipit lobortis nisl ut aliquip ex ea commodo consequat. Duis autem vel eum iriure dolor in hendrerit in vulputate velit esse molestie consequat, vel illum dolore eu feugiat nulla facilisis at vero eros et accumsan et iusto odio dignissim qui blandit praesent luptatum zzril delenit augue duis dolore te feugait nulla facilisi. Lorem ipsum dolor sit amet, consectetuer adipiscing elit, sed diam nonummy nibh euismod tincidunt ut laoreet dolore magna aliquam erat volutpat. Ut wisi enim ad minim veniam, quis nostrud exerci tation ullamcorper suscipit lobortis nisl ut aliquip ex ea commodo consequat.
Duis autem vel eum iriure dolor in hendrerit in vulputate velit esse molestie consequat, vel illum dolore eu feugiat nulla facilisis at vero eros et accumsan et iusto odio dignissim qui blandit praesent luptatum zzril delenit augue duis dolore te feugait nulla facilisi. Nam liber tempor cum soluta nobis eleifend option congue nihil imperdiet doming id quod mazim placerat facer possim assum.
Lorem ipsum dolor sit amet, consectetuer adipiscing elit, sed diam nonummy nibh euismod tincidunt ut laoreet dolore magna aliquam erat volutpat. Ut wisi enim ad minim veniam, quis nostrud exerci tation ullamcorper suscipit lobortis nisl ut aliquip ex ea commodo consequat. Duis autem vel eum iriure

Unusual margins create a page that is difficult to read: this document has narrow top and outside margins, and wide bottom and inside margins

Margins that neatly frame a document keep the reader's eyes focused on the page:

Lorem ipsum dolor sit amet, consectetuer adipiscing elit, sed diam nonummy nibh euismod tincidunt ut laoreet dolore magna aliquam erat volutpat. Ut wisi enim ad minim veniam, quis nostrud exerci tation ullamcorper suscipit lobortis nisl ut aliquip ex ea commodo consequat. Duis autem vel eum iriure dolor in hendrerit in vulputate velit esse molestie consequat, vel illum dolore eu feugiat nulla facilisis at vero eros et accumsan et iusto odio dignissim qui blandit praesent luptatum zzril delenit augue duis dolore te feugait nulla facilisi. Lorem ipsum dolor sit amet, consectetuer adipiscing elit, sed diam nonummy nibh euismod tincidunt ut laoreet dolore magna aliquam erat volutpat. Ut wisi enim ad minim veniam, quis nostrud exerci tation ullamcorper suscipit lobortis nisl ut aliquip ex ea commodo consequat.
Duis autem vel eum iriure dolor in hendrerit in vulputate velit esse molestie consequat, vel illum dolore eu feugiat nulla facilisis at vero eros et accumsan et iusto odio dignissim qui blandit praesent luptatum zzril delenit augue duis dolore te feugait nulla facilisi. Nam liber tempor cum soluta nobis eleifend option congue nihil imperdiet doming id quod mazim placerat facer possim assum.
Lorem ipsum dolor sit amet, consectetuer adipiscing elit, sed diam nonummy nibh euismod tincidunt ut laoreet dolore magna aliquam erat volutpat. Ut wisi enim ad minim veniam, quis nostrud exerci tation ullamcorper suscipit lobortis nisl ut aliquip ex ea commodo consequat. Duis autem vel eum iriure

Balanced margins make the page more readable

The top and bottom margins are now equal, and the outside margin has increased enough to leave white space between the text and the edge of the page. A dense, dark page can look so forbidding that a reader may not attempt to read it.

Binding methods should be considered when determining margins. For example, a hard bound book such as a yearbook needs a wide inside margin. A narrow inside margin could result in graphics or text being obscured. Many manuals are bound by a wire or a plastic comb binder which requires the paper to have holes punched through for the binding. Information too close to a margin can be cut out during the binding process. To avoid binding problems a document's final format should be considered early on in the design process.

Margins are important to publications with simple bindings, such as folded newsletters. Folded newsletters have *facing pages* with large inside margins. Facing pages are the two pages, a left page and a right page, that you see when you hold a book or magazine open. Each page has a wide inside margin where the page folds. The margins of facing pages combined together are called a *gutter*. Gutters are any area, between any type of guides (such as Margin guides), where text is not printed. In folded publications, wide inside margins create a large gutter that prevents type from printing off the page. Gutters also act as visual transitions between the pages as well as leaving ample space for the newsletter's vertical fold:

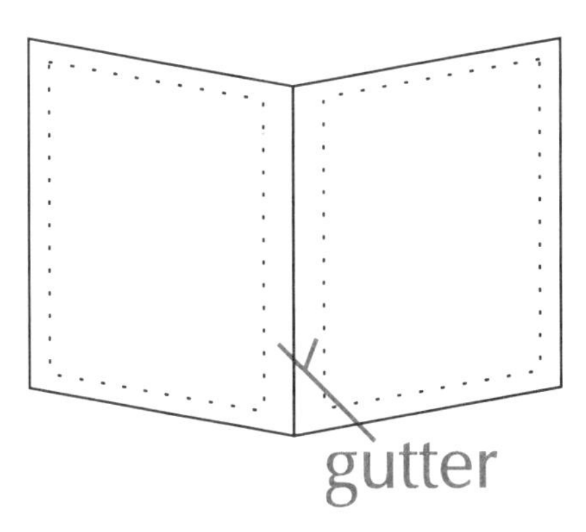

A gutter is needed to keep the text on a page and not in the fold

Gutters are also important for publications where the binding method will consume some of the inner margin space, such as when room must be left for the holes in a 3-ring binder.

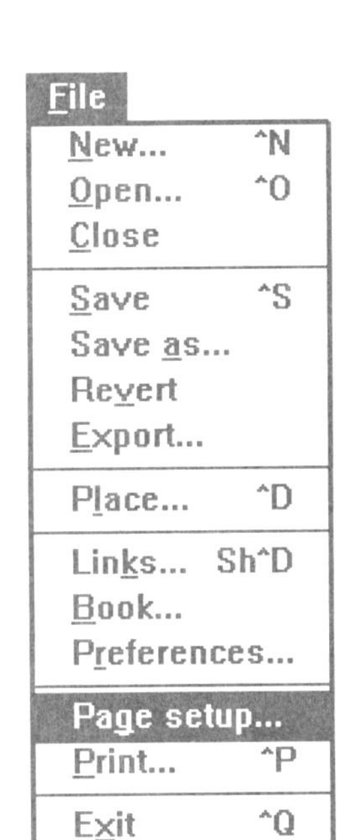

Using the same margins on each page helps maintain consistency throughout a publication. If the top margin is two inches on the first page, then each page should have a two inch top margin. The margins should not vary from page to page.

In PageMaker, margins appear on the page as pink lines, which are *nonprinting Margin guides*. Margin guides are called nonprinting because although they are visible on the screen, they do not appear on a printout. The margins for a whole publication can be changed using the Page setup command from the File menu. Any changes made in this dialog box take effect for the entire publication:

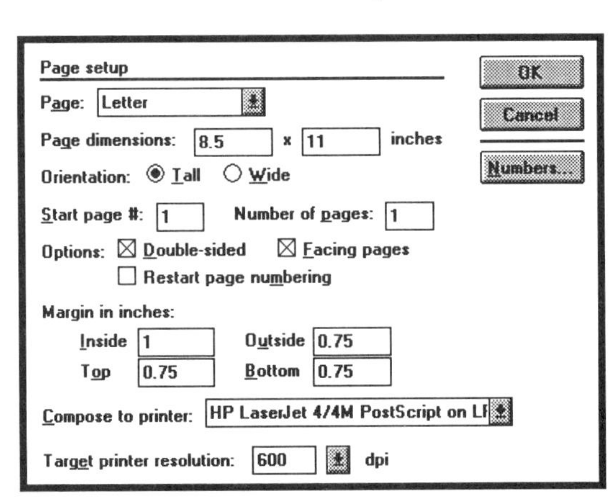

Margins are defined using the Page setup dialog box

For publications that have facing pages, the *inside margin* is the margin that will be near the binding, and the *outside margin* is the margin opposite the binding. The *top margin* and *bottom margin* are the white spaces at the top and bottom of the page, respectively.

Practice 3

You have been asked to create a flyer to promote the California Sunshine Company beverages. In this Practice you will manipulate the margins in the new publication.

1) START WINDOWS AND PAGEMAKER

2) CREATE A NEW PUBLICATION

a. From the File menu, select the New command. The Page setup dialog box is shown.
b. Verify that the Page option is Letter, the Orientation is Tall, and that the Double-sided and Facing pages options are selected.
c. Select OK to create the new publication. Note the blue and pink margin lines that appear on the page.

3) CHANGE THE INSIDE AND OUTSIDE MARGINS

a. From the File menu, select the Page setup command. The Page setup dialog box appears.
b. Type 2 for the Inside margin.
c. Press Tab to highlight the Outside margin entry. Type 1.5 to replace the current value.
d. Select OK. Note that because you increased the inside and outside margins, the inside and outside Margin guides have moved closer together. Now there is less space between the Margin guides, and more space in the margins. Notice that the Margin guides line up with the 2 inch mark and the 7 inch mark of the horizontal Ruler at the top of the screen.

4) CHANGE THE TOP AND BOTTOM MARGINS

a. From the File menu, select the Page setup command. The Page setup dialog box appears.
b. Type 2 for both the Top and Bottom margins.
c. Select OK. Note how the top and bottom margin lines have moved closer together. Notice that now there is even less space for the text on the page, and the Margin guides line up with the 2 inch mark and the 9 inch mark of the vertical Ruler.

5) CHANGE ALL THE MARGINS AT ONCE

a. From the File menu, select the Page setup command.
b. Change the margins to the values for the promotional flyer:

Inside: 1	Outside: 1
Top: 0.75	Bottom: 1

c. Select OK. The margins are changed to these settings.

6) SAVE THE PUBLICATION

a. From the File menu, select the Save command.
b. Type CH5PRACT in the File name box and select OK. PageMaker adds the proper extension (.PM5) and saves the publication under the name CH5PRACT.PM5.

5.7 Establishing a Layout with Grids

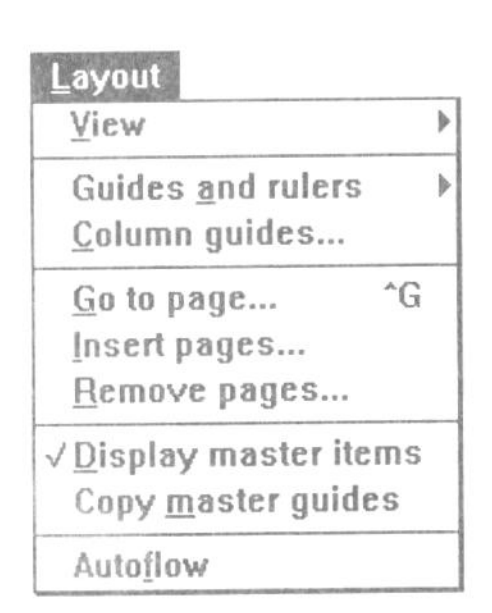

A *grid* is a pattern that is used to line up text and graphics in a consistent and precise manner and does not appear when the document is printed. By employing a grid in a publication's design, each page of the publication has the same basic organization.

By looking at a publication's thumbnail sketches, a pattern usually emerges that can be used to determine the grid:

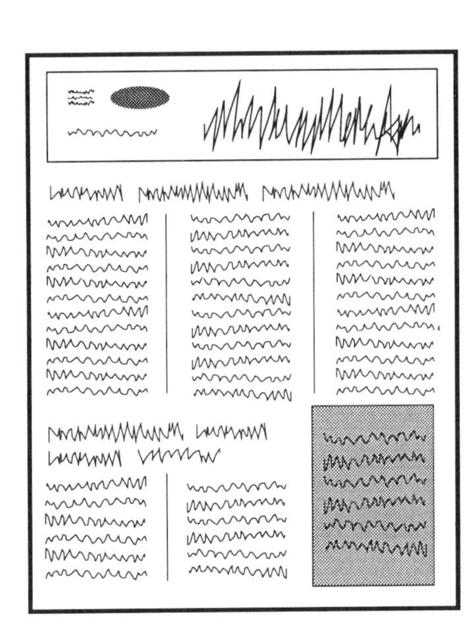

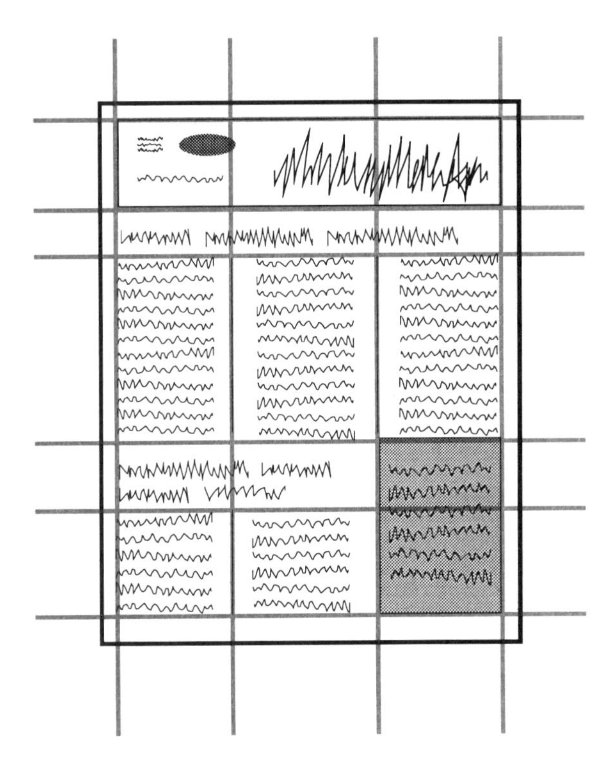

The elements in a thumbnail sketch are usually arranged in a manner that resembles a grid, so that by sketching gridlines over the thumbnail, the grid pattern emerges.

Creating a grid from a thumbnail sketch is a skill that you will develop with practice. It is important to look for patterns in the publication: vertical columns of text, horizontal alignments of headlines, graphics, headings or subheadings, etc. Most grids will be fairly simple, including from 1 to 7 vertical columns and 3 to 5 horizontal sections. If your grid is much more complex it may be an indication that either your design is too elaborate, or you are not looking for *groups* of elements in the thumbnail. Try to pare down the grid, indicating only major groups or sections in the thumbnail.

Up to 40 grid lines may be created in PageMaker using nonprinting guide lines:

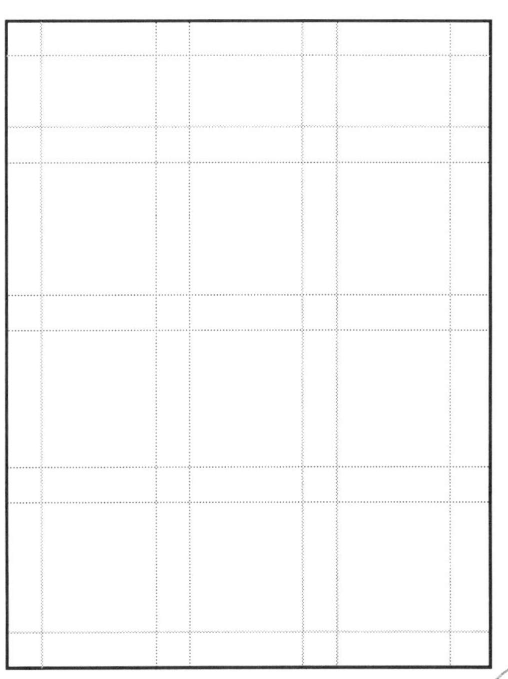

Blank page with a three column grid

Grids are composed of different types of nonprinting guides. One of the most commonly used guides are *Ruler guides*. Ruler guides are created by first placing the pointer on either the vertical or horizontal Ruler. The mouse button is then held down and the pointer dragged onto the page. An aqua Ruler guide appears which can then be positioned anywhere on the page by dragging. Ruler guides can be removed, added, or repositioned on a page without changing other pages.

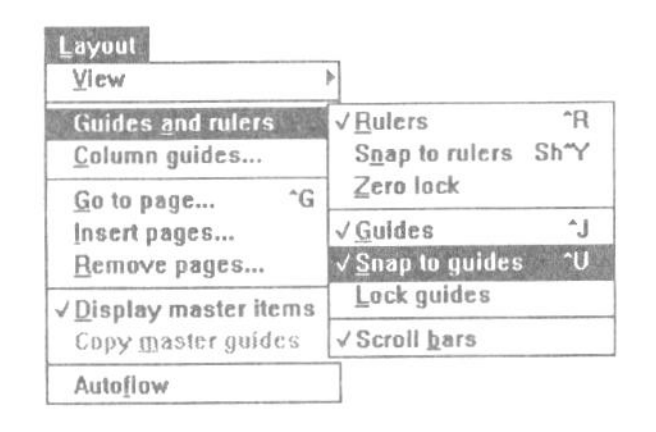

PageMaker has a *Snap to guides* feature that helps you place text and graphics on the grid with precision. The Snap to guides command in the Guides and rulers submenu "snaps" or "jumps" any mouse tool, text block, or graphic that is near a guide exactly to the guide. For example, when placing text with a loaded Text pointer, the pointer will "snap" into place when moved near a grid line. This feature is turned on or off using the Guides and rulers submenu from the Layout menu, or with the keyboard shortcut `Ctrl+U`.

5.8 Master Pages

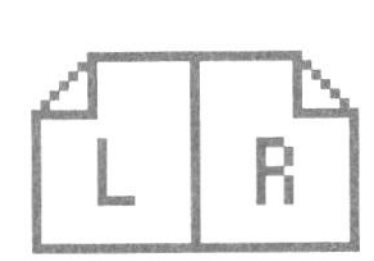

Grids are especially effective in publications that have many pages because they help maintain consistency. However, in a larger publication it would be tedious to set up the same grid on each page by hand. To solve this problem PageMaker has special pages called *Master Pages*. Anything placed on the Master Pages automatically appears on each page in the publication. There are separate Master Pages for left and right pages.

Master-page icons are displayed in the lower-left corner of the screen, with an "L" in the left page icon and an "R" in the right page icon. Clicking on either causes both the left and right Master Pages to appear. When creating grids one thing to keep in mind is that when a horizontal Ruler guide appears on one Master Page it will always appear on the other. Vertical Ruler guides may be created on one page without appearing on the other.

Practice 4

In this Practice, you will create a grid for the promotional flyer using Ruler guides on the Master Pages. You will also use the Snap to guides command. Start PageMaker and open the CH5PRACT.PM5 publication if you have not already done so.

1) *DISPLAY THE MASTER PAGES*

Click on one of the Master-page icons [L|R] in the lower-left corner of the screen. The Master Pages are displayed, and the Master-page icons are highlighted.

2) *CREATE A HORIZONTAL RULER GUIDE*

a. Select the Pointer tool from the Toolbox and place the pointer anywhere in the horizontal Ruler.
b. Hold down the mouse button and drag the pointer down, away from the Ruler and onto the page. A Ruler guide (an aqua-colored line) follows the pointer, and the position of the Ruler guide is shown on the vertical Ruler.
c. When the Ruler guide is lined up with the 5 inch mark on the vertical Ruler, release the mouse button.

3) *CREATE VERTICAL RULER GUIDES*

a. Place the mouse pointer anywhere in the vertical Ruler .
b. Drag the pointer to the right, away from the Ruler and onto the left Master Page. A Ruler guide follows the pointer.
c. When the Ruler guide is in the middle of the left page, near the 4½ inch mark on the horizontal Ruler, release the mouse button:

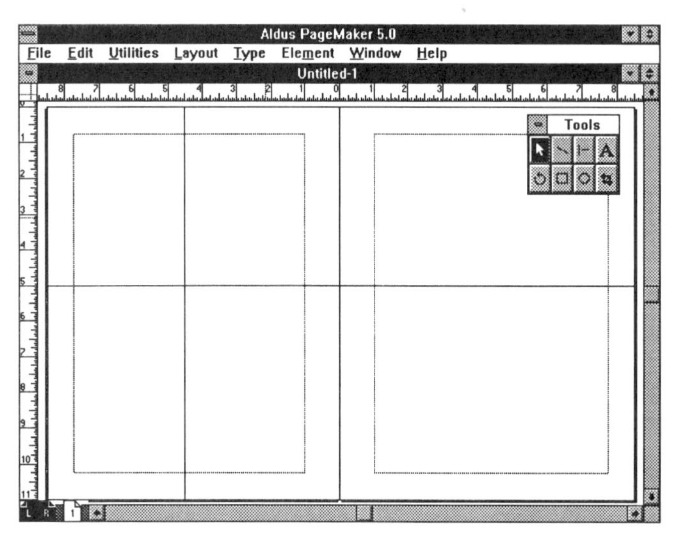

5

d. Place a vertical Ruler guide on the right page, near the 3 inch mark on the horizontal Ruler. You have now created a simple grid!

4) *REMOVE A GUIDE*

a. Place the pointer on the vertical Ruler guide that you placed in the left page.
b. Drag the Ruler guide back into the vertical Ruler, off the pasteboard. When the mouse button is released, the Ruler guide disappears.

5) *USE THE SNAP TO GUIDES COMMAND*

a. Click on the page 1 icon [1] at the bottom of the screen. Page 1 is displayed, and the page 1 icon is highlighted. The Ruler guides shown on the page are the guides you placed on the right Master Page.
b. Use the Place command from the File menu to place the CALIFSUN.WMF file anywhere on the page.
c. Drag the graphic you just placed on the page over to where the two grid lines intersect. Drag it slowly so that the corner of the graphic passes over the intersection of the grid lines. Notice how the graphic seemed to stick at the corner of the grid lines.
d Drag it back and forth slowly over the grid lines a few more times to get a feel for the Snap to guides feature. Note that the graphic will also snap to Margin guides because they are also guides.
e. From the Layout menu, select Guides and rulers, and from the submenu deselect Snap to guides.
f. Drag the graphic again over the intersection of the grid lines. Notice how the graphic flows freely at the corner of the grid lines.
g. Press `Ctrl+U` to turn on Snap to guides. Drag the graphic over the intersection and notice how it snaps to the guides again.
h. Remove the vertical Ruler guide from Page 1 by dragging it off the page.

Check - Your page should be similar to:

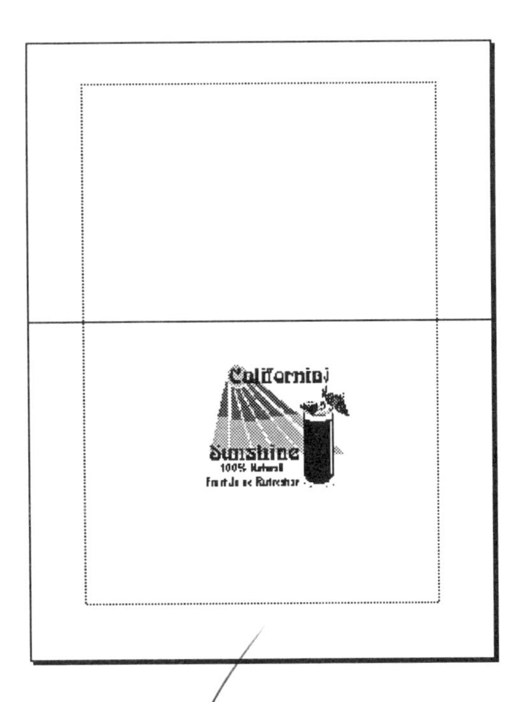

6) *SAVE THE MODIFIED PUBLICATION*

5.9 Columns

5

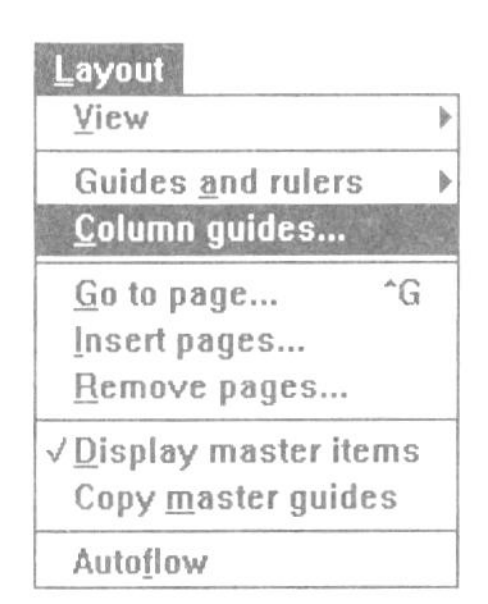

Most publications including magazines, newspapers, tabloids, newsletters, and mail order catalogs are formatted using columns. Two, three, and five column layouts are the most typical, except for newspapers, which generally use five to seven columns.

After roughing out layout ideas in thumbnail sketches, it should become obvious how many columns are needed in a publication's design. Similar to the Ruler guides, *Column guides* are nonprinting; they do not appear on the final printout. They are just lines on the screen to help with the publication's layout. Column guides appear blue in contrast to the pink-colored Margin guides and aqua-colored Ruler guides.

Column guides are created by executing the Column guides command from the Layout menu (`Alt+L C`). When the command is executed the Column guides dialog box is displayed, with default settings for Number of columns and Space between columns:

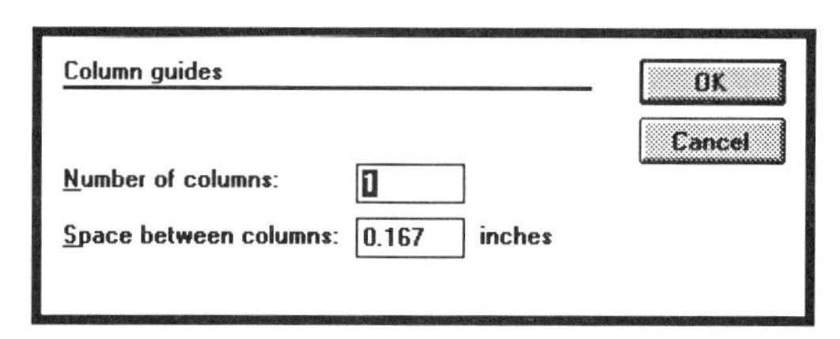

The Column guides dialog box

The Number of columns can be set to any whole number up to 20, as long as the columns will fit on the page. The Space between columns indicates the width of the gutters between the columns. Remember that gutters are the areas between any type of guides (such as Column guides) where text is not printed:

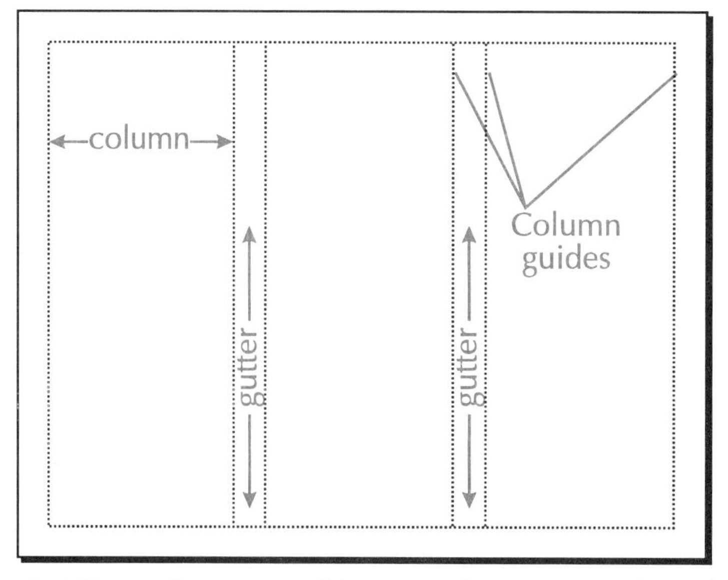

Gutters between columns are white space that separates the columns

The width of the columns should influence the font you select. If the columns are narrow, the font and size should be small. For wide columns of text, such as two-thirds of the page width or a whole page width, the font and size should be readable for the longer line length. Remember, creating a successful design requires experimentation, so try using several kinds of type to determine which one best suits a document's purpose and audience. You should also consider the alignment of the text for each column size. In narrow columns, body text usually reads best when formatted ragged right (aligned left). While fully justified text appears neat and orderly, spacing problems can occur in narrower columns if there are few words on each line:

Ragged Right

Lorem ipsum dolor sit amet, consectetuer adipiscing elit, sed diam nonummy nibh euismod tincidunt ut laoreet dolore magna aliquam erat volutpat. Ut wisi enim ad minim veniam, quis nostrud exerci tation ullamcorper suscipit lobortis nisl ut aliquip ex ea commodo consequat. Duis autem vel eum iriure dolor in hendrerit in vulputate velit esse molestie consequat, vel illum dolore eu feugiat nulla facilisis at vero eros et accumsan et iusto odio dignissim qui blandit praesent luptatum zzril delenit augue

Justified

Lorem ipsum dolor sit amet, consectetuer adipiscing elit, sed diam nonummy nibh euismod tincidunt ut laoreet dolore magna aliquam erat volutpat. Ut wisi enim ad minim veniam, quis nostrud exerci tation ullamcorper suscipit lobortis nisl ut aliquip ex ea commodo consequat. Duis autem vel eum iriure dolor in hendrerit in vulputate velit esse molestie consequat, vel illum dolore eu feugiat nulla facilisis at vero eros et accumsan et iusto odio dignissim qui blandit praesent luptatum zzril delenit augue

In narrow columns, justified text can have rivers of white between the words

Notice the large spaces between words in the justified columns. When there are few words on each line, the spaces between them needed to justify the text are too large. This causes a *river* of white space within the text. A river is when twisting, vertical channels of white space appear within a text column. The ragged right text is easier to read at these short line lengths.

Other problems that can occur with multiple columns are *widows* and *orphans*. A widow is a single line from the beginning of a paragraph that is alone at the end of a column. It is widowed from the rest of the paragraph. An orphan is a single line from the end of a paragraph that is alone at the beginning of a column. It is orphaned from the rest of the paragraph:

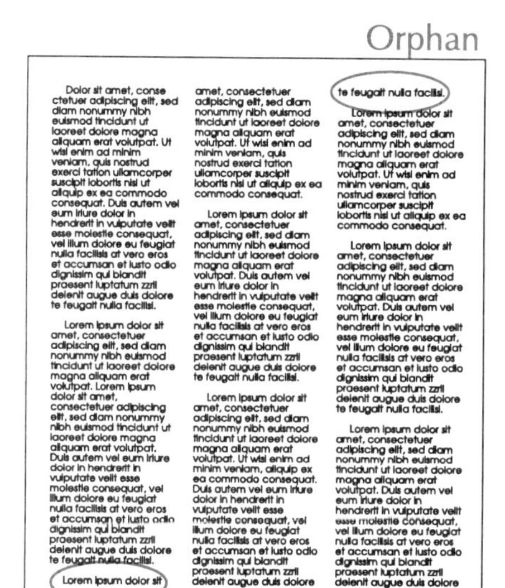

Widows and orphans should be avoided when possible

Widows and orphans make reading difficult, and are a sign of sloppy editing. The more columns a document has, the more chances there are of widows and orphans occurring. If the text in your document has many short paragraphs, it is a good idea to consider designs with only one or two columns.

Practice 5

In this Practice you will create Column guides that appear throughout an entire publication, including page 1 where you are creating the promotional flyer. Start PageMaker and open the CH5PRACT.PM5 publication if you have not already done so.

1) DISPLAY THE MASTER PAGES

Click on one of the Master Page icons (the page icons marked "L" and "R") in the lower-left corner of the screen. The Master Pages are displayed.

2) EXECUTE THE COLUMN GUIDES COMMAND

From the Layout menu, select the Column guides command. The Column guides dialog box is displayed.

3) TRY DIFFERENT VALUES OF COLUMNS AND GUTTERS

a. Type 3 for the Number of columns, and 0.5 for the Space between columns, and select OK. Notice on each page the blue Column guides that outline the columns and gutters. Each Master Page is displayed with three columns of equal width, and a half-inch gutter between the columns.
b. Select the Column guides command from the Layout menu again.
c. Type 6 for the Number of columns, and 0.1 for the Space between columns, and select OK. Each Master Page is displayed with six columns of equal width, and five 0.1 inch gutters between the columns.

5

4) SET THE NUMBER OF COLUMNS TO 2

a. Select the Column guides command from the Layout menu.
b. Type 2 for the Number of columns, and 0.25 for the Space between columns. Select OK. Each Master Page is displayed with two columns of equal width, and one 0.25 inch gutter between the columns.

5) VIEW THE COLUMNS ON PAGE 1

Click on the page 1 icon at the bottom of the screen. Page 1 is displayed. Notice how the Column guides you created on the Master Pages appear on this page. The Ruler guide and the graphic you placed in Practice 2 are also displayed. Move the graphic to the second column and resize proportionally to fit exactly across the column. Align the bottom of the graphic with the horizontal Ruler guide.

6) PLACE SOME TEXT IN THE FIRST COLUMN

a. Choose Place from the File menu, highlight the PRAC5.TXT file, and select OK. The Text-only import filter dialog box is displayed.
b. Select OK to accept the default options. After the file is processed, the pointer is changed to the loaded Text pointer.
c. Move the loaded Text pointer just under the Ruler guide, and next to the left margin of the first column. The pointer should be lined up in the corner of the Ruler guide and the Margin guide. Click once to place the text. The text flows to the shape of the column. Notice the red triangle in the bottom windowshade handle, indicating there is more text to be placed.
d. Click the Pointer tool once on the red windowshade handle to load it with the hidden text. The pointer changes to the loaded Text pointer.
e. Line up the loaded Text pointer with the Ruler guide and the left Column guide of the second column. Click once to place the text. Notice that all of the text in that file has been placed (the bottom windowshade handle is empty).

7) SAVE THE PUBLICATION

Check - Your page should be similar to:

5.10 Typefaces, Type Styles, and Fonts

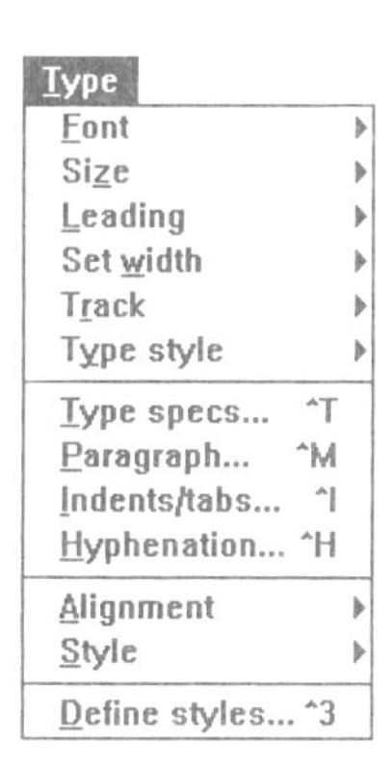

Because publications are based on printed words, choosing a font, size, and style are important design decisions. Chapter Three introduced fonts, type sizes, and type styles and how to manipulate them in PageMaker. Here we will examine them in more detail and consider their impact on document design.

As a quick review, each typeface belongs to one of two categories, *serif* and *sans serif* (sans is French for "without"). Serifs are the small extensions found on the ends of letters. The publishing world has long debated whether serif or sans serif typefaces are easier to read. When we read text our eyes recognize, or scan, whole words and not individual letters. Because the ends of serif letters extend outwards toward other letters, serif type appears closer together and scans easier. The continuity between the letters that serif typefaces have is more noticeable as the letters get smaller. Therefore, serifs are more popular for body text and sans serifs are more popular as titles, where the serif is not needed because of the larger type size.

Each letter of type is composed of different parts. Knowing and understanding each part helps to position type and choose the right typeface for each publication:

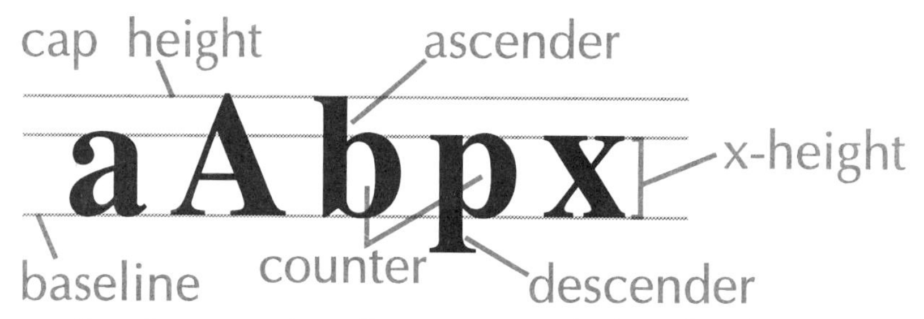

Typefaces vary but all are composed of similar elements

Ascenders and *descenders* are the parts of lowercase letters that rise up above or hang down below letters. The *x-height* is the height of the lowercase x, which also refers to the height of lowercase letters, not including ascenders and descenders. *Counters* are the empty spaces completely surrounded by a letter, such as the center of an "o". The *cap height* is the height of the capital letters. Ascenders can be as high as the cap height, lower, or even rise above the cap height, depending on the design of the typeface. The *baseline* is the imaginary line where the bottom of the letters sit, and the line that the descenders hang below. The baseline will be important later in this chapter.

All of these characteristics can affect design decisions to use or not use a specific typeface. Remember from Chapter Three that typeface sizes are measured in *points*, where one point is 1/72 of an inch. Before desktop publishing, printers hand set metal pieces of type into frames. The height of the metal pieces determined the point size of a font:

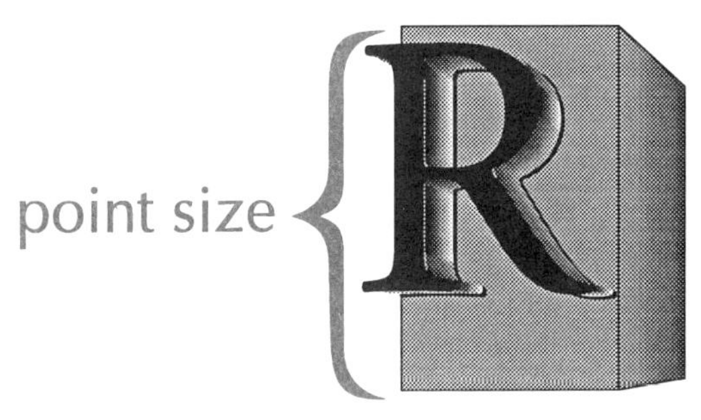

A character in metal type

With desktop publishing and electronic font design, the point size of each font is determined by the space in which the font designer creates the new font. Because typefaces are measured this way, the actual size of the characters can vary. The x-height of characters can also vary from typeface to typeface. For example, a typeface with a small x-height appears smaller than a typeface with a large x-height, and sometimes actually takes up less space:

step step **step**

x-height

Different typefaces of the same point size

The amount of text you need to print, the shape of the space where the text is (narrow columns or wide pages), and the size of the type are all factors that contribute to the typeface decisions.

In addition to changing a typeface's style, a typeface's size can be reduced or enlarged. Twelve-point, eleven-point, and ten-point type are the most commonly used sizes for body text. However, each typeface varies in size because of the different x-heights, cap heights, and shapes. Overall, twelve-point Times is smaller than twelve-point Avant Garde:

> This paragraph contains the same number of words as the other paragraph, only the typefaces are different. This paragraph contains the same number of words as the other paragraph.

> This paragraph contains the same number of words as the other paragraph, only the typefaces are different. This paragraph contains the same number of words as the other paragraph.

Times (top) and Avant Garde, both 12 points

Each of these paragraphs consists of the same amount of text, but is printed in different fonts. The top paragraph is twelve-point Times, and the bottom paragraph is twelve-point Avant Garde. Notice how the same amount of text needs more lines in Avant Garde. Type differences are a major consideration when designing longer documents. Choosing a different typeface could make a difference of several pages.

Typefaces for headings and headlines do not have to be the same as the text. A contrasting type style can help to separate the heading from the text. Having a sans serif title and serif body text is a common mixture that usually works well. The sans serif titles are easier to read and the different typeface clearly sets the titles apart from the text.

Type *styles* indicate standard variations of typefaces. For example, Palatino, Helvetica, and Avant Garde can each be converted to bold, italic, underline, or any combination of the three:

Palatino regular, **bold**, *italic*, underline

Normal type is generally called *regular,* although *book* and *roman* are also popular terms that indicate regular style. Using different type styles in the same publication can help indicate different levels of information. A title in bold appears to be one level above the same size title in regular style because bold type has a stronger appearance. Italics are usually read in a softer voice. Type styles are powerful statements in design that can visually change the meaning of words and should be used with care.

Since the main purpose of typefaces is to make our thoughts visible, different typefaces can convey different thoughts and feelings:

creepy casual

light RADICAL

MODERN Antique

There are many different typefaces for different circumstances

As you can see, words on a page need not appear lifeless or flat. Keep in mind appropriateness when deciding which type style to use. The typeface should fit the purpose and the audience of the publication.

After considering typefaces and styles, there is another category called fonts. Traditionally, a *font* includes a point size, style, and typeface. For example, twelve point size, bold style, and Avant Garde typeface combine to form one font: twelve-point Avant Garde bold. Each font includes a complete set of type characters, including capital letters (uppercase), small letters (lowercase), punctuation, numbers, symbols ($,%, ®), and other characters such as foreign letters (£, é, ö).

Each font must be purchased separately from the company that holds the copyright to it. Building a full library of many different fonts used to be expensive. However, in the past few years the prices of fonts have dropped, making it easier for the average desktop publisher to own an extensive font library. Prices have dropped partially because it is easier to create fonts on a computer, which means there are more fonts to choose from, and because of competition between makers of

5

fonts. Also, because the number of people who are using desktop publishing has increased, the prices of fonts can be lowered and the companies can still make a profit. Now with CD ROM technology, companies are selling CD ROMs that contain 500 fonts for $200! Some different font examples are shown below. (You may not be able to access all of these fonts on your printer.)

Sans Serif

Akzidenz Grotesk: ABCDEFGHIJKLMNOPQRSTUVWXYZ
abcdefghijklmnopqrstuvwxyz 1234567890 !@#$%&*?

Arial: ABCDEFGHIJKLMNOPQRSTUVWXYZ
abcdefghijklmnopqrstuvwxyz 1234567890 !@#$%&*?

Avant Garde: ABCDEFGHIJKLMNOPQRSTUVWXYZ
abcdefghijklmnopqrstuvwxyz 1234567890 !@#$%&*?

Block: ABCDEFGHIJKLMNOPQRSTUVWXYZ
abcdefghijklmnopqrstuvwxyz 1234567890 !••$%&*()•-/?••;:.

Gill Sans: ABCDEFGHIJKLMNOPQRSTUVWXYZ
abcdefghijklmnopqrstuvwxyz 1234567890 !@#$%&*()+-/?<>;:.

Helvetica: ABCDEFGHIJKLMNOPQRSTUVWXYZ
abcdefghijklmnopqrstuvwxyz 1234567890 !@#$%&*?

Decorative

Ad Lib: ABCDEFGHIJKLMNOPQRSTUVWXYZ
abcdefghijklmnopqrstuvwxyz 1234567890 !@#$

Chok: ABCDEFGHIJKLMNOPQRSTUVWXYZ
abcdefghijklmnopqrstuvwxyz 1234567890 !@#$%&*?

Linotext: ABCDEFGHIJKLMNOPQRSTUVWXYZ
abcdefghijklmnopqrstuvwxyz 1234567890 !@#$%&*()+-/?<>;:.

OCR-A: ABCDEFGHIJKLMNOPQRSTUVWXYZ
abcdefghijklmnopqrstuvwxyz 1234567890 #$?

Zapf Chancery: ABCDEFGHIJKLMNOPQRSTUVWXYZ
abcdefghijklmnopqrstuvwxyz 1234567890 !@#$%&()+-/?<>;:.*

Zapf Dingbats: ✡✢✣✤✥✦✧★☆✪✫✬✭✮✯✰✱✲✳✴✵
❀❁❂❃❄❅❆❇❈❉❊❋❏❐▼◆❖◗❘❙❚ ➔✕✖✗✘✙✚✐ ✁✂✃✄☎✆☛✝

Serif

Adobe Caslon: ABCDEFGHIJKLMNOPQRSTUVWXYZ
abcdefghijklmnopqrstuvwxyz 1234567890 !@#$%&*()+-/?<>;:.

Adobe Garamond: ABCDEFGHIJKLMNOPQRSTUVWXYZ
abcdefghijklmnopqrstuvwxyz 1234567890 !@#$%&*()+-/?<>;:.

Benguiat: ABCDEFGHIJKLMNOPQRSTUVWXYZ
abcdefghijklmnopqrstuvwxyz 1234567890 !@#$%&*?

Berkeley Book: ABCDEFGHIJKLMNOPQRSTUVWXYZ
abcdefghijklmnopqrstuvwxyz 1234567890 !@#$%&*?

Bodoni: ABCDEFGHIJKLMNOPQRSTUVWXYZ
abcdefghijklmnopqrstuvwxyz 1234567890 !@#$%&*?

Bookman: ABCDEFGHIJKLMNOPQRSTUVWXYZ
abcdefghijklmnopqrstuvwxyz 1234567890 !@#$%&*?

Cochin: ABCDEFGHIJKLMNOPQRSTUVWXYZ
abcdefghijklmnopqrstuvwxyz 1234567890 !@#$%&*?

Ellington: ABCDEFGHIJKLMNOPQRSTUVWXYZ
abcdefghijklmnopqrstuvwxyz 1234567890 !@#$%&*?

New Century Schoolbook: ABCDEFGHIJKLMNOPQ
RSTUVWXYZ abcdefghijklmnopqrstuvwxyz 12345678

Palatino: ABCDEFGHIJKLMNOPQRSTUVWXYZ
abcdefghijklmnopqrstuvwxyz 1234567890 !@#$%&*?

Times: ABCDEFGHIJKLMNOPQRSTUVWXYZ
abcdefghijklmnopqrstuvwxyz 1234567890 !@#$%&*()+-/?<>;:.

Times New Roman: ABCDEFGHIJKLMNOPQRSTUVWXYZ
abcdefghijklmnopqrstuvwxyz 1234567890 !@#$%&*()+-/?<>;:.

5.11 Headings and Subheads

Headings and subheads are used as visual cues in text to point out key ideas or topics. The term *subhead* just refers to a level of heading lower than the top level. If you removed everything from a publication except the headings, you would essentially be left with an outline of each story.

Headings are important visual transitions between stories and between major ideas within stories. As the heading levels get lower, the heading is either smaller or placed differently, or both. At the lower heading levels the reader reaches more specific topics deeper into the main story, and the smaller size or less prominent placing of the heading indicates the lower level of importance. If the headings get larger again, the reader knows that they are either at a new topic or a completely new story. It is the size and style of the type and the placement of the heading that gives the reader information about their location within a document.

When creating headings in a document use the design concepts that you have learned. Choose an appropriate and readable font. Place the headings so that they achieve the right amount of balance in your design. Be consistent with the size, style, and placement of each heading level. Be sure that the headings help the focus and flow of a page's design, and work with (not overwhelm) other design elements:

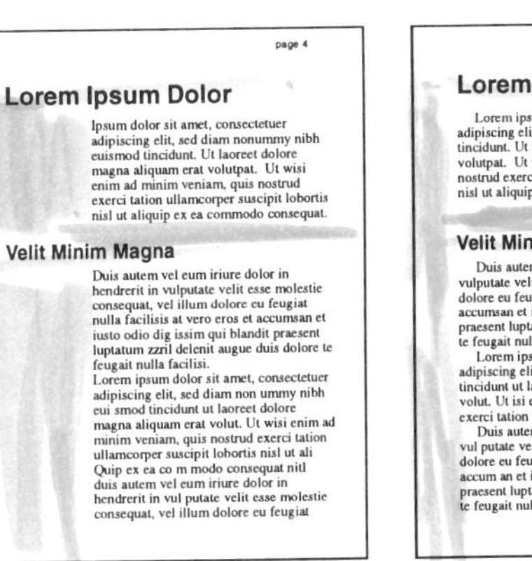

Three of the many ways to use headings in a layout

The illustration above shows three different ways to use headings effectively. Notice how other elements of the document's design influence the placement of the heading. In the first document, the headings are pulled out of the text to create tension in the big white space of the left margin. In the middle document, the text covers the full width of the page, and the headings share the same margins. Also, there is considerable white space between levels so that the second heading is not lost in the text. In the third document, the text is separated from the rest of the page with a vertical rule. The heading is placed outside the rule to create tension, although it does not cross the rule which would then create too much tension.

When choosing point sizes for multiple levels of headings in one publication, one general rule is to have the size of each heading level separated by at least two points. The size differences between text and headings should be enough to distinguish between the text and each level of heading, and two points are the minimum difference that is noticeable. For example, if you chose twelve-point type for the text, the titles or headlines should be at least fourteen points. When you have many levels of headings, an alternative to multiple sizes of fonts is to add a bold style. A subhead could even be the same size as the body text, but bold. Just be sure the different heading levels are distinguishable from the text and from each other:

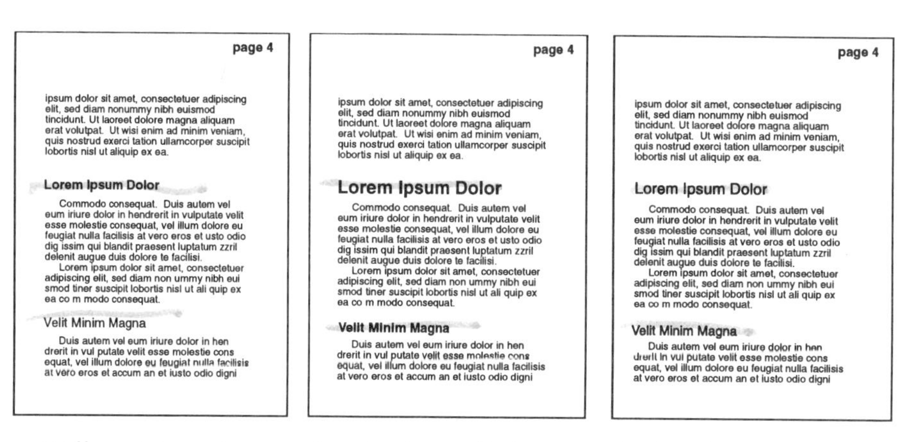

Different font sizes and styles help distinguish the levels of headings

In the picture above, the headings on the first page are one point apart in size; the text is eight-point, the top heading is ten-point, and the lower heading is nine-point. It is difficult to tell if the two headings are of equal size, or which heading is the higher level. In the middle page, the higher heading level is sixteen-point, the lower level is twelve-point, and the text is eight-point. Each level is different by four points, which clearly defines the levels of headings for the reader. The headings on the last page vary in size and font; they are Helvetica bold twelve-point and ten-point, two points apart from each other and from the text. The size difference is just enough to comfortably separate the headings, and the sans serif font contrasts with the serif font of the text to separate them further.

Practice 6

In this Practice, you will add headings to the promotional flyer. Start PageMaker if you have not already done so and open the CH5PRACT.PM5 publication.

1) *CREATE THE HEADLINE*

a. Select the Text tool and place the cursor in the top-left corner of the first column. Type: `Have a California Sunshine Holiday!`
b. Triple-click on the text to highlight it.
c. Select the Type Specs command from the Type menu (`Ctrl+T`) and change the Size to 48 points and the Style to Bold. Select OK.
d. With the Pointer tool, select the text block containing the headline you just typed. Resize the text block to fit exactly across both columns, from the left margin to the right margin. The text will be on two lines like this:

Have a California
Sunshine Holiday!

Move the text block so that the top of it aligns with the top Margin guide.

5

2) CREATE A HEADING IN THE TEXT

a. Zoom in to the body text in the second column. Locate the line *Sunshine Winter Punch* just above the recipe ingredients.

b. Using the Text tool, triple-click on the line of text to highlight it. Using the Type specs command, make the text 18 points in size and bold in style.

3) SAVE THE PUBLICATION

Check - Your page should be similar to:

5.12 Leading

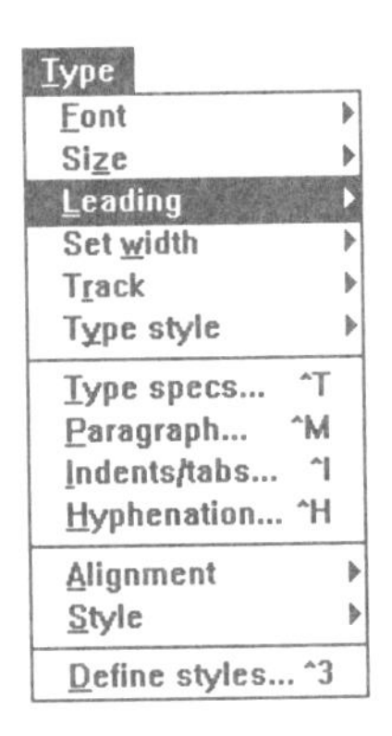

The spacing between lines of text is called *leading* (pronounced "ledding"). The term leading originates from the metal bars that typesetters used decades ago to create space between the lines of text. In desktop publishing, leading refers to the space between two reference points on each line of type:

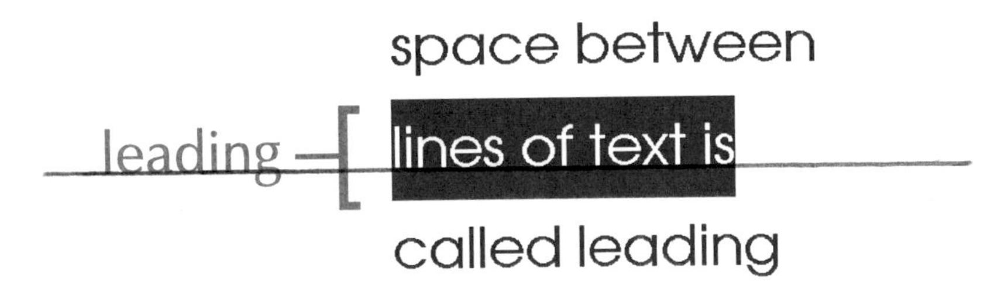

The leading slug

The highlighted area in the picture above is called a *slug* and indicates where the leading is considered to be. Notice that the baseline of the typeface separates the top two-thirds of the slug with the bottom third.

5

The size of leading is measured by the height of the slug. Leading is measured in points, just like fonts, and the two are generally mentioned together. For example, you would say "Palatino ten on twelve" which means ten-point Palatino type with twelve points of leading.

Leading affects many aspects of a document. The overall weight of the text, the darkness of the page, and the ability to relate text to other text varies by the amount of leading used:

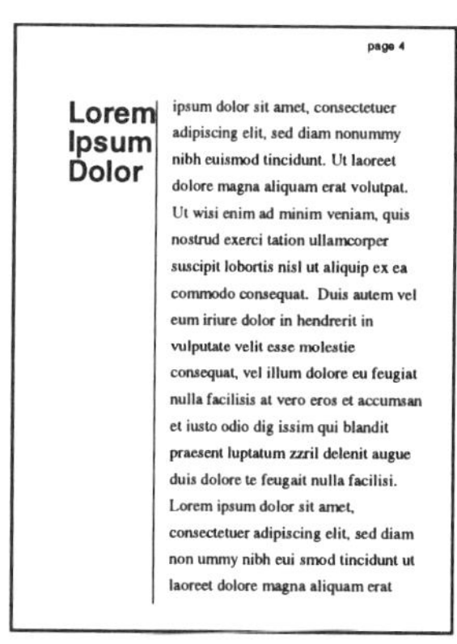

Different values of leading on the same size type

Lines of text need ample space between them to allow the reader's eyes to focus and scan each line easily and confidently:

> This is an example of leading: ten-point Times on ten points of leading (written as 10/10). Leading is an important part of document design. When choosing leading values, consider your other design choices. This is an example of ten-point Times on ten points of lead.

> This is an example of leading: ten-point Times on twelve points of leading (written as 10/12). Leading is an important part of document design. When choosing leading values, consider your other design choices. This is an example of ten-point Times on twelve points of lead.

> This is an example of leading: ten-point Times on sixteen points of leading (written as 10/16). Leading is an important part of document design. When choosing leading values, consider your other design choices. This is an example of ten-point Times on sixteen points of lead.

Different leading values affect the color of the page

In the previous example of ten-point leading, the spaces between the words (horizontal spaces) are as large or larger than the vertical spaces between the lines. The text is visually crowded, and the reader finds it difficult to scan individual lines. The middle example uses twelve points of leading, and the individual lines of text stand out more clearly. The bottom example shows that when the leading is considerably large, the white space between the lines begins to stand out and the eye has to travel too far to scan the lines.

Leading is an important part of document design. When choosing leading values, consider your other design choices. The longer the line length of text, the more leading that is needed to distinguish the lines from each other. The font used also influences the amount of leading; text with a large x-height has less white space between the lines and therefore needs more leading.

In PageMaker the leading values can be set for different text blocks individually. From the Type menu, the Leading command displays a submenu that contains choices in points for leading, an Auto leading option, and an Other leading command:

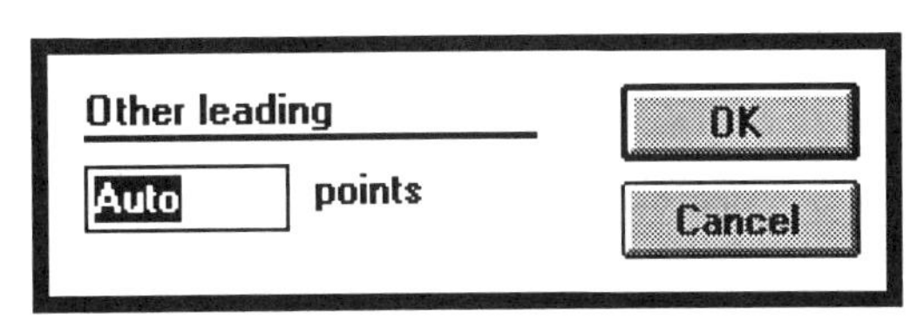

The Other leading dialog box

The Other leading command displays a dialog box where you may type in any amount of leading desired. The Auto leading option automatically sets the leading to 120% of the point size. Any leading set from the Leading command is immediately applied to text that has been selected. Leading can also be set using the Type specs command from the Type menu.

Practice 7

In this Practice you will manipulate the leading for several lines of text and finish the promotional flyer. Start PageMaker if you have not already done so and open the CH5PRACT.PM5 publication.

1) MOVE THE TEXT BLOCK

a. Place a horizontal Ruler guide at the 2.5" mark on the vertical Ruler.
b. With the Pointer tool, move the body text block in the first column upwards to the Ruler guide you just placed.
c. Pull the bottom windowshade handle down to the bottom margin. Some text flows from the second column into the first column.

2) CHANGE THE LEADING FOR THE INGREDIENTS

a. Using the Actual size view, zoom in to the text in the second column. Locate the list of recipe ingredients, just under the heading *Sunshine Winter Punch*. With the Text tool, select the entire list of ingredients.
b. From the Type menu select the Leading command and choose 36 point. The leading is now very large, and the lines of text are spread apart.
c. Highlight the line that says "2 liters ginger ale" by triple-clicking on it. The black highlight is the slug, indicating the leading. Notice how big a 36 point slug is!
d. Highlight the entire ingredients list again, and from the Type menu select the Leading command and choose Other. The Other leading dialog box appears. Type 8 and

select OK. The leading is now very small, and the lines of text are close together. Notice how the letters on one line overlap the letters on another line. Highlight one line of text and see how small the slug is now.

e. Again, highlight the entire ingredients list. From the Type menu, select the Type specs command. The Type specs dialog box is shown.

f. Click on the down arrow next to Leading to display the list of leading options. Choose 18 points of leading, then select OK. The leading between the lines of text is increased, and the lines of text are farther apart.

3) *FORMAT THE FLAVORS LIST*

a. Scroll over to the first column, and locate the list of juice flavors. Select the entire list, and then use the Alignment command from the Type menu to center the text.

b. From the Type menu, select the Type specs command. Change the Size to 18 point, the Type style to Italic, and type in 24 for the Leading. Select OK. The list of juice flavors is bigger and each line of text is spread further apart.

4) *SAVE THE PUBLICATION*

<u>Check</u> - Your page should be similar to:

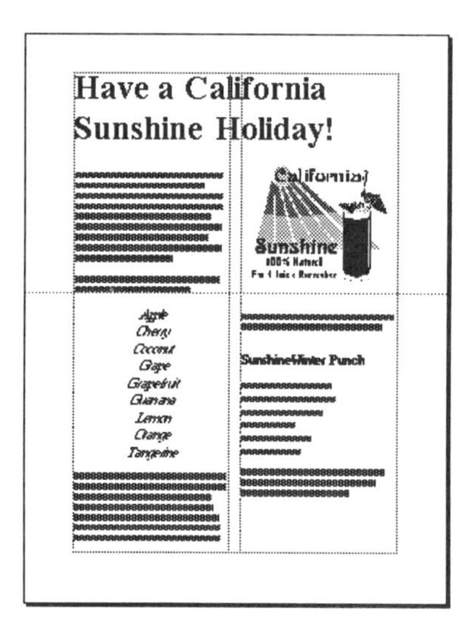

5) *PRINT THE PUBLICATION*

Examine your printout. Look at each different type style, the leading differences, graphic size and placement, and the overall layout.

6) *MAKE SOME CHANGES*

a. You have decided to improve on the design. Start by placing an insertion point in the headline with the Text pointer. From the Type menu select the Alignment command and choose Align center to center the headline.

b. You think that maybe the graphic in the second column would look better at the bottom of the column instead of at the top. With the pointer tool, move the graphic to the bottom of the second column, then move the text block from the bottom of the second column up to the Ruler guide below the headline. Using the Text tool, delete any blank lines in the top of the text block to line up both columns.

c. Comparing the two columns, you have decided that the first column is light in weight, with plain text and lots of white space in the middle, and the second column is heavy in weight, with a dark graphic and a dark heading, and some busy text differences. To balance the page better, you think the list of flavors should appear darker. Highlight the list of flavors in the first column. Choose the Type specs command from the Type menu, and change the Font to Helvetica and the Type style to Bold and Italic. Select OK to make the changes.

7) SAVE THE PUBLICATION

Check - Your page should be similar to:

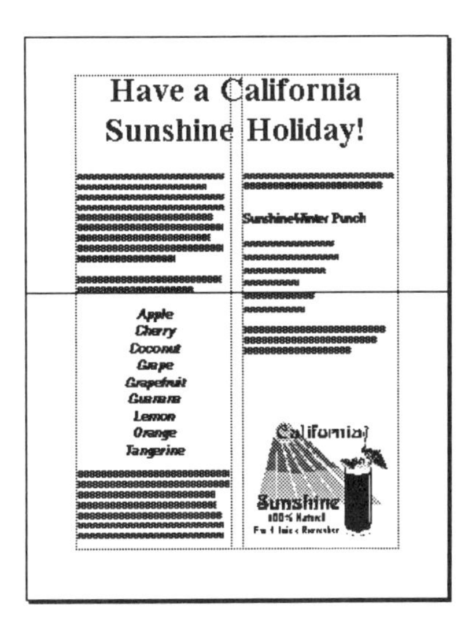

8) PRINT THE PUBLICATION AND EXIT PAGEMAKER

Compare this printout with the previous one. Look at the differences and the overall effect of the changes you made. Which design is better, and why? What other changes would you make to improve the design, and why?

Chapter Summary

This chapter introduced design concepts and PageMaker tools that help to implement different designs. The four major design concepts are: Appropriateness, Balance, Focus and Flow, and Consistency. All of these design concepts work together. For example, if the focus of a page is clear and the eye follows a natural path around the page, then the page is usually balanced. If the weight of each element is appropriate to the publication's purpose and audience, then the focus falls in the proper place and there is a natural path created around the page.

Graphic elements such as dingbats and rules help maintain consistency throughout a document and increase the readability of the document. Running headers and running footers are also visual cues that help the reader.

Planning a publication is a process that begins by writing down its purpose and audience. Thumbnail sketches are then drawn and revised. The next steps are done using PageMaker: creating the grid, creating and placing the masthead or title, placing and formatting graphics and text.

The purpose and the intended audience of the publication need to be thoroughly analyzed. It is important to know the who, what, where, why, and how of the audience.

Designers use small drawings called thumbnail sketches to rough out the overall design of a publication. The small thumbnail sketches are easy and quick to draw, and give an idea of how the finished product will look.

The spaces between the body of a document and the edges of the page are the margins. Margins can be set through the Page setup command in the File menu and affect the entire publication. Margins are indicated by pink, non-printing margin guides.

Grids are a network of guides that help align text and graphics on a page. They are nonprinting guides, which means they are visible only on the computer screen, and do not show on a printout. Ruler guides are the most common type of nonprinting guide. They are created by dragging the pointer from the vertical or horizontal Ruler. The Snap to guides command from the Layout menu helps to fine tune the alignment of text and graphics by automatically pulling the edge of a nearby element exactly to a guide.

Grids are usually created on the Master Pages. Any element placed on the Master Pages will appear on every page in the document.

Columns can be set up automatically through the Column guides command from the Layout menu. Columns are an integral part of many layouts, including newsletters and full books. The space between the columns, called the gutter, is specified in the Column guides dialog box.

X-height, ascenders, descenders, and cap height are all characteristics of typefaces. By varying these attributes, the typeface can convey feelings visually. These characteristics are also important because each typeface takes up a different amount of space vertically and horizontally on the page. The typefaces chosen for each publication are important design decisions.

Serif typefaces are best used as body text, and sans serif typefaces are best used as headings. Different styles of typefaces, such as italic or bold, can further distinguish between headings and subheads (lower heading levels). The point size of headings should be at least two points apart from each level and from the size of the body text.

Leading (pronounced "ledding") is the spacing between the lines

5

Leading (pronounced "ledding") is the spacing between the lines of text. It is measured in points, just like text, and is automatically set to 120% of the text point size. However, the leading should vary with the line length, text size, and font choice to make the document more readable.

Vocabulary

Ascenders - Parts of lowercase letters that extend above the x-height.

Baseline - Imaginary line that the bottom of the letters appear to rest on.

Cap height - Height of capital letters.

Column guides - Blue-colored nonprinting guides that indicate columns and gutters on the publication page.

Counters - The empty spaces in some letters, such as the center of an "o".

Descenders - Parts of lowercase letters that hang down below the baseline.

Dingbat - A decorative symbol.

Facing pages - The left page and a right page that are visible when a publication is open.

Font - A specific combination of a point size, style, and typeface.

Format - The physical specifications of the finished publication, such as the size, materials, and binding.

Gutter - Blank space that separates columns or pages.

Layout - The way text and graphics are arranged on each page.

Leading - Spacing between lines of text.

Margin - Blank space between the edges of the page and the text on the page.

Margin guides - Pink-colored nonprinting guides that mark indicate the margins on a page.

Master Pages - Special pages, identified as left and right, that contain the elements appearing on all pages in a publication.

Nonprinting guides - Lines used for aligning text and graphics that appear on the screen but do not appear on a printout.

Readability - How easily the reader can understand the publication.

Regular type - Indicates plain type, as opposed to italic or bold (*book* and *roman* are also terms for regular type).

Ruler guides - Lines created by dragging away from the horizontal or vertical ruler, used for aligning text and objects.

Rules - Straight lines used as graphics in a layout.

Running footers - Text and graphics that appear in the bottom margin of every page.

Running headers - Text and graphics that appear in the top margin of every page.

Slug - The area of leading around text.

Snap to guides - Forces a text block or graphic to cling to a nearby guide.

Subhead - A level of heading lower than the top level.

Thumbnail sketches - Small hand-drawn pictures of the final publication, used for experimenting with designs.

Type styles - Variations of a typeface, such as italic or bold.

Visual cue - A repeated pattern or object that the reader identifies with an element or specific part of the publication (like a drop cap at the beginning of every chapter).

Weight - The relative lightness or darkness of an element on a page, or the page itself.

White space - Blank areas around and between the elements on a page.

X-height - The height of a lowercase x, a measurement used for comparisons between letters and typefaces.

Reviews

Sections 5.1 — 5.5

1. What is the difference between layout and format?
2. a) List the four concepts of document design.
   b) Explain how you would use each of the concepts in the design of a promotional flyer.
3. a) What are the seven steps used to plan a publication?
   b) Which of these steps uses pencil and paper, and which uses the computer?
4. a) What are some questions you would ask yourself when analyzing an audience for a publication?
   b) How do the answers to the questions in part (a) affect your design?
5. a) Create two thumbnail sketches, one for the first page and one for the second page of a two-column newsletter. Put a masthead, text, and two graphics on the cover page. Put text and three graphics on the second page.
   b) Create a second thumbnail sketch for the same pages of the newsletter, improving on your first design.
   c) List the specific improvements you made and why you think they are improvements.
   d) The audience for your newsletter has been identified as teenagers. What changes would you make to your design and why?

Sections 5.6 — 5.9

6. a) What is the purpose of a margin?
   b) Where are margins found on a page?
   c) Which binding requires a larger inside margin: a ring binder, or a simple fold? Why?
7. What is meant by facing pages?
8. What should be considered when determining inside and outside margins?
9. a) When you change the margins using the Page setup dialog box from the File menu, what pages does your change affect?
   b) Describe the steps you would take to change the margins in a publication.
10. a) What is a grid?
    b) How does a grid help your designs?
11. a) What is meant by nonprinting guides?
    b) Are Margin guides nonprinting guides? Are Ruler guides? Are Column guides?
    c) How does the width of columns in a publication influence the font used for the text?

12. Describe the steps necessary to create one vertical Ruler guide.
    Click + drag a line off the vertick ruler

13. a) What is the Snap to guides command used for? *Snaps or jumps any mouse tool, text block or graphic that is near a guide exactly to the guide.*
    b) List two ways of turning off the Snap to guides command.
    Layout, guides or Ctrl + U

14. a) How do you display the Master Pages on the screen? *Click on either left or right master pages icons*
    b) Name three reasons you would use the Master Pages.

15. What is the space between columns called, and what is it used for?
    Gutter

16. What are widow and orphans? Give an example of each in a thumbnail.
    Widow = single line from the beg. of a ¶ that is left alone at the end of a column
    Orphan = single line from the end of a ¶ that is left alone at the beg. of a column

Sections 5.10 — 5.12

17. a) What is x-height and how does it affect your design? *height of lowercase x + all lower case letters*
    b) What is an ascender and how is it related to the x-height? *Part of lowercase that rises above the letter.*
    c) What is a baseline? What is a descender? How are they related?
    Baseline -- imaginary where the bottom of the letters sit. Descenders are parts of lowercase letters that hang down below the letters.

18. Is twelve-point Avant Garde text exactly the same size as twelve-point Times text? Why or why not? *No - Different X-heights, cap heights, + shapes.*

19. List three styles of typeface. Give two examples of where you would use each style.
    Bold, italic, underline

20. What is meant by a subhead? How does it relate to a heading and to body text?
    A level of heading lower than the top level. Important visual transition between stories + between major ideas within stories

21. a) What are the units used to measure leading? *The height of the slug, measured in points*
    b) Name the two different commands from the Type menu that allow you to change the leading. *Type / Type Specs* *Type / Leading*

Exercises

1. California Sunshine has decided to produce a promotional flyer which offers a free bottle of one of its eight fruit-flavored beverages. The flyer should be 5.5" by 8.5" (half of letter size paper), there is a logo about 2.5" wide by 2" tall, one coupon 3" wide by 2" tall, a heading, and body text describing each of the eight delicious flavors.

   a) On paper, write down the purpose of the flyer and the characteristics of the audience.

   b) Design two thumbnail sketches of the flyer experimenting with the placement of the elements. Keep in mind the purpose and audience as you sketch the designs.

   c) Indicate the typefaces, sizes, and other specifications next to each thumbnail.

   d) Pick the best thumbnail and use the Master Page to create a grid from the sketch of this single-sheet flyer.

   e) Place the CALIFSUN.WMF logo, resizing it proportionally and moving it to the desired location. Draw a rectangle as a graphic representation of the coupon, and move it to the desired location.

   f) Place GENERIC.TXT as the text. Resize, flow, adjust the fonts and leading, and move the text as necessary for your design. Delete any extra text. Create your own headlines.

   g) Save the flyer naming it CSFLYER and then print a copy.

2. A local artist is having an art show next month. She has asked you to create a 5.5" by 8.5" flyer containing her biography, logo, and a photograph of her best painting.

   a) On paper, write down the purpose of the flyer and some characteristics of the possible audience.

   b) Design two thumbnail sketches of the flyer, keeping in mind its purpose and audience.

   c) Indicate the typefaces, sizes, and other specifications next to each thumbnail.

   d) Pick the best thumbnail and use the Master Page to create a grid from the sketch of this single-sheet flyer.

   e) Place GENERIC.TXT as the biography body text, PHOTO.WMF as the photo, and GRAPHIC.WMF as the logo. Resize, move, adjust fonts, and delete any extra text as necessary. Create any headlines needed.

   f) Save the flyer naming it ARTAD and then print a copy.

g) Another artist has joined the show at the last minute, so now the flyer needs to be revised to contain both biographies, one picture for each artist, and no logos. Draw two thumbnail sketches of a revised flyer.

h) Include any specifications next to each thumbnail.

i) Use the Save As command to create a different file for the revised publication, naming it ARTAD2.

j) On the Master Page, change the grid for the new flyer as necessary, using your best thumbnail as a guide.

k) Use the Copy and Paste commands to create the second artist's biography and photograph. Resize the text and graphics as necessary.

l) Save the revised publication and then print a copy.

3. A local group is sponsoring a Thanksgiving dinner for area senior citizens. Create an 8.5" by 11" poster to announce the dinner. Include the location, time, date, cost, a brief menu, and the sponsor. Include the information that the dinner is for the area elderly. One graphic, which would be a line drawing, can be used in the poster.

   a) Design two thumbnail sketches of the poster. Experiment with the placement of the elements contained in the poster. Keep in mind the purpose and audience as you design.

   b) Indicate the typefaces, sizes, and other specifications on the thumbnails.

   c) Pick the best thumbnail and use the Master Page to create a grid from the sketch of the poster.

   d) Using the Story Editor write some brief text for the poster, including headlines. Return to the layout and resize, adjust fonts and leading, and move the text as necessary.

   e) Place GRAPHIC.WMF as the graphic. Resize and move as necessary.

   f) Save the poster naming it THANPOST and then print a copy.

4. Zawacki Orchards is planning to offer home-baked pies and other goodies for the holidays. They need a brochure to mail to people on their mailing list announcing their new phone-order home-baked goods. It should include information about the orchards, a listing of the products with a photo, and the phone number for orders. Because it will be mailed, the brochure will be printed on 11" wide by 8.5" tall paper, folded into thirds, and stapled. The outside of the brochure will be blank, and the inside will contain the printed information.

   a) Write down the purpose of the brochure and the audience's characteristics.

   b) Design two sets of thumbnail sketches for the brochure, keeping in mind the purpose and audience.

c) Indicate typefaces, size, and other specifications next to each thumbnail sketch.

d) Pick the best thumbnail and use the Master Page to create a grid from the sketch. You can turn the orientation of the page by clicking on the **Wide** radio button in the Page Setup dialog box.

e) Place PHOTO.WMF as the photo. Resize as necessary.

f) Place GENERIC.TXT as the text. Resize, flow, adjust the fonts and leading, and move the text as necessary for your design. Delete any extra text. Create your own headlines.

g) Save the brochure naming it ZAWBROCH and then print a copy. Fold the brochure into thirds.

5. Your best friends are getting married and have asked you to make the program that will be handed out at the ceremony. The program will be printed on 8.5" by 11" paper and folded in half like a book so that each page is 5.5" wide by 8.5" tall. Only the inside will contain printed information. Include the order of ceremonial events and the words to a song.

   a) Design two thumbnail sketches for the inside of the program. Experiment with the placement of the different elements. Keep in mind appropriateness, balance, focus and flow, and consistency as you sketch the designs.

   b) Pick the best thumbnail and use the Master Page to create a grid from the sketch. You can turn the orientation of the page by clicking on the **Wide** radio button in the Page Setup dialog box.

   c) Place GRAPHIC.WMF for any graphics you have included. Resize as necessary.

   d) Using the Story Editor write the text. Return to the layout and resize, adjust fonts and leading, and move the text as necessary.

   e) Save the program naming it WEDPROG and then print a copy. Fold the paper in half to form the program.

6. You work in the public relations department of *New House Incorporated*, a company that assembles and distributes pre-fabricated housing. *New House* has just merged with *Green Power*, a company that produces environmentally-aware electrical supplies. The merger has generated a new name for the conglomerate, *Power House Inc*. Your task is to design a letter explaining this merger to the general public, encouraging them to buy stock in the company, and reassuring them that the products will retain the same quality as always. The letter will be printed in the *New York Times*, and should include the logo of the new company and a photograph of the CEO.

   a) Write down the purpose of the letter and characteristics of the audience.

   b) Design two different thumbnail sketches of the letter. Experiment with the placement of the text, photo, and logo keeping in mind the purpose and audience.

c) Indicate the typefaces, sizes, and other specifications next to each thumbnail.

d) Pick the best thumbnail and use the Master Page to create a grid from the sketch.

e) Place PHOTO.WMF as the photo and GRAPHIC.WMF as the letterhead. Resize and move as necessary.

f) Place GENERIC.TXT as the main text in the letter, but create your own names and addresses. Resize, flow, adjust the fonts and leading, move the text as necessary for your design. Delete any extra text.

g) Save the letter naming it POWERLET and then print a copy.

7. Ivy University has asked you to design a calendar that can be sent to alumni. Important university, social, and sports events will be indicated on the calendar, along with the university's logo. The month, days of the week, and numbers of each day should also be included.

a) Design two thumbnail sketches for one month of the calendar which will be printed on paper 8.5" wide by 11" high.

b) Indicate the typefaces, sizes, and other specifications next to each sketch.

c) Pick the best thumbnail and use the Master Page to create a grid for the calendar. You can turn the orientation of the page by clicking on the **Wide** radio button in the Page Setup dialog box. Use solid rules to draw the seven columns and five rows needed for each month, and a rectangle for the border.

d) Produce the page for the month of September. Enter information such as the opening day of the university, beginning of classes, alumni day, and important sports and social events.

e) Place Ivy's logo IULOGO.WMF and resize proportionately as necessary.

f) Save the calendar naming it CALENDAR and then print a copy.

5

8. Ivy University needs a two column flyer which describes the University to student applicants. The text for the flyer is the first three paragraphs of the file IVYPROMO.TXT. Below is a thumbnail of the flyer designed by Ivy's Art Department chair Philip Crangi:

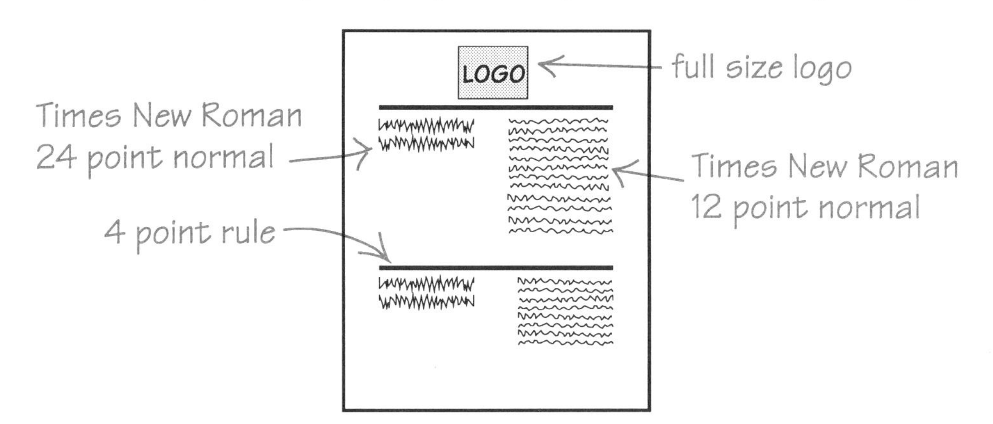

Phil Crangi's thumbnail sketch with specifications

a) Use the Master Page to create a grid based on Mr. Crangi's thumbnail sketch. Use both the Column guides command and Ruler guides for the grid.

b) Place IVYPROMO.TXT and delete all of the text except the first three paragraphs. Resize, flow, adjust fonts as necessary to follow the design in the thumbnail sketch above.

c) Place the University logo IULOGO.WMF. Draw the rules using the Straight line tool and the Line command.

d) Save the flyer naming it IVYFLY1A and print a copy.

e) Now that you have created the flyer using Mr. Crangi's design, Ivy University has asked you to submit a similar flyer of your own design. Create two thumbnail sketches of a promotional flyer that contain the same text and graphics as Mr. Crangi's. You may change the layout, delete the rules, or add other graphic elements as you see fit.

f) Indicate the specifications such as typeface and size next to the thumbnails.

g) Create a new file and use the Master Page to make a grid based on your best thumbnail sketch.

h) Place the same text and graphic as in the first flyer. Resize, flow, adjust the fonts and leading as necessary for your design.

i) Save the flyer naming it IVYFLY1B and print a copy.

9. The Department of Skin Injury and Disease at Ivy University needs a single sheet flyer containing its course descriptions. The text for the flyer will come from the file IVYPROMO.TXT. Below is a thumbnail of the three-column flyer designed by Ivy's graphic artist Judy Crangi:

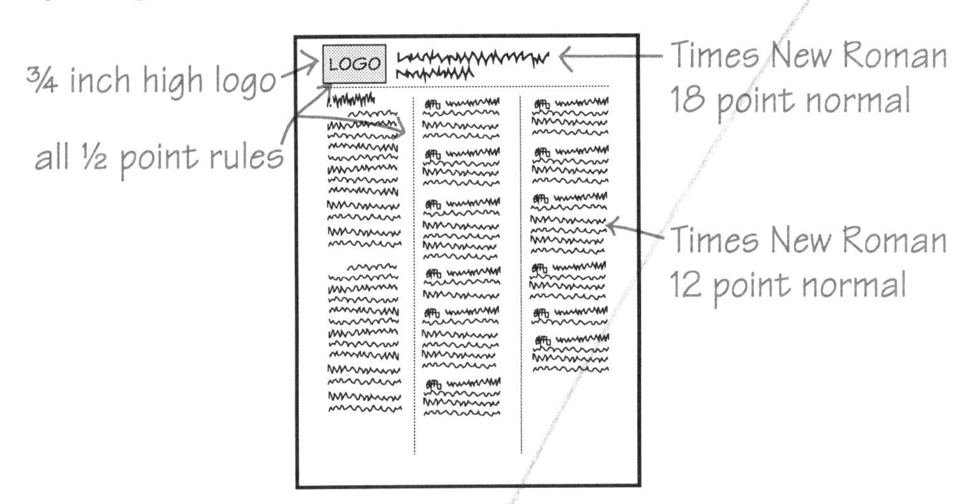

Judy Crangi's thumbnail sketch with specifications

a) Use the Master Page to create a grid based on Mrs. Crangi's thumbnail sketch. Use both the Column guides command and Ruler guides for the grid.

b) Place IVYPROMO.TXT and delete all of the text except the course descriptions. Resize, flow, adjust fonts as necessary to follow the design in the thumbnail sketch above.

c) Place the University logo IULOGO.WMF, resize proportionately and move as necessary. Draw the rules using the Straight line tool and the Line command.

d) Save the flyer naming it IVYFLY2A and print a copy.

e) Now that you have created the flyer using Mrs. Crangi's design, Ivy University has asked you to submit a similar flyer of your own design. Create two thumbnail sketches of a promotional flyer that contain the same text and graphics as Mrs. Crangi's. You may change the layout, delete the rules, or add other graphic elements as you see fit.

f) Indicate the specifications such as typeface and size next to the thumbnails.

g) Create a new file and use the Master Page to make a grid based on your best thumbnail sketch.

h) Place the same text and graphic as in the first flyer. Resize, flow, adjust the fonts and leading as necessary for your design.

i) Save the flyer naming it IVYFLY2B and print a copy.

In the following exercises you will revise publications created in exercises from previous chapters. To do this, the contents of the original publication will be moved onto the Pasteboard. A new grid will then be created on the Master Page based on your new design. The text and graphics are then moved back from the Pasteboard to the publication page and reformatted as necessary.

10. Now that you have learned the factors that determine good design, Aztec Café has asked you to redesign the one page flyer named ACBROCH which you created in earlier chapters. The flyer will be handed out by local merchants in the hope of attracting new customers to the Café.

    a) Open ACBROCH and print a copy for review. In this exercise you will revise the original file.

    b) Create two thumbnail sketches of new designs for the flyer. Experiment with the placement of different elements, keeping in mind the purpose and audience.

    c) Indicate the typefaces, sizes, and other specifications next to the thumbnails.

    d) Pick the best thumbnail. Move the contents of ACBROCH onto the Pasteboard and then create a grid for your new design on the Master Pages.

    e) Using the elements you moved onto the Pasteboard, create the new flyer based on your thumbnail.

    f) Save and then print a copy of the revised ACBROCH.

11. You have now learned much more about design since last working on Deborah Debit's résumé. She would like you to redesign it, using your new skills to create a better résumé.

    a) Open DDRESUME and print a copy for review. In this exercise you will revise the original file.

    b) Create two thumbnail sketches of new designs for the résumé. Experiment with the placement of different elements, keeping in mind the purpose and audience.

    c) Indicate the typefaces, sizes, and other specifications next to the thumbnails.

    d) Pick the best thumbnail. Move the contents of DDRESUME to the Pasteboard and then create a grid for your new design on the Master Pages.

    e) Using the elements you moved onto the Pasteboard, create the new résumé based on your thumbnail.

    f) Save and then print a copy of the revised DDRESUME.

12. In previous chapters you created a menu for Aztec Cafe, but it looked unprofessional since you lacked the necessary design and PageMaker skills. Now having gained those skills you will be able to give the menu the professional look it needs to impress customers.

   a) Open ACMENU and print a copy for review. In this exercise you will revise the original file.

   b) Create two thumbnail sketches of new designs for the menu, keeping in mind the audience and purpose.

   c) Indicate typefaces, sizes, and other specifications next to the thumbnails.

   d) Pick the best thumbnail. Move the contents of ACMENU onto the Pasteboard and then create a grid for your new design on the Master Pages.

   e) Using the elements you moved onto the Pasteboard, create the new menu based on your thumbnail.

   f) Save and then print a copy of the revised ACMENU.

Chapter Six:
Brochures & Newsletters

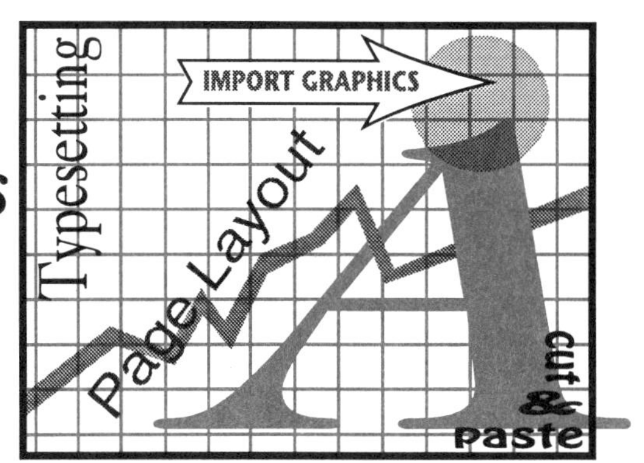

Lock guides

Rotation

Element - Bring to front

Element - Send to back

Element - Rounded corners

Layout - Display master items

Objectives

After completing this chapter you will be able to:

1. Identify different styles of bindings.
2. Manipulate the page size and orientation.
3. Effectively use columns in grids.
4. Identify the elements of a brochure and newsletter.
5. Layout a brochure and a newsletter using PageMaker.
6. Rotate objects in a publication.
7. Use shaded boxes and rules as graphic design elements.
8. Round the corners of a rectangle.
9. Create running headers and footers in a publication.

6

In this chapter the design skills learned in the previous chapter are utilized to create a brochure and a newsletter. Individual design elements and issues considered in producing both a brochure or newsletter are covered, as are special graphical elements that can be used in any publication.

6.1 Brochures and Newsletters

Brochures and newsletters are two types of publications that can be designed for many different purposes. Like all publications, the style and presentation of each is defined by both the purpose and the audience of the publication. Imagine, for example, a brochure with the purpose of educating people about dental care, and the audience of children. The brochure would need to appeal to a certain age group and be read and understood by them. A possible design for this brochure would include using colored paper, cartoon drawings, large fonts, and a limited vocabulary.

6.2 Bindings

One characteristic that is determined by the purpose and audience is the publication's *binding*, the method that keeps the pages together. Brochures and newsletters can be bound in many styles:

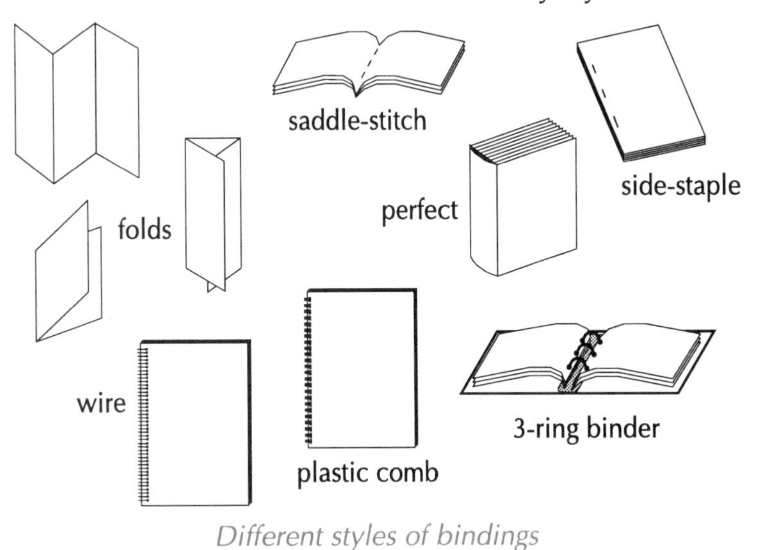

Different styles of bindings

Brochures that are printed entirely on one sheet of paper can be folded into sections (two-fold or three-fold), or left unfolded which is known as a *flyer*. Some brochures that have many pages are bound, either by *saddle stitch* (sewn or stapled down the middle), *side stapled* (stapled down the side), or *perfect bound*, which is glued with a flat binding. Other methods include *wire, plastic comb,* and *3-ring* binding. These last three methods require punching holes into the pages. Similarly, newsletters can be constructed of folded paper or bound. If they have a small circulation, newsletters can even be just stapled together at one corner.

The style of the binding must take into consideration the method of distribution (how it gets to the reader), the budget available to the project, and how much text and graphics must be included. A three-fold brochure or a bound brochure can be mailed and displayed more easily than a flyer or two-fold brochure. Also, a bound or three-fold publication is more elegant than the two-fold or flyer types; therefore, it is more likely to be picked up from a display by a customer. For brochures that are distributed through a display, the publication itself must capture the readers attention and persuade them to take a copy.

Practice 1

In this Practice you will determine the binding, purpose, audience, and other factors for different projects. Write down the answers to the questions on paper.

1) DETERMINE THE FORM AND DISTRIBUTION FOR A BROCHURE

You have been asked to design a brochure for a vacuum cleaner company.

Purpose: To sell mail-order vacuum cleaners.
Audience: 250,000 suburban homes in the United States.
Contents: 4 pictures of vacuums, 6 paragraphs of text, 1 reply card.

a. How do you think the brochure should be bound? Include the page size and be specific about the binding or folding. Why did you choose this method and size?
b. What method of distribution would you use? Why? Does the method of distribution fit the binding style you chose?

2) DETERMINE THE AUDIENCE AND DISTRIBUTION FOR A NEWSLETTER

You have been asked to design a bimonthly newsletter for a small candle factory (100 employees).

Purpose: To keep employees informed about company policies, new facilities, incentives, benefits.
Contents: Stories, lists, drawings, and photographs.
Binding: 1 sheet of 8.5" by 22" paper, folded in half to create 4 pages.

a. Define the audience.
b. What method of distribution would you use? Why?

3) DETERMINE THE SPECIFICATIONS FOR A NEWSLETTER

You have been asked to design a bimonthly newsletter for the members of a museum society.

Purpose: To inform members about upcoming events and exhibits, and educate them about museum-related subjects.

a. Define the audience.
b. List some possible contents.
c. How do you think the newsletter should be bound? Include the page size and be specifics about the binding or folding. Why did you choose this method and size?
d. What method of distribution would you use? Why? Does the method of distribution fit the binding style?

6.3 Page Size and Orientation

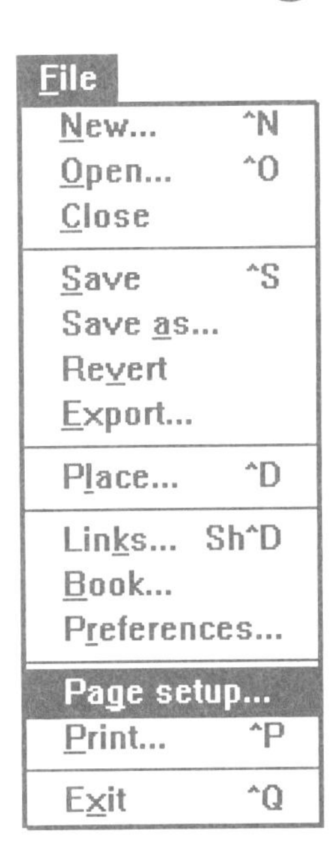

Before starting to sketch the thumbnails of a new design you must determine the size of the paper to be used. There are several standard sizes of paper. Using a standard paper size can keep production costs low, especially for a publication with small circulation. Odd sizes can be printed and cut, but the more custom specifications you have, the more expensive it is to produce the publication. For smaller jobs it is best to choose a standard size page such as:

Letter	(8.5" by 11")
Legal	(8.5" by 14")
Tabloid	(11" by 17")
A4	(210mm by 297mm)

For folded publications, the possibilities of different folds combined with different size papers are endless.

The *orientation* of the paper is another design decision. Orientation refers to the direction the paper faces in relation to the text and graphics. There are two ways to orient paper: *portrait* and *landscape.* Using regular letter size paper as an example, portrait orientation indicates that the paper is viewed as 8.5" wide and 11" tall. Portrait is also sometimes referred to as *Tall.* Landscape orientation indicates that the paper is viewed as 11" wide and 8.5" tall and is sometimes called *Wide*:

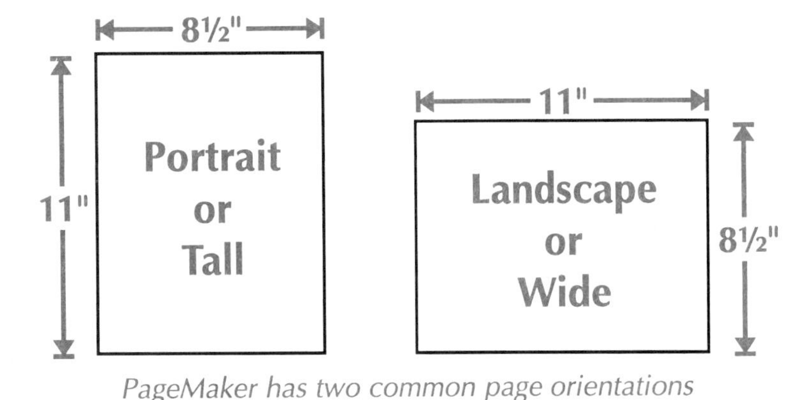

PageMaker has two common page orientations

In PageMaker, you can specify the size and orientation of the paper and number of pages in the Page setup dialog box:

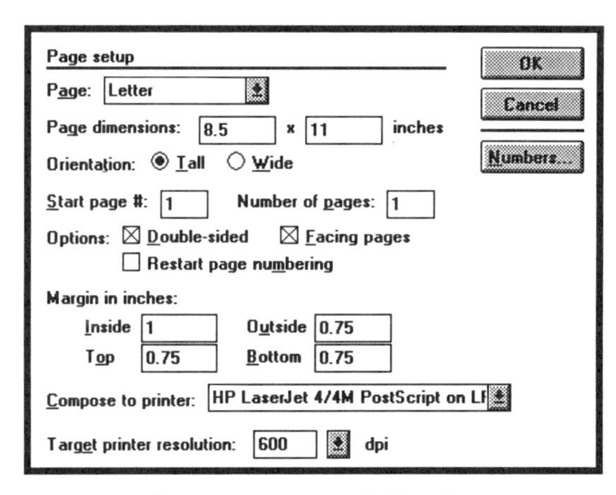

The Page setup dialog box

The Page option has a collapsible list of pre-set page sizes to choose from. Different choices will be available here depending on the printer selected for the Compose to printer. If the desired size is not listed, you can create your own page size by choosing Custom as the Page option and entering numbers for the Page dimensions. The Orientation of the paper can be specified by choosing either the Tall or Wide radio buttons. For two page documents or longer, the number of pages needed can be entered as the Number of pages option.

Practice 2

In this Practice you will experiment with different page sizes and orientations. Start Windows and PageMaker if you have not already done so.

1) CREATE A NEW, PORTRAIT, LETTER SIZE PUBLICATION

a. From the File menu, select the New command. The Page setup dialog box is shown.
b. Verify that the Page option is Letter and the Orientation is Tall. These are the defaults.
c. Select OK to create the new publication. Notice that the page is 8.5" wide and 11" tall as shown by the horizontal and vertical Rulers.

2) CHANGE TO TABLOID SIZE

a. From the File menu, select the Page setup command.
b. In the Page setup dialog box, choose Tabloid for the Page option.
c. Select OK. Note how the page is still oriented as portrait and is now tabloid size (11" wide and 17" tall) as shown by the Rulers.

3) CHANGE TO LANDSCAPE ORIENTATION

a. From the File menu, select the Page setup command.
b. Select Wide for the Orientation option.
c. Select OK. The page is still tabloid size, but is now oriented as landscape (17" wide by 11" tall).

6

4) *CHANGE TO A PORTRAIT, LEGAL SIZE*

a. From the File menu, select the Page setup command.
b. For the Page option, choose Legal.
c. Select Tall as the Orientation.
d. Select OK. Note how the page is now legal size and oriented as portrait (8.5" wide by 14" tall).

5) *CHANGE TO A CUSTOM SIZE*

a. From the File menu, select the Page setup command.
b. For the Page option, choose Custom.
c. Type 7 and 7 for the Page dimensions option.
d. Select OK. The page is now 7" by 7".

6) *CHANGE TO A LANDSCAPE, LETTER SIZE*

a. Execute the Page setup command.
b. For the Page option, choose Letter.
c. Select Wide for the Orientation.
d. Select OK. A letter size page is oriented as landscape.

7) *SAVE THE PUBLICATION*

a. From the File menu, select the Save command.
b. Type BROCHURE in the File name box and select OK. PageMaker adds the proper extension (.PM5) and saves the publication under the name BROCHURE.PM5.

6.4 Columns in Brochures and Newsletters

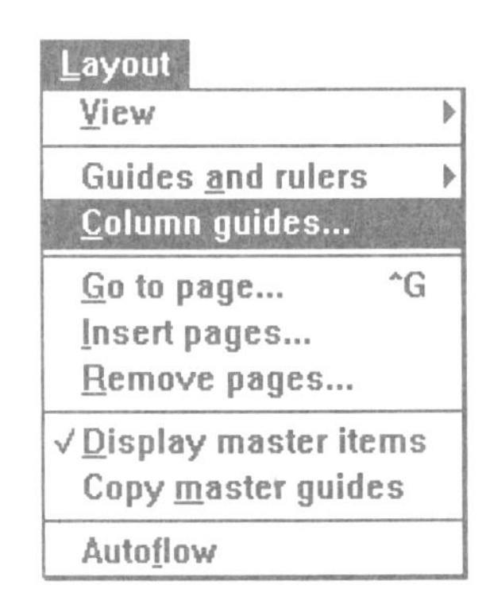

You learned in Chapter Five that you can create a grid using the Column guides command to generate columns automatically and finish the grid with manually-placed Ruler guides. By placing the guides on the Master Pages, the grid will appear on each page in the publication. For newsletters and brochures, using columns in a grid is essential to an effective design.

A grid based on columns is an excellent way of keeping the layout consistent throughout a brochure or newsletter. From the thumbnail sketches you can determine the number of columns to use. Placing text and graphics within the column guidelines helps to precisely line up each element in the layout, and resizing graphics is easier because you can visually see the graphic's outline in relation to the columns. The sizes of the text blocks and the graphics become related to each other, as each text block and graphic are usually units of one, two, or three columns in width.

When the Column guides command is executed, gutters are created between the columns. In a folded publication the gutters (the space between the columns) often determine where the folds appear. A three-fold (tri-fold) brochure is a good example. By orienting the page to Wide and assigning three columns per page on the Master Page, the folds will occur in each of the resulting gutters:

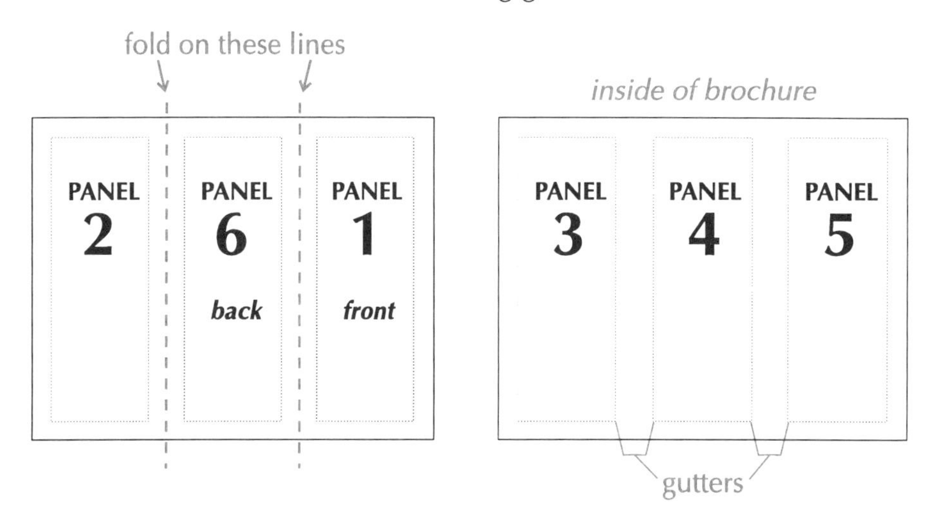

A three-fold brochure, printed on both sides

Enough space should be allotted in the gutter for a margin on each side of the fold. As shown in the picture above, if the margins around the edge of the page are 0.5 inches, the gutter at the fold should be about 1 inch, which allows for approximately 0.5 inches on each side of the fold.

In some designs, text and graphics will be placed across a fold. This practice is acceptable if handled carefully, but beware of small text or graphics crossing a fold—sometimes they can be obscured. It is safer to cross folds with larger objects, such as big graphics or extra large fonts that will not be lost in the crease.

The number of columns per page dictates how flexible the grid is. Two column layouts are the least flexible, because the text and graphics fit either in one column or across the whole page; there is often not enough diversity to create an interesting layout. There are times when graphics are sized differently than the exact width of a column, but these occasions are rare and care must be taken to work the graphic smoothly into the design. Three and five column layouts are usually the most flexible newsletter layouts because the odd number allows for more variation of text block and graphic placement and size:

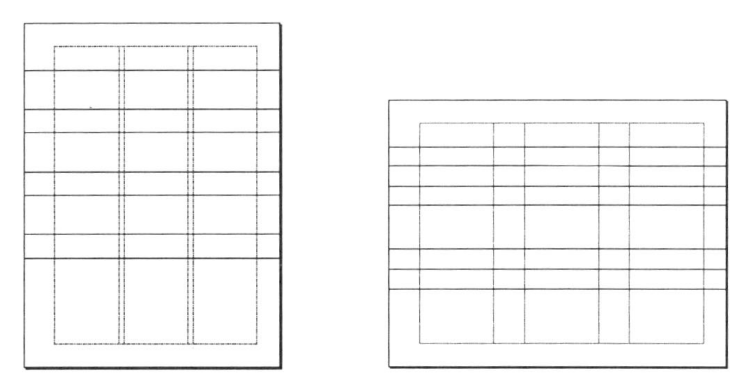

Grids are the basis of every layout

6

6.5 The Lock Guides Command

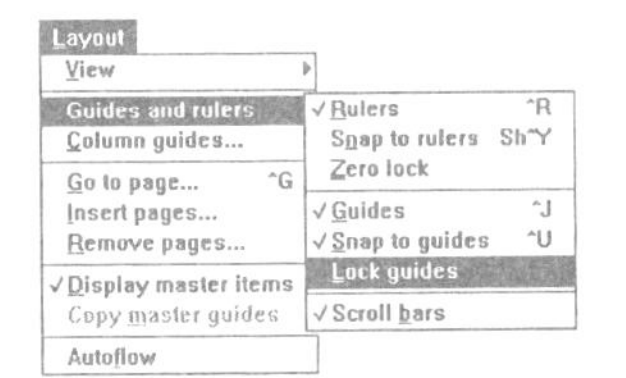

When using grids, the *Lock guides* feature allows you to move text and graphics on the grid without inadvertently moving the nonprinting guides. Lock guides secures all the guides in the entire publication, so that you cannot move them. If you need to move the guides, Lock guides can be turned off, freeing the guides. This feature is turned on or off using the Guides and rulers submenu from the Layout menu.

6.6 Page Setup for Brochures

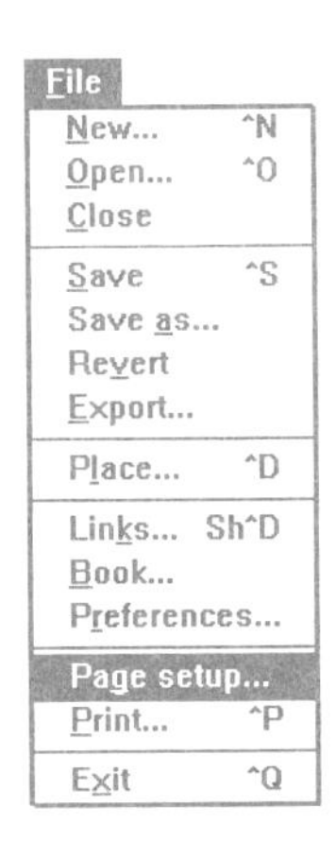

Brochures are usually designed to be printed on one piece of paper and then folded. Therefore, using only one page to set up the grid is ideal for a brochure.

In the Page setup dialog box there are two check-box options, Double-sided and Facing pages, that are used to set up PageMaker publications. The default option is to have both Double-sided and Facing pages options selected. These defaults cause the margins to be labeled as inside and outside and both facing pages to be displayed. By deselecting the Double-sided and Facing pages options, the margins are labeled right and left and only one page appears in PageMaker. PageMaker now handles each page as though it will be printed on only one side.

Practice 3

In this Practice you will create a layout of 3 columns to be used as guidelines for the panels of a brochure. You will then add Ruler guides to enhance the grid and print out a blank brochure. Start PageMaker and open the BROCHURE.PM5 file if you have not already done so.

1) *ADJUST THE PAGE SETTINGS FOR A BROCHURE*

a. From the File menu, select the Page setup command.
b. In the Page setup dialog box, change these settings:

    Number of pages: 2
    Double-sided and Facing pages options: deselected
    Left, Right, Top, and Bottom margins: 0.5 inches

    Be sure that the Compose to printer and Target printer resolution settings are correct for your printer.
c. Select OK to make the changes. A letter size page in a landscape orientation is displayed with 0.5 inch margins.

2) *CREATE A 3 COLUMN FORMAT FOR THE PUBLICATION*

a. Click on the Master-page icon [R] in the bottom-left corner of the screen. The Master Page is displayed.
b. From the Layout menu, select the Column guides command. The Column guides dialog box is displayed.

c. Type 3 for the Number of Columns and 1 for the Space between columns.
d. Click on OK. The Master Page is displayed with three columns of equal width and two one-inch gutters between the columns.

3) *LOCK THE GUIDES*

a. With the Pointer tool, drag the leftmost column guide to the 2 inch mark. Notice that the guide is moveable.
b. From the Layout menu, select Guides and Rulers and from the submenu select the Lock guides command.
c. With the Pointer tool, try to drag the Column guide back to the left margin. Notice that the guide cannot be moved, because the Lock guides feature is on.
d. From the Layout menu, select Guides and Rulers and from the submenu select the Lock guides command to turn it off. Drag the Column guide back to the left margin.
e. Select the Column guides command and type 3 for the Number of columns to reset the Column guides.

4) *DRAW ON THE MARGINS TO CREATE BOXES*

a. Select the Rectangle tool. Place the cross-hairs pointer over the upper-left corner of the far left column.
b. Drag the cross-hairs to the bottom-right corner of that column. Release the mouse button. A rectangle is created exactly the size of the column. (Part of the rectangle might not be shown on the screen because it is overlapped by the guides.)
c. Repeat the procedure and draw rectangles on the margins of the other two columns.

5) *VIEW THE COLUMNS ON PAGES ONE AND TWO*

a. Click on the page 1 icon at the bottom of the screen. Page 1 is displayed. Notice how the columns and rectangles that you created on the Master Page also appear here.
b. Now click on the page 2 icon. Page 2 is displayed. Note that the Master items, in this case three rectangles, appear here exactly as they do on page 1 and the Master Page.

6) *SAVE AND PRINT THE PUBLICATION*

7) *FOLD THE BROCHURE*

a. Place the two pages back-to-back, with the rectangles facing outwards on both sides and lay them on a table.
b. Treating both sheets as one piece of paper, fold in the right third of the paper towards the middle so that one full rectangle from the bottom side is showing, including half of the gutter. Crease the fold.
c. Fold in the left third of the paper, so that the rectangle and half of the gutter is showing. Crease the fold. You have created a blank brochure! Note how the rectangles, that exactly match the columns, are centered on each page. They represent the area that you would place text and graphics in a brochure. A blank brochure such as this one can be used to sketch in the approximate placement of the elements, similar to a thumbnail sketch but on a larger scale.

6

6.7 Elements of a Brochure

All brochures, regardless of how they are folded or bound, have certain elements in common. Each has a *cover page*, or a *title area* that contains the title or headline. For example, a flyer-style brochure does not have separate panels and therefore needs an area selected to stand out as the title. Another element is the *body*, which is the main section of the brochure and is composed of the text and graphics. At the end (or on the back) of the brochure can be other elements, depending on the specific purpose of the brochure, such as an *indicia* or a *reply card*. An indicia is the space used for mailing, including the return address, mailing label, and postal codes. A reply card is a self-addressed card, usually with mail codes that the reader cuts or tears out:

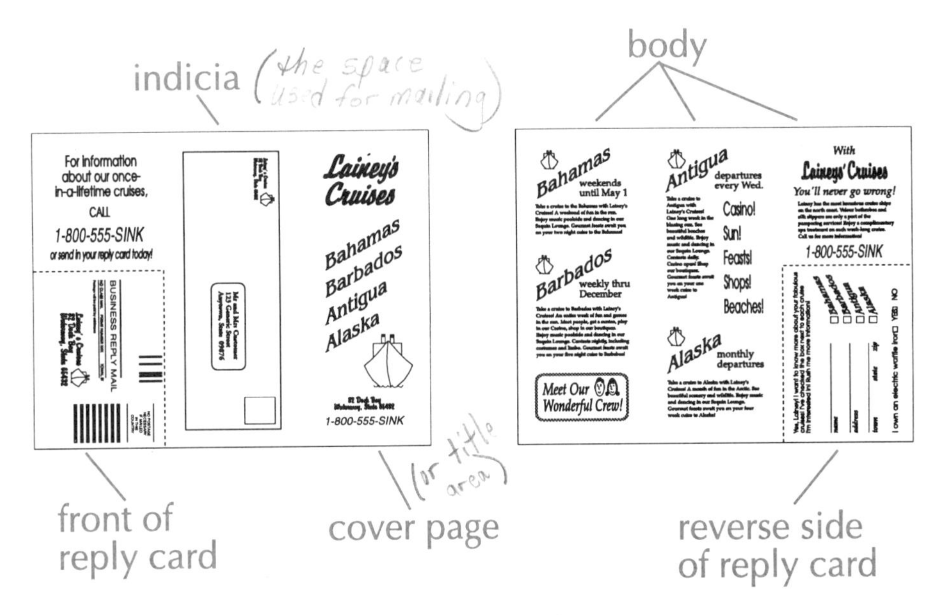

A three-fold brochure

The physical elements of the brochure vary by binding. Flyer-style brochures are flat sheets of paper that are printed either on one side or two sides. Folded brochures start out as one sheet of paper and are folded, usually into thirds, to create several pages called *panels*. A panel is the section of a piece of paper that becomes a flat, page-like area when the paper is folded. For example, a three-fold brochure has six panels. Longer brochures are saddle-stitched with staples, and the sides of paper are called pages instead of panels.

6.8 Design for Brochures

In Chapter Five you learned what makes a publication design effective, including basic guidelines for all documents. As with any publication, brochures have a few special considerations:

Appropriateness

It is important to keep the elements in a publication appropriate for the purpose and audience. A brochure is usually a short document and choosing the few graphics and paragraphs that can reasonably fit can be a difficult task. Each word or picture has greater importance because there are so few of them. Appropriateness is especially important on the front panel or cover of a brochure. It is the cover that grabs the readers eye—or dissuades it.

Balance

The balance of elements on a page is crucial to holding the reader's interest. In a brochure not only does each panel have to balance, but any panels that are viewed at the same time should balance with each other. For example, the three inside panels of a tri-fold brochure will be viewed at the same time so it is important that they balance as a single unit, as well as individually. Care must also be taken when balancing each panel individually, because the narrow dimensions of the panels offer limited layout choices.

Focus and Flow

The focus and flow of each page in a document is vital to helping the reader understand the intended message. In a smaller document such as a brochure, it is important that the reader's eye flow smoothly through the entire brochure from beginning to end. The focus and flow on each panel, as well as throughout the brochure, must be carefully considered to ensure that it is suitable to the purpose and audience.

Consistency

Because a brochure is usually a short document, graphical elements such as dingbats and rules are not usually effective in maintaining consistency. However, from their past experiences with brochures the reader expects concise, specific information in a small format. The brochure should be consistent with the reader's expectations and should only contain pertinent information.

Here is a brochure before and after a thorough re-design:

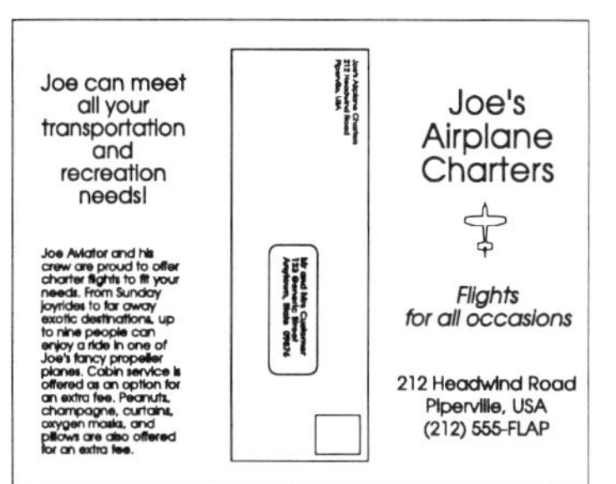

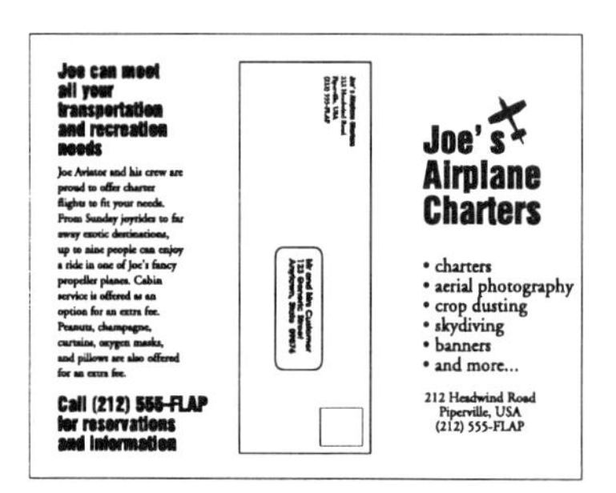

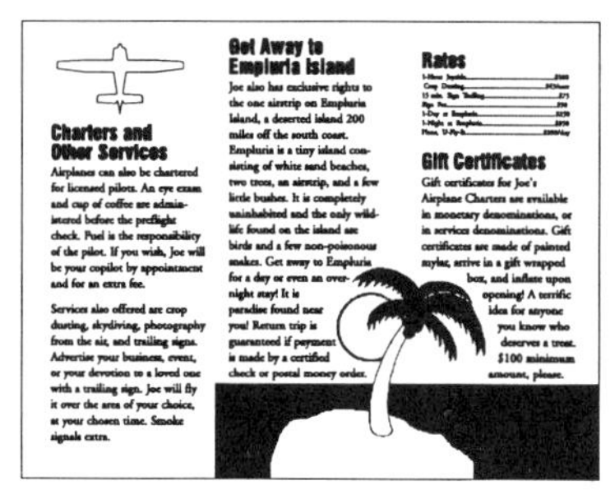

Before (top) and after (bottom) a brochure makeover

6

6

The contrast between the covers of the two brochures above illustrates how appropriateness can influence the reader. When a potential reader glances at the top brochure's cover, the only information they can gather is the name of the business and the type of business it is. The picture and the phrase *Flights for all occasions* are not specific enough to tell the reader anything more. On the bottom brochure's cover the vague phrase is changed into a list of services offered. The reader can now get a clear idea of what services the business provides, and the list is appropriate because it conveys information in a concise manner. The last item in the list, *and more...*, entices the reader to pick up the brochure in order to find out what other related services are available.

The three inside panels of the top brochure are good examples of a layout that is too balanced and therefore boring. Each separate panel is evenly covered with a graphical element at the top and text below, contributing to the dull uniformity of the panels. From the repetitive layout and the even visual tone of these panels the reader has difficulty finding an "entry point" into the text. The three inside panels should also balance as a whole, because they will be viewed at the same time. With the title of the business as the only heading, the reader has no idea what the contents is of the four long paragraphs, and most likely will not want to read the text to find out.

The bottom brochure shows an improved layout with the three panels balanced and possessing sufficient tension. Differences between the graphics and text divide the panels into approachable sections. The addition of headings, in the same font as the business title on the cover and a different font from the text, adds interest to the three panels. Here, headings break up the text, letting the reader know at a glance what is in the text, and providing contrasting weight to break up the page. The text itself has been changed to a serif font in the same type size as the top brochure, but with a smaller x-height that adds visual space between the lines of text. Leading has been increased to further lighten the visual weight of the text, making the text more inviting to the reader.

Note how the graphic has been enlarged and moved to the bottom corner to *bleed* off of the page. The word "bleed" indicates that the graphic is printed right up to and off of the edge of the paper. Bleeds can provide variations in layouts that create interest for the reader. By using a bleed that spans two panels in this brochure, a much bigger difference is created between the weight of the graphic and the weight of the text, adding interest to the page. The text wrap around the graphic also adds visual interest to the page. Headings, graphics, and the text wrap combine to create more "entry points" for the reader and a more pronounced focus and flow across the three panels.

6.9 Rotating Objects

When laying out a publication you may need to rotate a text block or a graphic. For example, on the mailing area of a brochure the address information will face in a different direction than the text and graphics on the other panels and therefore needs to be rotated.

The Rotation tool is used to rotate text and graphics. After selecting the object to be rotated with the pointer, the Rotation tool is chosen from the Toolbox which changes the pointer to a starburst shape. The starburst is then placed over the object at the point around which the object is to be rotated (the center of rotation). Dragging straight to the right draws a handle on the screen, then continuing to drag the starburst in a circular direction rotates the object. The mouse button is released when the object is at the desired angle.

Practice 4

In this Practice you will place graphics and text in a brochure. Start PageMaker and open the BROCHURE.PM5 publication if you have not already done so.

1) *REMOVE THE RECTANGLES*

a. Click on the Master-page icon in the bottom-left corner of the screen. The Master Page is displayed with the three rectangles you created.
b. From the Edit menu choose the Select all command to select all of the rectangles.
c. Press the Delete key to delete all the rectangles.

2) *PLACE GRAPHICS ON PAGE 1*

a. Click on the page 1 icon to display page 1. Note that the rectangles you removed from the Master Page are also gone from page 1.
b. Place GRAPHIC.WMF in the panel on the far right. When the brochure is folded, this panel will be the front panel (see Section 6.5 about folding). Align the graphic with the left margin. Resize the graphic proportionately (hold down the Shift key while dragging with a corner handle) to fit exactly between the Column guides. Move the graphic to about halfway down the column.
c. Place a second copy of GRAPHIC.WMF in the panel on the far left. This panel is the second panel the reader will see. Resize the graphic proportionately so that it fits exactly between the Column guides. Move the graphic to the bottom of the column so that it is similar to:

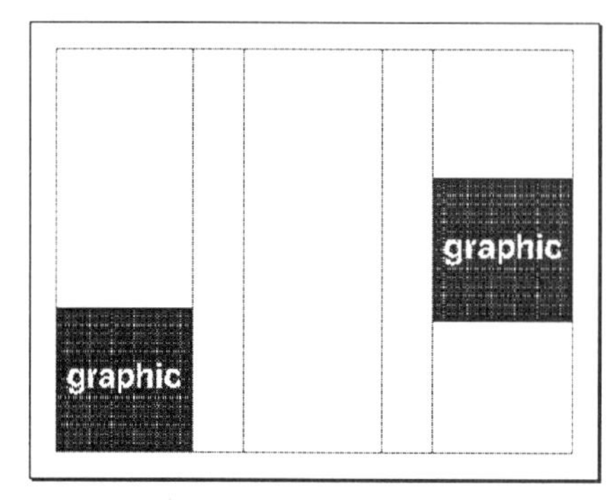

3) *PLACE GRAPHICS ON PAGE 2*

a. Click on the page 2 icon in the bottom-left of the screen. Page 2 is displayed. When the brochure is folded, the three panels on page 2 will be the inside of the brochure.
b. Place GRAPHIC.WMF in the panel on the far left. Instead of resizing proportionately, stretch the graphic horizontally to fit exactly across the column, inside the Column guides. Move it to the top of the column.
c. Place another copy of GRAPHIC.WMF in the middle panel. Resize the graphic so that its width is at most half the column wide and its height is half the column's height. Align the graphic to the lower-left corner of the column:

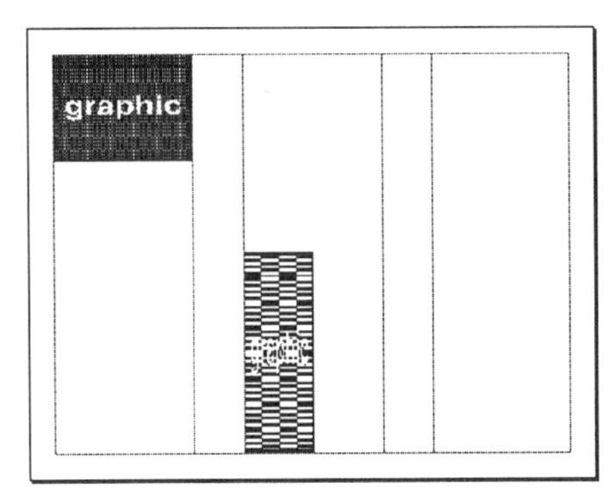

4) *PLACE TEXT ON PAGE 1*

a. Click on the page 1 icon to view page 1. Place GENERIC.TXT starting at the top-left corner of the left column. This will be the second panel the reader sees and the text should begin here.
b. Roll up the bottom windowshade handle of the text block until it is just above the graphic:

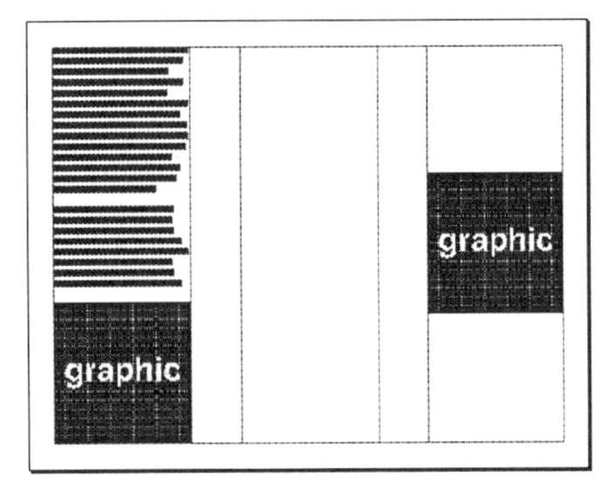

c. Click once on the red triangle in the bottom windowshade handle to load the hidden text into the pointer. The Pointer tool changes to the loaded Text pointer.

5) *PLACE TEXT ON PAGE 2*

a. Click on the page 2 icon to view page 2. Place the text from the loaded Text pointer in the left panel starting just under the graphic.
b. Continue placing the text into the second column, rolling the bottom windowshade handle up to just above the narrow graphic. Click on the red windowshade handle to load the Pointer tool.
c. Place the text from the loaded Text pointer over the narrow graphic, creating another text block in the second column. Resize the text block using the corner handles to fit the blank space next to the narrow graphic. Again click on the red windowshade handle to load the Pointer tool.

d. Place the remaining text in the third column:

6) *MAKE A TITLE ON THE FRONT PANEL*

a. Click on the page 1 icon to view page 1. With the Text pointer, place an insertion point in the panel on the far right. This is the front panel of the brochure.
b. Type `The Title` and change the text to 36 point Helvetica bold. If you do not have Helvetica, use Arial or another sans serif font. Center the text and move it to just above the graphic.

7) *INDICATE THE MAILING AREA*

The middle panel will be the back of the brochure when it is folded, and it is the area where the mailing label and stamp will go. To indicate that this is the mailing area, you will put a label in this panel that is rotated in the direction the address and mailing information will face.

a. In the middle panel, type `mailing area` and change it to 24 point Helvetica italic. Center the text and move it to about halfway down the column.
b. Select the text block with the Pointer tool, then choose the Rotation tool from the Toolbox (). Move the starburst over the "g" in the words "mailing area".
c. Drag the starburst to the right to draw a handle, then continue to drag in a circular motion. Release the mouse button when the text is facing the left panel (the rotating handle will be pointing down). If the text is not facing to the left or is not straight, rotate it again in the same manner.

<u>Check</u> - Your pages should be similar to:

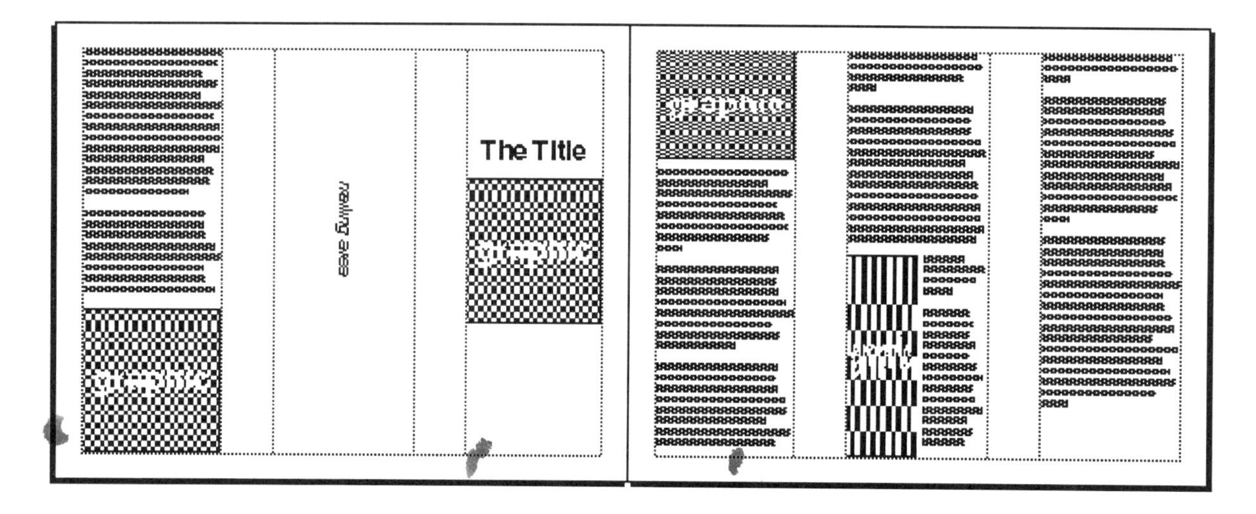

8) SAVE AND PRINT THE PUBLICATION

Save the publication and print a copy. After the file has been printed, Close the publication.

9) FOLD THE BROCHURE

Print the publication and put the two sheets of paper back to back. Place them on the table so that the inside of the brochure faces you, right side up. Fold the right side panel in, then the left panel just as you did in Practice 3. The front of the brochure should be on the cover.

6.10 Elements of a Newsletter

All newsletters, regardless of how they are folded or bound, have certain elements in common. Each has a cover page, consisting of a *masthead*, some text, and graphics. A masthead is the section at the top of the cover page that contains the title and other publication information. Aside from the masthead, the amount of text and graphics on the cover page can vary. Some fancy newsletters resembles magazines with glossy, color covers with a photo, the masthead, and two or three phrases called *teasers* that give a glimpse of the key articles in that issue:

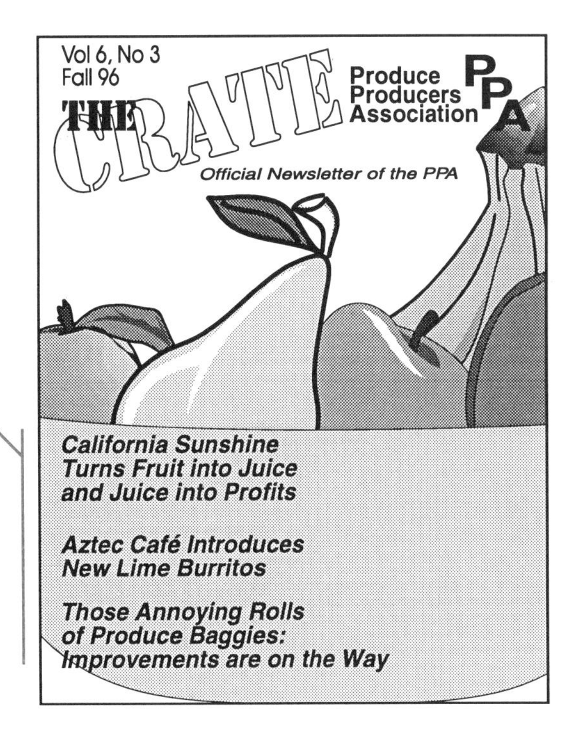

Some newsletters look more like magazines

Only newsletters with a large budget are so deluxe, most are not as fancy. Usually, there is a masthead and the text of at least one story, with graphics, on the cover page:

Vol 6, No 3
Fall 96

THE CRATE

Produce Producers Association — PPA

Official Newsletter of the PPA

California Sunshine Profits are Up

Dolor sit amet, consectetuer adipiscing elit, sed diam non ummy nibh euismod tincidunt ut laoreet volutpat.

Ut wisi enim ad minim veniam, quis nostrud exerci ulorper suscipit lobortis sequat. Duis eu feugiat nulla facilisis at vero eros et accumsan et iusto odio dignissim qui blandit praesent l suscipit lobortis sequat. Duis eu feugiat nulla facilisis at vero eros et accumsan et iusto odio dignissim qui blandit upt te feugait nulla facilisi.

Lorem ipsum dolor sit amet, concing elit, sed diam nonummy nibh euismod tincidunt ut laoreet dolore magna aliquam erat volutpat. Lorem ipsum dolor si dolor volutpat ut wisi vedolor t ampat. Duis autem vel eum iriure vt iusto odio dign badit praes lum zzril delenit augue duis dolore te feugait nulla facilisi.

Lorem ipsum dolor sit amet, consectetuer adipiscing elit, sed diam nonummy nibh euismod tunt ut laopat. Lorem ipsum dolor sit amet, consectetuer adipiscing elit, sed diam nonummy nibh euismod tincidunt ut laoreet erat volutpat.

Ut wisi enim ad minim veniam, quis nostrud exe ipsum dolor ut wisi vena corpolle lor wisi dolor veniat corpus magnus ut wisi vena crearci tation ullamcorper suscipit lobortis nisl ut aliquip ex ea commodo consequat.

Dolor sit amet, consectetuer adipiscing elit, sed diam euism sit ut wisi vena corper utod tincidunt ut laoreet volutpat. Ut wisi enim ad min psu adipiscing elit, sed diam nonu mmy nibh euismod tinpat.

——— *Sylvia Peartridge*

Aztec Café Introduces Fresh Lime Burritos

Dolor sit amet, consectetuer adipiscing elit, sed diam non ummy nibh euismod tincidunt ut laoreet volutpat.

Ut wisi enim ad minim veniam, quis nostrud exerci ulorper suscipit lobortis sequat. Duis e at vero eros et accumsan et iusto odio dit l suscipit lobortis sequat. Duis umsan et nulla facilisi.

Lorem ipsum dolor sit amet, concing elit, sed diam nonummy nibh euismod tincidunt ut laoreet dolore magna aliquam erat volutpat. Lorem ipsum dolor sit ampat. Duis autem vel eum iriure vel illum dolore eu feugiat nulla facilisis at vero eros et accumsan et iusto odio dign badit praes lum zzril delenit augue duis dolore te feugait nulla facilisi.

Lorem ipsum dolor sit amet, consectetuer adipiscing elit, sed diam nonummy nibh euismod tunt ut laopat. Lorem ipsum dolor sit amet, consectetuer adipiscing elit, sed diam nonummy nibh euismod tincidunt ut laoreet erat volutpat.

Ut wisi enim ad minim veniam, quis nostrud exerci tation ullamcorper suscipit lobortis nisl ut aliquip ex ea commodo consequat.

Dolor sit amet, consectetuer adipiscing elit, sed diam euismod tincidunt ut laoreet volutpat. Ut wisi enim ad minim veniam, quis nostrud ex sequat. Duis eu feugiat nulla facilisis at vero eros.

——— *Ned Peachleton*

In This Issue:

Garble lorem gooba..2
Jooler po Yuter........3
Dolor ipsum............3
Chell.......................4
Rewfrol towe...........4

Most newsletters have stories right on the cover

For all newsletters, fancy or plain, the masthead is one of the most important design elements. It sets the tone for the whole publication and must therefore be appropriate to the purpose and audience. Customarily, a masthead includes at least the title of the newsletter, the name and logo of the organization producing it, the date of publication, and a volume number:

The masthead contains a great deal of important information

A masthead can be thought of as a visual signature. It makes a newsletter stand out from the other publications that find their way onto the desks or into the mailboxes of busy people.

While a masthead appears only once, a logo can appear on many pages. The logo identifies the publication with a particular organization or company; it is therefore usually best to show the logo in several places. However, be consistent with the use of the logo.

6

The body of the newsletter is composed of text and graphics that convey the publication's purpose. A common element associated with newsletters is a *sidebar*, which is a narrow column placed next to a story that contains related information. Another common element is the *credit box* that includes circulation information, names of contributing writers, copyright information, etc. The credit box is sometimes also called the masthead. It is customarily placed in the body of the newsletter within the first few pages.

Each individual story within the body of the newsletter may have features that are specific to newsletters and newspapers:

Aztec Café Introduces Fresh Lime Burritos

by Ned Peachleton

Lorem ipsum dolor sit amet, concing elit.

Dolor sit amet, consec tetuer adipiscing elit, sed diam non ummy nibh euismod tincidunt ut laoreet volutpat.

Ut wisi enim ad minim veniam, quis nostrud exe rci ulorper sus cipit lob ortis sequat. Du is e at vero eros et accumsan et iusto odio dit l suscipit lobortis sequat. Duis ipsup vena enimull msan et nulla facilisi.

Lorem ipsum dolor sit amet, concing elit, sed diam nonummy nibh euismod tincidunt ut laoreet dolore magna aliq uam erat volutpat. Lorem ipsum dolor sit ampat. Duis autem vel eum iriure vel illum at vero eros et accumsan et iusto odio dign badit praes lum zzril delenit augue duis dolore te feugait nulla facilisi.

Lorem ipsum dolor sit amet, consectetuer adipiscing elit, sed diam nonummy nibh euismod tunt ut laopat. Lorem ipsum dolor sit amet, consectetuer adipiscing elit, sed diam nonummy

duis dolore te feugait nulla facilisi

nibh euis diam nonummy mod tincidunt ut laoreet exerci tatidolore ummy gooloron ullamcorper suscipit lobortis dolor ut wisi nisl ut aliquip. ■

Newsletter and newspaper stories have many special features

A *by-line* is the identification of who wrote a story—usually the author's name. The by-line appears either at the beginning or at the end of the story. The type is usually the same font as the text, italic or bold (not regular), and about the same size as the text. A *kicker* is an opening phrase that appears just before the text in larger type. It is usually a lead-in sentence, meaning the reader naturally continues on to the first sentence of the text. The kicker is designed to grab the reader's attention, hold their interest, and give them a better idea of what the story is about. A *pull quote* is a copy of a phrase from the story that is set in much larger type than the text, yet is located in or near the text block. The pull quote is usually set in between two rules to separate it from the body text. Pull quotes are similar to kickers in that they are a way to grab the reader's attention. An *end sign* is a dingbat or other graphical indicator that is placed at the end of each story, usually right after the last punctuation in the last sentence, signaling the reader that they do not need to look for more text. It can be either a generic dingbat such as a box or diamond, or a small graphic related to the purpose or audience, such as part of a logo or an object.

As with any publication, it is important to plan ahead and design your newsletter before you actually place text and graphics in PageMaker. A well-planned newsletter reads smoothly and looks appealing to potential readers.

6.11 Design for Newsletters

6

The basic design guidelines covered in Chapter Five apply to all documents. As with any publication, newsletters have a few special design considerations:

Appropriateness

The contents of a newsletter are targeted to one audience, therefore it helps to have the layout and other graphical concerns appropriate to that same audience. Newsletters can have complicated layouts with many sizes and shapes of fonts, text, and graphics, so consider the appropriateness of each element you incorporate into your design.

Balance

In Chapter Five you learned that tension on a balanced page can interest the reader. In a newsletter tension is important because with many levels and types of information, a perfectly balanced page layout would deter the reader from even beginning to explore that page. To help create a natural balance and tension on a newsletter page, use an odd number of columns. The odd number has a small amount of tension to begin with, and from this will usually follow a balanced tension between all the elements on the page.

Focus and Flow

In a complex publication such as a newsletter, the focus and flow of each page must be fine tuned because of the multiple graphics and text blocks. If the focus and flow is not carefully planned, the page can appear too busy. Be sure that each page has a focal point (an element that appropriately catches your eye first) which is usually a main story heading or a graphic. Then check that the eye travels (flows) from the focal point around the page to end at the least important element.

Consistency

Used consistently throughout a newsletter, visual cues such as end signs and company logos help the reader quickly identify parts such as story endings and sections. However, be careful not to use the same visual cue for two different newsletter elements. For example, using a grey shaded box behind any text will set the text apart from the surrounding stories. But if you also use a grey shaded box to highlight a headline, the reader may think the headline and shaded text are related. Keep the visual cues as unique from each other as possible.

The illustration on the next page shows the cover page and second page of a newsletter before and after a thorough re-designing:

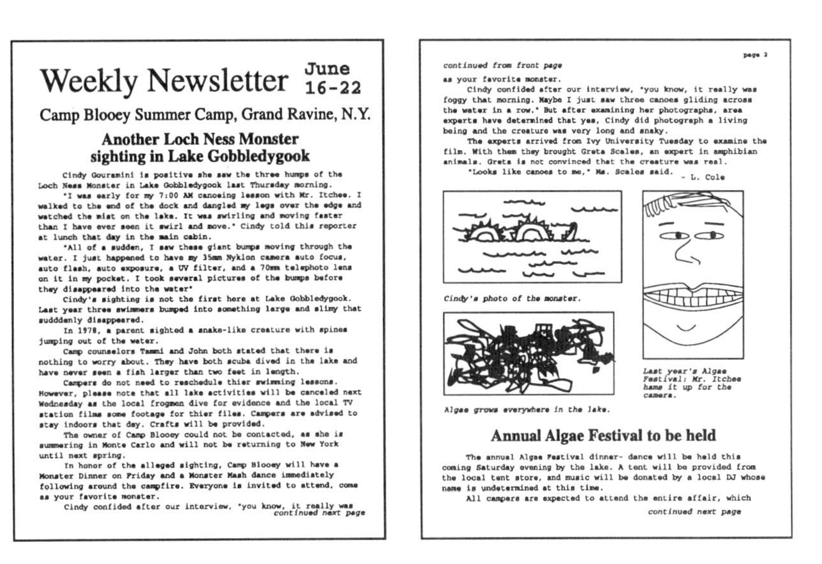

Weekly Newsletter June 16-22

Camp Blooey Summer Camp, Grand Ravine, N.Y.

Another Loch Ness Monster sighting in Lake Gobbledygook

Cindy Gouramini is positive she saw the three humps of the Loch Ness Monster in Lake Gobbledygook last Thursday morning.

"I was early for my 7:00 AM canoeing lesson with Mr. Itchee. I walked to the end of the dock and dangled my legs over the edge and watched the mist on the lake. It was swirling and moving faster than I have ever seen it swirl and move." Cindy told this reporter at lunch that day in the main cabin.

"All of a sudden, I saw these giant bumps moving through the water. I just happened to have my 35mm Nyklon camera auto focus, auto flash, auto exposure, a UV filter, and a 70mm telephoto lens on it in my pocket. I took several pictures of the bumps before they disappeared into the water"

Cindy's sighting is not the first here at Lake Gobbledygook. Last year three swimmers bumped into something large and slimy that sudddenly disappeared.

In 1978, a parent sighted a snake-like creature with spines jumping out of the water.

Camp counselors Tammi and John both stated that there is nothing to worry about. They have both scuba dived in the lake and have never seen a fish larger than two feet in length.

Campers do not need to reschedule thier swimming lessons. However, please note that all lake activities will be canceled next Wednesday as the local frogmen dive for evidence and the local TV station films some footage for thier files. Campers are advised to stay indoors that day. Crafts will be provided.

The owner of Camp Blooey could not be contacted, as she is summering in Monte Carlo and will not be returning to New York until next spring.

In honor of the alleged sighting, Camp Blooey will have a Monster Dinner on Friday and a Monster Mash dance immediately following around the campfire. Everyone is invited to attend, come as your favorite monster.

Cindy confided after our interview, "you know, it really was

continued next page

page 2

continued from front page

as your favorite monster.

Cindy confided after our interview, "you know, it really was foggy that morning. Maybe I just saw three canoes gliding across the water in a row." But after examining her photographs, area experts have determined that yes, Cindy did photograph a living being and the creature was very long and snaky.

The experts arrived from Ivy University Tuesday to examine the film. With them they brought Greta Scales, an expert in amphibian animals. Greta is not convinced that the creature was real.

"Looks like canoes to me," Ms. Scales said. - L. Cole

Cindy's photo of the monster.

Algae grows everywhere in the lake.

Last year's Algae Festival: Mr. Itchee hams it up for the camera.

Annual Algae Festival to be held

The annual Algae Festival dinner- dance will be held this coming Saturday evening by the lake. A tent will be provided from the local tent store, and music will be donated by a local DJ whose name is undetermined at this time.

All campers are expected to attend the entire affair, which

continued next page

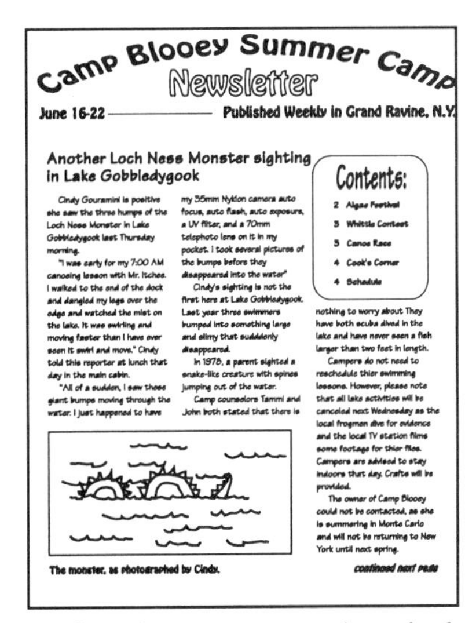

Camp Blooey Summer Camp Newsletter

June 16-22 —— Published Weekly in Grand Ravine, N.Y.

Another Loch Ness Monster sighting in Lake Gobbledygook

Cindy Gouramini is positive she saw the three humps of the Loch Ness Monster in Lake Gobbledygook last Thursday morning.

"I was early for my 7:00 AM canoeing lesson with Mr. Itchee. I walked to the end of the dock and dangled my legs over the edge and watched the mist on the lake. It was swirling and moving faster than I have ever seen it swirl and move." Cindy told this reporter at lunch that day in the main cabin.

"All of a sudden, I saw these giant bumps moving through the water. I just happened to have my 35mm Nyklon camera auto focus, auto flash, auto exposure, a UV filter, and a 70mm telephoto lens on it in my pocket. I took several pictures of the bumps before they disappeared into the water"

Cindy's sighting is not the first here at Lake Gobbledygook. Last year three swimmers bumped into something large and slimy that sudddenly disappeared.

In 1978, a parent sighted a snake-like creature with spines jumping out of the water.

Camp counselors Tammi and John both stated that there is nothing to worry about. They have both scuba dived in the lake and have never seen a fish larger than two feet in length.

Campers do not need to reschedule thier swimming lessons. However, please note that all lake activities will be canceled next Wednesday as the local frogmen dive for evidence and the local TV station films some footage for thier files. Campers are advised to stay indoors that day. Crafts will be provided.

The owner of Camp Blooey could not be contacted, as she is summering in Monte Carlo and will not be returning to New York until next spring.

Contents:

2 Algae Festival
3 Whittle Contest
3 Canoe Race
4 Cook's Corner
4 Schedule

The monster, as photographed by Cindy.

continued next page

Camp Blooey - page 2

continued from front page

In honor of the alleged sighting, Camp Blooey will have a Monster dinner on Friday and a Monster dance immediately following around the campfire. Everyone is invited to attend, come as your favorite monster.

Cindy confided after our interview, "you know, it really was fogy that morning. Maybe I just saw three canoes gliding across the water in a row." But after examining her photos, area experts have determined that yes, Cindy did photograph a living being and the creature was very long and snaky.

The experts arrived from Ivy University Tuesday to examine the film. With them they brought Greta Scales, an expert in amphibian animals. Greta is not convinced that the creature was real.

"Looks like canoes to me," Ms. Scales said. — L. Kole

Annual Algae Festival to be held

The annual Algae Festival dinner- dance will be held this coming Saturday evening by the lake. A tent will be provided from the local tent store, and music will be donated by a local DJ whose name is undetermined at this time.

All campers are expected to attend the entire affair, which begins with chips and dip appetizers at 6:00 P.M. Dinner will be buffet style, with tacos and spaghetti as the main course choices. Scalloped potatoes and rutabaga will be the vegetable choice, and dessert is yellow cake.

Dress is formal, so all campers must wear thier green uniforms with shined shoes, buttons, and medals. Absolutely no other jewelry allowed. Gloves are optional.

Prizes will be awarded to the following categories: Best Lindy, Best Jitterbug, Best Squirm, Best Woodchopper's Ball, Best Twist. All these categories refer to individual dances. The prizes will consist of: First prize, a large pizza and a bottle of soda, second prize, a triple-decker submarine sandwich, third prize, a birch bark canoe. Food prizes have been donated by SuperSubs. — W. [illegible]

Last year's Algae Festival: Mr. Itchee hams it up for the camera.

Algae grows everywhere in the lake.

Before (top two pages) and after (bottom two pages) a re-design

Notice the difference between these two newsletters. One simple modification, such as the change here from a one-column format to a three-column format, can completely alter the appearance of a document. The overall look of the newsletter is changed to a more professional, readable document. The top newsletter's cover page is one big block of text. Even the masthead and centered headline blend into the long lines of text. In fact, it is difficult to tell where the masthead ends and where the headline begins. The bottom newsletter has a three column layout with a left-justified headline. With the addition of a table of contents and graphic it is much more inviting to read.

The fonts used in these newsletters illustrate clearly the difference an appropriate font can make. The top newsletter has a plain masthead in a serif font. In the bottom newsletter, the masthead is in a fun typeface that resembles the signs found in parks and campgrounds. This is appropriate for a summer camp newsletter. The text and headlines have been changed to a sans-serif typeface that resembles handwriting, appropriate for the light reading subjects found in a summer camp newsletter.

It is easy to see how unbalanced the two pages of the top newsletter are compared to each other. One page is completely text, while the other has a grouping of photos that is flanked in by two areas of text, above and below. Here it is difficult to tell which photograph is associated with which story. In the bottom newsletter, the photos are more evenly distributed between the two pages. The photo that belongs with the cover story has been moved to the cover, and the two photos on the second pages have been rearranged so that they are not clumped together. Notice the rule on the second page that separates the end of the cover story from the other story and photos. Also, by rearranging the elements so that they balance just enough, the focus and flow of the reader's eye on the pages is correctly placed.

Practice 5

In this Practice you create a newsletter by using Column guides and Ruler guides to make a grid, then placing the masthead, text, and graphics in the publication. Start Windows and PageMaker if you have not already done so.

1) START A NEW PUBLICATION

a. From the File menu, select the New command. The Page setup dialog box is shown.
b. Type in a 2 for the Number of pages and select OK to create the new publication.

2) CREATE 3 COLUMNS ON THE MASTER PAGES

a. Click on one of the Master-page icons in the bottom-left corner of the screen. The Master Pages are displayed.
b. From the Layout menu, select the Column guides command. The Column guides dialog box is displayed.
c. Type 3 for the Number of columns and select OK. Each of the Master Pages are displayed with three columns of equal width and two 0.167 inch gutters between the columns.

3) ENHANCE THE GRID WITH RULER GUIDES

Using the Pointer tool, create horizontal Ruler guides at these locations on the vertical Ruler:

1.25 inches	5.5 inches
2.75 inches	6.0 inches
3.25 inches	

4) VIEW THE COMPLETED GRID AND CREATE THE MASTHEAD

a. Click on the page 1 icon at the bottom of the screen. Page 1 is displayed. Notice how the Column and Ruler guides that you created on the right Master Page also appear here.
b. With the Text pointer place an insertion point in the top margin. Type `Ivy University Newsletter`, highlight the words, and change the size to 60 point.
c. With the Pointer tool, move the text block down so that it fits between the top Margin guide and the Ruler guide at the 2.75 inch mark.

6

5) *PLACE THE GRAPHIC ON PAGE 1*

Place GRAPHIC.WMF on page 1. Align the left side of the graphic with the left guide of the second column. Align the top of the graphic with the Ruler guide at the 5.5 inch mark on the vertical Ruler. Stretch the graphic horizontally to fit completely across the second and third columns.

6) *PLACE THE TEXT ON PAGE 1*

a. Place GENERIC.TXT starting in the left column at the 3.25 inch Ruler guide.
b. Continue the story to the second column, using the 3.25 inch Ruler guide. In the second column you will need to roll the windowshade handle up to the Ruler guide at the top of the graphic, so that the text appears above the graphic, then continue placing the text below the graphic. Do the same for the third column.
c. When you reach the end of the third column, you will have text left to place (as indicated by a red triangle in the windowshade handle). Ignore the leftover text; we will pretend that the first story exactly fits on the front page. Remember to align the top of the upper text blocks with the Ruler guide at the 3.25 inch mark.
d. With the Text tool, type `This is the cover story headline` in 28 point Helvetica Bold above the story and below the Masthead (between the 2.75 inch and 3.25 inch Ruler guides). Resize the text block to fit across all three columns and align the bottom of the text block with the Ruler guide at the 3.25 inch mark. Align the text to the left margin.

Check - Your page should be similar to:

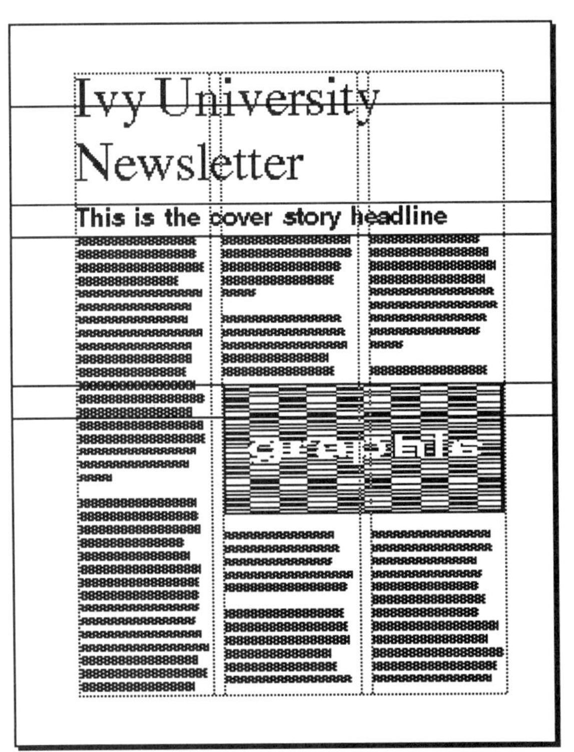

7) *PLACE THE GRAPHICS ON PAGE 2*

a. Display page 2 on the screen. Place another copy of GRAPHIC.WMF in the first column, aligning the top of the graphic with the Ruler guide at the 1.25 inch mark. Stretch it horizontally to fit across the column.
b. Place GRAPHIC.WMF again, this time in the bottom of the center column. Stretch it to fit across the column.

8) PLACE THE TEXT ON PAGE 2

a. Place GENERIC.TXT onto page 2 starting below the upper-left graphic. Leave about one line of space under the graphic. Fill the column with text.
b. Continue the story to the second column, aligning the top of the text block with 1.25 inch Ruler guide. Extend that text block to the Ruler guide at the 5.5 inch mark on the vertical ruler. Do the same for the third column, ending the story at the 5.5 inch Ruler guide. Ignore the leftover text; we will pretend that the story exactly fits.
c. Type `A story of interest to the readers` across the top of the page. Make the headline 28 point Helvetica bold. Resize the text block to fit across all three columns and align the bottom of the text block with the Ruler guide at 1.25 inches. Align the text to the left margin.
d. Place GENERIC.TXT again onto page 2 as the second story, starting in the second column at the Ruler guide at the 6 inch mark. Roll up the windowshade handle to just above the graphic, fitting the text block to the space above the graphic.
e. Continue the story to the second column. Align the top of the text block in the third column with the 6 inch Ruler guide. End the story at the bottom margin. Ignore the leftover text; we will pretend that the story exactly fits.
f. Type `Here is a small story`, in 28 point Helvetica bold, across the top of the second story. Resize the text block to fit across both columns and align the bottom of the text block with the Ruler guide at 6 inches. Align the text to the left guide of the second column.

Check - Your page should be similar to:

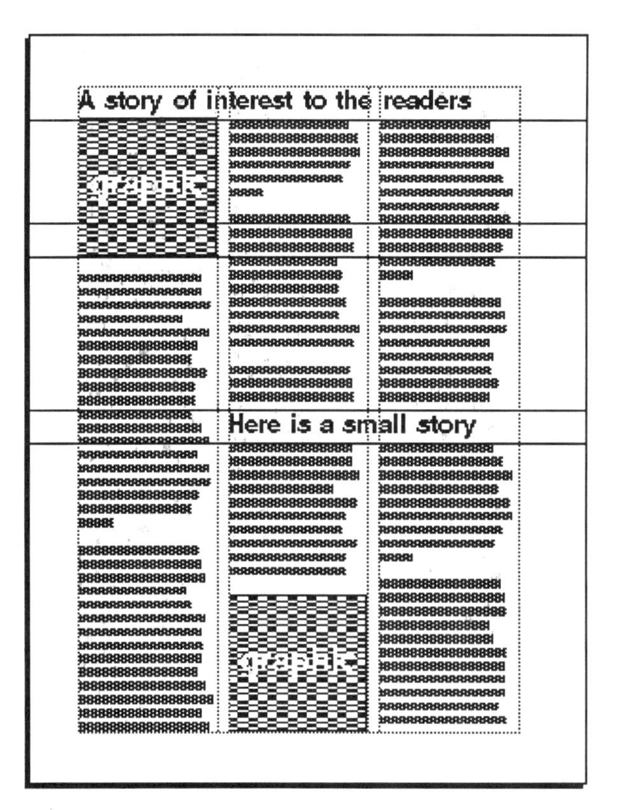

9) SAVE, PRINT, AND CLOSE THE PUBLICATION

a. Save the publication as NEWSLETT.
b. Print a copy of NEWSLETT.PM5.
c. Close NEWSLETT.PM5.

6

6.12 Using Drawing Tools in Publications

Designs often include rules (lines), shaded boxes, or outlines of various shapes. The drawing tools that PageMaker provides can help create such special elements.

Rules can be important in a design. For brochures, rules can separate topics or add emphasis to titles. In newsletters they are used to separate columns of text or to strengthen the weight of a headline:

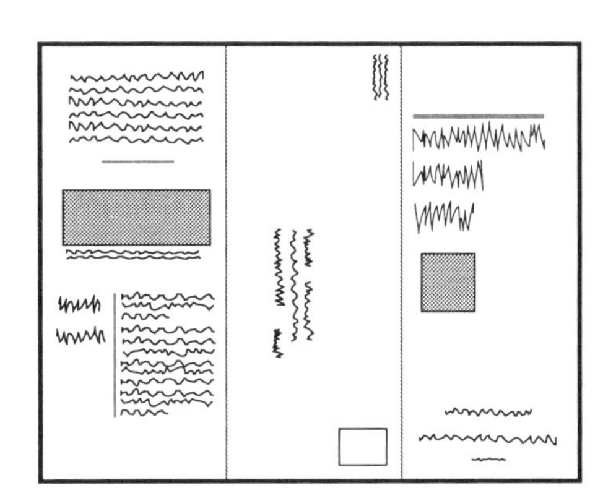
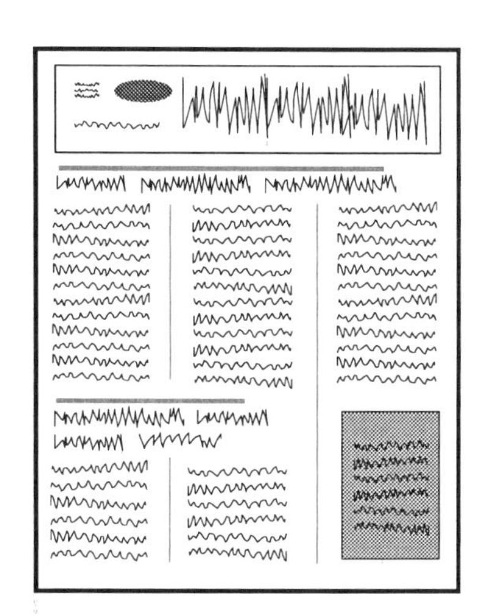

Publication designs benefit from the use of rules

Geometric shapes can also enhance designs. Shaded boxes (rectangles) and ovals of different sizes and shades can be used to highlight sections of a publication. For example, a table of contents on the cover page of a newsletter might have a light grey box behind it, acting as a frame to set it apart from the rest of the text:

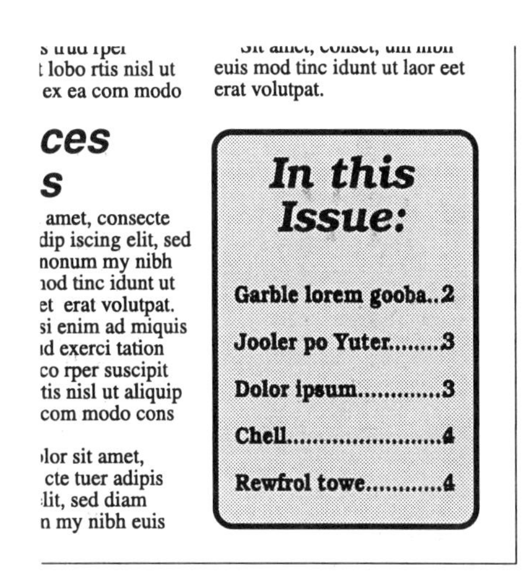

A small table of contents looks more important and is easier to find on a page when it is highlighted by a shaded box

When text is framed by a shaded shape, it acts as a graphic element in the page design. The shading darkens the area enough that it should be treated as a graphic, and positioned on the page so that it balances with the other graphics and does not compete for the focus or interrupt the flow of the reader's eye around the page.

Shaded boxes are often used in the design of a masthead. The shaded box sets the masthead off from the rest of the page and gives the appearance of greater importance. It also serves to unite all the individual parts of the masthead into a well-defined single unit:

A shaded box defines the boundaries of a masthead

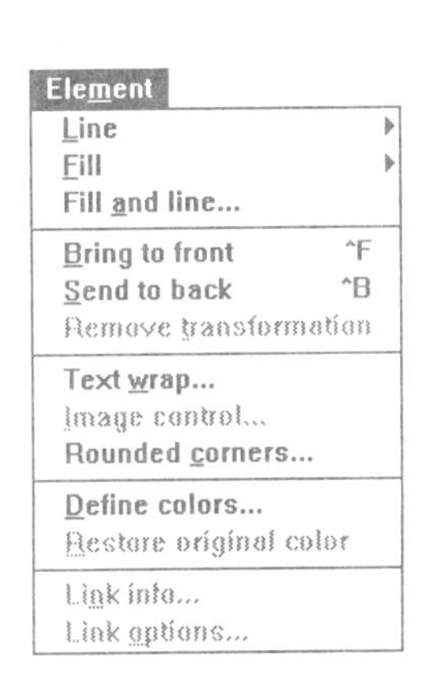

When working with graphics, it is sometimes necessary to use two other Element commands: Bring to front and Send to back. When there is more than one text block or graphic occupying the same space on a page, the elements are stacked on top of each other. Sometimes an object that should be in the front is behind another element, which covers or obscures it:

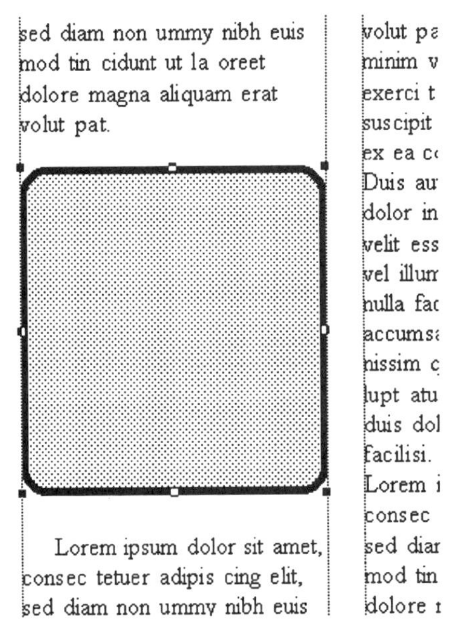

This shaded box is stacked above the text

When this occurs, the text is obscured and only the shaded box can be seen on the page. If the text block is selected, then the Bring to front command (`Ctrl+F`) moves the text block in front of any other elements, in this case over the shaded box. Or, to move the selected box to the back, the Send to back command can be selected from the Element menu (`Ctrl+B`) and the shaded box will be behind the text:

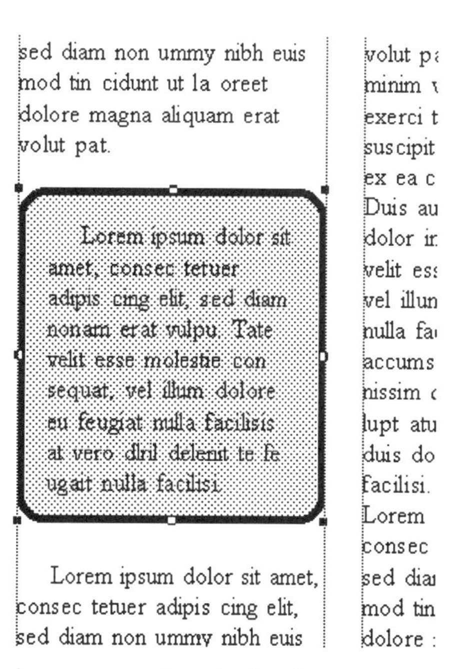

The shaded box has been moved to the back, exposing the text

6.13 The Rounded Corners Command

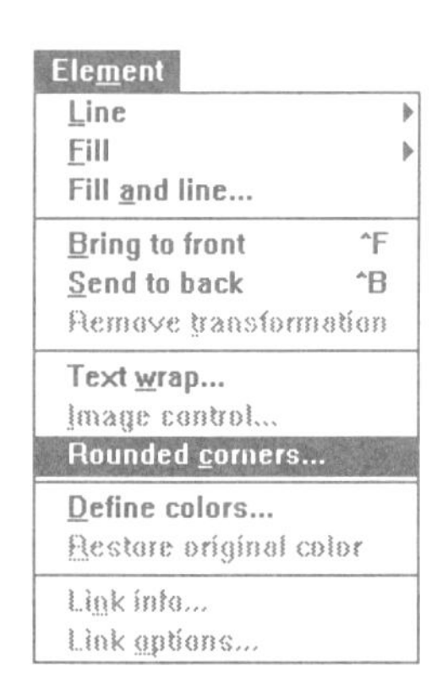

To customize the corners of rectangles, PageMaker has a Rounded corners command, accessible from the Element menu. When the Rounded corners command is selected, the Rounded corners dialog box appears with six choices of various corners:

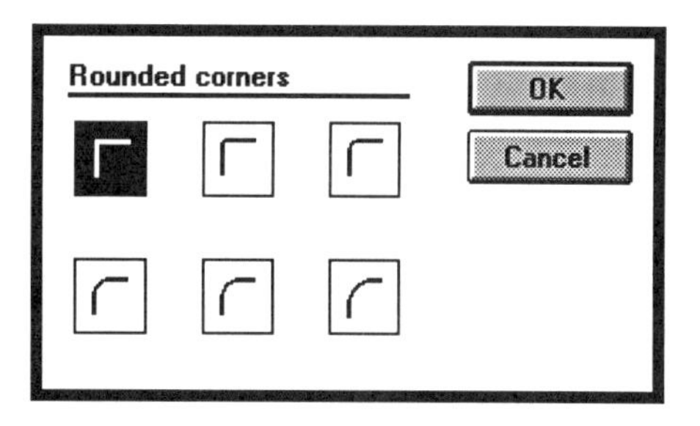

The Rounded corners dialog box

You can apply any of the six choices to a selected object. It is important to have an object selected when you first choose the Rounded corners command. If no object is selected, then the corner you choose in the dialog box immediately becomes the default. This means that every rectangle you draw afterwards will have that kind of corners.

Practice 6

In this Practice you create a shaded box with rounded corners and use it to emphasize a section of the brochure you created in Practice 4. Start Windows and PageMaker if you have not already done so.

6

1) OPEN THE BROCHURE.PM5 PUBLICATION

2) RE-FORMAT THE TEXT IN THE PARAGRAPH

a. Click on the page 2 icon at the bottom of the screen to display page 2 if it is not already shown.
b. Place an insertion point in the last paragraph in the third column.
c. From the Type menu, select the Paragraph command. The Paragraph specifications dialog box is displayed.
d. For both the Left and Right Indents, type `0.25` and select OK to make the formatting changes. The paragraph is indented a quarter of a inch from the left and the right.

3) DRAW A FILLED RECTANGLE AROUND THE LAST PARAGRAPH OF TEXT

a. Select the Rectangle tool.
b. Move the cross-hairs to the last paragraph, the bottom paragraph in the third column.
c. Start with the cross-hairs just above the last paragraph, on the left column guide. Drag the cross-hairs down and to the right. Release the mouse button when the rectangle extends across to the right column guide and ends below the paragraph.

4) ROUND THE CORNERS ON THE RECTANGLE

a. The rectangle should still be selected from the previous step. From the Element menu, select the Rounded corners command. The Rounded corners dialog box is displayed.
b. Select the corner with the most roundness (bottom row, far right), then select OK to make the change to the rectangle. The corners of the rectangle are now rounded.

5) FILL THE RECTANGLE WITH 20% BLACK

a. From the Element menu, select the Fill command. The Fill submenu is displayed.
b. Select 20%. The rectangle is filled with grey (20% black) and obscures text below.

6) SEND THE RECTANGLE TO THE BACK

From the Element menu, select the Send to back command. The Rectangle is moved to the back, behind the paragraph text.

7) BRING THE RECTANGLE TO THE FRONT AND BACK AGAIN

a. From the Element menu, select the Bring to front command. The Rectangle is moved to the front again, and the paragraph text is hidden.
b. From the Element menu, select the Send to back command. The Rectangle is moved to the back layer and the paragraph text is visible again.

Check - Your page should be similar to:

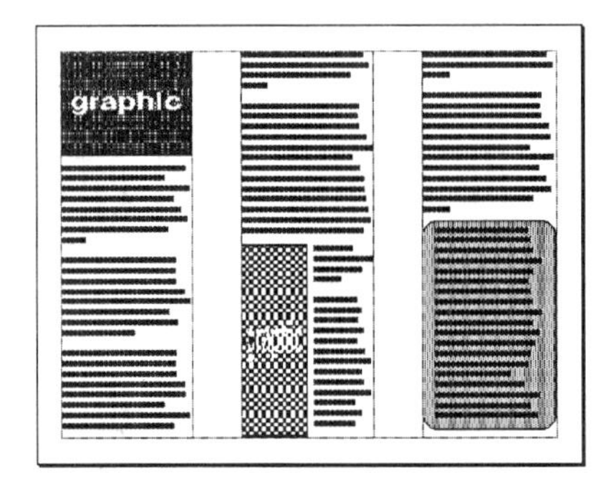

8) *SAVE AND PRINT THE PUBLICATION*

9) *FOLD THE BROCHURE*

a. Place the two pages back-to-back, with the printed sides facing outwards on both sides and lay them on a table.
b. Fold the brochure in the same manner as you did in Practices 3 and 4.
c. Close the publication.

6.14 Using Running Headers and Footers

Running headers and *footers* are text and graphics that appear in the margins of all the pages in a publication. Exceptions to where they would appear are the cover page and sometimes the last page. Headers refer to the contents of the top margin, while footers refer to the contents of the bottom margin.

Headers and footers can contain text blocks, graphics, or both. Depending on the specific purpose of the header or footer you may wish to have just a section name and page number, a logo and page number, or just a logo. If the purpose is to identify the publication, then the page number can appear with either the logo of the organization, the title of the publication as it appears in the masthead, or with the publication date or issue information:

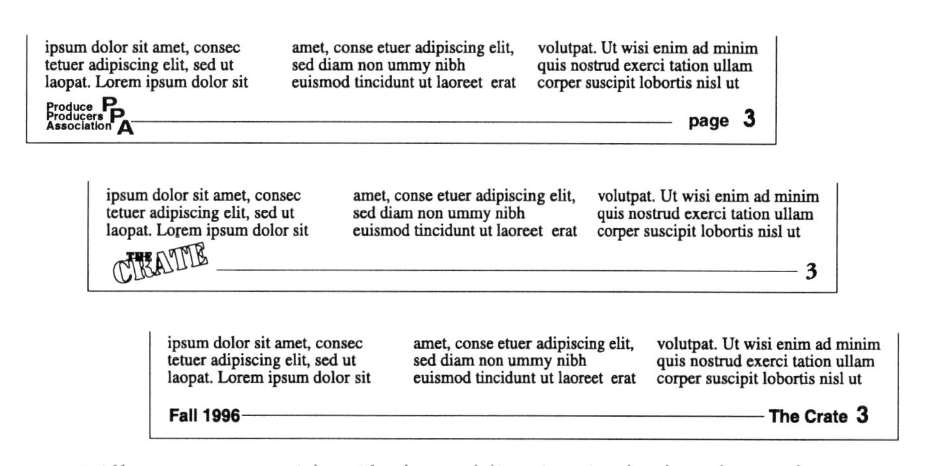

Different ways to identify the publication in the header or footer

Notice in the examples above that a simple rule has been included in the footer. Rules in the header or footer can add a framing effect to the page, enhancing the body of the page, yet alerting the reader that there is information in the margin.

Another purpose the header or footer may have is to identify a section of the newsletter, or the topic of a page:

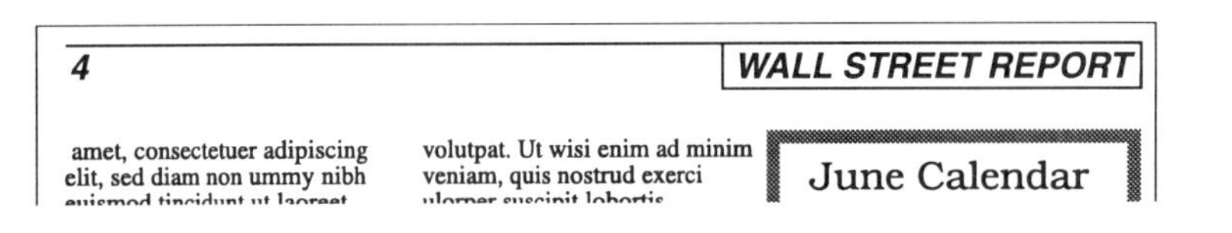

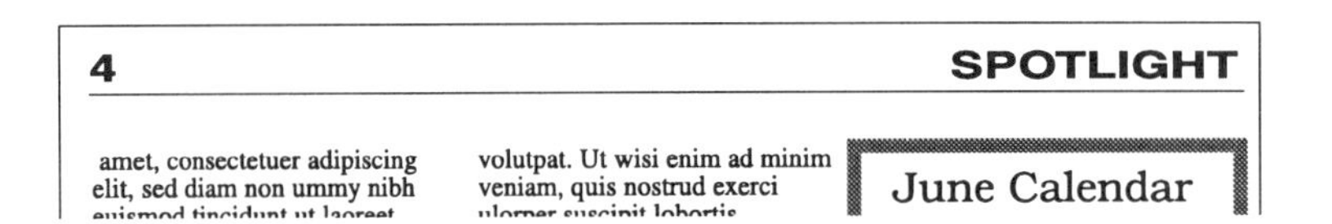

Headers can identify sections for the reader

Like any repetitive element, it is important to keep headers and footers consistent throughout a document. In PageMaker, maintaining consistency in the headers and footers is easy by using the Master Pages. Anything that is placed on the Master Pages appears throughout the document.

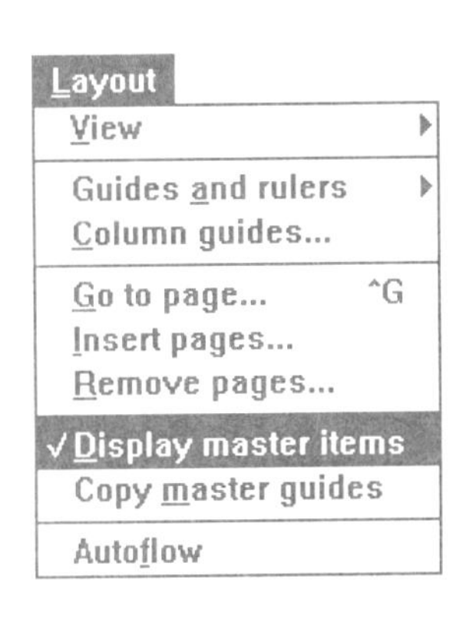

There are places, such as the cover page, where you may not want the Master items to appear. The Display master items command from the Layout menu clears the Master items from any page or facing pages that are currently displayed. Removing Master items from a page does not affect the rest of the publication.

Page numbers are usually placed in the header or footer of a publication. PageMaker has an automatic numbering process that uses *page-number markers*. By placing markers on the Master Pages, the page number is automatically calculated and appears in the same location on every page. Page-number markers are placed on a Master Page by placing an insertion point with the Text pointer, and then pressing `Ctrl+Shift+3`.

The page-number marker will look different, depending on which page it is on. On the left Master Page it appears as LM and on the right Master Page it appears as RM:

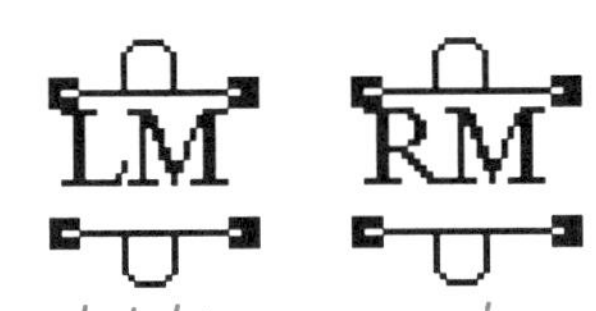

Left and right page-number markers

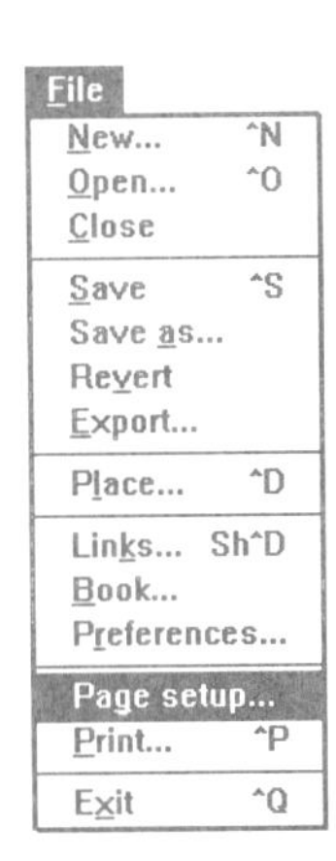

The page-number markers can be manipulated just like text; you can change the font, size, leading, alignment, etc. from the Type menu. The style of the actual numeral that appears on the page can be changed using the Page numbering dialog box, chosen from the Page setup dialog box from the File menu. Arabic, Roman or alphabetic numbering schemes can be selected:

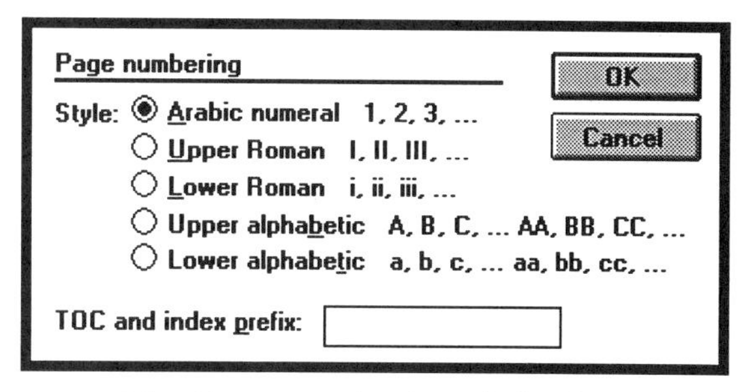

The Page numbering dialog box

Page numbers are just a part of what can go in headers and footers. Any information to help the reader is useful, but be careful that keep the headers and footers light enough in weight so that they are in the background of the page. The most important part of the page is the body of the page.

Practice 7

In this Practice you create a header in the newsletter with a page number and a rule. Start Windows and PageMaker if you have not already done so.

1) OPEN THE NEWSLETT.PM5 PUBLICATION

2) DISPLAY THE MASTER PAGES

Click on the Master-page icons at the bottom left corner of the screen. The Master Pages are displayed.

3) PLACE A PAGE-NUMBER MARKER ON THE LEFT MASTER PAGE

a. Zoom in at 75% and scroll over to the top-left corner of the left Master Page.
b. Select the Text pointer and place an insertion point in the first column.
c. Press `Ctrl+Shift+3` to place a page-number marker. Note that the page-number marker is LM, for left marker.
d. Place a vertical Ruler guide on the left Margin guide of the page, and a horizontal Ruler guide at the ⅜ inch mark on the vertical ruler.
e. Use the Pointer tool to select the text block that contains the page-number marker.
f. Move the text block up so that the top windowshade handle is aligned on the horizontal Ruler guide, and the left side of the text block is aligned with the vertical Ruler guide.

4) DRAW A RULE IN THE TOP MARGIN OF THE LEFT MASTER PAGE

a. Use the scroll bars to display as much of top margin of the left Master Page as you can. Place a vertical Ruler guide on the right Margin guide of the page.
b. Select the Straight line tool. Starting just to the right of the page-number marker, draw a line across the top of the page, ending at the vertical Ruler guide. The rule should be about even with the middle of the "M" in the page-number marker.

Check - Your top margin should be similar to:

LM

5) PLACE A PAGE-NUMBER MARKER ON THE RIGHT MASTER PAGE

a. Scroll over to the top right corner of the right Master Page.
b. Select the Text pointer and place an insertion point in the third column.
c. Press `Ctrl+Shift+3` to place a page-number marker. Note that the page-number marker is RM, for right marker.
d. Place an insertion point in the page-number marker and format it as right aligned.
e. Place a vertical Ruler guide on the right Margin guide of the page.
f. Use the Pointer tool to select the text block that contains the page-number marker.
g. Move the text block up so that the top windowshade handle is aligned on the horizontal Ruler guide, and the right side of the text block is aligned with the vertical Ruler guide.

6) DRAW A RULE IN THE TOP MARGIN OF THE RIGHT MASTER PAGE

a. Use the scroll bars to display as much of top margin of the right Master Page as you can. Place a vertical Ruler guide on the left Margin guide of the page.
b. Select the Straight line tool. Starting just to the left of the page-number marker, draw a line across the top of the page, ending at the left vertical Ruler guide. The rule should be about even with the middle of the "R" in the page-number marker.

Check - Your top margin should be similar to:

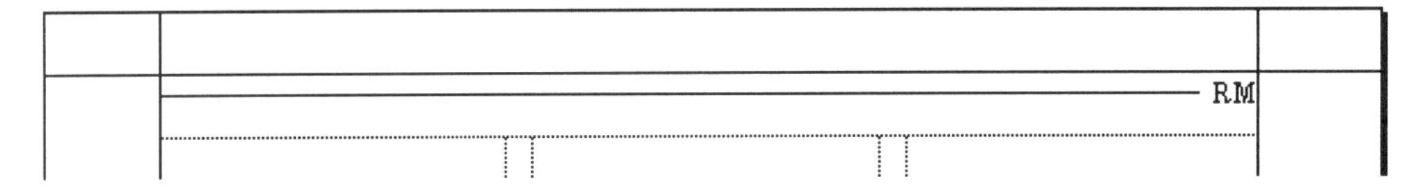

7) VIEW THE HEADER ON PAGE 1

Click on the page 1 icon at the bottom of the screen. Page 1 is displayed. Zoom into the top margin. Notice that the rule appears in the margin, and the number "1" is in the upper-right corner.

8) REMOVE THE HEADER FROM THE COVER PAGE

The cover of a newsletter is page 1 of the publication. However, it is customary to not have items such as the header and footer appear on a newsletter's cover. Therefore you need to remove them from page 1 only.

a. From the Layout menu, choose the Display master items command to deselect it. Note that the header, consisting of a rule and page number, is gone from page 1.
b. From the Layout menu, choose the Display master items command again to select it. The header has reappeared on page 1.
c. Choose the Display master items command once again to deselect it. Note that the header is once again gone from page 1.

9) VIEW THE HEADER ON PAGE 2

Click on the page 2 icon at the bottom of the screen. Page 2 is displayed. Zoom into the top margin. Notice that the rule appears in the margin, and the number "2" is in the upper-left corner.

10) SAVE THE PUBLICATION AND PRINT THE FILE

Chapter Summary

The audience and purpose define the style and presentation of a publication. Brochures and newsletters can be bound in many different ways, including saddle-stitched and perfect bound. Another consideration of any publication is the page size of the end product and the orientation, portrait (tall) or landscape (wide).

The Column guides feature in PageMaker can be used to mark off the margins of individual panels in a folded brochure. When using narrow columns, it is important to consider the column width in conjunction with font size, alignment, and leading. Columns are usually the basis for a grid, which organizes the layouts.

A brochure has many separate design elements, such as a cover page, reply card, indicia, and body. These elements unique to a brochure will influence the design guidelines.

Objects such as text blocks or graphics can be rotated by using the Rotation tool.

A newsletter also has many separate elements, such as a masthead, teasers, pull quotes, by-lines, and kickers. As with any publication, there are design considerations unique to newsletters because of their elements.

PageMaker drawing tools can be used in a publication to create graphical elements such as rules and shaded boxes. The Rounded corners command can be used to vary the degree of roundness in rectangle corners. The Bring to front and Send to back commands move objects occupying the same space on a page above or below each other.

Running headers and footers are text and graphics that appear in the margins of all the pages in a publication, except the cover. By creating any header or footer on the Master Pages, they will automatically appear on every page. Placing page-number markers on the Master Pages will automatically number each page in a publication.

Vocabulary

3-ring binder - A method of binding pages together that involves punching holes in the pages and placing them through three rings.

Bleed - Printing off of the edge of a page.

Body - The main section of a publication, usually consisting of text and graphics.

By-line - The identification of the author of a story.

Cover page - The front page of a publication.

Credit box - A small section located within a publication that includes circulation information, names of contributing writers, editors, and artists, and copyright information.

End sign - A dingbat or other graphical indicator placed at the end of a story, signaling the end of a story.

Footer - See running footer.

Flyer - A sheet of paper, any size, not folded or bound in any way.

Header - See running header.

Indicia - The space on a publication used for mailing purposes, including the return address, mailing label, and postal codes.

Kicker - An opening phrase or lead-in sentence, printed in large type, that appears just before the body text in a story.

Landscape - A page orientation that indicates the paper is viewed more wide than tall. Also called wide.

Masthead - The section at the top of a newsletter's cover page that contains the title and other periodical information.

Orientation - The direction of the page's dimensions, either tall (portrait) or wide (landscape).

Panels - The section of paper that becomes a flat, page-like area when the paper is folded.

Perfect bound - A glued binding that is flat along the spine.

Plastic comb - A binding where the pages are held together by a plastic cylinder with curved, wide teeth.

Portrait - Page orientation where the paper is viewed more tall than wide. Also called tall.

Pull quote - A copy of a phrase from a story that is set in larger type than the body text, and located in or near the text of the story.

Reply card - A self-addressed card, usually with mailing codes that indicate postage paid by addressee, that the reader detaches and returns by mail.

Running footers - Text and graphics that appear in the bottom margins of all the pages in a publication.

Running headers - Text and graphics that appear in the top margins of all the pages in a publication.

Saddle stitch - A method of binding where sheets of paper are sewn or stapled down the center, then folded at the stitching.

Side stapled - A method of binding where sheets of paper are stapled down one side.

Sidebar - A narrow column placed next to a story that contains related information.

Spiral wire - A method of binding where the pages are held together by a spiral wire running through holes along one margin.

Tall - Page orientation that indicates the paper is viewed as Portrait—more tall than wide.

Teasers - Phrases printed on a publication's cover that give a preview of the main articles inside.

6

Title area - Part of a brochure that contains the title or headline.

Wide - Page orientation that indicates the paper is viewed as Landscape—more wide than tall.

Reviews

Sections 6.1 — 6.4

1. a) List four different styles of bindings.
   b) For each of the four binding styles listed, give an example of an actual published document with that binding.

2. List the names and dimensions of three standard sizes of paper.

3. a) What is landscape orientation?
   b) What is portrait orientation?
   c) How do you change the orientation of a publication?

4. Why would you use columns in brochures? In newsletters?

Sections 6.5 — 6.10

5. Would you use double-sided, facing pages when laying out a brochure or newsletter? Why?

6. List four common elements in a brochure.

7. List four special design considerations associated with brochures.

8. List the steps needed to rotate an object.

9. List six elements in a newsletter.

10. List four special design considerations associated with newsletters.

Sections 6.11 — 6.13

11. Explain where you might use rules to enhance the layout of a newsletter.

12. List the steps needed to round the corners of a rectangle.

13. Explain where you might use a shaded box in both a brochure and a newsletter. Exactly what text would be emphasized with the box?

14. a) What does the Bring to front command do?
    b) What does the Send to back command do?

15. On a left Master Page, what does a page-number marker look like?

16. List the steps necessary to remove Master-page items from page 1 of a publication.

Exercises

1. Silent Waters Sanctuary, a local nature preserve, has asked you to create an informative three-fold brochure to be distributed by display. The unfolded size of the brochure is 8.5" by 11". Include three graphics in your design, each at least 1" wide by 3" tall.

   a) On paper, write down the purpose of the brochure and the characteristics of the audience.

   b) Design two different sets of thumbnail sketches for the brochure, including the inside and the outside. Experiment with the placement of different elements. Keep in mind the purpose and audience. Consider adding graphical elements such as rules and rectangles to your design.

   c) Indicate the typefaces, sizes, and other specifications next to each thumbnail.

   d) Create a new publication, entering 2 for the Number of pages option in the Page setup dialog box, along with any other options needed for the brochure. Pick the best inside and outside thumbnail sketches and use the Master Page to create a grid.

   e) Place copies of GRAPHIC.WMF to represent the three graphics. Copy and paste, resizing as necessary.

   f) Place GENERIC.TXT as the text. Resize, flow, adjust the fonts and leading, and move the text as necessary for your design. Delete any extra text. Create your own headlines.

   g) Save the brochure naming it PRESERVE and print a copy. Place the pages back to back and fold into thirds.

2. Brown's Bus Adventures, a small New England bus tour company, has hired you to produce a catalog brochure of their fall tours. The three-fold 8.5" by 11" brochure will be mailed to past customers, and also distributed by display. Include two 1.5" by 1.5" photos and one 2" by 2" photo. There are four tours: Fall Foliage Frolic, Halloween in Hartford, A Pilgrimage to Plymouth Rock, and A Mohawk Trail Holiday. Include the titles of these tours and some generic text as descriptions.

   a) On paper, write down the purpose of the brochure and the characteristics of the audience.

   b) Design two different sets of thumbnail sketches for the brochure, including the inside and the outside. Experiment with the placement of different elements. Keep in mind the purpose and audience. Consider adding graphical elements such as rules and rectangles to your design.

   c) Indicate the typefaces, sizes, and other specifications next to each thumbnail.

d) Create a new publication, entering 2 for the Number of pages option in the Page setup dialog box. Pick the best inside and outside thumbnail sketches and use the Master Page to create a grid.

e) Place PHOTO.WMF to represent the three photographs. Copy and paste, resizing as necessary.

f) Place GENERIC.TXT as the text. Resize, flow, adjust the fonts and leading, and move the text as necessary for your design. Delete any extra text. Create your own headlines.

g) Save the brochure naming it BUSTOUR and print a copy. Place the pages back to back and fold into thirds.

3. The citizens of Muon, a very small town, have asked you to layout a monthly newsletter for them. Each month they will send you the text and graphics. For the first issue, the newsletter will be one sheet of 8.5" by 11" paper, printed on two sides (you will print two pages and place them back to back). You are also given these specifications:

    - masthead: make a masthead by typing `Muon Monthly News` and changing the font to 48 point Times New Roman
    - headlines for articles: *Muon council holds annual meeting, Police get new car, Harvest Dance a success* (each article has one photo)

a) On paper, write down the purpose of the newsletter and the characteristics of the audience.

b) Design two different sets of thumbnail sketches for the newsletter, including the front of the page and back. Experiment with the placement of different elements, keeping in mind the purpose and audience. Consider adding graphical elements such as rules and rectangles to your design.

c) Indicate the typefaces, sizes, and other specifications next to each thumbnail.

d) Create a new publication, entering 2 for the Number of pages option and deselecting the Double-sided option in the Page setup dialog box. Pick the best thumbnail sketch and use the Master Page to create a grid.

e) Start on page 1 and create the masthead as indicated above. Continue by placing PHOTO.WMF as any photos that are in the design on both pages one and two, resizing as necessary.

f) Create the headlines for each article, format them, and place according to your design. Place LONG.TXT as text for the articles. Resize, flow, adjust the fonts and leading, and move the text as necessary for your design. You may find it necessary to copy and paste some of the text if you need extra.

g) Save the newsletter as MUONNEWS and print a copy. Place the pages back to back to simulate two-sided printing.

4. The Ivy University music department needs a four-page, monthly newsletter for everyone associated with the music department: music majors, orchestra members, faculty, etc. Each page will be the standard 8.5" by 11". You are given these additional specifications:
   - masthead: make a masthead by typing `University Music News` and changing the font to 48 point Times New Roman
   - headlines for articles: *Music department sees enrollment increase, Dr. Phlat offers banjo course, IU Music Department is world-renowned, The Ivy Chanters need altos, What's in a waltz?, Faculty focus: Dr. Greta Pyannoe* (each articles has one photo)

   a) On paper, write down the purpose of the newsletter and the characteristics of the audience.

   b) Design two different sets of thumbnail sketches for the newsletter, including sketches of the front page and a representative inside page. Experiment with the placement of different elements, keeping in mind the purpose and audience. Consider adding graphical elements such as rules and rectangles to your design.

   c) Indicate the typefaces, sizes, and other specifications next to each thumbnail.

   d) Create a new publication, entering 4 for the Number of pages option in the Page setup dialog box. Pick the best sketches and use the Master Pages to create one grid for all pages.

   e) Start on page 1 and create the masthead as indicated above. Continue by placing PHOTO.WMF as any photos that are in the design on the appropriate pages, resizing as necessary.

   f) Create the headlines for each article, format them, and place according to your design. Place LONG.TXT as text for the articles. Resize, flow, adjust the fonts and leading, and move the text as necessary for your design. You may find it necessary to use more than one copy of the LONG.TXT text to fill up all of the articles.

   g) Save the newsletter naming it IVYMUSIC and print a copy. Assemble so that it is similar to a four-page newsletter.

5. An upscale bookstore has hired you to create their monthly flyer containing the month's events. You are given these specifications:
   - 8.5" by 11" paper folded in half to create a brochure with four 8.5" by 5.5" pages
   - distributed in stacks at the door and the register of the bookstore
   - graphics: three 1.5" wide by 2" high portrait photos of authors, one 2" by 2" photo for children
   - text: a paragraph introductory greeting, 3 book signing events, one paragraph of children's events

   a) On paper, write down the purpose of the brochure and characteristics of the audience.

   b) Design two different sets of thumbnail sketches for the brochure. Experiment with the placement of the different elements, keeping in mind the purpose and audience. Consider adding graphical elements such as rules and rectangles to your design.

c) Indicate the typefaces, sizes, and other specifications next to each thumbnail.

d) Create a new publication, entering 2 for the Number of pages option in the Page setup dialog box. Pick the best thumbnail sketch and use the Master Pages to create a grid.

e) Place PHOTO.WMF to represent the four photos. Copy and paste, resizing as necessary.

f) Place GENERIC.TXT as the text. Resize, flow, adjust the fonts and leading, and move the text as necessary for your design. Delete any extra text. Create your own headlines.

g) Save the brochure naming it BOOKSTOR and print a copy. Place the pages back to back and fold in half.

In the following exercises you will revise publications created in exercises from previous chapters. You may need to redesign the entire publication, or just add a page to the existing file. The contents of the original publication may need to be moved onto the Pasteboard, and a new grid created on the Master Page based on your new design. The text and graphics can then be moved back to the publication page and reformatted as necessary.

6. In Chapter 5 Exercise 4 you created a brochure for Zawacki Orchards named ZAWBROCH, but left the outside panels blank. In this exercise you will design and create the outside panels including a cover, back mailing panel, and list of products offered.

   a) Open ZAWBROCH and insert a second page by executing the Page setup command from the File menu and entering 2 for the Number of pages option.

   b) Design two thumbnail sketches for the three outside panels, keeping in mind that the brochure will be folded into thirds. Consider adding graphical elements such as rules and rectangles to your design.

   c) Indicate typefaces, sizes, and other details on the thumbnails and then select the best sketch.

   d) Create the three outside panels based on your thumbnail using the PageMaker drawing tools where necessary.

   e) Save the revised ZAWBROCH and then print a copy. Place the pages back to back and fold into thirds.

7. In Chapter 5 Exercise 5 you created a wedding program named WEDPROG, but left the outside panels blank. In this exercise you will design a front cover that includes the date, time, location of the ceremony, and the names of the bride and groom.

   a) Open WEDPROG and insert a second page by executing the Page setup command from the File menu and entering 2 for the Number of pages option.

b) Design two thumbnail sketches for the cover. Consider adding graphical elements such as rules and rectangles to your design.

c) Indicate typefaces, sizes, and other details on the thumbnails. Keep in mind the ceremony at which the program will be handed out in making your selections.

d) Create the cover based on your best thumbnail using PageMaker's draw tools where necessary.

e) Save the revised WEDPROG and then print a copy. Place the pages back to back and fold in half.

8. In Chapter 5 Exercise 9 you produced a two column flyer (named IVYFLY2B) for Ivy University's Department of Skin Injury and Disease. The Department now wants the flyer redesigned as a folded brochure 8 1/2" tall by 5 1/2" wide. The inside will contain the text of the original flyer with any additional text flowing to the back of the brochure. The front cover should be bold and eye catching.

   a) Open IVYFLY2B. Using the Page setup command from the File menu, change the Orientation option to Wide and insert a second page by entering 2 for the Number of pages option.

   b) Design two thumbnail sketches for both the inside and cover of the brochure. Consider adding graphical elements such as rules and rectangles to your design.

   c) Indicate typefaces, sizes, and other specifications next to the thumbnails.

   d) Pick your best thumbnail sketch and rearrange the grid on the Master Page as necessary for the new design.

   e) Produce the pages for the new brochure allowing text to flow to the back page of the brochure if necessary.

   f) Save the revised IVYFLY2B and then print a copy. Place the pages back to back and fold in half.

Chapter Seven:
Advertisements, Awards, & Invitations

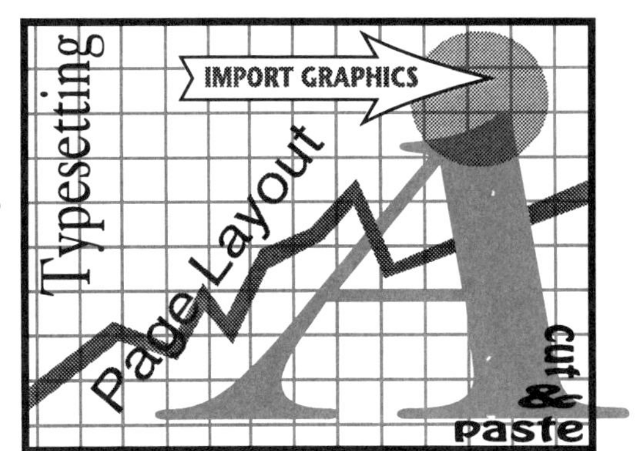

Element - Text wrap

Window - Control palette

CHARSET.PT5

Skewing

Objectives

7

After completing this chapter you will be able to:

1. Identify the elements of an advertisement.
2. Discuss design concepts of advertisements.
3. Use logos effectively in designs.
4. Create forms and coupons in publications.
5. Flow text around graphics using the Text Wrap command.
6. Select one object from overlapping objects.
7. Use the Control palette for formatting text and graphics.
8. Design effective signs, awards, and invitations.
9. Print character sets.
10. Use a dingbat as a graphic element in a publication.
11. Rotate objects using the Control palette.
12. Create folded invitations.
13. Skew an object using the Control palette.

7

Design skills learned in previous chapters are combined to create interesting and effective advertisements in this chapter. Using logos in designs is covered, as well as designing and creating forms, coupons, awards, and invitations. The powerful Control palette is also introduced, as is rotating and skewing objects.

7.1 Advertisements

When a company has a message to communicate to a specific audience, they often use advertisements. There are two major categories of printed ads: *published* and *distributed*. Published advertisements appear within a publication such as a newspaper, magazine, or newsletter. Distributed advertisements are flyers or small brochures that are distributed by mail or by hand, or posted on a bulletin board or in a window. In either case the design and size of an advertisement is influenced by its surroundings, such as where it appears or where and how the publication is distributed.

7.2 Types of Advertisements

One type of advertisement is an *informative ad* where the purpose is to educate the audience about a product. Such advertisements can vary based on the amount of information to be communicated. They can announce a new product, showing the product with little or no text, or containing a large amount of text.

A typical informative advertisement

Another type is the *sale advertisement*. Here the purpose is to inform the targeted audience about items that are being sold at a special price for a limited time, or are "on sale." In most cases, specific information about the sale items is also included.

A sale advertisement

A third type is the *emotional advertisement*. Perfume and jewelry companies often make use of such advertising. This type uses graphics and text that are not directly related to the product, but that communicate an emotion or an attitude. The audience then associates the feeling they have from the ad with the product. This type of advertising is gaining in popularity.

Emotional advertising: What is this an ad for?

Bear in mind that the product to be promoted is not always a retail item. It can be a company, a service, or a line of products with the same brand name. Many times the purpose of the advertisement is to maintain a public image by continuing or increasing public awareness. This type is called an *exposure advertisement*. It begins or continues a relationship between the targeted audience and the company. Corporate public-relations departments use this type of advertising to uphold or change the public image of a company.

Exposure advertising is common on billboards

7.3 Elements of Advertisements

All advertisements have two elements in common: *copy* and *advertiser identification*. Copy refers to the text used in an ad, and the advertiser identification is either a logo, name and address, or title that identifies the advertiser:

All advertisements have copy and advertiser identification

Beyond these two common elements, each ad has an individual structure that varies with the product, purpose, audience, and type of advertisement.

Practice 1

In this Practice you will identify different types of advertisements and their separate elements. Write your answers on paper.

Answer the following questions for each of the three advertisements shown above.

a. What type of advertisement is it? Why?
b. Would it be a published ad or a distributed ad? Why?
c. Which elements are the copy and which are the advertiser identifications?

7.4 Design for Advertisements

In Chapter Five you learned the factors that make a good design, including some basic guidelines for all publications. As with any publication, advertisements have a few special considerations:

Appropriateness

There is relatively little text in most advertisements, therefore what text does appear is of great importance and must be appropriate. In Chapters Three and Five we discussed different fonts and their ability to communicate feelings and images. The visual communication of text is the key to most advertisements. Large text takes on the characteristics of a graphical element, communicating messages through shape, weight, and placement. Because of this, many advertisements make use of fonts from the decorative or *display* families.

Balance

The relative balance of all the elements is dictated by the purpose of the advertisement. The placement of the elements is based not only on relative weight, balance, and tension in the layout, but also on each element's order of importance. For example, large type is considered a graphical element that also has textual importance, and therefore has a heavy visual weight. Likewise, the company's address will usually be in a smaller font and therefore less of an influence on the design.

Focus and Flow

The focus and flow determine how the consumer sees and interprets an advertisement. Do you want the consumer to remember the name of the company and not the product? Or do you want the consumer to remember the product and not the name of the company? Is the location of the company more important than the product? The flow or the focus must make this apparent.

Consistency

Repetition of the same style or theme through all of the advertisements a company uses is imperative if the ads are to be remembered by the consumer. For example, every few years the two large cola companies change their advertisement campaigns. When they do, you have been used to seeing the old advertisement campaign for at least three years. Familiar logos and common themes were used consistently.

This illustration shows a restaurant advertisement before (left) and after a thorough re-design:

Before (left) and after (right) an advertisement makeover

The advertisement on the left is overwhelmed by the "Now through February 28" phrase in a huge italic font. Because of its size, the text works as a strong graphic element in the design, and becomes the inappropriate focus of the page. The same phrase is placed near the bottom of the ad in the makeover, appropriate in size and location. There is no focus or flow in the ad on the left, as all the elements are jumbled together and unbalanced. By placing the food items into a bulleted list, a sense of structure is added to the advertisement on the right which in turn balances the ad and creates a proper focus and flow in the design. Adding the ribbon-like graphic frame to two sides of the ad strengthens the balance.

7.5 Using Logos in Designs

A logo represents the ideas and objectives of a company. To take full advantage of a logo it should appear as many places as possible, such as stationery, business cards, company vehicles, products, and packaging. By placing the logo everywhere, it increases exposure to customers and they begin to recognize it and identify it with the company. This is called a *corporate identity*:

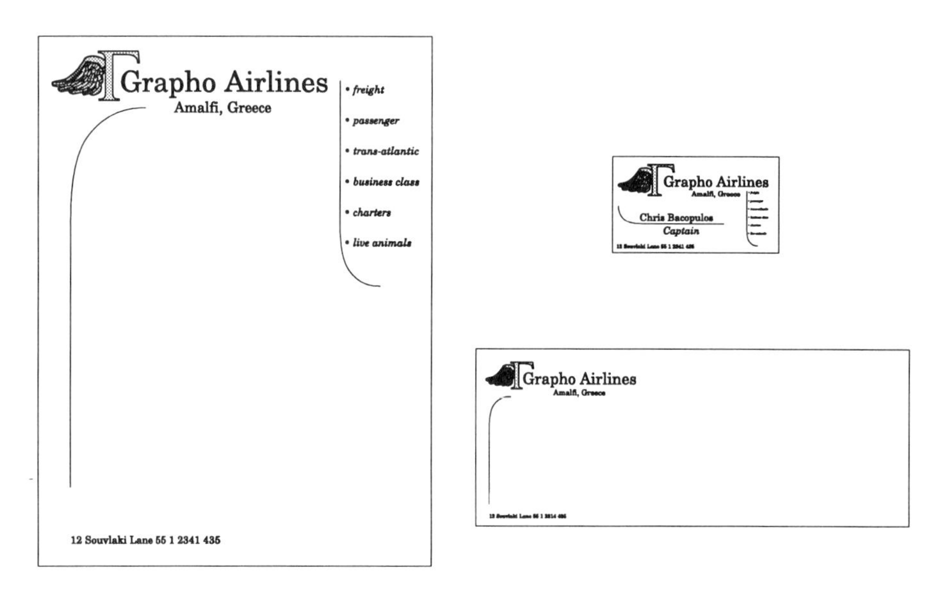

The corporate identity of an airline

There are many ways to incorporate a logo into a design. The logo can be placed in the header or footer, used as a bullet in a list, or displayed in the masthead of a newsletter. You may also slightly change a logo by resizing, rotating, or stretching it to adapt to a design. Remember to use the Master Pages to help you place a logo permanently in a design.

In the advertisement makeover shown in Section 7.4, notice the treatment of the Aztec Café logo. The logo in the advertisement on the left is the only information that identifies the restaurant. In the ad on the right, the logo appears next to the name of the restaurant and is then repeated at the bottom of the ad, next to the address. The repetition of the logo strengthens the consumer's identification of the restaurant. To maintain consistency the same logo should also be placed on any other advertisements it prints, as well as on menus, matches, napkins, and signs.

PageMaker, because of its limited drawing tools, is not usually used to create the logo itself. Instead, a graphics program such as CorelDraw, Adobe Illustrator, or Aldus Freehand is used to create the logo, which is then exported as a file. The logo file can then be imported into PageMaker with the Place command, and formatted and sized as necessary.

7.6 Forms and Coupons

Some advertisements, such as sale ads, may have a form or coupon within the design for the consumer to cut out and redeem. When designing an advertisement that includes one of these elements, be sure the form or coupon is useable; leave sufficient room to write in the requested areas. The easier the coupon is to use, the more likely consumers are to use it.

The placement of the ad in the publication, and the coupon or form in the ad, are both important. Coupons are generally located at the bottom-right corner (where the reader's eye usually lands last in the flow) of an advertisement. To make it easier for the consumer to cut out the coupon, the ad should be located in the bottom-right corner of a right-hand page:

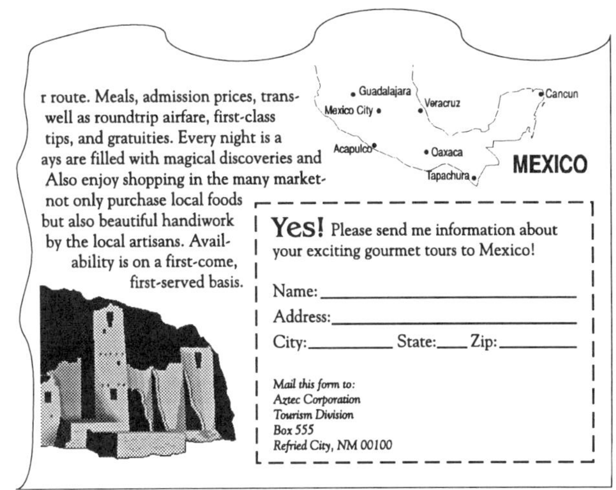

A coupon in the corner of the advertisement is easier for the consumer to use

When creating coupons and forms in PageMaker, the Line command from the Element menu is used to select dotted, dashed, and thin lines. A rectangle can be drawn using these styles to indicate the area that is to be cut out.

Practice 2

In this Practice you will begin creating an advertisement by making a coupon that is to be filled out and mailed by the consumer.

1) ***START WINDOWS AND PAGEMAKER***

2) ***CREATE A NEW PUBLICATION***

   a. From the File menu, select the New command. The Page setup dialog box is shown.
   b. Type 6 for the Top margin and select OK to create the new publication. The dimensions of the work area are now 6.75" wide and 4.25" high. This is the size of the advertisement that will eventually be created.

3) *DRAW THE COUPON OUTLINE*

a. Place a vertical ruler guide at the 4.75" mark on the horizontal ruler.
b. Select the Rectangle tool.
c. Move the pointer to the intersection of the Ruler guide and the bottom Margin guide. Drag the cross-hairs up and to the right, drawing a rectangle 3" wide and 2" high.
d. From the Element menu, select the Line command and format the rectangle with a 1 point dashed line.

4) *ADD THE TEXT*

a. Move the vertical Ruler guide from the 4.75" mark to the 4.875" mark (halfway between 4.75" and 5").
b. Select the Text tool. Create an insertion point and type the following text:

```
Please send me more information about the California
Sunshine Home Juicer.
```

c. Resize the text block to fit inside the coupon. Position it near the top of the coupon, with the left side of the block aligned on the Ruler guide:

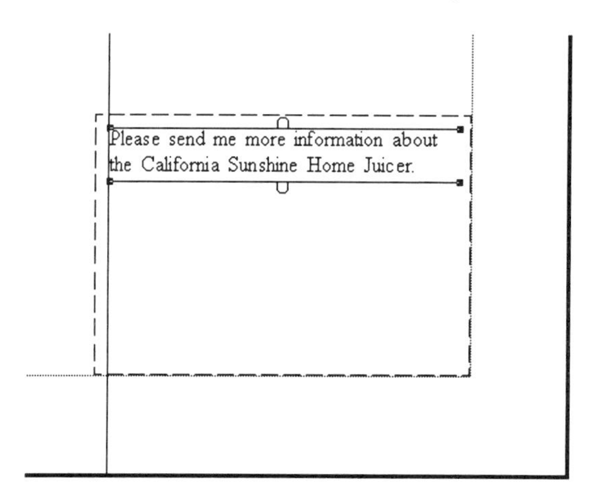

d. Start a new text block with the following text:

```
Name:_______________________________________
Address:____________________________________
City:______________  State:___  Zip:________
```

Use the underscore character to create the lines.
e. Resize the text block to fit inside the coupon and place it below the other text block, aligning the left side of the block with the Ruler guide. You may need to modify the underscores to get the text to fit on each line.
f. Start a new text block with the following text:

```
Mail this coupon to:
California Sunshine Consumer Relations
78932 Ground Road
San Jerdi, CA 89373
```

Make the text in this block ten-point type.
g. Resize the text block to fit inside the coupon, place it below the other text block, and align with the Ruler guide. Remove the Ruler guide.

Check - Your coupon should be similar to:

Please send me more information about
the California Sunshine Home Juicer.

Name: ______________________________

Address: ____________________________

City: __________ State: ___ Zip: _________

Mail this coupon to:
California Sunshine Consumer Relations
78932 Ground Road
San Jerdi, CA 89373

5) *SAVE THE PUBLICATION*

Save the publication using the name CSADVERT.

7.7 Flowing Text Around Graphics

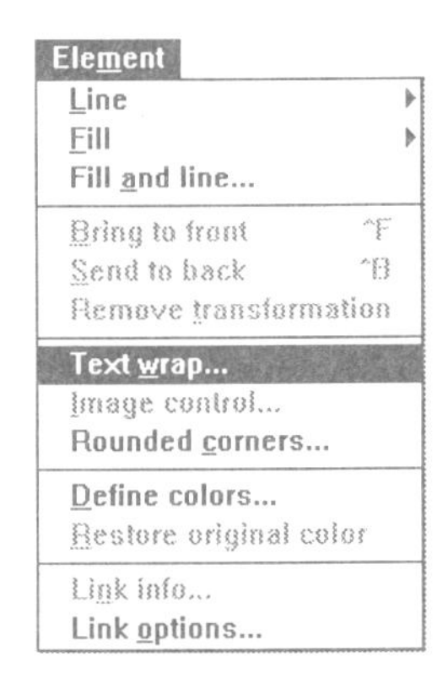

There may be an occasion where the text in your design should closely follow the edge of a graphic. It is possible to wrap text around a graphic using the Text wrap command from the Elements menu. By first selecting the object or objects that you want the text to wrap around, then executing the Text wrap command, a dialog box is shown:

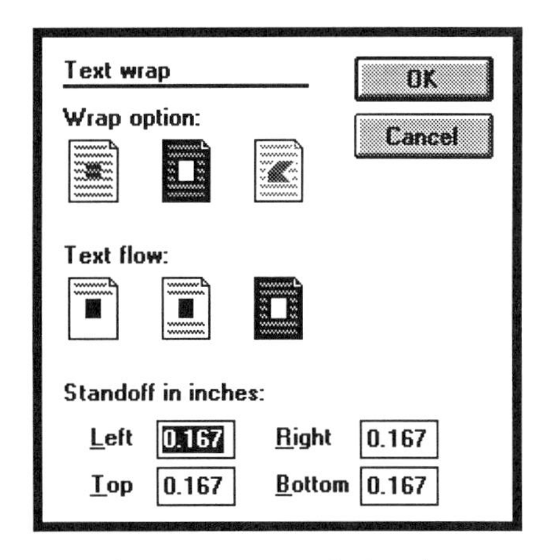

The Text wrap dialog box

Within the dialog box is a row of icons under Wrap option. Choosing the leftmost option allows the text to flow over the graphic. The middle Wrap option wraps text around a graphic. The rightmost option is highlighted when the object has had Text wrap applied and the boundaries of the object have been altered.

After selecting a Wrap option, the Text flow options become active allowing you to select the option suitable for the situation. The leftmost Text flow option stops the text at the graphic and continues the text on the next column (or page for a single column publication). The middle option continues the text after the graphic, but leaves blank space on the sides of the graphic. The rightmost option flows text to completely surround the graphic.

The Standoff in inches option describes how far the *boundaries* will be from the edge of the graphic. The boundaries are dotted lines that define the area that the text flows around. The default setting of 0.167" (12 points) is usually sufficient.

After setting the desired options and selecting OK, the graphic is shown with dotted lines called *boundaries* around it:

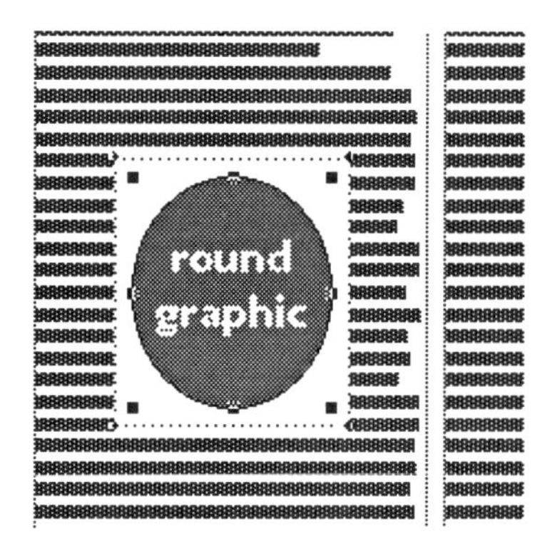

Default boundaries are rectangular

The text wraps completely around the graphic at the boundaries.

7.8 Customizing Text Wrap Boundaries

When the Text wrap boundaries around a graphic are manipulated into a new shape, the boundaries are said to be *customized*. Custom boundaries can be adjusted to follow the contours of an individual graphic by dragging the small handles at the corners. New handles can be created by clicking once on the dotted line boundary:

This boundary has been adjusted and new handles added to customize the wrap shape

The handles can be dragged along the boundary to the desired position. If there are too many handles, they can be deleted individually by sliding one along the boundary and into another handle. The two handles then combine together.

7.9 Selecting One Object From a Stack

In a complex design it may become necessary to select an object that, although visible, is overlapped by some other object(s). For example, a graphic that has had text wrapped around it is completely visible, but it is overlapped by the text block. When you try to select the graphic by clicking on it, you might select the text block instead if it is on the top layer. One way to select the desired object is to use the Send to back command from the Element menu to move the top, selected object to the back layer. This process may be repeated until the desired object is on the top and can be selected.

An alternative method of selecting a stacked or overlapped object is to use the Control key. Each time you click on the object while holding down the Control key, another layer is selected. The desired object will be selected when you reach its layer. This method does not rearrange the objects in a stack, but simply allows an object on a lower layer to be selected.

An object may also be selected by dragging the mouse pointer to create a *marquee* box around it. A marquee box is the blinking, dashed-line box that appears while you drag the Pointer tool. It disappears when the mouse button is released, and any objects completely surrounded by the marquee box are selected. This method, called *marquee selecting*, is useful when selecting more than one object at once.

Practice 3

In this Practice you will wrap text around two graphics. Start PageMaker and open the CSADVERT.PM5 file if you have not already done so.

1) PLACE AND ALIGN THE LOGO

a. Place CALIFSUN.WMF anywhere and resize proportionally until the logo is about 2" wide.
b. Place a horizontal Ruler guide at 6.5" and then move the logo so that the top is aligned with the Ruler guide and the right side is on the right margin:

2) PLACE THE COPY

Place CSJUICE.TXT starting under the Ruler guide at the left margin. Pull down the bottom windowshade handle so that all of the text is visible. The text flows over the logo and part of the coupon.

3) WRAP THE TEXT AROUND THE COUPON

a. Select the dashed-line rectangle around the coupon.
b. From the Element menu, select the Text wrap command.
c. Choose the middle icon for the Wrap option and select OK to accept the default settings. The dotted text-wrap boundaries appear and the text wraps around the side of the coupon.

4) WRAP THE TEXT AROUND THE LOGO

a. Select the logo with the Pointer tool. You may need to hold down `Ctrl` when clicking to select it.
b. Execute the Text wrap command. Choose the middle Wrap option and select OK to accept the defaults. The text wrap boundaries appear around the logo and the text does not go beyond the boundaries.
c. Drag the upper-left boundary handle down to the horizontal Ruler guide, then over to the corner of the logo, right next to the sun or the letter C in the word "California." The boundaries will change, following the edges of the logo more closely:

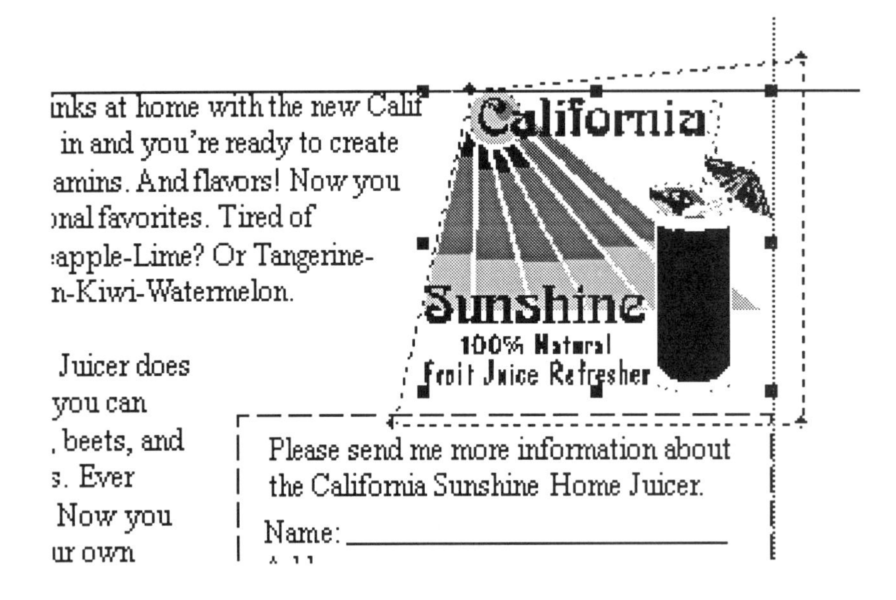

d. Drag the upper-right boundary handle down to the Ruler guide to straighten the top boundary.

5) CREATE A HANDLE ON THE LEFT BOUNDARY

a. Click once on the left boundary, about two-thirds of the way down the side of the logo, at the bottom of the S in the word "Sunshine." A handle appears on the boundary.
b. Drag the bottom-left handle to the right, until the boundary between this corner handle and the one you just created is vertically straight.

6) ADJUST THE BOTTOM BOUNDARY

The text in the coupon may be different if the bottom boundary of the logo extends into the coupon. Drag each of the handles of the bottom boundary upwards until the boundary is on the dashed line of the coupon. The text in the coupon will be returned to normal.

7) FINISH THE ADVERTISEMENT

a. Create an insertion point in the blank area above the Ruler guide and below the top Margin guide. Type `NEW California Sunshine Home Juicer!` and set it to 24 point type.

Check - Your advertisement should be similar to:

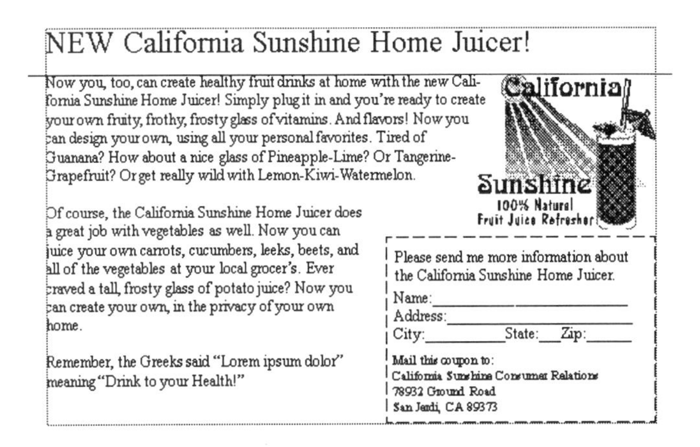

b. Save and print a copy of your advertisement.
c. Close the file.

7.10 The Control Palette

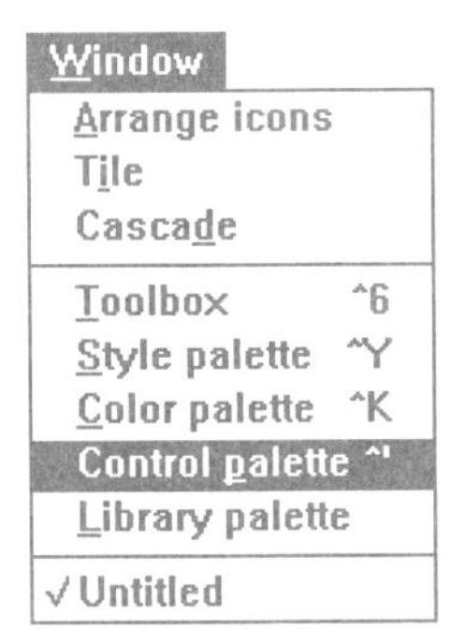

Most of the techniques for formatting text and graphics that you have already learned can be performed using the *Control palette*. The Control palette is displayed by choosing the Control palette command from the Window menu, or by using the keyboard shortcut `Ctrl+'` (the Control key and the single-quote key). The palette not only contains shortcut commands for many formatting options, but also tracks the positions of both the mouse pointer and objects in the publication. In addition, the Control palette displays specifications such as the exact dimensions of a graphics to the thousandth of an inch which allows you to format text and objects with precision.

The contents of the Control palette change depending upon what is selected in the publication. When no objects are selected, the Control palette simply displays the position of the mouse pointer on the screen, relative to the horizontal and vertical rulers. The X coordinate is its position on the horizontal Ruler, and the Y coordinate is the position on the vertical Ruler:

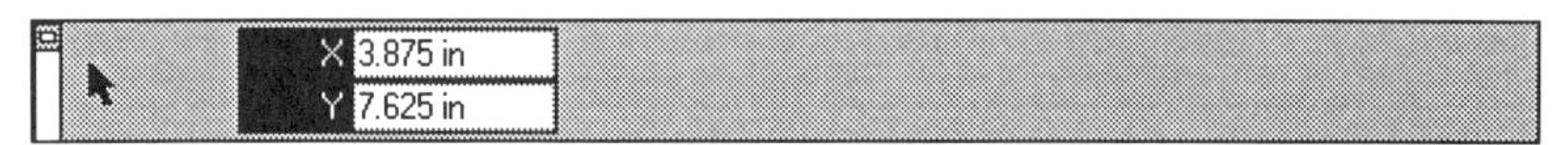

The Control palette with no objects selected

When a graphic or text block is selected, the Control palette displays the X and Y coordinates of a reference point on the object. The reference point selected corresponds with the location of the enlarged handle on the *Proxy* in the Control palette. The Proxy is a diagram of the object's reference points, using handles to illustrate their location:

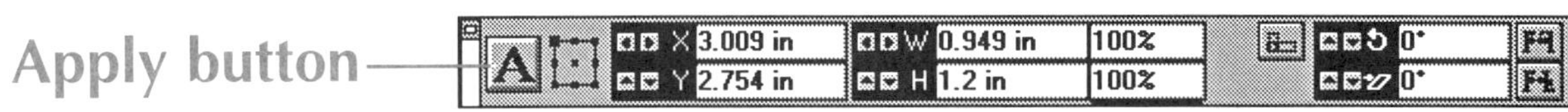

The Control palette with a text block selected

The Control palette with a graphic selected

The W and H measurements are the Width and Height of the graphic. New values, in inches or in percentages, can be entered directly into the Control palette. They are then applied to the graphic by either pressing Enter or clicking on the Apply button at the far left of the palette.

7.11 The Control Palette and Text

When the Text tool is selected there are two views of the Control palette available: character view and paragraph view. The displayed view is chosen by clicking on the character view button or the paragraph view button.

Character view has buttons for formatting type styles and fields for type size, leading, tracking, and other character formats:

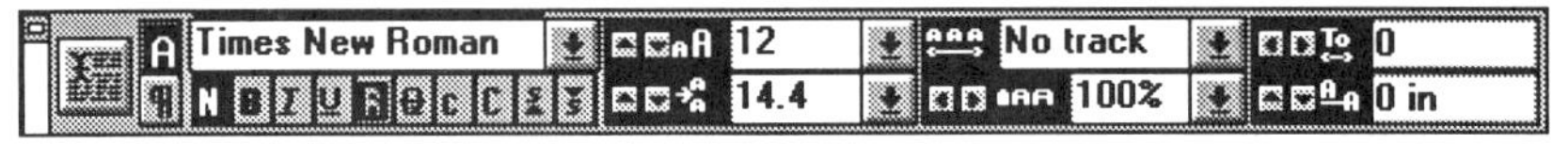

The Control palette—character view

The current font.

Type styles: Normal (plain), Bold, Italic, Underline, Reverse, Strikethrough.

Case options: Small caps, All caps.

Position options: Superscript, Subscript.

Type size (top) and leading.

Tracking (top) and width (Chapter Ten).

Paragraph view has buttons for formatting alignment and fields for the cursor's position, left, right, and first-line indents, and other paragraph formats:

The Control palette—paragraph view

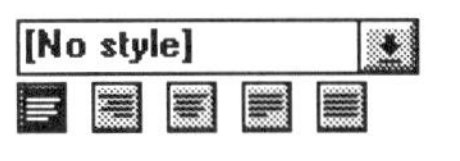

The current style (top) and paragraph alignments: left, right, centered, justified, and force justified.

The position of the cursor (upper left). Indents: left, first line, and right.

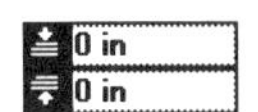

Space before (top) and after the paragraph.

The Control palette can be moved by placing the pointer in the blank area below the Close box and dragging. Clicking on the Close box in the upper-left corner closes the palette, as does executing the Control palette command or pressing `Ctrl+'` again.

7.12 Signs and Awards

The design concepts and techniques you have learned so far can be put to use creating signs, posters, and award certificates for various occasions.

Signs and Posters

A sign or poster is meant to catch the reader's attention from a distance, so keep in mind the cliché "bigger is better" and make the most important element as big as you can. Large text is a necessity. It may help to hold your thumbnail sketch at arm's length and see what element will be noticed first from a distance. Once the poster catches the reader's attention, they will move closer to read the rest of the text, which should be in a medium sized font.

Award Certificates

When designing an award certificate, be sure to identify the presenting company or organization, the reason for the award, a blank area for the recipient's name, and the date. Other elements, such as a logo, places for other signatures, or blank areas for seals will vary by the purpose of the award. Use an appropriately fancy font for an official look to the award, and add a border to frame the text. The Rectangle tool and various line settings will help you create unique borders. Just as with a sign or poster, be sure that the elements are large enough to be read from a distance, and that the most prominent element is appropriate.

For both signs and awards, the Master Pages are the key to consistency. By creating an entire blank sign or award on a Master Page, the main elements will be unalterable when working on page 1. Just the changing data, such as names and dates, need to be typed in on page 1.

7

Practice 4

In this Practice you will create a blank award on the Master Pages, then fill in a recipient's name on page 1. Start PageMaker if you have not already done so.

1) *ADJUST THE PAGE SETTINGS FOR AN AWARD*

a. From the File menu, select the New command. The Page setup dialog box is shown.
b. Change these settings:

    Orientation: Wide
    Double-sided and Facing pages options: deselected
    Left, Right, Top, and Bottom margins: 1 inch

   Be sure that the Compose to printer and target printer resolution settings are correct for your printer.
c. Select OK to make the changes. A letter size page in a landscape orientation is displayed with 1 inch margins.

2) *CREATE A BORDER AND GRID FOR THE BLANK AWARD*

a. Click on the Master-page icon in the bottom-left corner of the screen. The Master Page is displayed. You will create all of the blank award on the Master Page.
b. With the Rectangle tool, draw a rectangle exactly the size of the margins. Begin with the tool at one corner of the Margin guides and drag diagonally to the opposite corner.
c. From the Element menu, use the Line command to format the rectangle as a 12 point, solid line.
d. Place horizontal Ruler guides at the 3", 4", and 6" marks on the vertical Ruler.

3) *ENTER SOME TEXT AND FORMAT IT USING THE CONTROL PALETTE*

a. Create an insertion point and type `Ivy University`. Highlight the text.
b. From the Window menu, open the Control palette (`Ctrl+'`). The Control palette appears at the bottom of the screen.
c. Click on the arrow next to the Type size option field (12). A pop-up list appears. Scroll down in the list and select 72. The text is now 72 points in size.
d. Click on the arrow next to the Font option. Scroll down in the pop-up list and select Zapf Chancery. The text now appears in an appropriate, ornate font.
e. With the text still highlighted, change the Control palette from character view to paragraph view by selecting the paragraph view button.
f. Click on the center alignment button to center-align the text.
g. With the Pointer tool, move the text block so that the bottom of the Text block rests on the 3" Ruler guide.

4) *ENTER THE REST OF THE TEXT AND FORMAT IT*

a. Create a new insertion point and type `Certificate of Completion`. Highlight the text.
b. Change the Control palette to character view by selecting the character button.
c. Make the type size 36 points and the font Zapf Chancery using the Control palette as you did in step 3. Change the Control palette to paragraph view. Click the center align button to center the text.

d. With the Pointer tool, move the text block so that the bottom of the Text block rests on the 4" Ruler guide.
e. Create a new insertion point and type the following, using 20 underscore characters for the line:

    This is to certify that ________________ has completed the courses necessary to complete the program for this certificate.

   Highlight the text.
f. Make the type size 24 points. The font should already be Times New Roman. Click on the italic button [I] to format the text as italic.
g. With the text still highlighted, change the Control palette from character view to paragraph view by selecting the paragraph view button [¶].
h. Enter values of 1 for both the left and right indents [0 in] [0 in] and click on the Apply button. The text is indented. With the Pointer tool, move the text block so that the bottom of the text block is on the 6" Ruler guide.
i. Create a new insertion point and type 15 underlines, press Enter for a new paragraph, and type `Dean's Signature`. Highlight both lines of text.
j. Format the highlighted text as right-aligned with a right indent of 2 using the right-align button and the right-indent field on the Control palette. Switch the Control palette to character view and format the text as 18-point Times New Roman italic.
k. With the Pointer tool, move the text block so that the top of the text block is on the 6" Ruler guide.

5) *CHANGE THE GUIDES*

a. Now that the blank award is finished, the Ruler guides used to set it up should be removed and new guides put in to help line up the recipient's name. Remove all of the horizontal Ruler guides.
b. The Control palette displays the exact location of Ruler guides as you move them. Using the Control palette display, place vertical Ruler guides at exactly 5" and 7.5" on the horizontal Ruler.

6) *INSERT A NAME ON PAGE 1*

a. Display page 1. The entire blank award appears on the page.
b. Create an insertion point anywhere on the page. Type `Bruce Presley` and use character view of the Control palette to format the text as 18 point type.
c. Select the text block using the Pointer tool. Use the Control palette to size the text block exactly 2.5" wide. Move the text block to the blank line, and fit it perfectly between the Ruler guides.

Check - The publication should be similar to:

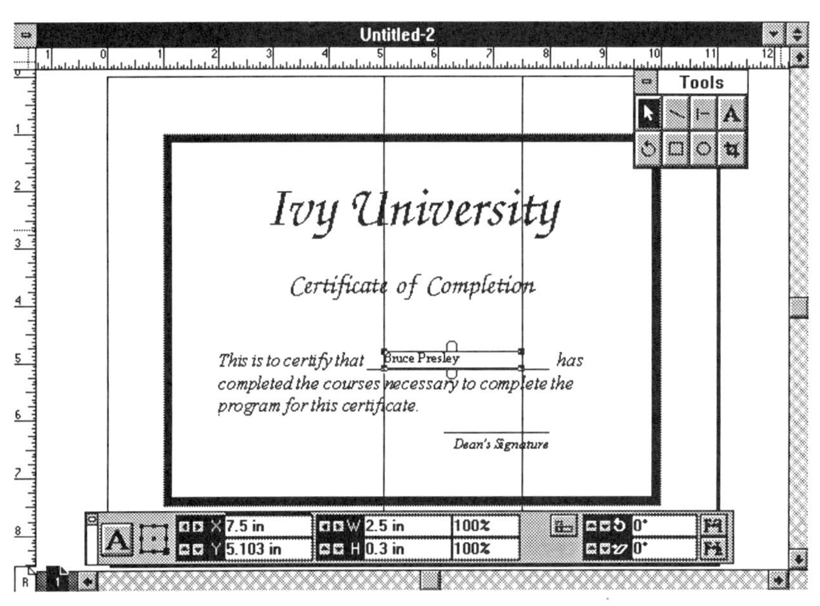

7) SAVE, PRINT, AND CLOSE THE PUBLICATION

Save the publication as IUAWARD, print a copy, then close the publication.

7.13 Dingbats

On some occasions, a dingbat can be used as a graphical element in a design. The dingbat is formatted and manipulated just like text because it actually is a text character. If it is large enough, however, it visually acts as a graphic element.

To choose a dingbat, you need to know what characters are available. Opening CHARSET.PT5 displays all of the available characters (called a *character set*) for any font:

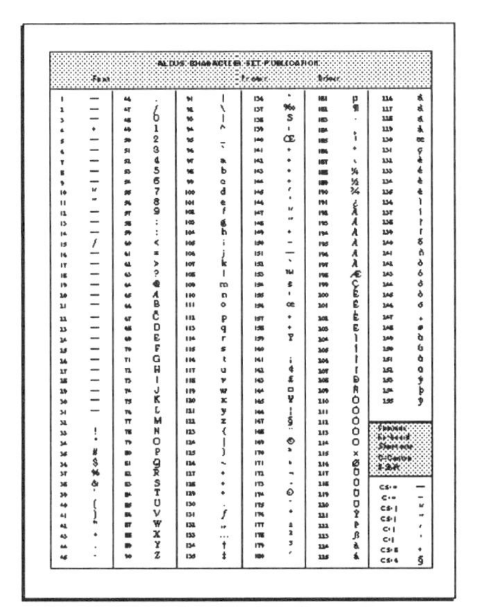

A character set for the Bookman font

Placing the Text tool within the publication, selecting all, and choosing a font will display all of the characters for that font. Also displayed are the special code numbers, called *ASCII* (pronounced "ask-ee") *codes*, that you need to type into the computer to make the character appear:

136	ˆ	181	µ	226	â
137	‰	182	¶	227	à
138	Š	183	·	228	ä
139	‹	184	¸	229	å
140	Œ	185	¹	230	æ
141	•	186	º	231	ç
142	•	187	»	232	è
143	•	188	¼	233	é
144	•	189	½	234	ê
145	‘	190	¾	235	ë
146	’	191	[illegible]	236	ì

Close-up of the Bookman character set, showing ASCII codes

Decorative fonts such as Symbol, Zapf Dingbats, and Wingdings contain many dingbats. Printing out a character set of a decorative font shows the ASCII code for all dingbats. Dingbats are placed by first creating an insertion point in the publication, then holding down the `Alt` key while typing `0` and the three digit ASCII code on the numeric keypad of the keyboard. The code must be typed in using the numeric keypad, not the numbers above the letter keys. The Num Lock does not affect entering codes. For example, placing a dingbat with an ASCII code of 163 requires holding down the `Alt` key and typing the number `0163` on the numeric keypad.

Practice 5

In this Practice you will print out character sets of decorative fonts and then add a dingbat to the award created in the previous practice. Start PageMaker if you have not already done so.

1) OPEN THE CHARSET.PT5 PUBLICATION

2) CHANGE THE FONT OF THE CHARACTER SET AND PRINT A COPY

a. Zoom in to the top half of the publication. Note the columns of ASCII codes and characters.
b. With the Text tool, create an insertion point on any of the characters (not the ASCII codes). From the Edit menu, execute the Select all command (`Ctrl+A`) to highlight all of the characters.
c. Using the Type menu, change the font to Times New Roman. The characters change to reflect the new font.
d. Print a copy of the publication. At the top of the printout, write the name of the font. Note all the special characters available.
e. Change the font of the characters to Wingdings. (If you do not have Wingdings, choose Zapf Dingbats or Symbol.)
f. Print a copy of the publication. Write the name of the font at the top of the page. Note how these characters differ from the previous printout.

3) PRINT COPIES OF OTHER CHARACTER SETS, AND CLOSE THE FILE

a. If they are available, print out character sets for other decorative fonts:

Zapf Dingbats
Symbol

Be sure to write the font name at the top of each printout.

b. Close the file, selecting No at the Save Untitled before closing? message box.

4) OPEN THE IUAWARD.PM5 PUBLICATION

5) VIEW THE MASTER PAGE

6) ADD A LARGE DINGBAT TO THE AWARD

a. You have decided to add a large, decorative dingbat to all of the awards, and will therefore place the dingbat on the Master Page. Look at your printout of the Wingdings character set. ASCII code number 174 resembles a seal that is appropriate to awards. (If you do not have Wingdings, choose a dingbat on your character set printout that resembles a foil seal or other appropriate shape.)

b. Place a vertical Ruler guide at the 3" mark.

c. Create an insertion point near the bottom of the award. Zoom in to the insertion point. The cursor may be difficult to see because of the border. Make the font Wingdings and the size 100 points. The cursor will now be very large.

d. Hold down the `Alt` key and type `0174` on the numeric keypad of your keyboard. The dingbat appears.

e. Select the text block with the Pointer tool. Use the Control palette to size the text block to 1.5" wide, then align the right side of the text block with the Ruler guide you just placed. Align the bottom of the text block with the bottom Margin guide, keeping the right side of the text block on the vertical Ruler guide.

f. Remove the vertical Ruler guide at 3". Display page 1. Note the seal on the award.

Check - Your award should be similar to:

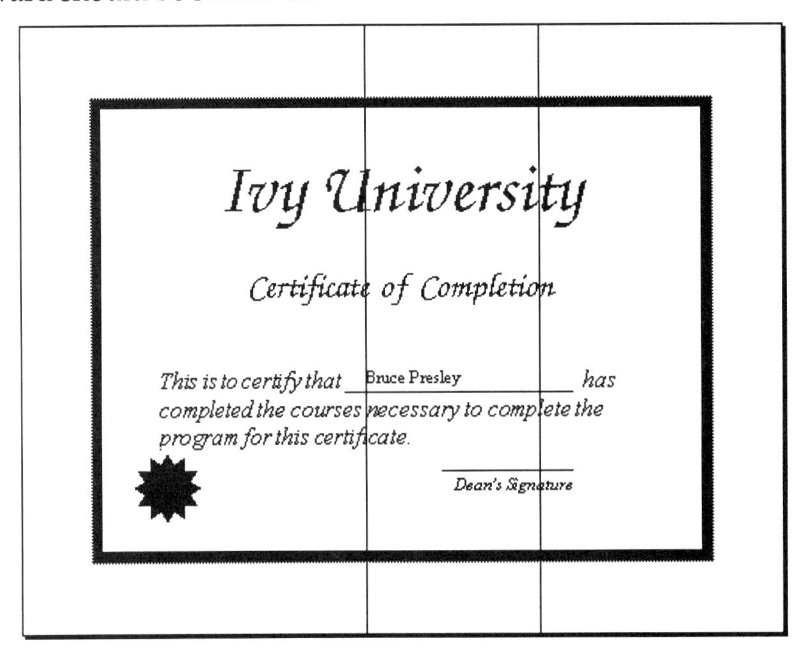

7) SAVE, PRINT, AND CLOSE THE AWARD

Save the publication, print a copy, then close the publication.

7.14 Invitations

Most of the design concepts and techniques presented so far also apply to creating invitations for any occasion. When designing an invitation, remember that the guest who receives it will interpret the reason, atmosphere, and intention of the occasion from the text, graphics, and physical format, so your intended message should be clear. The physical format of the design also influences the message through a special kind, color, shape, or size of paper.

The most common designs for invitations have centered text in a script font that resembles handwriting. This format is appropriate for weddings, dances, and other formal occasions. However, for other events such as a child's birthday party or an open house, an asymmetrical layout in a modern font would be more suitable.

A helpful way to make multiple invitations is to divide the blank page into four equal sections with Ruler guides and Column guides. The thumbnail sketches for the invitation are then based on a one-sided invitation, one-quarter of the page in size. After choosing a design from the sketches, the invitation is then created in one-quarter of the page:

One 4.25" by 5.5" invitation

Four invitations can be produced by first executing the Select all command to ensure that all elements are selected, then using the Copy and Paste commands to fill out the rest of the page:

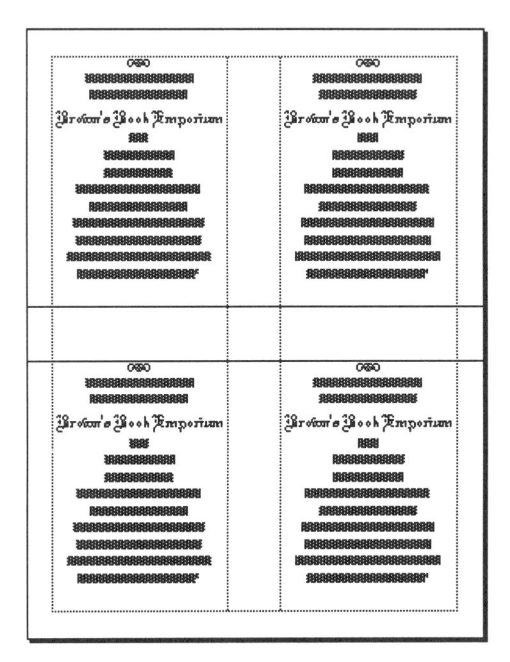

Four invitations on one page

7.15 Rotating with the Control Palette

In Chapter Six you learned how to use the Rotation tool to rotate text and graphics. The Control palette allows objects to be rotated with precision. When a graphic or a text block is selected, the rotation field appears on the far right of the Control palette:

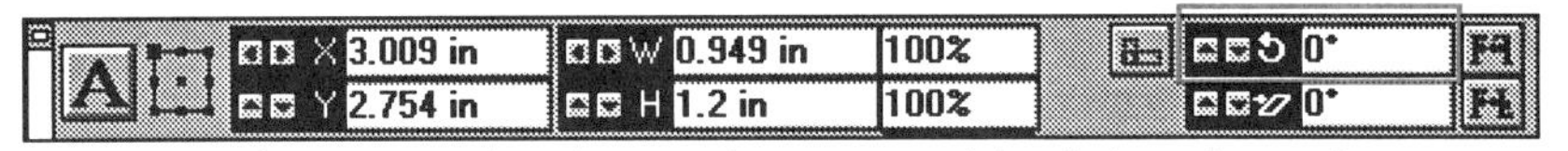

The Control palette when a text block is selected

The selected object is rotated by typing in the number of degrees to be rotated. A positive number of degrees rotates an object counter-clockwise, and a negative number is clockwise. Pressing Enter or clicking on the Apply button will rotate the object.

It is important to note that the selected object will rotate around a point defined by the selected reference point on the Proxy. If the center reference point is chosen (indicated by being larger than the other handles) the object will rotate around its center. You may change the selected reference point by clicking on the desired handle in the Proxy.

Practice 6

In this Practice you will create a page of four invitations for a bon voyage party. Start PageMaker if you have not already done so.

1) ADJUST THE PAGE SETTINGS FOR A QUARTER-PAGE INVITATION

a. From the File menu, select the New command. The Page setup dialog box is shown.
b. Change these settings:

    Double-sided and Facing pages options: deselected
    Left, Right, Top, and Bottom margins: 0.5 inches

   Be sure that the Compose to printer and Target printer resolution settings are correct for your printer.
c. Select OK to accept these values. A letter size page is displayed with one-half inch margins.

2) CREATE THE GRID

a. Display the Master Page, then display the Control palette (`Ctrl+'`).
b. From the Layout menu, execute the Column guides command. Enter `2` for the Number of columns option and `1` for the Space between columns option and select OK.
c. Place a horizontal Ruler guide at the 5" mark on the vertical Ruler, and another horizontal Ruler guide at the 6" mark on the vertical Ruler. Use the display on the Control palette to help place the Ruler guides exactly at 5" and 6".

3) ADD SOME TEXT

a. Display page 1. Note how the page is divided into four sections, each with a half-inch margin. Zoom in to the upper-left quarter of the page.
b. Create an insertion point near the top Margin guide and type the following:

```
Bon Voyage!
Our friend Bonnie Lorin is going to Antarctica for a
year to study! We will all miss her. Come and help us
wish Bonnie good luck!
```

c. Using the Control palette in character view, make all of the text Helvetica. Make the words `Bon Voyage!` 36 points and the rest of the text 18 points.
d. Using the Pointer tool, align the top of the text block with the top Margin guide.

4) ADD AN APPROPRIATE DINGBAT AND ROTATE IT

a. Using the Text tool, create a new insertion point below the text. With the Control palette, select the Zapf Dingbats font and enter a point size of `100`. Click on the apply button. Note the very large cursor on the page.
b. An airplane dingbat in the Zapf Dingbat font has the ASCII code of 40. Hold down the `Alt` key and type `0040` on the numeric keypad. The airplane dingbat appears.
c. With the Pointer tool, select the text block containing the dingbat. On the Control palette, select the center handle on the Proxy, then double click in the Rotation field. Type `90` and click on the Apply button. The dingbat is rotated so that the airplane now points upwards.

d. Place a horizontal Ruler guide at the 4.25" mark on the vertical Ruler. Align what is now the bottom of the text block containing the dingbat with the Ruler guide, and the left of the text block along the left Margin guide.

5) ADD THE REST OF THE TEXT

a. Create a new insertion point below the horizontal Ruler guide at the 4.25" mark on the vertical Ruler. Type the following text, pressing Enter at the end of each line to create new paragraphs:

```
Buffet Dinner
Friday, May 6
From 7 PM - ?
Bonnie & Deb's Apt.
23 Rick Drive, Foville
BRING A FRIEND!
```

b. Highlight all of the new text and make it Helvetica.
c. Using the paragraph view of the Control palette, give the highlighted text a left indent of 1.5".
d. Move this new text block upwards, and align the bottom of the text block with the horizontal Ruler guide at the 4.25" mark.
e. Remove the Ruler guide.

<u>Check</u> - Your invitation should be similar to:

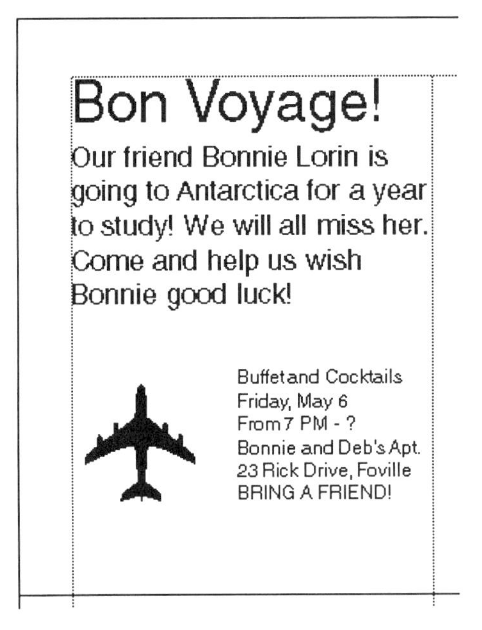

6) COPY THE INVITATION INTO THE REST OF THE PAGE

a. Zoom out to the Fit in Window view.
b. From the Edit menu, execute the Select all command (`Ctrl+A`) to select all the text blocks in the invitation.
c. From the Edit menu, execute the Copy command (`Ctrl+C`). All of the text blocks are copied to the clipboard.

d. From the Edit menu, execute the Paste command (`Ctrl+V`). The text blocks are pasted slightly below and to the right of the original text blocks.
e. With the Pointer tool, drag the pasted text blocks to a blank quarter of the page. The text blocks will all move together. Be sure the outline of the dragged block is aligned to the top of the quarter before you release the mouse button.
f. From the Edit menu, execute the Paste command again, and drag the pasted copy to a blank quarter of the page. Repeat for the last empty quarter of the page.

Check - The page should be similar to:

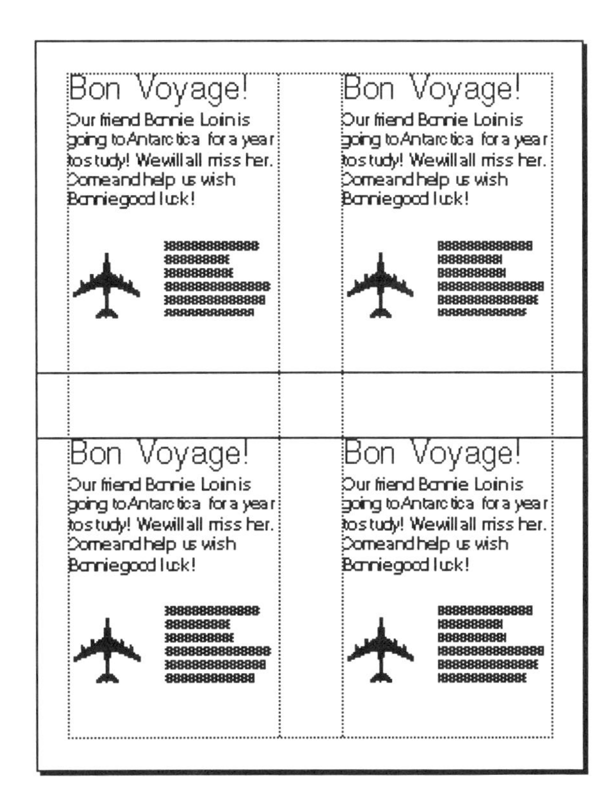

7) SAVE, PRINT, AND CLOSE THE PUBLICATION

a. Save the publication using the name BONVOYAG. Print a copy and then Close the publication.
b. Cut the printout into equal quarters to separate the four invitations.

7.16 Folded Invitations

Some occasions may require an invitation with an inside and an outside, rather than the flat, one-sided kind created in the previous practice. These alternative invitations are printed one to a page, then folded to resemble a greeting card. In order to have the elements in the correct positions for a folded invitation, the text that will appear inside is laid out on one quarter of the page and the outside text on the opposite quarter of the page:

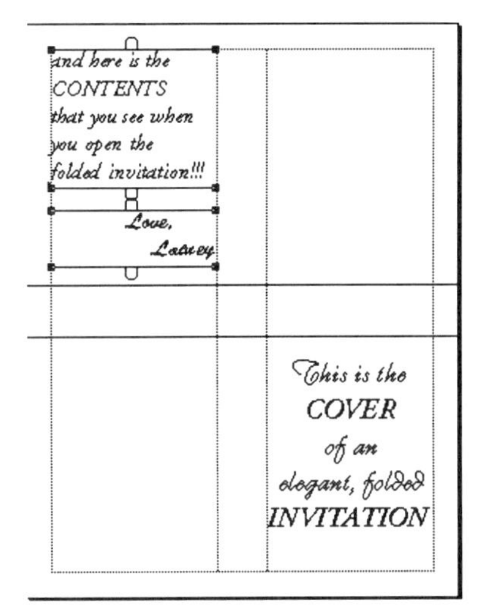

The initial layout of a folded invitation

The inside text is then rotated 180° and appears upside-down:

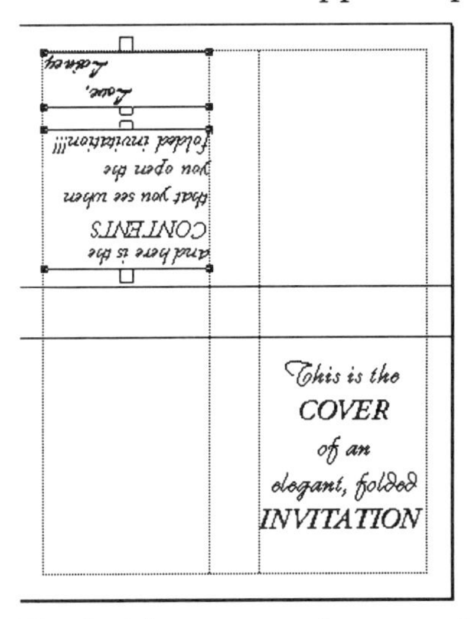

The inside text must be rotated

The printed page can then be folded into quarters to resemble a greeting card:

A folded invitation

For a different look to the invitation, create the design in a landscape orientation:

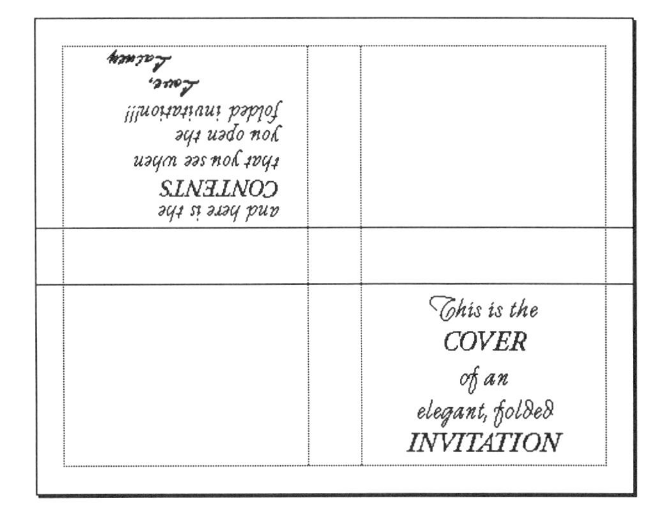

A landscape invitation

and fold the finished product so that it opens upwards:

The landscape invitation folded

7.17 Skewing an Object

Some designs for invitations, signs, or any publication may require fancy effects for graphics and text. The Control palette allows you to transform objects by *skewing* them with precision. Skewing means to slant an object:

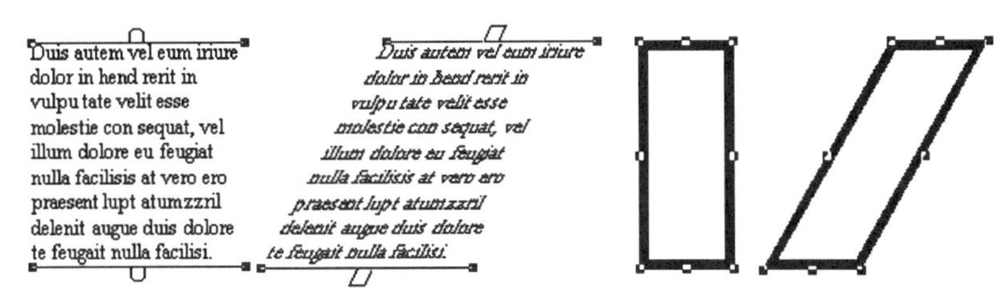

Both text blocks and graphics can be skewed, in this case by 30°

An object can be slanted up to 85° from its original position.

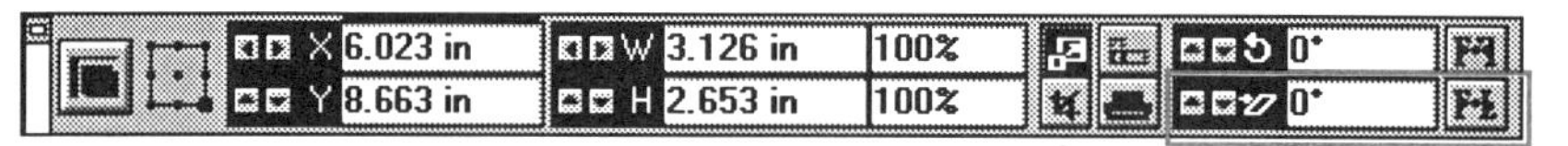

The Control palette when a graphic is selected

Skew

Text blocks or graphics can be skewed by first selecting the object and then typing in the number of degrees to be skewed from its original position. Pressing Enter or clicking on the Apply button will skew the object. Entering a positive number of degrees skews the object to the right, and a negative number skews the object to the left.

It is important to note that the reference point defined on the Proxy will remain fixed, and the object will skew from that point. If the bottom-right handle is chosen (indicated by being larger than the other handles) the top of the object will skew left or right and the bottom will remain stationary. If the top-right handle is chosen as the reference point, the bottom of the object will skew left or right and the top will remain stationary.

Practice 7

In this practice you will create a folded invitation for a party. The design will include a skewed dingbat. Start PageMaker if you have not already done so.

1) ADJUST THE PAGE SETTINGS FOR A FOLDED INVITATION

a. From the File menu, select the New command. The Page setup dialog box is shown.
b. Change these settings:

 Double-sided and Facing pages options: deselected
 Left, Right, Top, and Bottom margins: 0.5 inches
 Orientation: Wide

 Be sure that the Compose to printer and Target printer resolution settings are correct for your printer.
c. Select OK to make the changes. A letter size page is displayed with one-half inch margins.

2) CREATE THE GRID

a. Display the Master Page, then display the Control palette.
b. From the Layout menu, execute the Column guides command. Enter 2 for the Number of columns option, 1 for the Space between columns option, and select OK.
c. Use the display on the Control palette help place horizontal Ruler guides at exactly 3.75" and 4.75". You now have a grid marking off the margins of the invitation.

3) DRAW A GRAPHIC AND SKEW IT

a. Display page 1. Note how the page is divided into four sections.
b. In the bottom-right quarter of the page, draw a rectangle with the Rectangle tool. Use the Control palette to size the rectangle exactly 1" wide and 3.25" high.

c. From the Element menu, use the Line command and Fill command to format the rectangle with a line of None and a fill of 20%.
d. On the Control palette, double click in the Skew field. Type `-35` and click on the Apply button. The rectangle is now skewed 35° to the left.
e. Move the skewed rectangle in the bottom-right quarter of the page so that the upper-left corner is aligned with the Column guide and the horizontal Ruler guide at 5.75".

4) COPY AND PASTE THE SKEWED RECTANGLE

Copy the skewed rectangle, and paste a copy into the upper-left quarter of the page. Align the pasted copy with the upper-left corner of the Margin guides.

5) ADD TEXT TO THE FRONT COVER

a. In the bottom-right quarter of the page, create an insertion point and type the following text:

```
The Greenbaum Museum
invites you
to a private showing
```

Start each line with a new paragraph.
b. Use the Control palette to format the text to Bookman 24 point Bold. Center the text.
c. Place a horizontal Ruler guide at the 6" mark on the vertical ruler. Align the top of the text block you just created to the horizontal Ruler guide at 6". Remove the Ruler guide.

6) ADD TEXT TO THE INSIDE

a. In the top-left quarter of the page, create an insertion point and type the following text, just as it appears:

```
Cuckoo for Dada
a collection of dadaistic art
on display through december 2
special private showing
for museum members only
saturday, september 27
5 pm to 9 pm
wine and cheese served
```

b. Use the Control palette to format the text as Bookman 12 point Bold. Select the text block with the Pointer tool, and use the Control palette to make the block exactly 2.75" in width.

7) SKEW THE TEXT BLOCK

a. On the Control palette, double click in the Skew field. Type `35` and click on the Apply button. The text block is now skewed 35° to the right.
b. Place a horizontal Ruler guide at the 1" mark on the vertical Ruler. Move the skewed text block so that the upper-right corner is aligned with the Column guide and the horizontal Ruler guide at 1":

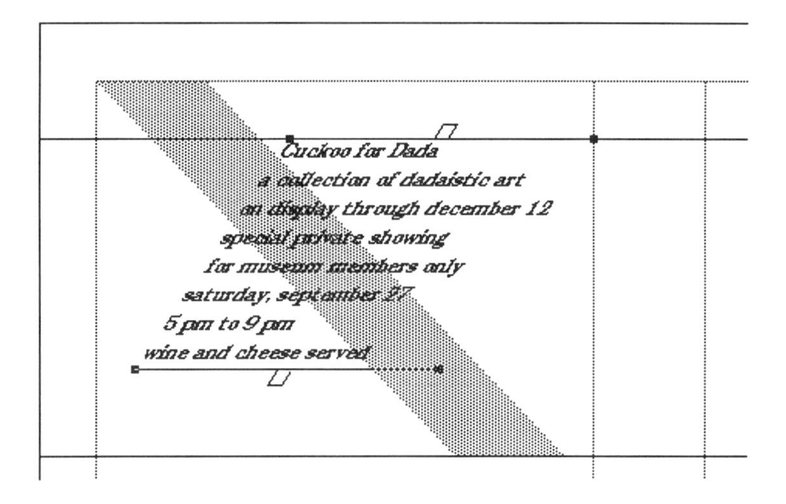

Remove the Ruler guide.

8) ROTATE THE INSIDE CONTENTS

a. With the Pointer tool, select the skewed text block and the skewed rectangle that occupy the upper-left corner of the page.
b. On the Control palette, select the center handle on the Proxy, then double click in the Rotation field. Type `180` and click on the Apply button. The text and graphic are rotated upside-down.

Check - The page should be similar to:

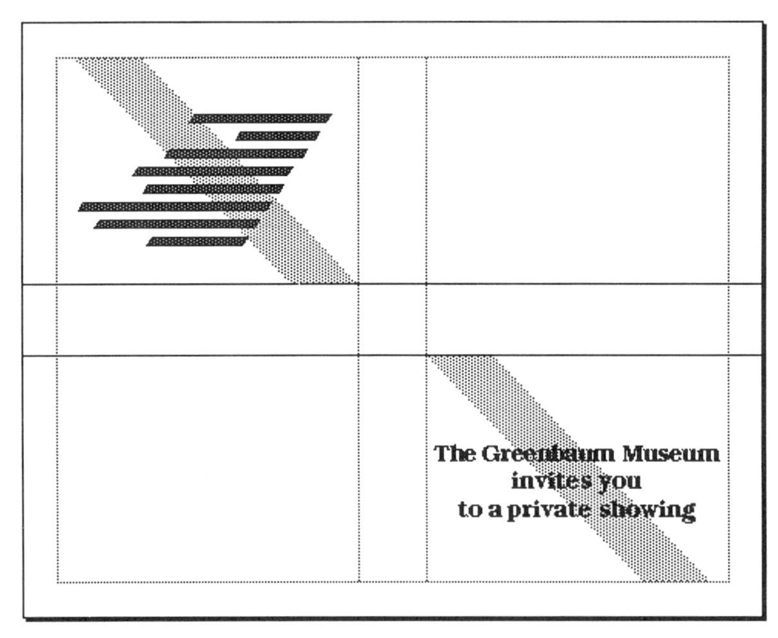

9) SAVE, PRINT, AND CLOSE THE PUBLICATION

a. Save the publication using the name DADAINV. Print a copy, then Close the file.
b. Fold the printout, printed side outwards, in half the short way. Fold the paper again in half, with the outside text on the outside.

10) EXIT PAGEMAKER AND WINDOWS

Chapter Summary

There are two major categories of printed advertisements: published and distributed. Published ads appear in publications, and distributed ads are manually given to the audience.

Advertisements, whether published or distributed, are split into four major types: informative, sale, emotional, and exposure. Every advertisement contains copy, which is the text, and advertiser identification such as a company name or logo.

Design considerations for advertisements are similar to those for other publications: appropriateness, balance, focus and flow, and consistency. The contents of the ad must be appropriate for the targeted audience, the layout of the ad must balance and have a fitting focus and flow, and the ad must be consistent with other items from the advertiser.

Using logos repetitively in a design and across many designs can increase the consistency of the design(s). By using similar designs with different media, a corporate identity is created.

Forms and coupons in advertisements should be large enough to be useable. If they are to be cut out, they should be in an accessible location so that they can be easily used by the audience.

Text can be flowed around graphics by using the Text wrap command from the Element menu. The boundaries that the wrapped text follow can be customized by moving boundary handles and creating new handles.

Single objects can be selected from a stack of objects by three methods: using the Send to back command until the desired object is selectable with the Pointer tool, using the Pointer tool to marquee select the object, or by holding down the Control key while clicking on the object until it is selected.

The Control palette offers shortcuts for formatting text, text blocks, and graphics; the format options available change depending upon what type of object is selected in the publication. A Proxy, displaying a selected reference point where formatting will occur, is contained in most views of the Control palette.

Signs and awards can be created in PageMaker just as any other publication. Printing out a character set of a decorative font will show the ASCII codes for different dingbats that can be used to make effective signs and awards. The numeric keypad is used to type in the ASCII code for each special character (`Alt+0`+three digit ASCII code).

Invitations can be made by either printing four to a page, or by printing an inside and an outside on one page and folding the finished product into a greeting card. The inside text needs to be rotated 180° so that it will appear upright on the folded invitation. The Control palette can rotate the text and graphics with precision. Text and graphics can also be skewed, or slanted, with the Control palette.

Vocabulary

Advertiser identification - Either a logo, name and address, or title that identifies the advertiser

ASCII codes - Three digit numbers typed on the numeric keypad needed to access special characters in a font.

Boundaries - Dotted lines that define the area text flows around.

Character set - All the characters available for a font.

Control palette - A window that contains precise formatting commands and displays the coordinates of objects.

Copy - The text used in an ad.

Corporate identity - The common theme that is created by repeatedly placing the same logo in a similar manner on all things associated with a company.

Customized boundary - Text wrap boundary that is moved from its original position or changed from its original shape.

Display font - Fonts from the decorative family often used in ads.

Distributed advertisements - Ads in the form of flyers or small brochures that are distributed by mail, by hand, or posted in public.

Emotional advertisement - A type of ad where the graphics and text used are not related directly to the product, but they communicate an emotion or an attitude that is then associated with the product.

Exposure advertisement - A type of ad that begins or continues a relationship between the targeted audience and the company or product.

Informative advertisement - A type of ad where the purpose is to educate the audience about a product or topic.

Marquee box - Temporary blinking box drawn by dragging the Pointer tool used to select groups of objects.

Marquee selecting - Surrounding objects to be selected with a marquee box.

Proxy - Control palette diagram of an object's reference points.

Published advertisements - Ads that appear within a publication such as a newspaper, magazine, or newsletter.

Sale advertisement - A type of ad where the purpose is to inform the targeted audience about items that are being sold at a special price for a limited time.

Skewing - Slanting an object a certain degree to the left or to the right.

7

Reviews

Sections 7.1 — 7.5

1. List the four different types of advertisements.

2. What are the two common elements of advertisements?

3. List three separate design considerations that apply specifically to advertisements.

4. How is a logo related to a corporate identity?

Sections 7.6 — 7.9

5. Where should a coupon be placed in an advertisement and why?

6. Explain how you would create the outline of a coupon.

7. List the steps required to wrap text around a graphic.

8. a) What is a customized boundary?
   b) How do you add a handle to the boundary?
   c) How do you delete a handle from the boundary?

9. List three methods of selecting an object that occupies the same area where there are many other objects.

Sections 7.10 — 7.17

10. a) What is the Control palette used for?
    b) How does the contents of the Control palette change?

11. a) What is the Proxy?
    b) How do you select a reference point?

12. a) What does a character set consist of?
    b) Why do you need ASCII codes?
    c) How must you enter the ASCII code?

13. a) List the steps needed to rotate objects with the Control palette.
    b) How do you rotate an object counter-clockwise? Clockwise?

14. List two different formats of invitations.

15. a) What is meant by skewing?
    b) List the steps necessary to skew an object.
    c) How do you skew an object to the left? To the right?

Exercises

1. In Section 7.4 of this chapter two versions of an advertisement for Aztec Café's lunch buffet are displayed. Aztec's owner thinks that both ads are too crowded and would like you to design an ad that does not contain a list of the foods served.

    a) Design two thumbnail sketches for the advertisement which will be 6.5" wide and 9" tall. Include the Aztec Café's logo in your designs, and consider adding graphical elements such as rules to your design. Indicate typefaces, sizes, and other specifications next to each thumbnail.

    b) Create a new publication, deselecting the Double-sided option and entering 1 for the left, right, top, and bottom margins in the Page setup dialog box. Pick the best thumbnail sketch and use the Master Page to create grid.

    c) Place AZTECAFE.WMF, the logo, in the advertisement and resize proportionately, copy and paste, and move as necessary.

    d) Using the Story Editor write any text necessary for the advertisement. Return to the layout and resize, adjust fonts and leading, and move the text as necessary.

    e) Save the advertisement naming it ACLUNCH and then print a copy.

    f) Aztec has decided to run an advertisement for its luncheon buffet in a local magazine. Because of the high cost of advertising the ad will have to fit a space 3" wide by 4" long. Using thumbnail sketches redesign the ad above reducing the information it contains, but being careful to maintain the look of the larger ad. Remember that consistency is important in an advertising campaign.

    g) The publication ACLUNCH should still be open. Use the Save as command from the file menu to save the publication under a new name, ACLUNCH2.

    h) Move the contents of ACLUNCH2 onto the Pasteboard and then change the margins so that the work area is 3" wide by 4" high. Pick your best thumbnail sketch and create a grid on the Master Page.

    i) Using the elements you moved onto the Pasteboard, create the new advertisement based on your thumbnail.

    j) Save the publication and print a copy.

2. California Sunshine has decided to sponsor a rock band, The Sunshines, and has asked you to the cover for their latest compact disc as well as an advertisement for the CD. The band has four members: Johnny Lemon, Sheila Heart, Michael Porter, and Beth Brown. The CD will be titled *Hello Sunshine Goodbye Rain* and contain four songs: You are My Sunshine, Sunny Days are Here Again, Oranges and Lemons, and Hello Sunshine Goodbye Rain.

a) Design two sets of thumbnail sketches for the cover and back panel of the compact disc. The dimensions of both are 4.75" wide by 4.75" high. As the Band's sponsor, California Sunshine expects its logo to be included on the CD cover. Make sure that the back includes the names of the band's members and the song titles. Consider rotating elements, using text wrap, and skewing objects.

b) Create a new publication, entering `4.75` for both Page dimensions options, `2` for the Number of pages option, `0.167` for all margins, and deselecting the Double-sided option in the Page setup dialog box. Pick the best thumbnail sketches and create a grid on the Master Page.

c) Place CALIFSUN.WMF, the logo, in the publication. Resize and move as necessary. Create any text needed then resize, adjust fonts, and move blocks as necessary.

d) Save the cover naming it CSROCK and then print a copy.

e) Design two thumbnail sketches for the CD's advertisement. The ad will be 6.5" wide by 9" tall. Include a coupon for the CD which can be sent with a check for $9.95 to California Sunshine Consumer Products, 78932 Ground Road, San Jerdi CA 89373. Keep in mind the purpose and audience as you sketch, and make sure that the advertisement is consistent with the CD cover. The cover should be shown full size in the ad. Consider rotating elements of the ad and using text wrap around the CD cover and coupon.

f) Create a new publication, deselecting the Double-sided option and entering `1` for the left, right, top, and bottom margins in the Page setup dialog box. Pick the best thumbnail sketch and use the Master Page to create grid.

g) Using the Story Editor write any text necessary for the advertisement. Return to the layout and resize, adjust fonts and leading, and move the text as necessary. To copy the CD cover from CSROCK, open the publication, select the cover, execute the Copy command, and then paste it into the advertisement.

h) Save the advertisement naming it CSROCKAD and print a copy.

3. In Exercise 2 you created an 8.5" x 11" advertisement (CSROCKAD) for a compact disc made by the rock band The Sunshines. The band's sponsor, California Sunshine, would also like to run a smaller ad for the CD in newspapers and magazines. Since the CD's release, the title song *Hello Sunshine Goodbye Rain* as well as the lead singer, Michael Porter, have both received considerable publicity. Therefore, the new ad should mention both prominently.

   a) Design two thumbnail sketches for the advertisement so that it contains a coupon similar to the one used for CSROCKAD. The ad will be 5" wide by 4" tall. Since this ad is smaller it will not contain the CD cover, but should be consistent with the design of the larger ad. You will need to use the Text wrap command to fit both text and a coupon in the ad.

   b) Create a new publication, deselecting the Double-sided option in the Page setup dialog box. Adjust the margins so that the work area is 5" wide by 4" tall. Pick the best thumbnail sketch and create a grid on the Master Page.

c) Place CALIFSUN.WMF, the logo, in the publication. Resize and move as necessary. Create any text needed then resize, adjust fonts, and move text blocks as necessary for your design.

d) Save the ad naming it CSRKAD2 and then print a copy.

4. Ivy University Press is about to publish a gardening book titled *How Does Your Ivy Grow?* by botanist Dr. Ivana Green. You have been asked to design both the front and back covers for the book which will measure 7" wide by 9" tall. Ivy University wants its logo used on both the front and back.

   a) Design two sets of thumbnail sketches for the front and back covers. Include the following in your designs:

      - Ivy University logo
      - a brief description of the book's contents
      - Ms. Green's photograph
      - Ms. Green's biography: graduated Ivy University in 1954, chairperson of the University's Botany department since 1981, married with three children, author of six books including the best seller *Ivy, Ivy On the Wall*
      - two quotes: "I love everything Ivana writes. This is her best book since *The Death of Ivy*". (John Talbot, Southern University) and "Ivana you have done it again! I can never look at ivy again without thinking of you". (Lillian Andrews, American Ivy Association)

      Consider using graphical elements, rotated text, or skewed elements in your design. Indicate typefaces, sizes, and other specifications next to each thumbnail.

   b) Create a new publication, entering 2 for the Number of pages option and deselecting the Double-sided option in the Page setup dialog box. Pick the best thumbnail sketch and create a grid on the Master Page.

   c) Place IULOGO.WMF, the logo, in the publication and resize proportionately, copy and paste, and move as necessary. Place PHOTO.WMF for Ms. Green's picture and format as necessary.

   d) Using the Story Editor write any text necessary for the book covers. Return to the layout and resize, adjust fonts and leading, and move the text as necessary.

   e) Save the publication naming it IVYBOOK and then print a copy.

5. Each year Ivy University Press awards its prestigious Hortense Hollaway book prize. This years winner is Ivana Green for her book *How Does Your Ivy Grow?* You are to design the award which is to be printed on 11" wide by 8.5" tall paper.

   a) Design two thumbnail sketches for the award, keeping in mind the purpose and audience. Include the University's logo in your design. Consider using graphical elements and dingbats in the design.

   b) Create a new publication, selecting Wide, deselecting the Double-sided option, and entering 1 for the Left, Right, Top, and Bottom margins in the Page setup dialog box. Pick the best thumbnail sketch and create a grid on the Master Page.

c) Place IULOGO.WMF, the logo, in the publication. Resize and move as necessary. Create any text and graphics needed then resize, adjust fonts, and move as necessary for your design.

d) Save the award naming it IVYAWARD and then print a copy.

6. Ivy University Press is planning a party to celebrate Ivana Green's winning the Hortense Holloway Book Prize for her book *How Does Your Ivy Grow?* The party is to be held at 6:00 PM on Saturday, May 14 at Bookman Hall on the Ivy University campus. You have been asked to produce an invitation 4.25" wide by 5.5" tall for the party.

a) Design two thumbnail sketches for the invitation, keeping in mind design elements used for the cover of Ms. Green's book (see Exercise 4). Consider using graphical elements and dingbats in the design.

b) Create a new publication, deselecting the Double-sided option and entering 0.5 for the left, right, top, and bottom margins in the Page setup dialog box. Pick the best thumbnail sketch and create a grid on the Master Page, keeping in mind that there will be four invitations on a page.

c) Place any graphic files needed, such as IULOGO.WMF or PHOTO.WMF, then resize and move as necessary. Create the text and any graphics needed for your design, then resize, adjust fonts, and move as necessary for your design.

d) Copy and paste the invitation into the empty three-quarters of the page so that there are four invitations.

e) Save the invitation naming it INVITE and then print a copy. Cut the page into four invitations.

f) Ivana Green now changes her mind and wants a fancier folded invitation. Design two sets of thumbnails for the invitation, including sketches for the cover and the inside. Use design elements from INVITE and from the book cover to keep the design consistent. You might consider placing Ms. Green's biography and photograph PHOTO.TIF on the left inside page.

g) Create a new publication, deselecting the Double-sided option and entering 0.5 for the left, right, top, and bottom margins in the Page setup dialog box. Pick the best thumbnail sketch and create a grid on the Master Page, keeping in mind that the page will be folded into quarters to produce the invitation.

h) Place any graphic files needed, such as IULOGO.WMF or PHOTO.WMF, then resize and move as necessary. Create the text and any graphics needed for your design, then resize, adjust fonts, and move as necessary for your design. Remember to rotate the text that will be on the inside pages 180° using the Control palette.

i) Save the folded invitation naming it INVITE2 and then print a copy. Fold the invitation so that it is ready for Ms. Green's approval.

7. In Chapter 5 Exercise 7 you created a calendar for Ivy University (named CALENDAR) that included only the month of September. The University would like you to add the fall months of October and November.

   a) Open CALENDAR and add pages for the additional months by executing the Page setup command from the File menu and entering 3 for the Number of pages option.

   b) Draw two thumbnail sketches, redesigning the calendar. Keep in mind the design considerations for a sign or poster as you sketch.

   c) Pick your best thumbnail and make any necessary changes to the grid on the Master Page for your new design. Layout the pages for the new months and make any needed changes to the month of September.

   d) Save the revised CALENDAR and then print a copy.

8. Aztec Café is planning a party for its best customers to be held at the restaurant (1413 Encinada Boulevard, Grande, CA 10023 phone 308-555-8432) on Friday, March 4 at 6:30 PM. You are to design a folded invitation with copy printed on the cover and two inside pages. The left inside page might contain a list of Aztec favorites to be served at the party. Owner Juan Hernandez wants both his name and Aztec Café's logo used in the invitation.

   a) Design two thumbnail sketches for the invitation, keeping in mind design elements used for other Aztec Café publications. Include the logo and Juan Hernandez in your design, and consider using other graphical elements and dingbats as well.

   b) Create a new publication, deselecting the Double-sided option and entering 0.5 for the left, right, top, and bottom margins in the Page setup dialog box. Pick the best thumbnail sketch and create a grid on the Master Page, keeping in mind that the page will be folded into quarters to produce the invitation.

   c) Place AZTECAFE.WMF, then resize and move it as necessary. Create the text and any graphics needed for your invitation, then resize, adjust fonts, and move as necessary for your design. Remember to rotate the text that will be on the inside pages 180° using the Control palette.

   d) Save the folded invitation naming it ACINV, print a copy, and fold the invitation.

7

Chapter Eight:
Long Publications

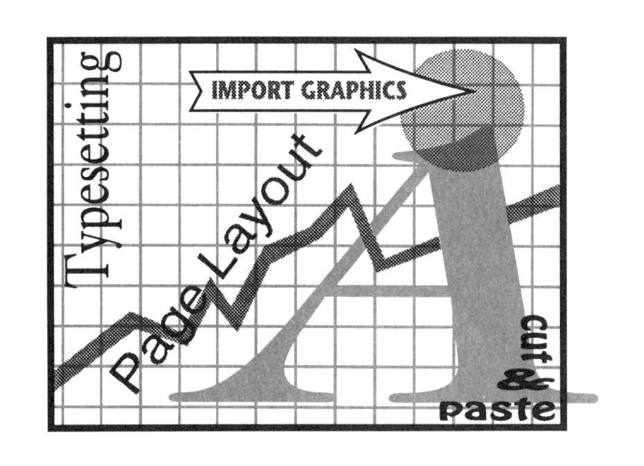

Type - Style

Type - Define styles

Window - Style palette

Type - Paragraph

Layout - Autoflow

Layout - Insert pages

Layout - Remove pages

Inline graphics

Utilities - Create TOC

Objectives

After completing this chapter you will be able to:

1. Understand the design considerations necessary for long publications.
2. Use styles to create a consistent look.
3. Work with multiple column text and Autoflow.
4. Insert and remove pages.
5. Use printing options to save time and paper.
6. Create and modify inline graphics.
7. Create and format headers and footers with page numbers on the Master Pages.
8. Have PageMaker create a table of contents for a publication.

8

Publications you have created so far have been short, 4 or 5 pages at the most. Desktop publishers must be prepared to deal with longer, multi-page documents such as newspapers (as opposed to newsletters), annual reports, yearbooks, catalogs, textbooks, and reference manuals. Longer publications pose a number of problems, not the least of which is their size. This chapter introduces design considerations for longer documents, as well as PageMaker commands which make the creation and modification of such documents easier.

8.1 Design for Long Publications

In Chapter Five you learned about the factors that produce a good design, including four basic guidelines for all documents:

- Appropriateness
- Balance
- Focus and Flow
- Consistency

Each of these guidelines has special applications in a longer document.

Appropriateness

Appropriateness involves making choices about typeface, margins, graphical elements, etc. so that the document sends the right message to the intended audience. In a long publication it is also important to consider *readability*—making certain that your design is easy to read, page after page. For example, a typeface that works well in a half-page advertisement may become difficult to read in a 500 page textbook.

Balance

You already know that absolute balance is boring. However, in a long document balance can add stability, increasing the reader's ability to find and focus on important information.

Focus and Flow

There are usually many different topics and subtopics (or levels) of information in a long publication. It is important to employ techniques such as headings and subheadings to indicate these levels to the reader. For example, in this text each section is preceded by a solid black line followed by the section number and title. The Practices are preceded by a dotted blue line and the word "Practice." Consistent use of these headings allows the reader to easily locate the beginning of a new section and distinguish between Practices and readings.

Consistency

Consistency will ensure that the reader is able to locate desired information from page to page or chapter to chapter. The dotted blue line used to indicate a Practice section is used in each chapter in this text. When you see this you know that a Practice is next, no matter which chapter you are in.

8

8.2 Styles - The Key to Consistency

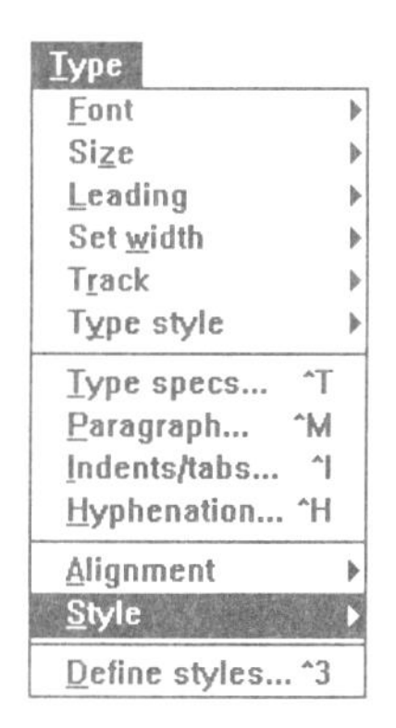

Styles are PageMaker's way of helping you automate consistency and, while they may be used in any document, they are especially helpful in longer publications. A *style* is a named group of text and paragraph formatting options which can all be applied by selecting the Style command from the Type menu:

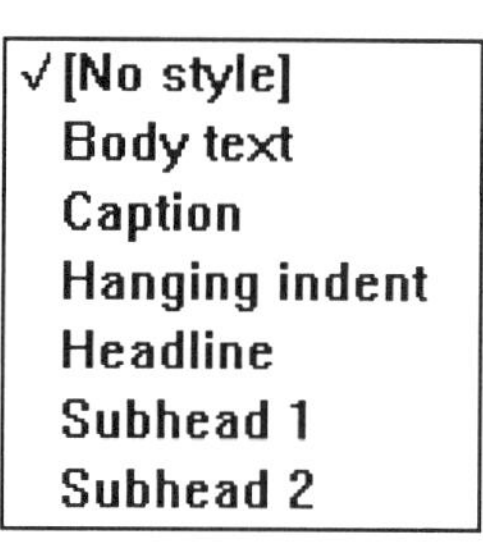

These styles are defined in every new publication

The Style submenu lists 6 predefined styles as well as a No style option. The current style is indicated with a check mark.

To apply a style, the Text tool is selected and the pointer clicked in the paragraph to be formatted, placing the insertion point in that paragraph. To apply a style to a block of paragraphs, they are first highlighted. Then the desired style is selected from the Style submenu. The defined text and paragraph formatting options for that style (including font, size, style, alignment, leading, etc.) will then be applied. To remove a style, the insertion point (or highlight) is placed in the desired paragraph and the style set to No style.

Obviously, using styles save time. Simply selecting the style name applies formatting options which could require 3 or 4 commands to set. However, styles also create a consistency from page to page and chapter to chapter because a paragraph which is formatted with the Headline style on one page will have the same appearance as a Headline style paragraph on the next page, or 20 pages later. Additionally, styles can be copied from publication to publication, making it easy to maintain a consistent look from document to document. This is especially useful in a periodical such as a magazine which is produced each month.

Practice 1

In this Practice you will create a new publication and apply different styles.

1) START PAGEMAKER AND CREATE A NEW PUBLICATION

2) IMPORT A TEXT FILE

a. From the File menu, select the Place command.
b. Select the PRAC-8.TXT file and click on OK in the Text-only import filter box.
c. Place the pointer in the upper-left corner of the document and click. The text is placed.

3) APPLY THE HEADLINE STYLE

a. Select the Text tool from the Toolbox. Zoom in so that the text is readable.
b. Click once in the first paragraph, the line which says "This is a Headline."
c. From the Type menu, execute the Style command. (Note: this is the Style command, not the Type Style command.) A submenu of available styles is shown.
d. Select the Headline style. The font, style, and size of the current paragraph are changed and surrounding paragraphs are unchanged:

This is a Headline

Obviously, using styles save time. Simply selecting the style name applies formatting options which could require 3 or 4 commands to set. However, styles also create a consistency from page to page and chapter to chapter.

This is a Subhead
A paragraph which is formatted with the Headline style on one page will be the same as a Headline paragraph on the next page. Additionally, styles can be copied from publication to publication, making it easy to maintain a consistent look from document to document. This is especially useful

4) APPLY THE SUBHEAD 1 STYLE

a. The Text tool should still be selected. There are two paragraphs which read "This is a Subhead." Click once in the first one, near the top of the document.
b. From the Type menu, execute the Style command.
c. From the Style submenu, select Subhead 1. The font, style, and size of the current paragraph are changed.
d. Locate the next "This is a Subhead" paragraph and apply the Subhead 1 style to it. Note that this paragraph is given exactly the same font, style, and size options as the previous subhead.

5) APPLY THE SUBHEAD 2 STYLE

a. The Text tool should still be selected. Click once in the paragraph which says "How to Apply a Style."
b. From the Type menu, execute the Style command and select Subhead 2.

6) FORMAT THE LIST AS A BLOCK

a. The next two paragraphs are a numbered list which will be formatted as a hanging indent. Click once in the paragraph which begins "1. First, select...".

b. Drag down into the next paragraph, creating a highlight.
c. From the Type menu, execute the Style command and select Hanging indent. Both paragraphs are formatted. Note that this style modified only the paragraphs, and not the font.

7) FORMAT THE BODY OF THE PUBLICATION

a. Using the Style command, format the remaining paragraphs as Body text.
b. Save the file as CH8PRACT.PM5. Your publication should be similar to:

This is a Headline

Obviously, using styles save time. Simply selecting the style name applies formatting options which could require 3 or 4 commands to set. However, styles also create a consistency from page to page and chapter to chapter.

This is a Subhead

A paragraph which is formatted with the Headline style on one page will be the same as a Headline paragraph on the next page. Additionally, styles can be copied from publication to publication, making it easy to maintain a consistent look from document to document. This is especially useful in a periodical such as a newsletter which is produced every month.

This is a Subhead

To apply a style, select the Text tool and click the pointer in the paragraph to be formatted. To apply a style to a block of paragraphs, highlight them first. Then select the desired style from the Style submenu. The defined text and paragraph formatting options for that style will then be applied. To remove the style, make sure that the cursor (or highlight) is in the desired paragraph and set the style to No Style.

How to Apply a *Style*

1. First, select the paragraph to be formatted. This may be done by clicking in the paragraph with the Text tool, placing the cursor in the paragraph.
2. Next, select the Style command from the Type menu, and choose the desired style name from the submenu.

8.3 *Defining Styles*

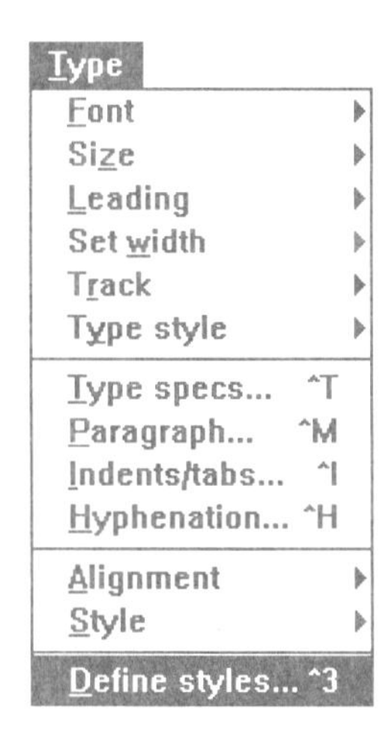

Existing styles can be redefined and new styles created at any time using the Define Styles command from the Type menu (`Ctrl+3`):

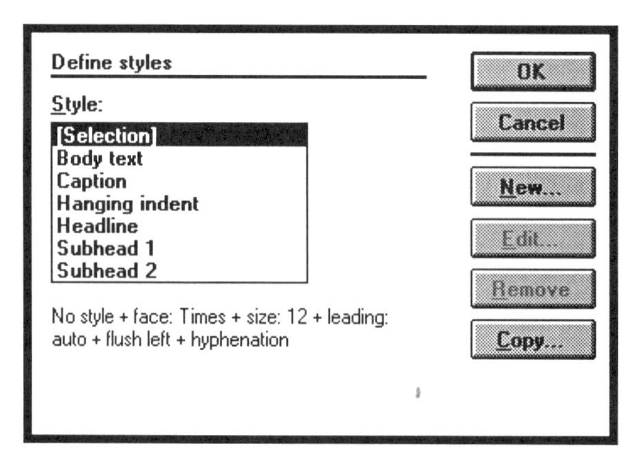

Styles can be created or modified using Define Styles

PageMaker shows the currently defined styles in the list. The six styles shown above are automatically created for every new publication. The Selection option is not an actual style, but shows the settings for the currently highlighted text including typeface, size, leading, and paragraph formats.

A style may be redefined by highlighting it in the list and then selecting Edit. The formatting options that you wish to change are then selected from the displayed dialog box:

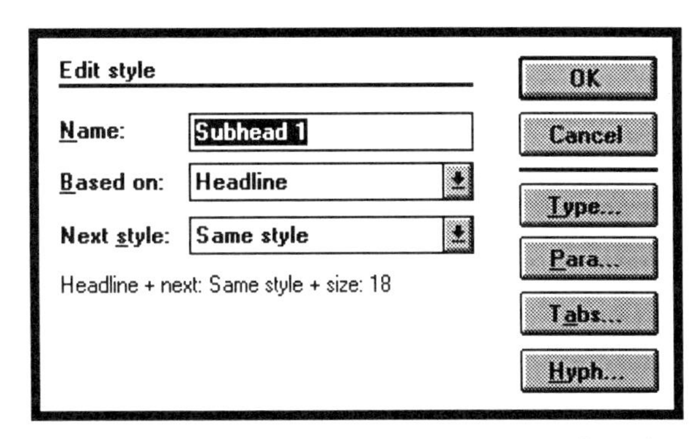

Options for the Subhead 1 style can now be changed

PageMaker groups the formatting options into Type, Para(graph), Tabs, and Hyph(enation). Selecting one of these buttons displays the standard dialog box for that option. For example, selecting Type displays the Type Specs dialog box where you can specify the type options for the selected style. Paragraph, tab, and hyphenation options can then be specified by selecting the appropriate button.

New styles are created by selecting the New button in the Define Styles dialog box. The Edit style dialog box is then displayed and you must supply a Name for the style. Type, Para, Tabs, and Hyph options can then be defined for the new style.

When creating or editing a style, multiple dialog boxes will be open at the same time. For example, when changing the font for a style, three overlapping dialog boxes are displayed: Define style, Edit style, and Type specifications. Selecting OK closes the top dialog box and displays the previous. In a complicated format, there could be seven or eight dialog boxes stacked up. Rather than selecting OK for each box, PageMaker has a shortcut. Holding down the Shift key and clicking OK (`Shift+OK`) closes all open dialog boxes. Any options set along the way will be retained, as if OK was selected for each box. Similarly, `Shift+Cancel` cancels all the dialog boxes, ignoring any options that had been selected. These shortcuts can be used whenever there are multiple dialog boxes open.

8.4 The Style Palette

PageMaker has a shortcut for applying styles. The Style palette command from the Window menu (`Ctrl+Y`) displays a listing of the available styles in a box similar to the Toolbox:

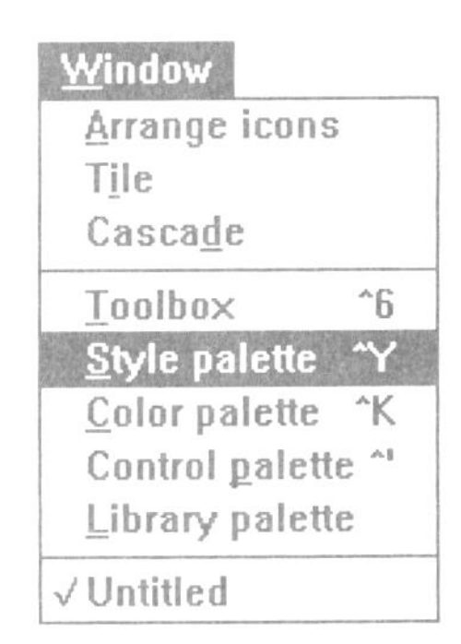

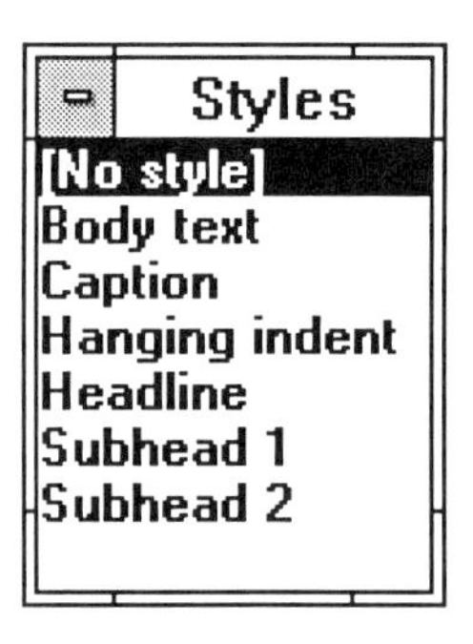

The Style palette is similar to the Toolbox

The Style palette can be dragged to a new location so that it does not obscure the material you are working on. It may be removed from the screen by clicking on its Close box or selecting Style palette again.

Clicking on a style name in the Style palette applies that style to the currently selected text. As with all formatting commands, it is important to place the insertion point in the proper paragraph or highlight the text to be formatted first, and then select the style.

Practice 2

In this Practice you will edit an existing style, create a new one, and use the Style palette. Start PageMaker and open the CH8PRACT.PM5 publication if you have not already done so.

1) EXECUTE THE DEFINE STYLES COMMAND

a. Select the Pointer tool from the Toolbox.
b. From the Type menu, select the Define Styles command. The Define styles dialog box is shown listing all of the currently defined styles.
c. The currently selected style should be [Selection]. Press the down-arrow key to highlight Body text. Directly below the list are shown the options for the Body text style.
d. Press down-arrow for each style, noting the different formatting options for each.

2) CHANGE THE SUBHEAD 1 STYLE

a. Using the mouse, click once on the Subhead 1 style, highlighting it.
b. Select the Edit button. The Edit style dialog is displayed.
c. Select the Type button. The Type specifications dialog box is shown. These are the type options currently assigned to the Subhead 1 style.
d. Change the Font to Helvetica.
e. Click on OK to remove the Type specifications dialog box.
f. Click on OK to remove the Edit style dialog box. The Define styles dialog box is shown. Note that the new font for Subhead 1, Helvetica, is listed below the list.
g. Select OK. All Subhead 1 style paragraphs ("This is a Subhead") are now displayed in Helvetica. Note that changing the style affected both Subhead 1 paragraphs.

3) CREATE A NEW STYLE

a. From the Type menu, select the Define Styles command.
b. Select New to create a new style.

c. On the Name line, type `My Headline`.
d. Click on the Type button. Make the font Helvetica, 24 points, and Bold.
e. In the Type specifications box, click on OK to return to Edit style.
f. Select the Para option and choose Center as the Alignment.
g. There are currently three dialog boxes open: Paragraph specifications, Edit style, and Define style. Holding down the Shift key, click on OK (`Shift+OK`). All three boxes are removed and the style is created.

4) *DISPLAY AND USE THE STYLE PALETTE*

a. From the Window menu, select the Style palette command. The Style palette is displayed. Note that the My Headline style created in the previous step is listed.
b. Place the pointer over the word "Styles" in the title bar of the Style palette.
c. Drag the pointer to the left. An outline of the Style palette moves with the pointer.
d. Release the mouse button. The palette is placed at the new position.
e. Drag the palette so that it is below the Toolbox.
f. Select the Text tool from the Toolbox.
g. Click in the headline at the top of the publication. Headline is highlighted in the Style palette indicating that the cursor is currently in a Headline style paragraph.
h. Click the pointer in the next paragraph. The Style palette indicates that this is a Body text paragraph.
i. Click in each of the remaining paragraphs, noting the style that is applied.

5) *APPLY A STYLE WITH THE STYLE PALETTE*

a. Place the cursor in the headline at the top of the publication. This is currently a Headline style paragraph as indicated in the Style palette.
b. Click on My Headline in the Style palette. The My Headline style is applied to the paragraph, changing its type and paragraph options to those you created in step 3.
c. From the Window menu, select the Style palette command. The palette is removed from the screen.
d. Press `Ctrl+Y`. The palette is again displayed.
e. Save and print the modified publication.

<u>Check</u> - Your publication should be similar to:

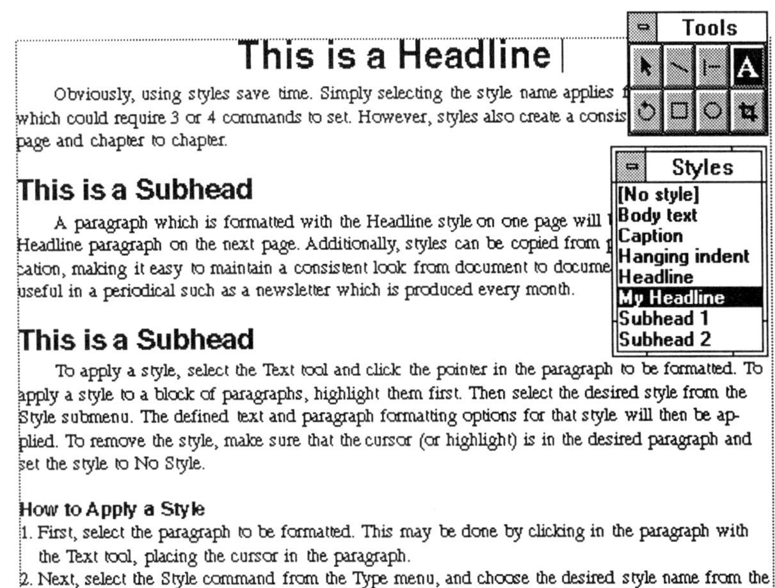

8.5 Indents

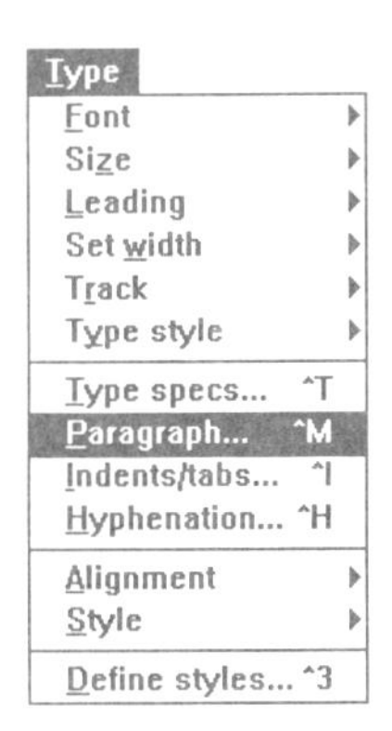

In a long document it may be necessary to alter the width of the lines in a specific paragraph using *indents*, either to set some information off from the rest of the document (such as a long quotation) or to create visual interest. Indents make the margins of a specific paragraph appear larger, and therefore the line length appears shorter. The default indent is 0", meaning that lines can extend from the left to the right margin. It is possible to set off a paragraph by specifying left and right indents. For example, it is possible to set the left and right indents to 1 inch, similar to:

> This is a justified paragraph with no indents. Each full line extends from the left margin to the right margin.
>
> > This paragraph is indented. The lines extend from the left to the right indent, making for a shorter line length.

Indents are set using the Paragraph command from the Type menu (`Ctrl+M`):

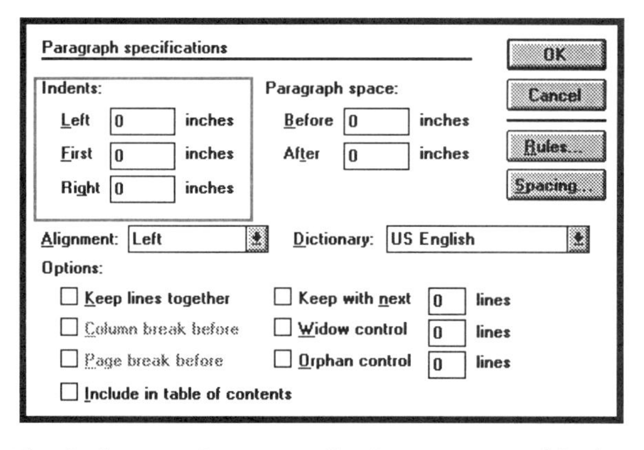

The indent options specify the amount of indent

To set an indent, simply enter the desired size(s) in the Left and Right options. Like all paragraph formats, setting an indent affects only the paragraph which currently contains the cursor or the highlighted block of paragraphs.

8.6 Hanging Indents and Bulleted Lists

Left and right indents are most commonly used to set off quotes, for outlines, and in bibliography entries. A special type of indent is the *hanging indent* where, as the name implies, the first line of the indented paragraph hangs out to the left over the lines below it. Hanging indents are useful when preparing lists, creating outlines, or including a standard bibliography in a research paper. On the next page is a bibliography entry, formatted with a hanging indent:

Canine, Butch S. *My Life as a Dog: A True-Life Story.* New York: Sirius Press, 1992.

The first line, which begins with the author's name, sticks out to the left from the rest of the bibliography entry. A hanging indent is created by specifying a negative value for the First line indent in the Paragraph dialog box:

Indents:

Left	0.5	**inches**
First	-0.5	**inches**
Right	1	**inches**

The negative First line indent creates the hanging effect

In the previous Practice you applied a predefined style named Hanging indent which contained a similar indent.

A special use for the hanging indent is in the creation of *bulleted lists*. A bulleted list is a unique way to vertically list separate items, sentences, or paragraphs using a special symbol or character to introduce each line. The following is an example of a bulleted list:

Today's Lunch Specials

- *Pizza Bianca* - A blend of four imported cheeses mixed with fresh herbs on a thin, crispy crust.
- *Insalata di Pollo* - Oak grilled chicken breast served with fresh salad greens, mozzarella, roasted peppers, and olives in a light vinaigrette.
- *Veal Chop* - Mesquite grilled with mushrooms.

In a bulleted list each item is a separate paragraph, formatted with a hanging indent. After creating the hanging indent, a bullet character such as an asterisk or the circular `Shift+Ctrl+8` character shown in the example above is added to draw attention to each item of the list. A Tab is used after the bullet to align the first line with the rest of the paragraph:

•→ *Pizza Bianca* - A blend of four imported cheeses mixed with fresh herbs on a thin, crispy crust.¶
•→ *Insalata di Pollo* - Oak grilled chicken breast served with fresh salad greens, mozzarella, roasted peppers, and olives in a light vinaigrette.¶
•→ *Veal Chop* - Mesquite grilled with mushrooms.¶

Tab

Enter

Bulleted lists do not show any order of importance within the list; each item is equally important. Numbered lists, also created with a hanging indent, show a priority of importance and should be used, for example, when listing directions or the steps in a recipe. The following recipe is an example of a numbered list created with a hanging indent:

1. Pour chicken broth into saucepan and bring to a boil.
2. Add noodles and cook for 5-7 minutes, stirring occasionally.
3. Reduce heat and add chicken chunks. Let simmer for 3-4 minutes.
4. Serve immediately with crackers.

Numbers are used as the "bullets" for this recipe because each step logically follows the previous one. If the noodles were added first, for example, they would probably burn in the bottom of the saucepan, ruining a potentially great supper!

Practice 3

In this Practice you will set and change paragraph indents and create a bulleted list. Start PageMaker and open the CH8PRACT.PM5 publication if you have not already done so.

1) *CREATE 1 INCH PARAGRAPH INDENTS*

a. Place the cursor anywhere in the paragraph which begins "A paragraph which is formatted . . .".

b. From the Type menu, select the Paragraph command.

c. Change the Left indent to `1`, the First to `0`, and the Right to `1`. Select OK to apply the changes. Your paragraph should be similar to:

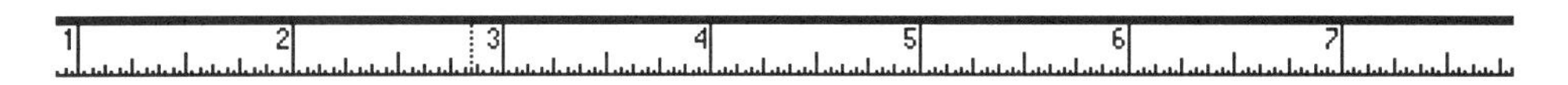

This is a Headline

Obviously, using styles save time. Simply selecting the style name applies formatting options which could require 3 or 4 commands to set. However, styles also create a consistency from page to page and chapter to chapter.

This is a Subhead

A paragraph which is formatted with the Headline style on one page will be the same as a Headline paragraph on the next page. Additionally, styles can be copied from publication to publication, making it easy to maintain a consistent look from document to document. This is especially useful in a periodical such as a newsletter which produced every month.

2) *CHANGE THE LEFT INDENT*

a. Make certain that the cursor is still in the indented paragraph. Press `Ctrl+M` to execute the Paragraph command. The current indent values are shown.

b. Change the Left indent to 0.5 and select OK. The left indent is reduced.

c. In the paragraph that begins "To apply a style ...", set a Left indent of `0.5`, First of `0`, and Right of `1`. Both paragraphs now have the same indents.

8

3) *MODIFY THE HANGING INDENT*

a. Place the cursor in one of the numbered steps at the bottom of the document. Execute the Paragraph command and note the current indent settings: 0.167 Left and -0.167 First. Cancel the Paragraph command.
b. We want to change the indents for both paragraphs at the same time, so create a highlight that extends from the step number 1 into step number 2.
c. Execute the Paragraph command. Change the current indents settings to Left 0.5, First -0.5, and Right 0.5. Select OK and both paragraphs are given the same indents. Note the position of the first line in each paragraph:

How to Apply a Style

1. First, select the paragraph to be formatted. This may be done by clicking in the paragraph with the Text tool, placing the cursor in the paragraph.
2. Next, select the Style command from the Type menu, and choose the desired style name from the submenu.

4) *CREATE THE BULLETS*

a. Move the cursor to the beginning of numbered step 1. Highlight the 1 and the period after it.
b. While holding down the Shift and Ctrl keys, press the 8 to create a bullet.
c. Highlight the 2 and the period after it at the beginning of numbered step 2. Press Shift+Ctrl+8 to create a bullet.
d. To make the bullet stand out more, reduce the First line indent to -0.25 for both bulleted steps.

Check - Your list should be similar to:

How to Apply a Style

- First, select the paragraph to be formatted. This may be done by clicking in the paragraph with the Text tool, placing the cursor in the paragraph.
- Next, select the Style command from the Type menu, and choose the desired style name from the submenu.

e. Save the publication and print a copy.
f. Close the publication.

8.7 Autoflow and Multiple Columns

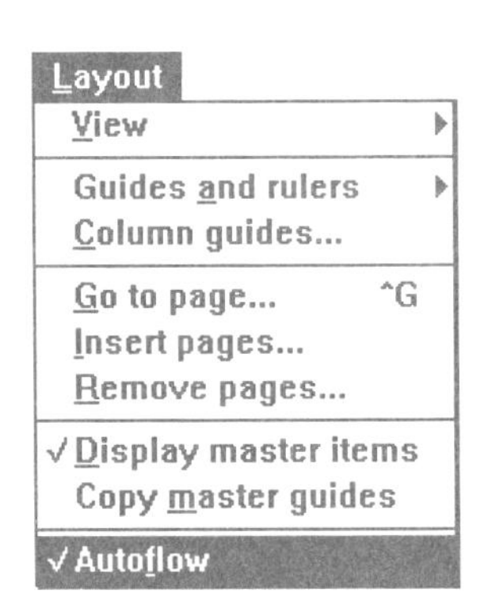

In Chapter Six you learned how to create multiple columns using the Column guides command in the Layout menu. While each page can have up to 20 columns of differing widths, 3 to 7 columns of equal width is the most common layout. Because consistency is especially important in longer documents, you should set your columns on the Master Pages. That way, the same column guides will automatically be placed on each page in the publication.

When a publication has many pages with multiple columns per page, it can be time-consuming to manually flow the text from one column to the next. Autoflow in the Layout menu instructs PageMaker to automatically flow any placed text into the next column. When it reaches the end of the page, Autoflow will create a new page and start flowing in the first column until all the text has been placed.

A check mark is shown next to Autoflow in the menu when it has been selected. When placing text, the loaded Text pointer also indicates that Autoflow is on:

The loaded Text pointer shape changes when Autoflow is selected

8.8 Adding and Removing Pages

It is possible to manually add and delete pages using the Insert pages and Remove pages commands from the Layout menu.

Layout
View
Guides and rulers
Column guides...
Go to page... ^G
Insert pages...
Remove pages...
√Display master items
Copy master guides
Autoflow

Insert pages is capable of creating any number of new pages and placing them either before or after the currently displayed page:

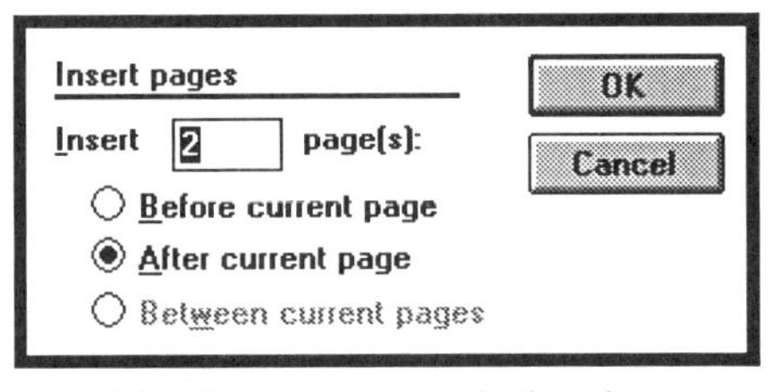

The Insert pages dialog box

If the document has facing pages new pages may be inserted between two existing pages by selecting Between current pages.

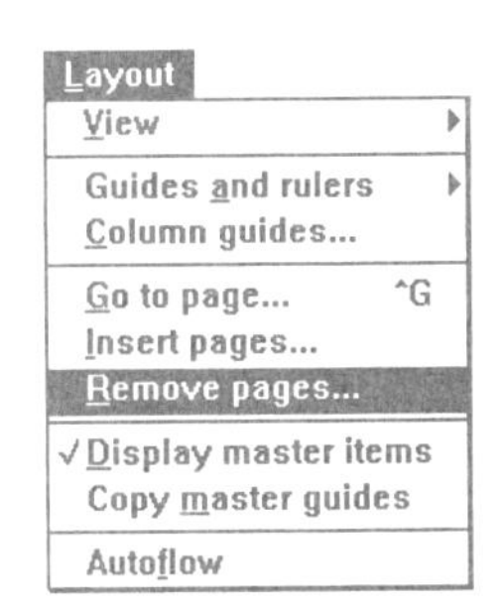

Remove pages deletes pages from a publication:

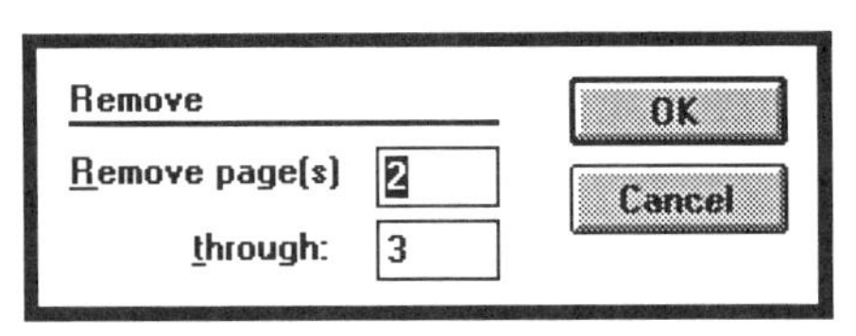

The Remove pages dialog box

Multiple pages may be removed, but they must fall in a continuous range. Because removing a page also removes all of the material on that page, PageMaker displays a warning:

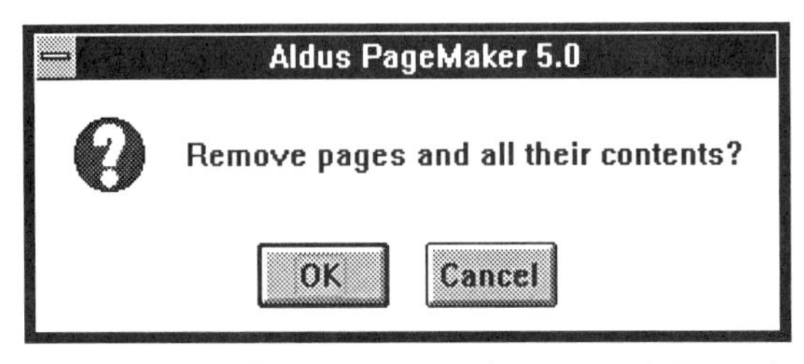

Removing a page also removes the material on that page

If a page is removed by mistake, immediately executing Undo will restore the page and its contents. Undo may also be used with the Insert pages command.

Practice 4

In this Practice you will create a new publication and experiment with Autoflow, columns, and adding and removing pages. Start PageMaker if you have not already done so.

1) *CREATE A NEW PUBLICATION WITH COLUMNS*

a. Using the New command, create a new publication. Page 1 is displayed.
b. From the Layout menu, select the Column guides command. Create 3 columns with .25 inch between each.
c. In the Layout menu, make sure that Autoflow is off (unchecked).

2) *IMPORT A TEXT FILE*

a. From the File menu, select the Place command (Ctrl+D).
b. Select the LONG.TXT file. Click on OK in the Text-only import filter box to accept the defaults.
c. Place the pointer in the upper-left corner of the first column and click to flow the text. The text flows to the bottom of the first column and stops.
d. Click on the red triangle in the windowshade handle at the bottom of the text block. The pointer is loaded.
e. Click at the top of the next column. The text flows to the bottom of the column and stops. To place all of the text this procedure would have to be repeated for each column on every page.

3) *DELETE THE PLACED TEXT*

a. From the Edit menu, execute the Select All command (Ctrl+A). All of the currently placed text blocks are selected.
b. From the Edit menu, select the Cut command (Ctrl+X). The text is removed.

4) *PLACE THE TEXT USING AUTOFLOW*

a. From the Layout menu, select the Autoflow command.
b. Display the Layout menu. Autoflow is on, as indicated by the check mark.
c. Execute the Place command and load LONG.TXT again. The loaded Text pointer now shows a curved arrow, indicating that the text will autoflow when placed.
d. Place the pointer in the upper-left corner of the first column and click to flow the text. The text flows to the bottom of the first column and then continues into the second and then third columns. When it reaches the end of the first page, PageMaker automatically creates two new pages and flows the text onto them:

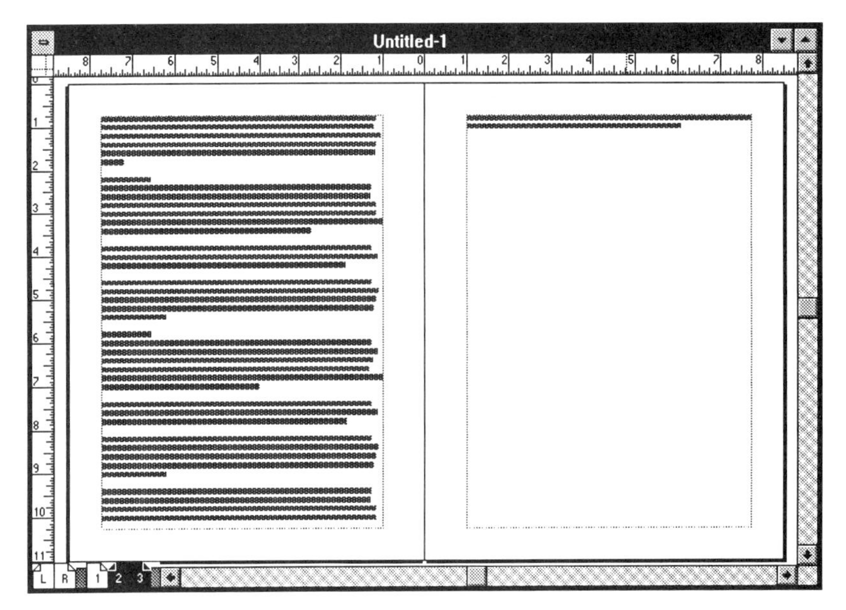

There is a problem with this, however. Because the column guides were applied to the first page, they appear on the first page only. In order to have columns on each page, the guides need to be placed on the Master Pages.

5) REMOVE ALL THE PAGES IN THE PUBLICATION

a. From the Layout menu, select the Remove pages command. The Remove dialog box is shown and set to remove pages 2 through 3, the currently displayed pages.
b. Change the Remove page(s) option to 1 and select OK.
c. PageMaker warns that the pages and their contents will be removed. This is what we want to do, so select OK. Pages 1 through 3 are removed. Because no pages are left in the publication, the Master Pages are displayed.

6) CREATE MASTER PAGE COLUMN GUIDES AND INSERT A NEW PAGE

a. From the Layout menu, select the Column guides command. Create 3 columns with .25 inch between each. The column guides are shown.
b. From the Layout menu, select Insert pages. The Insert pages dialog box is shown with the defaults of inserting 2 pages after the current page. Select OK. Pages 1 and 2 are added to the publication and page 1 is displayed.
c. Switch between pages 1 and 2. Because column guides were created on the Master Pages, the guides were added to both new pages automatically.

7) PLACE THE TEXT USING AUTOFLOW

a. Return to page 1.
b. Display the Layout menu and check that Autoflow is on.
c. Execute the Place command and load LONG.TXT.
d. Place the loaded Text pointer in the upper-left corner of the first column and click. The text flows from column to column and page to page.
e. Save the publication as JOURNAL.PM5.

Check - The second page of your publication should be similar to:

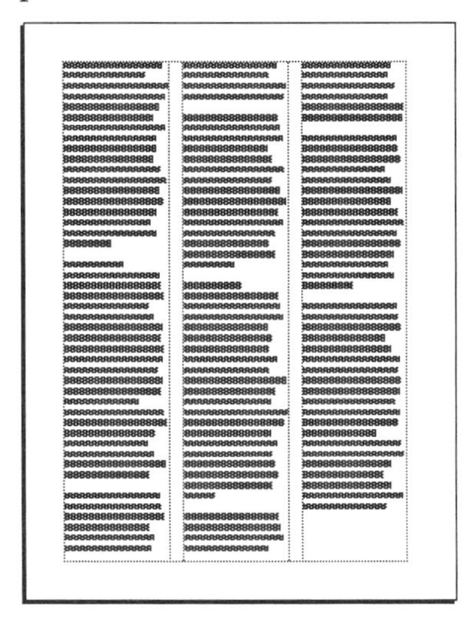

8.9 Printing Specific Pages

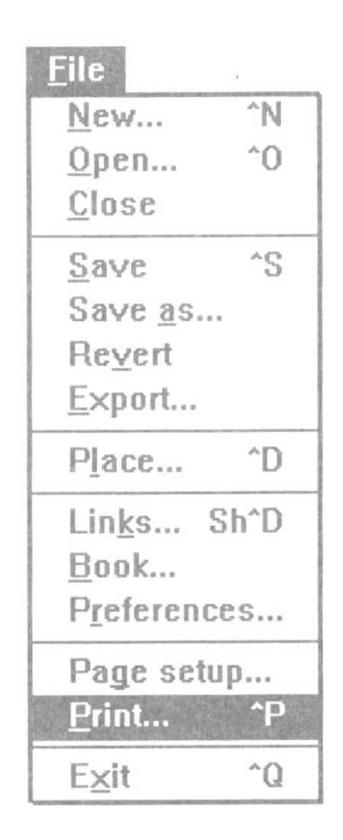

A single PageMaker publication can be hundreds of pages long. After making a correction or applying a formatting option you may wish to see a printout of a specific page or group of pages. This can be done using the Ranges option in the Print command's dialog box:

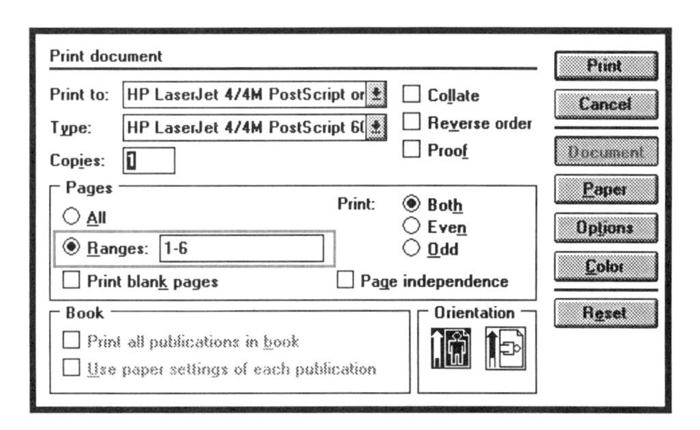

The Range option can be used to print specific pages

Ranges can be specified in a number of different ways:

Single Page—Simply type the page number to be printed as the Ranges:

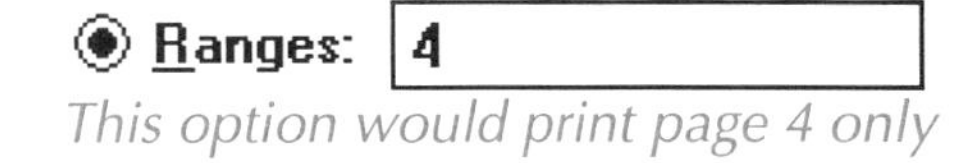

This option would print page 4 only

Range of Pages—List the first and last pages separated by a dash. The pages must be listed in ascending order:

Ranges: 1-6

This prints pages 1 through 6, inclusive

Group of Pages—List the page numbers separated by commas:

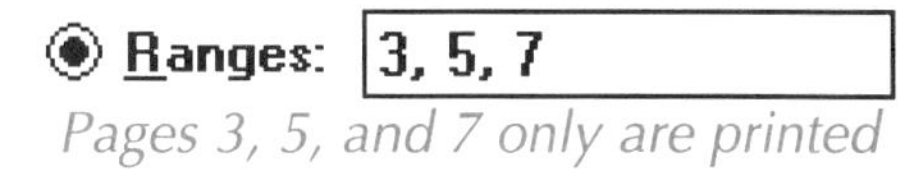

Pages 3, 5, and 7 only are printed

The range and group options may be combined:

◉ Ranges: 2, 5-7, 11, 29-

This option prints pages 2, 5 through 7, 11, and 29 to the last page in the document

Note the last entry, 29–. A dash may be supplied before or after a page number. When before, PageMaker prints the first page in the publication up to and including the supplied page number (entering –5 prints pages 1 through 5). When the dash is placed after a page number, PageMaker prints that page and all remaining pages.

8.10 Inline Graphics

Up to this point, text and graphics have been separate parts of a PageMaker publication. However, this can cause difficulty when changes are made to either the text or graphic. For example, below is a text block and an independent graphic placed in a column:

A text block and independent graphic

The text block is selected and its handles are visible. Adding text to the text block causes it to flow. The graphic, however, remains stationary and so the two overlap:

Text added to the text block

The solution to this problem is to use *inline graphics*. An inline graphic is placed in the text, and flows with it. Below is an example of an inline graphic:

Inline graphics are part of the text

The selected text block shows that the graphic is part of the block. Adding (or deleting) text no longer poses a problem because the graphic flows with the text:

Inline graphics flow with the text

There are other advantages to inline graphics as well. For example, a text block containing an inline graphic can be copied or moved and the graphic will stay with the text. Inline graphics are especially useful with photograph captions because they keep the caption text with the graphic at all times.

Inline graphics are created by selecting the Text tool instead of the Pointer when placing the graphic. To create an inline graphic, select the Text tool and create an insertion point before executing the Place command. When Place is then executed, the graphic is imported and placed inline at the position of the insertion point.

Practice 5

In this Practice you will add an inline graphic. Start PageMaker and open the JOURNAL publication.

1) PLACE AN INDEPENDENT GRAPHIC

a. Display page 2 and make sure that the Pointer tool is selected. From the File menu, select the Place command.
b. Select GRAPHIC.WMF.
c. Place GRAPHIC.WMF anywhere in the second column. The graphic is placed over top of the existing text. This type of graphic is called independent because it is not related to the text below it.
d. Click on the text block in the first column, selecting it.
e. Drag the bottom windowshade handle of the selected text block up. Text flows into the second column but the graphic remains unchanged.
f. Drag the windowshade handle back to the bottom of the column.
g. Click on the graphic, selecting it. Delete the graphic.

2) PLACE AN INLINE GRAPHIC

a. Select the Text tool. Zoom in so that you can read the text at the top of the second column.
b. Click on the blank line just after "`commodo con sequat.11`". An insertion point is created on the blank line.
c. From the File menu, execute the Place command. Select GRAPHIC.WMF. The graphic is placed as an inline graphic at the position of the insertion point, and the text below is moved to make room:

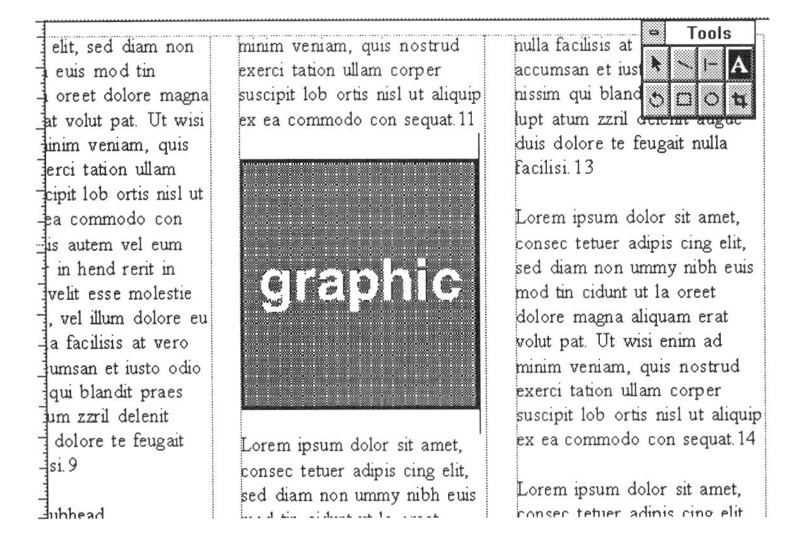

d. Switch to the Pointer tool. Click on the text block in the first column, selecting it.
e. Drag the bottom windowshade handle of the selected text block up. Text flows into the second column and the graphic flows with it.
f. Drag the windowshade handle back to the bottom of the column. The graphic flows back to its original position.

3) PRINT PAGE 2 ONLY

a. Save the modified publication.
b. From the File menu, select the Print command. The Print dialog box is shown.
c. Double-click in the Ranges box, highlighting the current contents.
d. Type 2, replacing the contents. Ranges is automatically selected.
e. Select Print. Only page 2, the page with the graphic, is printed.

8.11 Converting Between Inline & Independent Graphics

There may be times when you want to convert an independent graphic to an inline graphic, or vice versa. PageMaker makes this simple with the use of the Cut and Paste commands.

Inline to Independent

Select the inline graphic with the Pointer tool. Using the Edit menu, Cut the graphic to the clipboard. Execute the Paste command and the graphic is placed in the publication as an independent graphic.

Independent to Inline

Select the independent graphic with the Pointer tool. Using the Edit menu, Cut the graphic to the clipboard. Select the Text tool and place an insertion point in the text. Execute the Paste command and the graphic is placed at the position of the insertion point as an inline graphic.

In either case, the Copy command may be used in place of Cut if the original graphic should remain unchanged.

8.12 Modifying Inline Graphics

Once an inline graphic is in place, most paragraph formats can be applied to it. For example, an inline graphic can be centered in a text block by highlighting it with the Text tool and applying the Align center command. Similarly, leading, tracking, and spacing options can be applied. Standard graphic editing operations may also be performed. For example, an inline graphic can be cropped, sized, and rotated using the normal techniques.

PageMaker always applies Auto leading to an inline graphic. For this reason, a tall graphic can affect the line spacing of a paragraph when placed inline:

Don't forget our daily specials. Join the Aztec Café every Tuesday night for Night!

Don't forget our daily specials. Join the Aztec Café every Tuesday night for  Night!

Auto leading can change line spacing in paragraphs with inline graphics

One approach to solving this problem is to increase the leading for the entire paragraph. This can be effective if you have the vertical space. Another technique is to reduce the size of the graphic itself:

Don't forget our daily specials. Join

the Aztec Café every Tuesday night

Don't forget our daily specials. Join
the Aztec Café every Tuesday night
for Night!

Leading can change the feel of a paragraph, especially when inline graphics are involved

In the Story Editor, inline graphics appear as black boxes and may be formatted, but not edited as a graphic:

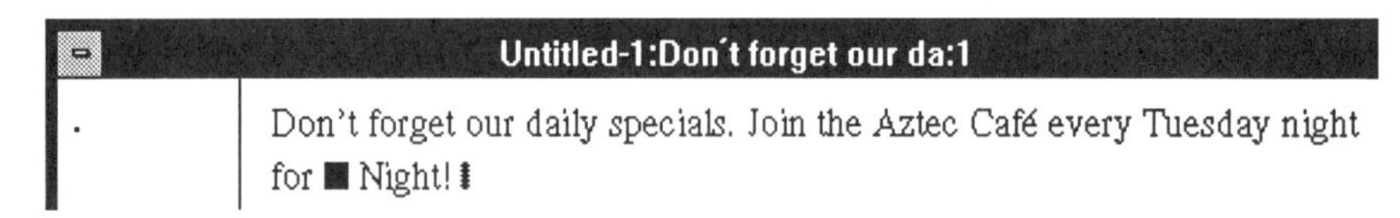

Practice 6

In this Practice you will modify and format an inline graphic. Start PageMaker and open the JOURNAL publication.

1) MODIFY AN INLINE GRAPHIC

a. With the Pointer tool, select the graphic in column 2.
b. From the Window menu, select the Control palette command. The Control palette is displayed with the information about the currently selected object, GRAPHIC.WMF.
c. Double-click on the width (W) percent, highlighting it. Type `50`, replacing the old value and press Enter. The width for GRAPHIC.WMF has been reduced by 50%.
d. Double-click on the height (H) percent, highlighting it. Type `50` and press Enter. The height for GRAPHIC.WMF has been reduced by 50% and text flows up from below it:

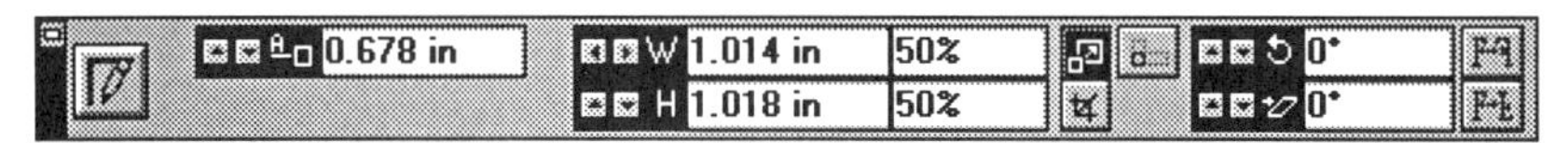

e. Click on the Control palette's Close box, removing it from the screen.

2) FORMAT AN INLINE GRAPHIC

a. Select the Text tool.
b. Highlight the inline graphic by triple-clicking on it with the Text tool.
c. In the Type menu, highlight the Alignment command. From the submenu, select Align center. The "paragraph" containing the inline graphic is centered.

3) ADJUST THE GRAPHIC'S LEADING

a. Because the graphic's size is not standard, the Auto leading default causes the text in the middle column below the graphic to not align with the text in the left and right columns:

pis cing elit, sed diam non
ny nibh euis mod tin
int ut la oreet dolore magna
uam erat volut pat. Ut wisi
n ad minim veniam, quis
trud exerci tation ullam
per suscipit lob ortis nisl ut
uip ex ea commodo con
uat. Duis autem vel eum
e dolor in hend rerit in
pu tate velit esse molestie
sequat, vel illum dolore eu
giat nulla facilisis at vero

minim veniam, quis nostrud
exerci tation ullam corper
suscipit lob ortis nisl ut aliquip
ex ea commodo con sequat.11

Graphic

Lorem ipsum dolor sit amet
consec tetuer adipis cing elit,
sed diam non ummy nibh euis

Lorem ipsum dolor sit am
consec tetuer adipis cing e
sed diam non ummy nibh
mod tin cidunt ut la oreet
dolore magna aliquam era
volut pat. Ut wisi enim ad
minim veniam, quis nostr
exerci tation ullam corper
suscipit lob ortis nisl ut al
ex ea commodo con sequa

Lorem ipsum dolor sit am

Using the Text tool, triple-click on the graphic.

b. In the Type menu, highlight the Leading command. Auto is checked in the submenu.
c. Select the largest value in the submenu, 36. The leading is reduced and the graphic overlaps some of the text.
d. Set the leading back to Auto.
e. The current paragraph has 12 point text with Auto leading. This means that the leading is really 14.4 points because PageMaker uses 120% of the point size for Auto (120% x 12 = 14.4). To have the text below the graphic line up with the other columns, the leading for the graphic must be a multiple of 14.4. Looking to the adjacent column, we see that the graphic takes up approximately 6 lines. 6 lines at 14.4 points each is 86.4 points leading. In the Type menu, highlight Leading and select Other.
f. Type the new value `86.4` in the Other dialog box and select OK. The leading around the graphic is slightly reduced but the text in all three columns is now aligned.
g. Save the publication.

8.13 Running Headers & Footers

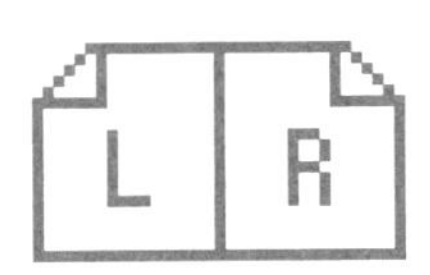

Running headers and footers play an important role in long documents. For example, in a textbook it is helpful to know both the title of the book and the current chapter name. In smaller publications such as manuals, having the section or division name or number makes it easier for the reader to locate needed information.

Some thought should be given to the material which appears in the headers or footers, and on which page. Information can be split across pages, so that, for example, the title is on the left page and the chapter name on the right.

Because they should appear on each page, headers and footers are best created on the Master Pages. Of course, the most common use for headers and footers is to print the current page number. To have PageMaker automatically insert the current page number at the insertion point, press `Ctrl+Shift+3`, which is displayed as LM on the left Master Page and RM on the right. When the document is printed, the actual page number is shown. A popular page numbering technique is to show the chapter number separated from the page number by some punctuation such as 8-18 or 8.18 to represent chapter 8, page 18.

The header or footer text should not overwhelm the page or distract the reader's eye. Therefore, a type size which is 1 or 2 points smaller than the body text is recommended. Italics make good headers / footers, but bold should usually be avoided. The LM and RM markers can appear in a block with other text and can be formatted by highlighting and then executing the desired formatting commands.

8.14 Tables of Contents

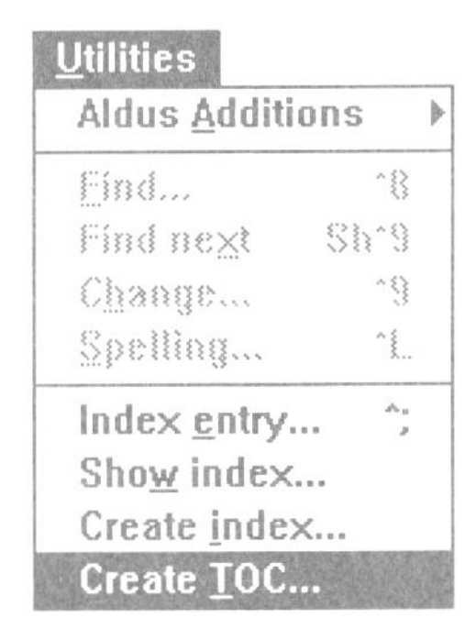

An important part of a long publication is the *table of contents* or TOC which lists important sections along with the page number where they can be found. Items in a TOC should include chapter titles, headings and subheadings, and section or division names.

Generating a table of contents for a manually-prepared document can be time consuming. Someone familiar with the subject of the publication must go through each page and create a list of important topics and page references. These must then be entered into the publication, formatted, and printed.

PageMaker can automatically generate a table of contents based on a Paragraph format. As the publication is created, you indicate the items to appear in the TOC by selecting Include in table of contents:

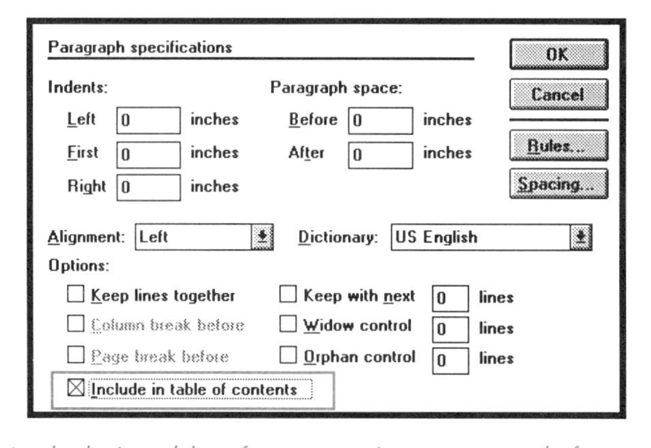

Include in table of contents is a paragraph format

The Include in table of contents option can also be included as part of a style, which can save time. The predefined styles Headline, Subhead 1, and Subhead 2 automatically have this option selected. In this textbook, the style for section headings like "8.14 Tables of Contents" above have Include in table of contents selected so that each section name and number appears in the TOC.

Once all of the paragraphs to appear in the TOC have been marked, either using the Paragraph command from the Type menu or by applying a style which contains the Include in table of contents option, executing the Create TOC command from the Utilities menu automatically creates the table. PageMaker finds each reference and creates a new text block containing the reference and its page number. The new block can be placed and formatted just like any other text. In fact, in anticipation of the need for formatting, PageMaker creates new styles such as TOC Heading 1 and TOC title, and applies them to the new text. You can then edit these styles as desired.

8.15 Printing Thumbnails

Earlier we discussed different ways to print ranges of pages in order to save time and paper. With a long document it is often useful to print *thumbnails*—smaller versions of each page. In Chapter Five you learned that it was important to produce small drawings of your designs before using the computer. After a document has been created you can have PageMaker print similar thumbnails so that you can evaluate your design over several pages. Thumbnails are created using the Paper option in the Print command's dialog box:

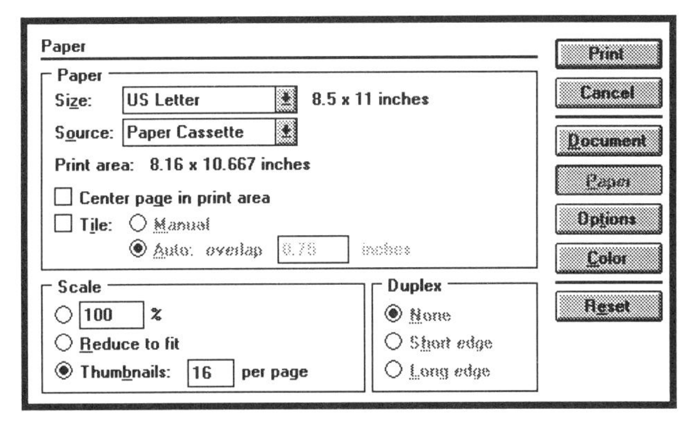

The Paper printing options

Selecting Thumbnails in the Scale box allows you to print from 2 to 1,000 miniature pages on each piece of paper, with 16 as the default value. The larger the number of thumbnails, the smaller each thumbnail is.

Practice 7

In this Practice you will add footers and have PageMaker create a simple table of contents. Different thumbnails will then be printed. Start PageMaker and open the JOURNAL publication.

1) CREATE THE RIGHT RUNNING FOOTER

a. We want the footers to appear on every page in the publication so they will be placed on the Master Pages. Display the Master Pages.

b. Select the Text tool.
c. Zoom in near the bottom-left corner of the right Master Page. Click in the first column to create an insertion point.
d. Type the footer text: `Journal of the Electro-Chemical Society`
e. Press Tab and type `Page` followed by a space.
f. We want the actual page number printed here. Press `Ctrl+Shift+3`. PageMaker displays RM which will be replaced by the actual page number when printed. Your footer (selected here to show the block) should be similar to:

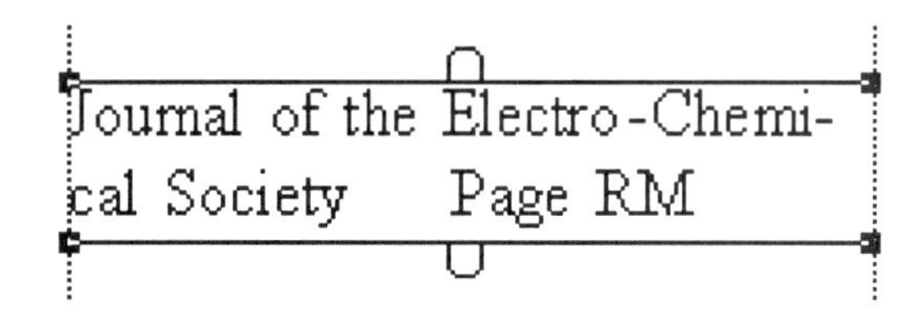

2) FORMAT THE FOOTER

a. Triple-click on the footer text.
b. From the Type menu, select the Type specs command and make the footer Size 11 point and Italic.
c. Right align the footer text.

3) PLACE THE FOOTER

a. Select the Pointer tool and click on footer text block.
b. Drag the right side of the footer text block to the end of the third column so that the footer text block now stretches across the three columns:

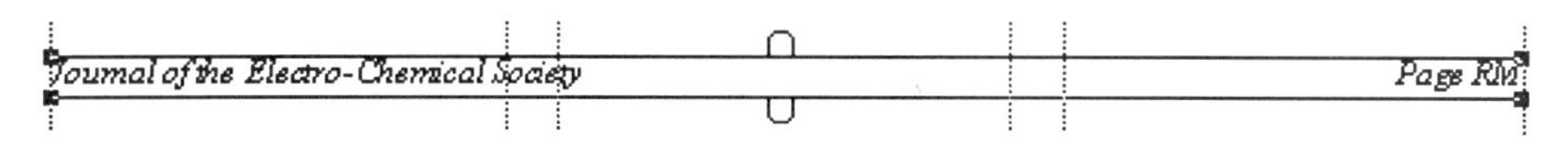

c. Drag the text block down so that the top of the block is aligned with the bottom margin of the page. Make certain that the top of your block is aligned with the bottom of your page, which places the block in the bottom margin.
d. Switch to view page 1. Zoom in to the bottom-right corner. Note that the correct page number is shown.
e. Switch back to the Master Pages.

4) COPY AND EDIT THE FOOTER

a. With the Pointer tool, select the footer text block.
b. From the Edit menu, execute the Copy command.
c. Scroll to the left Master Page.
d. From the Edit menu, execute the Paste command. Drag the text block to the bottom of page. Note that the RM page number marker has changed to LM because this text is now on the left Master Page.
e. Select the Text tool. Using Cut and Paste, edit the text so that the page number and Tab come before the journal name:

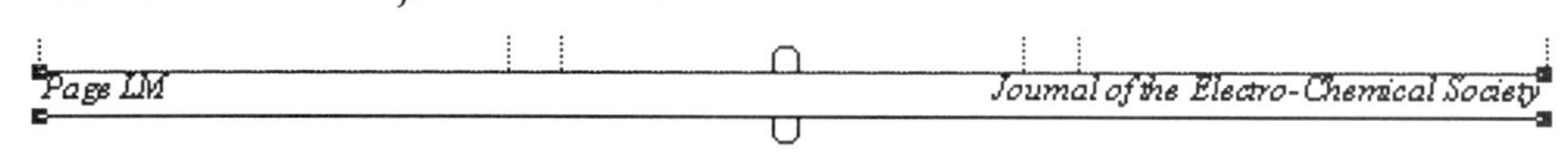

f. Switch to view page 2. Zoom in to the bottom and note the footer and page number.

5) APPLY STYLES WITH THE TOC OPTION SELECTED

a. There a 5 occurrences of the text "This is a Subhead" in the publication. Each is preceded by its number (1 through 5) and a dash. Locate each occurrence and apply the Subhead 1 style to it.
b. Using the Text tool, place the cursor in any one of the "This is a Subhead" paragraphs. Execute the Paragraph command and note that the Include in table of contents option is selected. When the TOC is generated each paragraph with the Subhead 1 style will be included. Cancel the Paragraph command.
c. Some text will flow out of the third column on page 2. Simply roll the text block up to the bottom margin.

6) CREATE A TABLE OF CONTENTS

a. We need a place for the table of contents to go. Using the Insert pages command, insert a single page after page 2.
b. From the Utilities menu, select the Create TOC command. The dialog box is shown. Select OK. PageMaker processes the publication and creates the TOC text block containing a page reference for each paragraph in the publication with the Include in table of contents option selected. The pointer changes to the loaded Text shape.
c. Click the pointer at the top of the first column on page 3. The table of contents text block is placed.
d. Drag the bottom-right corner of the text block across the three columns to the right side of the page. Your table should be similar to:

Contents

1—This is a Subhead **1**
2—This is a Subhead **1**
3—This is a Subhead **1**
4—This is a Subhead **2**
5—This is a Subhead **2**

e. Using the Window menu, display the Style palette. Note the new TOC styles. These styles could be edited to change the look of the table. Close the Style palette.
f. Save the publication.

7) PRINT FULL-SIZE AND THUMBNAIL VERSIONS

a. Use the Print command to print All of the publication.
b. We will now print the thumbnails. From the File menu, execute the Print command. In the dialog box, select Paper.
c. In the Scale options, select Thumbnails and Print the document. A thumbnail is printed for each page, each taking approximately 1/16 of the paper.
d. The size of the individual thumbnails can be changed. Execute the Print command again and select Paper. For the number of Thumbnails, type 4, replacing the 16. Select Print to produce a thumbnail for each page, each now taking approximately 1/4 of the paper.
e. Save the publication, then exit PageMaker and Windows.

Chapter Summary

This chapter describes several tools for working with long documents. When designing a long document, following the four basic design guidelines of Appropriateness, Balance, Focus and Flow, and Consistency are especially important. The first three increase the readability of the document, maintaining the reader's interest. Consistency allows the reader to locate needed information easily.

The key to consistency is the proper use of styles, which are named groups of character and paragraph formats. Selecting a style applies all of its formats to the selected paragraph(s) with a single command. Changing a formatting option in a style changes all of the text already formatted in that style. Usually applied with the Style palette, styles not only enforce consistency but also save time.

Styles are created and modified using the Define styles command in the Type menu. PageMaker automatically creates 6 predefined styles for every new publication including styles for body text, captions, headlines, and subheads. Modifying these styles is a good start to developing a comprehensive style sheet. Every new style must be given a name. After that, type, paragraph, tab, and hyphenation options can be defined for that style.

A useful paragraph format is the indent. Indents decrease the width of the lines in a paragraph, and may be applied to the left, right, or first line only in a paragraph. A special use for indents is the creation of a hanging indent, where the first line indent is set to a negative number. The causes the first line in a paragraph to hang out to the left above the rest of the text. Hanging indents are often used to format bibliographies or long quotes, and can be used to create bulleted and numbered lists.

Normally, PageMaker forces you to specify where the text block will begin and end when placing a file. When Autoflow is turned on, PageMaker automatically flows text from the top of a column to the bottom, and then continues at the top of the next column or page, automatically adding new pages as necessary. This option can save a great deal of time when placing text into multi-column, multi-page documents.

It is expected that during the layout process that some documents will need pages deleted or added. The Insert pages command can be used to add any number of pages to a publication, either before or after the currently displayed page. The Remove pages command deletes ranges of pages, specified by page number. Remove pages also deletes any items from the removed page, so PageMaker issues a warning before deleting the page.

8

It would be wasteful to reprint a long document just because a single page changed. For this reason the Print command allows any number of pages to be printed, either singly, or in continuous or non-continuous ranges.

An independent graphic retains its position on the page. An inline graphic is linked to a specific position in the text, so that if the text flows the graphic moves with it. An inline graphic is created by executing the Place command while the Text tool is selected. The imported graphic is then placed at the position of the cursor.

Inline graphics can be switched to independent by selecting the graphic with the Pointer tool, and then Cutting and Pasting it back into the publication. An independent graphic can be turned into an inline graphic by selecting it with the Pointer tool and Cutting it. The Text tool is then selected and used to place the cursor at the desired location for the graphic. When Paste is executed the graphic is placed inline.

Inline graphics may be stretched and sized with the Pointer tool. They can be aligned, have leading changed, and other paragraph formats applied with the Text tool.

Running headers and footers are text (and graphics) that appear in the top and bottom margin (respectively) of every page. Normally used for page numbers, headers and footers can contain other information that will help the reader of a long publication locate desired information: chapter names, section numbers or names, etc. Different text can appear on the left and right pages. Headers are footers are created on the Master Pages. Page numbers are included in a header or footer text by pressing `Ctrl+Shift+3`, which shows LM on the left Master Page and RM on the right.

A table of contents (TOC) lists important sections and their page numbers. These are especially important in long publications. Text to be included in a TOC can be identified using a paragraph formatting option. This option can also be included in a style. After all the desired text has been formatted, PageMaker can automatically generate and format a table of contents text block. This chapter just touched on the power of the TOC command. More information can be found in the PageMaker Help system and manuals.

Thumbnails are small versions of each page that can be printed for any publication. Multiple thumbnails, each representing a single page in the publication, can be printed on each piece of paper. Thumbnails are useful for reviewing the formatting and layout of a publication without wasting great amounts of paper.

8

Vocabulary

Bulleted list - Special use for a hanging indent where the first character is a bullet symbol (normally `Ctrl+Shift+8`).

Hanging indent - Indent where the first line hangs out to the left over the lines below it. Useful when preparing lists, outlines, or bibliography references. (This paragraph uses a hanging indent format.)

Indents - Decrease in the width of the lines in a paragraph created with the Paragraph command. Often used to set some information off from the rest of the document, indents can affect the left side, right side, or first line of a paragraph.

Independent graphic - Standard, non-inline graphic which is unaffected by text flow.

Inline graphic - A graphic placed inside the text, so that it flows with it.

Readability - Making a document's design easy to read, page after page.

Style - Named group of text and paragraph formatting options which can all be applied at the same time using a single selection from the Style command's submenu.

Table of contents / TOC - List of important sections in a document along with the page number where they can be found.

Thumbnails - Small versions of each page, usually printed several to a page.

Reviews

Sections 8.1 — 8.4

1. Give an example of how each of the four major design considerations listed below affects a long publication:

   a) Appropriateness
   b) Balance
   c) Focus and Flow
   d) Consistency

2. a) What is a style?
   b) How does using styles affect a document's design?

3. a) How are styles applied?
   b) Name the 6 predefined styles.

4. Describe the steps necessary to create a new style.

5. What four options are available when creating or redefining a style?

6. A style named Price List has been created and applied to several paragraphs. You now change the typeface of the style. What happens to the previously formatted Price List style paragraphs?

7. What is the quickest way to apply styles?

Sections 8.5 — 8.8

8. a) What is an indent?
   b) How is an indent created?

9. Name the 3 types of indents.

10. a) What is a hanging indent?
    b) Draw a thumbnail of a hanging indent.

11. a) What is a bulleted list?
    b) Draw a thumbnail of a bulleted list.
    c) How is a bulleted list created?
    d) What character is often used for the bullet?

12. a) What is Autoflow and how does it affect placing text in a publication?
    b) When is Autoflow most useful?
    c) How is Autoflow turned off and on?

13. a) Describe how to add 2 pages before the current page.
    b) Describe how to add 4 pages to the end of a publication.

14. a) How can pages be removed from a publication?
    b) What happens to the material on a page when that page is deleted?

Sections 8.9 — 8.12

15. Explain how to print just a single page in a multi-page document.

16. Show the option necessary to have PageMaker print the following pages:

    a) Just page 5.
    b) Pages 6 through 12.
    c) From the beginning of the document to page 11.
    d) From page 17 to the end of the document.

17. a) What is an inline graphic?
    b) What are the benefits of using inline graphics?
    c) Describe the steps necessary to import a graphic as an inline graphic (as opposed to an independent graphic).

18. a) What steps are required to convert an inline graphic to an independent graphic?
    b) What steps are required to convert an independent graphic to an inline graphic?

19. a) What Tool is used to format an inline graphic?
    b) Give 2 examples of formatting that may be applied to an inline graphic.

20. How are inline graphics displayed in the Story Editor?

Sections 8.13 — 8.15

21. a) What is a running header? A running footer?
    b) Give several examples of text that might be included in the running header / footer of a long publication.

8

22. a) What is a table of contents?
    b) How can items be marked as belonging in a publication's table of contents?

23. Describe the steps necessary to generate a table of contents for a publication.

24. a) What is a printed thumbnail?
    b) What are printed thumbnails used for?
    c) Describe the steps required to print thumbnails for an 8 page publication. What options do you have?

Exercises

1. Ivy University needs a promotional two-page, two-column flyer.

    a) Create a new PageMaker publication and create a two column grid on the Master Pages.

    b) With the Autoflow command turned on, place IVYPROMO.TXT starting at the top of the left column of page 1.

    c) Remove the section titled "Student Diversity..." and the accompanying text and table.

    d) Format the title "Ivy University The Ultimate...." in the Headline style

    e) Format each of the section headers (OUR CONTRIBUTION..., Department of Minor Skin..., Student Diversity...., and In Conclusion) in the Subhead 1 style.

    f) Format each of the course numbers and titles (i.e., 101 - Introduction to Adhesive Bandages) in the Subhead 2 style.

    g) Using the Define styles command create a new style named Instructor with 13-point Bookman italic type. Format the Faculty Member section (Dr. Phineas Itchee... Sal Strant) in the Instructor style.

    h) Format the rest of the paragraphs as Body text.

    i) Save the flyer naming it IVYFLYR1 and print a copy. The two pages should look similar to:

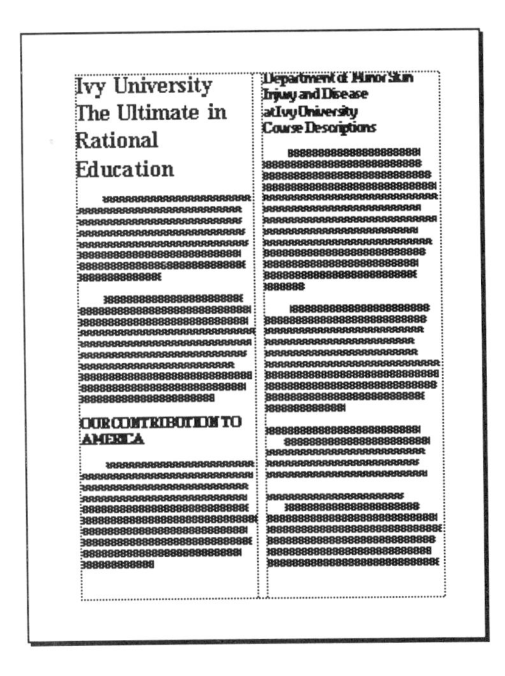

j) Ivy University wants you to create a new design for this flyer. Examine the printout of IVYFLYR1 and create two thumbnail sketches for a new design. Be sure to indicate the fonts, sizes, alignments, and other formatting information on your sketches.

k) Use the Save as command to save IVYFLYR1 as IVYFLYR2. In IVYFLYR2, move the contents of the two pages onto the pasteboard. Pick your best thumbnail and create a grid on the Master Pages.

l) Move the text from the pasteboard onto the publication pages. Reformat, move, and resize text blocks as necessary to fit your new design.

m) Save the publication and print a copy. Compare your new design with the first design. Which is better and why?

2. The Ivy University public relations department has reviewed the flyers created in Exercise 1 and would like the following changes made to IVYFLYR1:

   a) Open IVYFLYR1. Change the Body text style so that the first line indent is 0 (zero). Using the Story Editor, delete the tabs from the first lines of any paragraph defined as Body text. (You can search for a tab by entering `^t` as the Find what text.)

   b) Place the Ivy University logo IULOGO.WMF as an inline graphic just before each Subhead 1 paragraph. For each graphic, use the Control palette to resize the logo to 50% of its actual size. Center the logos.

   c) Arrange the text blocks so that all of the text fits on the two pages. If necessary, redefine the Subhead 1 or the Body text styles with a slightly smaller typeface to create more room.

   d) Save the edited flyer and then print a copy.

3. A scholarly journal is about to publish an article titled *The History of Computers* and needs the text formatted in three columns.

   a) Create a new PageMaker publication and set a two-column grid on the Master Pages.

   b) With the Autoflow command turned on, place COMPUTER.TXT starting at the top of the left column of page 1.

   c) Format the title *The History of Computers* by applying the Headline style.

   d) Format each of the numbered section headers (i.e., 1 Ancient Counting Machines) by applying the Subhead 1 style.

   e) Format the subheadings in section 15 by applying the Subhead 2 style.

   f) Apply the Body text style to the rest of the text.

   g) To make the article more interesting, photographs of some of the mentioned machines are to be added. Place PHOTO.WMF as an inline graphic at the ends of sections 3, 6, 7, and 9, and 16. Use the Control palette to resize it to a width and height of 1.5 inches.

h) Under each of the photographs add a caption that explains what is shown (i.e, in section 3 the caption should read *A Pascaline*.) Format the captions by applying the Caption style.

i) Edit the Caption style to centered Avant Garde. Note how the fonts in all of the captions change.

j) Format the numbered lists in sections 16 and 17 by applying the Hanging indent style.

k) Edit the Hanging indent style, making the typeface 10 point Avant Garde and changing the indents to Left 0.5", First -0.2", and Right 0.2".

l) Add a running footer to the publication that contains the title *The History of Computers* and the page number.

m) Add a blank page at the end of the document if needed and create a Table of Contents that contains each of the numbered section headings. Deselect the Display master items command from the Layout menu so that the footer does not appear on this page.

n) Save the article naming it HISTCOMP.

o) Print Thumbnails to check formatting and then make any needed changes.

p) Save your changes to HISTCOMP and print a full size copy.

4. The scholarly journal that will publish *The History of Computers* has reviewed the layout you created in Exercise 3 and would like to see the article reformatted for two columns.

   a) Sketch two thumbnails for a new, two-column design. Indicate the fonts, sizes, column and gutter widths, and other formatting information on your sketches.

   b) Open HISTCOMP.PM5 and use the Save as command to save a copy of this publication as HISTCOM2.

   c) Move the contents of the two pages onto the pasteboard by starting at the end of the publication and rolling up the windowshade handle. Pick your best thumbnail and create a grid on the Master Pages. Move the text from the pasteboard and onto the publication pages. Reformat, move, and resize as necessary for your new design.

   d) Edit the Headline and Subhead 1 styles to Helvetica.

   e) Edit the Subhead 2 and Body text styles to Bookman.

   f) Delete the old table of contents and create a new one on the last page.

   g) Save the publication. Print Thumbnails to check formatting and make needed changes.

   h) Save any changes to HISTCOM2 and then print a full size copy.

5. In Exercises 3 and 4 you formatted the article *The History of Computers* by following given instructions. The scholarly journal is pleased with the results, but believes that you are capable of producing a more imaginative format.

   a) Create at least two thumbnail sketches for formatting the article using various columns and additional graphics and photographs. Include either a header or footer and a table of contents. Be sure to show complete formatting information on your sketches.

   b) Select the best sketch, create a new PageMaker document, place COMPUTER.TXT, and then format the article based on your selected thumbnail. Place GRAPHIC.WMF and PHOTO.WMF for the graphics and photographs.

   c) Save the publication naming it HISTCOM3 and print Thumbnails to check the formatting. Make any needed changes.

   d) Save the changes and then print a full size copy.

6. Brown's Bus Adventures, a New England bus tour company, wants to put together a booklet of all their tours, with detailed itineraries for each tour. The booklet will be printed on 8.5" by 11" paper and stapled down the side. There are four tours to present: Fall Foliage Frolic, Halloween in Hartford, A Pilgrimage to Plymouth Rock, and A Mohawk Trail Holiday. Each page should have one tour on it, with at least two photographs. The bus company wants the table of contents on the cover, and one page of general tour information (reservation information, clothing suggestions, prices, etc.) at the end.

   a) Create at least two complete sets of thumbnail sketches for this six-page booklet. Include sketches for the cover, a sample tour page, and the information page. Consider formatting the booklet using various columns, graphic elements, and methods such as rotating and skewing. Be sure to indicate the necessary formatting information on your sketches.

   b) Select the best sketches and create a new publication. Create any headlines, Tour titles, etc. that you need.

   c) Place LONG.TXT as any text needed. (You may need to place this file twice to have enough text.) Place PHOTO.WMF throughout the publication for any photographs you need.

   d) Generate a Table of Contents and place it on the cover.

   e) Save the publication naming it BUSBOOK and print Thumbnails to check the formatting. Make any needed changes.

   f) Save the changes and then print full size copies. Assemble the copies and staple down the left side.

Chapter Nine:
Color & Graphics

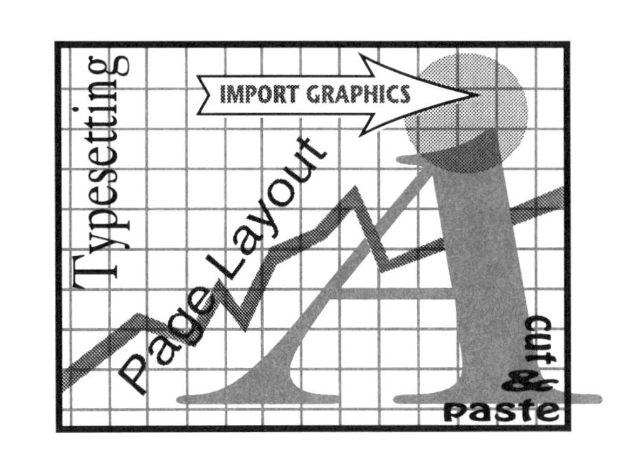

Window - Color palette

Element - Define colors

Spot color

Process color

Color separations

Knockout

Overprint

Cropping

Objectives

After completing this chapter you will be able to:

1. Understand the different color models and how they affect colors shown on the computer screen and when printed.
2. Define the differences between spot and process color, and understand the four color process.
3. Apply colors to text and graphics, and print color separations.
4. Use printing options related to color publishing.
5. Understand the reasons for using color matching systems.
6. Create new colors by mixing and using color matching libraries.
7. Create and apply tints.
8. Delete existing colors.
9. Create colors that overprint.
10. Understand the differences between bitmapped and vector graphics.
11. Trim graphics with the Crop tool.

9

Until recently, most desktop published documents were strictly black and white. Today, the desktop publisher must be prepared to work with a variety of color publications. Depending on the type of document, use of color can range from a single accent color to full color logos, type, and photographs. While desktop publishing programs have grown more adept at handling color, desktop color is still not an exact science. It is important to work closely with the printer who will produce the final document, from the earliest design stages right through to the final printing.

Most color publications are produced by a commercial printing company. When discussing "the printer" in this chapter, we are usually referring to the company printing your work, and not the output device attached to your computer.

9.1 Color Models

There are many different ways of describing or defining a color. These are called *color models*, and each has certain advantages and disadvantages when applied to a specific output device. For example, the *RGB color model* (Red, Green, and Blue) is useful when defining a color that will appear on a computer screen. This is because each tiny dot on the computer's screen, called a *pixel*, is actually composed of three smaller dots: one red, one green, and one blue. To display a colored pixel the computer varies the brightness of each of the three dots. A purple pixel, for example, might be created by having the red and blue dots shine brightly, and the green dot dimmed. White is created by having all of the dots on, and black by all of the dots off.

Most color printing is produced using the *CMYK* or *process color model*: Cyan (an aqua blue), Magenta (a bright purple), Yellow, and blacK. Millions of different colors can be created by overlapping layers of semi-transparent inks in each of the four colors. (For this reason, commercial printing is sometimes called *four color* work.) For example, to print the color green, a layer of yellow ink is printed over a layer of cyan. The percentages of each ink used determine the resulting color. White is the absence of any ink (assuming that you are printing on white paper), and black is its own ink (K).

Note the difference between these two color models. To create white on the screen, each of the three color dots is made to shine brightly, but to create white in commercial printing, no ink is used at all. While this is due to the ways that the two output devices create images, it means that there will always be differences between the colors displayed on the screen and colors produced on a printing press. **It is important to realize that the colors shown on the screen are approximations only.** You must check with your print shop to determine how the color will print.

9.2 Spot Color versus Process Color

There are two ways to produce color in printed documents; *spot color* and *process color*. Each is used for specific applications and PageMaker can handle either.

Spot Color

In spot color, the printer applies a separate ink for each color in the document. For example, this text is printed with two colors, black and blue. These are examples of spot colors. Adding a third color, say red, would require that the printer apply another layer of ink, this time red.

Process Color

With process color all of the colors in the publication are generated from the four CMYK inks. By layering different percentages of the four colors, thousands of colors can be produced. Adding a new color requires only that its components of cyan, magenta, yellow, and black be determined.

You know from Chapter One that ink is applied on a printing press using metal plates. Splitting the colors in a document into their different plates is called *separating*, and the different plates are called *separations*. When using spot color there will be one plate separated for each color in the document:

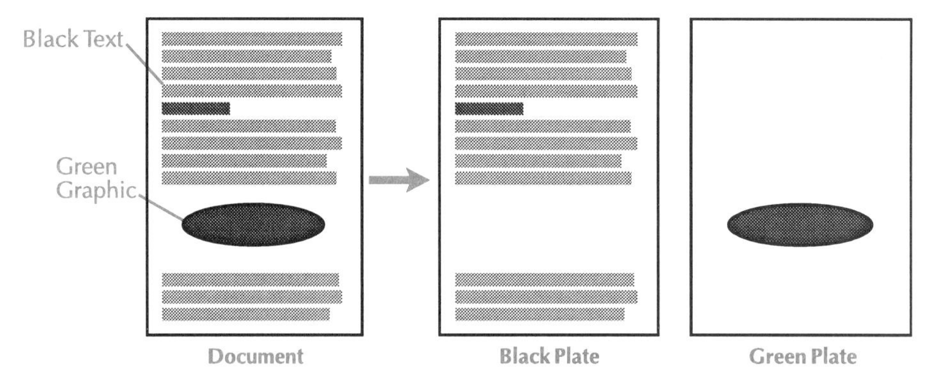

A two-color document separates into two plates, one for each color

In process color, there are always four plates (CMYK) no matter how many colors are in the publication:

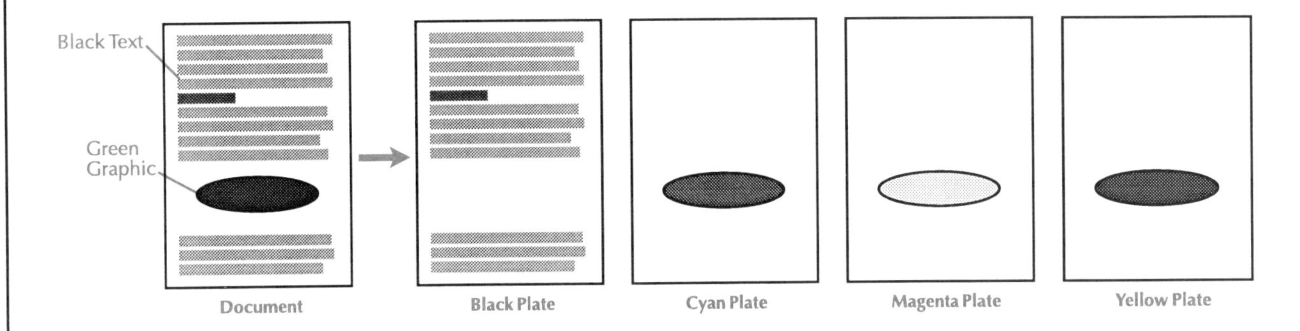

Choosing whether to use spot or process color depends on the job. Normally, spot color is used when there are three or less colors, or when using a special ink such as a metallic or fluorescent that cannot be approximated with process colors. A simple business card or letterhead might be printed using spot colors. Process color is used when there are four or more colors, or when there are full color photographs such as in a fashion magazine. Spot color is usually cheaper to produce than process color, especially for a simple publication with few colors.

9.3 Applying Colors

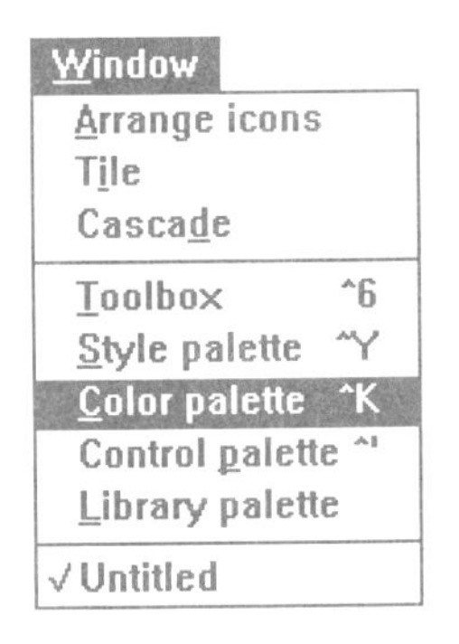

Color can be applied in a number of different ways. For example, the Type specifications dialog box has a Color option for creating colored type. However, the easiest way is to use the Color palette which is displayed using the Color palette command from the Window menu (`Ctrl+K`):

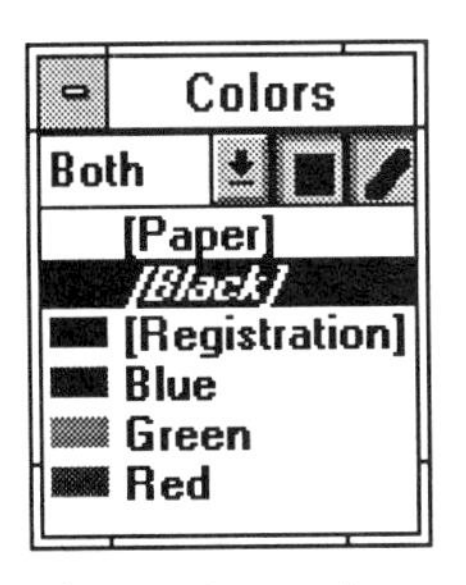

The Color palette

The default color, Black, is highlighted. Choosing a color from the palette applies that color to the selected text or graphic.

The four predefined colors are Red, Blue, Green, and Black. Two other "colors" are also defined. Any text or graphics set to Registration appears on each plate. This color is normally used by the printer to help keep the plates aligned during printing. Items set to Paper are printed as white, which is used to produce *reversed* text—white letters on a solid background. Red, Blue, and Green are spot colors, and because they are less complex, we will focus on using spot color first.

PageMaker can apply a color to the line or fill of a graphic. The buttons below the palette title indicate which:

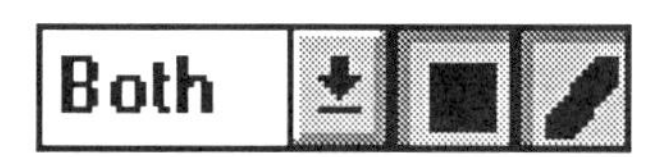

Color can be applied to the fill, line, or both

The default is to apply the selected color to Both the fill and the line. Clicking on a button sets just the fill (square) or just the line. This can also be changed with the drop-down menu to the left of the buttons.

Practice 1

In this Practice you will create a new publication and apply colors to both text and graphics.

1) START PAGEMAKER AND CREATE A NEW PUBLICATION

2) DISPLAY THE COLOR PALETTE

a. From the Window menu select the Color palette command. The palette is displayed. No objects are selected but Black is highlighted because it is the default color—any new text or graphic will be black.
b. If the palette obscures your publication, place the pointer over the palette title and drag it to the bottom right of the screen.

3) DRAW A RECTANGLE

a. From the Toolbox, select the Rectangle tool ().
b. Draw a large rectangle near the middle of the page. Black is highlighted in the Color palette indicating that the currently selected object (in this case the outline of the rectangle) is colored black.

4) CHANGE THE COLOR OF THE RECTANGLE

a. With the rectangle still selected, click on Blue in the Color palette. Both the fill and line of the rectangle are set to blue. In the Color palette the fill and line buttons are shown in blue, and Blue is highlighted.
b. In the Color palette, click on Green. The rectangle changes color and the Color palette is updated to show the selected object's color.
c. Click on Red, then Black, noting the changes to the rectangle and the Color palette.
d. Click on Paper. Anything with the color of paper is invisible. The rectangle disappears, and only its handles are shown.
e. Click on Blue. The rectangle is again shown.

5) CHANGE THE LINE COLOR OF THE RECTANGLE

a. In the Color palette, click on the line button. The fill button "pops out" and the drop-down menu reads "Line". Colors selected now will affect an object's line only.
b. Click on Red. The outline of the rectangle is made red. The fill button in the Color palette still shows blue, and the line button is now red.

6) COLOR SOME TEXT

a. Select the Text tool. In the white space below the rectangle type: `This is some test text`. Zoom in so that the text is readable.
b. Triple-click on the text, highlighting it.
c. From the Type menu, select the Type specs command. Set the Size to 36 points.
d. Click on the down-arrow for the Color option. The same colors in the Color palette are shown. Select Red.
e. Select OK to apply the formats. Zoom out and click anywhere to remove the highlight. The text is 36 points and Red.
f. With the Text tool, click in the text. The fill button shows red, the text's color.
g. Triple-click on the text, selecting it. Select Green from the palette and note the effects on both the text and in the palette. Click anywhere to remove the highlight and see the actual color.

7) SAVE THE FILE

Save the file as CH9PRACT. Your file should be similar to:

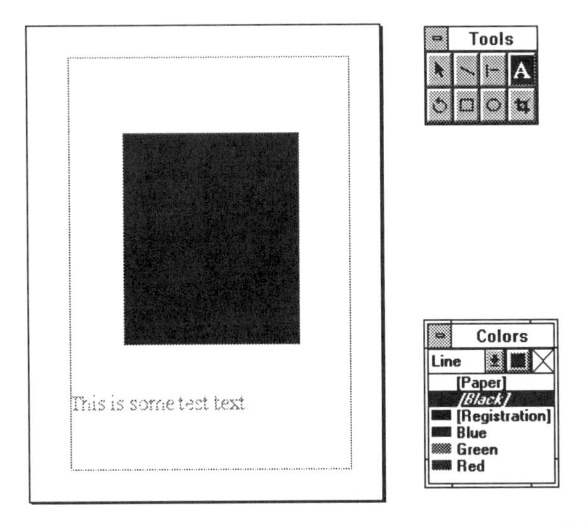

9.4 Printing Color Separations

PageMaker produces color separations during the printing process. Selecting the Color button on the Print dialog box displays options relating to color printing:

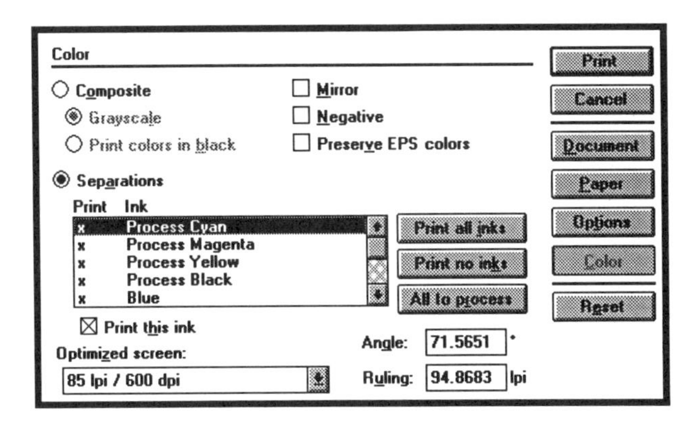

Color options for the Print dialog box

To print color separations, select the Separations option. Both process and spot colors are listed in the inks list. Colors that will print are indicated with an X. To print a non-selected color or to deselect a currently printing color, double-click on it.

All of the colors in the document can be printed by selecting Print all inks. Because PageMaker skips colors not in the document this is a fast way of printing separations for all colors. To switch back to black and white printing select Composite.

Practice 2

In this Practice you will print color separations for the publication created in the last Practice. Start PageMaker and open CH9PRACT.PM5 if you have not already done so.

1) *EXECUTE THE PRINT COMMAND*

a. From the File menu, select the Print command. The Print dialog box is displayed.
b. Select the Color button. The dialog box changes to show the color options.

2) *SET SEPARATION OPTIONS*

a. Select Separations. The ink list and buttons are no longer dimmed.
b. Using the arrows, scroll through the ink list. The four process colors (CMYK) and three spot colors (Blue, Green, Red) are listed. Only the process colors are currently selected.
c. Scroll to the top of the ink list. Double-click on Process Cyan. The X is removed and no plate for Cyan objects would be printed.
d. Select the Print all inks button. All of the inks are selected and shown with an X.

3) *PRINT THE SEPARATIONS*

a. Click on the Print button. PageMaker prints one page for each of the three spot colors in the current document. Note how only the objects for a single color appear on each printed page (plate): Green text, Blue rectangle, Red outline.
b. Save the file.

Note: The Separations option remains selected until you turn it off. To avoid printing separations you must set the Color options back to Composite the next time you print.

9.5 Color Separation Options

Options

Your printer will need to know which of the separation pages is to be printed in which color. They will also need to align the separate plates so that the document is printed properly. This process is called *registration* and you have probably seen color printing where one color was slightly mis-aligned. PageMaker can print a set of special marks on the outside of each page that identify the color and help the printer keep the registration aligned properly. These are selected using the Options button on the Print command's dialog box:

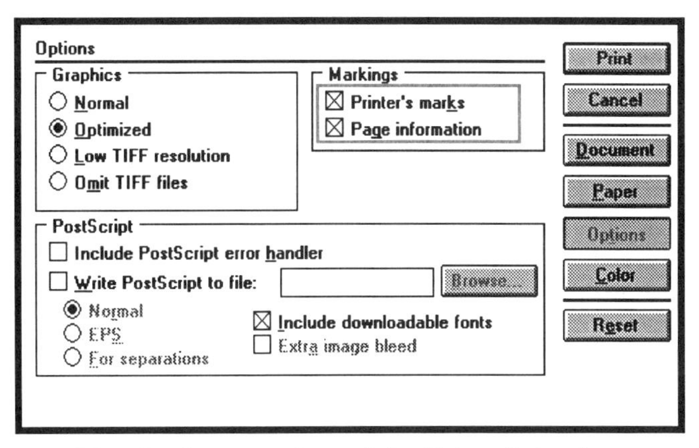

The Options section of the Print dialog box

Under Markings, selecting Printer's marks and Page information includes several important items on your printed pages:

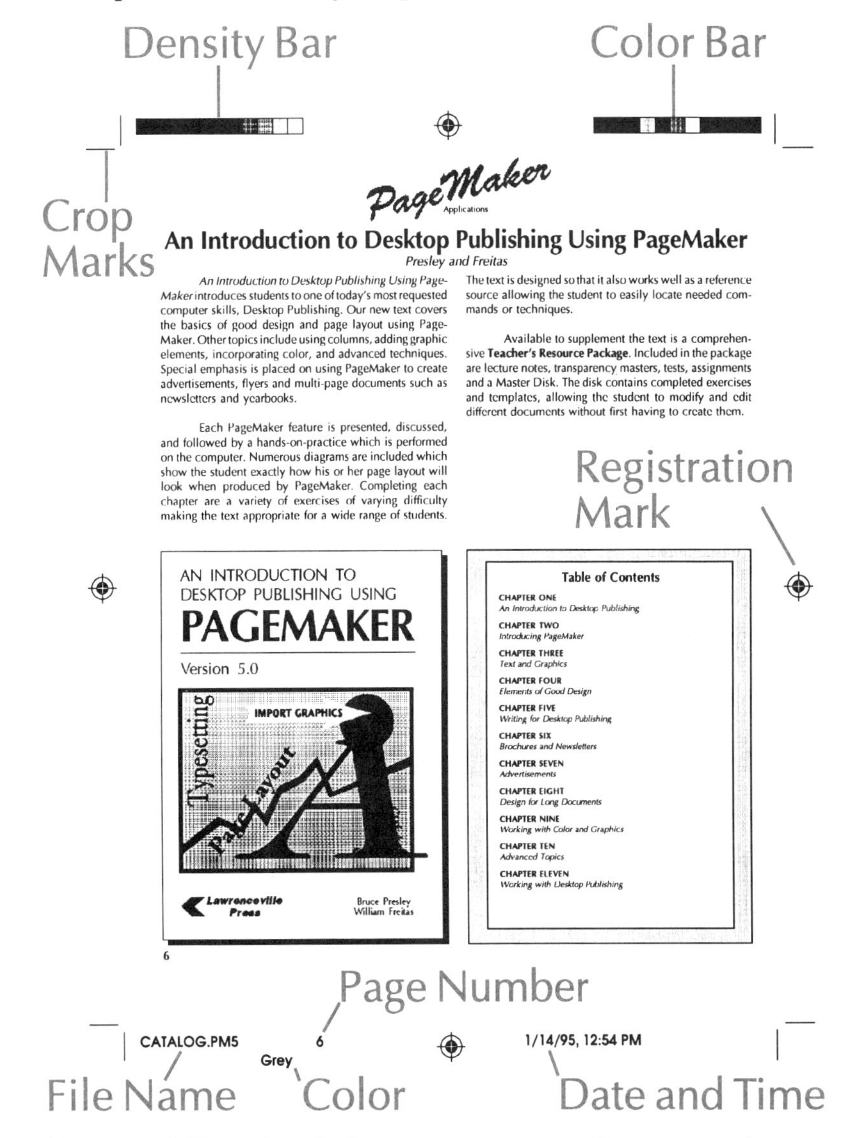

PageMaker Applications

An Introduction to Desktop Publishing Using PageMaker

Presley and Freitas

An Introduction to Desktop Publishing Using PageMaker introduces students to one of today's most requested computer skills, Desktop Publishing. Our new text covers the basics of good design and page layout using PageMaker. Other topics include using columns, adding graphic elements, incorporating color, and advanced techniques. Special emphasis is placed on using PageMaker to create advertisements, flyers and multi-page documents such as newsletters and yearbooks.

Each PageMaker feature is presented, discussed, and followed by a hands-on-practice which is performed on the computer. Numerous diagrams are included which show the student exactly how his or her page layout will look when produced by PageMaker. Completing each chapter are a variety of exercises of varying difficulty making the text appropriate for a wide range of students.

The text is designed so that it also works well as a reference source allowing the student to easily locate needed commands or techniques.

Available to supplement the text is a comprehensive **Teacher's Resource Package**. Included in the package are lecture notes, transparency masters, tests, assignments and a Master Disk. The disk contains completed exercises and templates, allowing the student to modify and edit different documents without first having to create them.

AN INTRODUCTION TO DESKTOP PUBLISHING USING **PAGEMAKER** Version 5.0

IMPORT GRAPHICS Typesetting Page Layout

Lawrenceville Press — Bruce Presley, William Freitas

Table of Contents

6

Crop Marks

Commercially printed documents are usually prepared on paper that is larger than the finished sized. *Crop marks* in each corner tell the printer where to cut (crop) the final page.

Density Bar and Color Bar

Printing presses need to be adjusted during the print run to ensure that inks are being applied correctly. The *density bar* helps the printing press operator determine that enough ink is being used and *color bars* show if the process colors are being accurately mixed.

Registration Marks

The four *registration marks* help the printer align the different colored plates. When a plate is out of alignment, gaps are visible between objects, and certain objects may be mis-colored.

File Name, Date, and Time

The name of the file, date, and time the file was printed are useful for making certain that the correct and most up-to-date plates are used.

Color and Page Number

When printing separations, there will be multiple plates per page. Your printer must know the page number and color of the plate in order to properly produce the publication.

Crop marks, density bars, color bars, and registration marks are printed by selecting Printer's marks. The file name, color, page number, and date information are produced by Page information.

9.6 Reduce to Fit

There will be times when you need to print a proof of a publication that is larger than the paper used in your printer. For example, newspapers are often printed on 11" x 17" paper but most laser printers can only print on 8.5" x 11" or 8.5" x 14" (legal). For this reason, the Print command dialog box includes a Reduce to fit option under Scale in the Paper options:

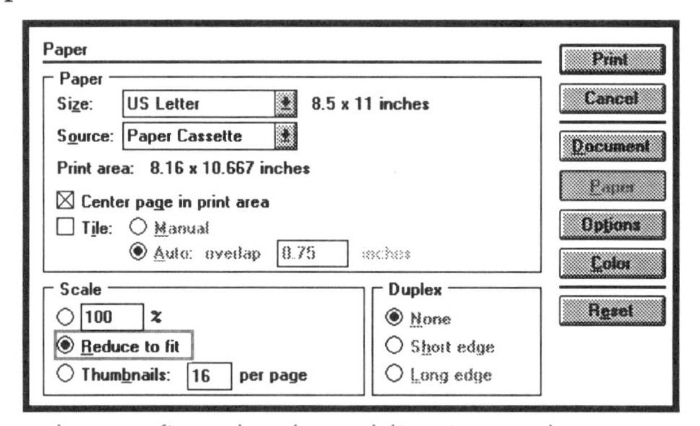

Selecting Reduce to fit scales the publication to the current paper size

Selecting Reduce to fit scales the publication down to fit your paper size. When Printer's marks or Page information is selected (described in Section 9.5), the publication size will be further reduced to show these marks as well.

Practice 3

In this Practice you will create a composite (black and white) printout with printing marks. Start PageMaker and open CH9PRACT.PM5 if you have not already done so.

1) EXECUTE THE PRINT COMMAND

a. From the File menu, select the Print command. The Print dialog box is displayed.
b. Select the Color button. Set the separations back to Composite.

2) SET PRINT OPTIONS

a. Select Options.
b. Under the Markings, select both Printer's marks and Page information.

3) REDUCE THE PUBLICATION PRINT SIZE

a. Select Paper.
b. Under Scale, select Reduce to fit.

4) PRINT THE PUBLICATION

a. Click on the Print button. PageMaker prints the publication in black and white only, using shades of grey to represent the different colors. Note the marks around the outside of the reduced page.
b. Save the file.

9.7 Creating New Colors

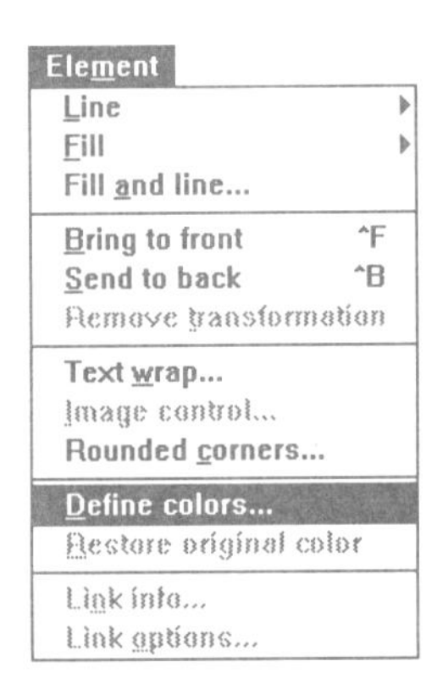

New colors are added to the Color palette using the Define colors command from the Element menu:

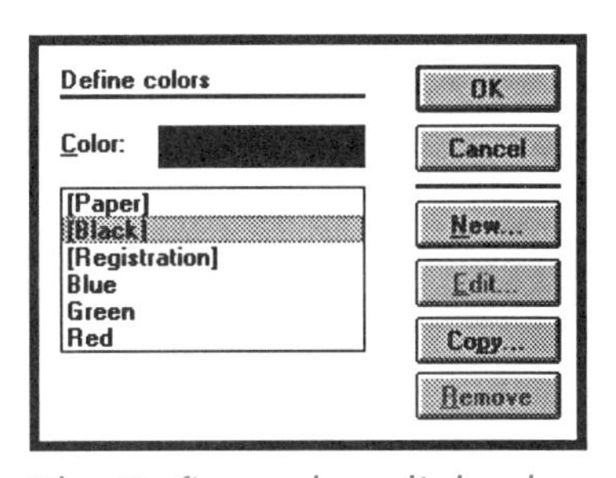

The Define colors dialog box

The three pre-defined spot colors are listed. Selecting New displays the Edit color dialog box:

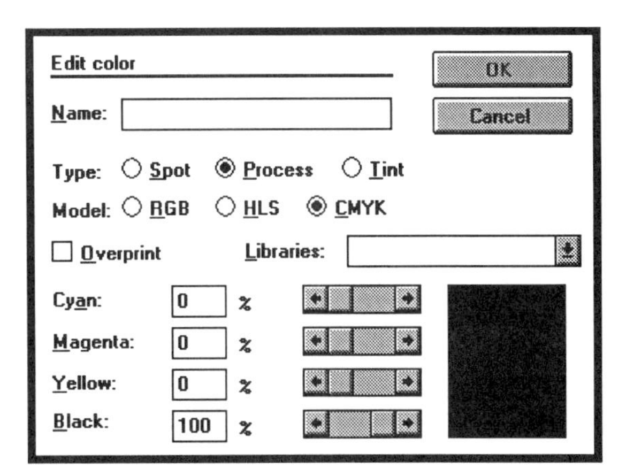

Colors can be created from scratch or added from matching systems

Added colors can be one of three different Types: a Spot color, a Process color, or a Tint which is a percentage of a previously defined color. The colors can be specified using three different color Models: red, green, blue (RGB), hue, lightness, saturation (HLS), and four-color process (CMYK). For most jobs CMYK should be selected.

Once you have selected the color Model, it is possible to mix your color using the color sliders the same way an artist mixes paint. The rectangle (or "color chip") next to the sliders shows the new color at the top and the old color at the bottom for comparison. It is important to remember that the color shown on the screen is only an approximation of the actual printed color:

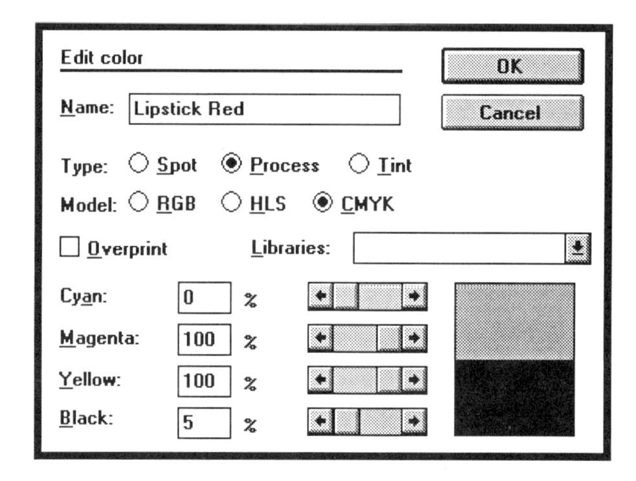

After the color has been mixed, you should give it a meaningful Name. The color can then be added to the Color palette by selecting OK twice.

9.8 Color Matching Systems

In order to ensure proper printed color a variety of *color matching systems* have been created. PageMaker supports the most common of these including the PANTONE matching system (PMS), Focoltone, TruMatch, TOYO, and Munsell. The color matching system helps to guarantee that a specific shade of red will always be that shade of red, regardless of where and when the publication is printed. For example, the color identified as PANTONE Red 032 will be the same whether printed in California, Massachusetts, or Japan.

For reasons discussed in Section 9.1, color matching systems cannot guarantee that the same shade of red will appear on your computer screen, but only provide a simulation of that color. Most color matching systems have *swatch books* that show samples of the printed colors, and these are available at most local graphics arts stores.

9.9 Adding Matching System Colors

Because the colors shown on the screen are approximations, to guarantee that the correct colors are used when the document is printed you should add colors using one of the color matching systems. These are accessed using the Libraries option on the Edit color dialog box:

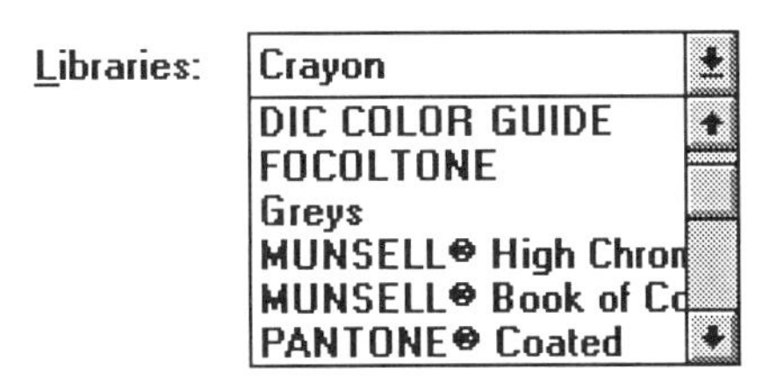

More libraries are available by scrolling

After selecting the desired library, PageMaker displays a large dialog box of available colors from which you may choose:

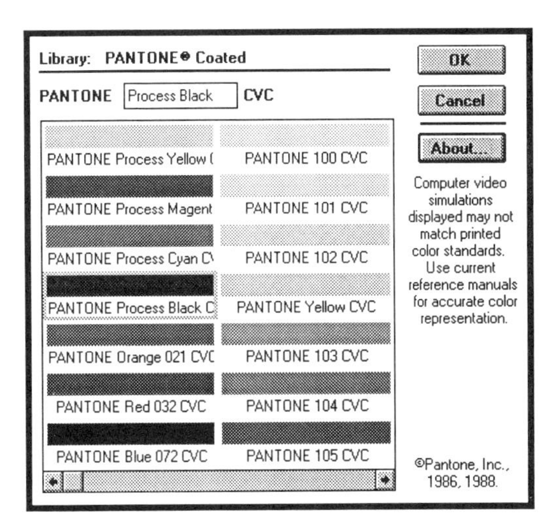

Color options will appear in full color on your screen

Choosing OK displays the selected color name and its CMYK (or other Model) values in the Edit color dialog box where they may be edited if necessary:

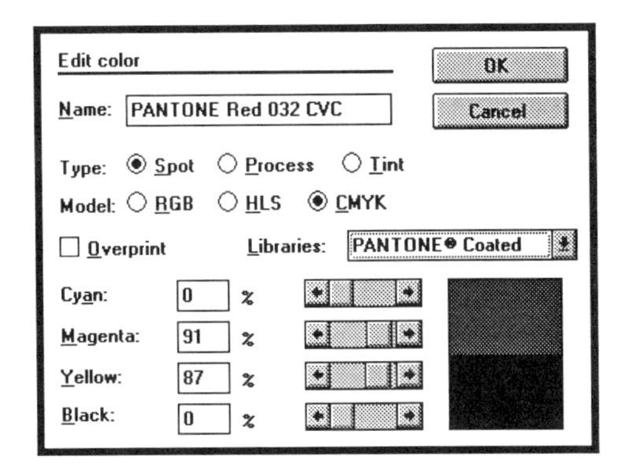

Selecting OK twice adds the color to your palette.

While color names and values may be edited, it is best to leave them unchanged. This is especially true for process colors because PageMaker will separate the color into the four CMYK plates based on the values specified in the Edit color dialog box. Also, your printer is expecting to find the color names printed on each plate (created by the Page information option). Changing a color's name without first checking with your printer will likely cause problems when it comes time to produce the printed publication.

Practice 4

In this Practice you will add two new colors, one from a matching system and one of your own mixing. Start PageMaker and open CH9PRACT.PM5 if you have not already done so.

1) *CREATE A NEW COLOR*

a. Make sure that nothing is selected. From the Element menu, select the Define colors command. The Define colors dialog box is displayed.
b. Select the New button. The Edit color dialog box is shown.
c. Name the color `My Color`. If not already, select Process as the Type and CMYK as the Model.

2) *MIX THE COLOR*

a. Set the Black to 0%.
b. Drag the Cyan slider to 100%. Note the color chip to the right of the sliders which shows the screen's approximation for the color cyan at the top.
c. Adjust the sliders to see 100% Magenta only, and then 100% Yellow only.
d. Adjust the four color sliders until you produce a color that you like.
e. Select OK. The color is shown on the Define colors box.
f. Select OK. The color is added to this document's palette. If not already visible, display the Color palette (`Ctrl+K`). The size of the palette can be adjusted by dragging its lower corners.
g. Select the rectangle. Using the Color palette, apply your new color to Both the line and fill of the rectangle.

3) *ADD A COLOR MATCHING SYSTEM COLOR*

a. Make sure that nothing is selected. In the Element menu, select Define colors.
b. Select the New button. The Edit color dialog box is shown. We will not enter a name for this color because we will use the color matching system's name.
c. Display the list of Libraries. Scroll through the list and select PANTONE® Uncoated. (The "uncoated" in the library name refers to a type of paper.) The PANTONE® Uncoated library is displayed.
d. Scroll through the colors. In PANTONE, each color is numbered, and uncoated colors are followed by the letters CVU. Locate color 3005 (in the blue spectrum).
e. Click on PANTONE 3005 CVU and select OK. The color is displayed on the Edit color dialog box and we can see that this color is made up of 100% Cyan, 30% Magenta, 0% Yellow, and 6% Black.
f. Select OK to return to Define colors and OK again to add the color to your palette.
g. Using the Text tool, triple-click on the text and make it PANTONE 3005.

4) PRINT THE PUBLICATION

a. Execute the Print command.
b. Select Paper. Under Scale, select 100%.
c. Select Options. Under the Markings, deselect both Printer's marks and Page information.
d. Click on Print. PageMaker prints the publication in shades of grey because Composite is still selected from the last Practice.
e. Save the file.

9.10 Effective Use of Color

Color can have dramatic effects on a publication, changing the way that your audience perceives your message. Color can also be expensive—adding a second color to a job can increase its printing cost by 50% to 75%, so it is important to make sure your color is used effectively and does not interfere with your message. Below are a few hints for getting the most out of your color.

Use Color Sparingly

You have earlier been warned about using too many fonts in a document to avoid the "ransom note" effect. The same is true about using too many colors, which can make a document look garish or distracting. Using the same color for three different rules (lines) is often more effective than using a different color for each. Some experts recommend using a palette of no more than 4 different colors. (Of course, some publications will require more.)

Use Care with Colored Text

Colored text can be difficult to read, especially a light colored ink printed on white paper. Yellow is a perfect example of this. Yellow text can be eye-catching and effective, but only when set at a large size, as in a headline or banner, or on a dark background such as large yellow letters on a purple or blue background. On the other hand, printing all the body text for this book in yellow would make it hard to read, limiting our ability to get the message to the reader. When using colored text, make sure that it is large enough and dark enough to be read easily by your audience.

Use Complementing Colors

Artists long ago developed a *color wheel* for examining the relationships between different colors. The colors from red to violet are arranged chromatically in a circle: red, red-orange, orange, orange-yellow, yellow, yellow-green, green, green-blue, blue, blue-violet, violet, and violet-red:

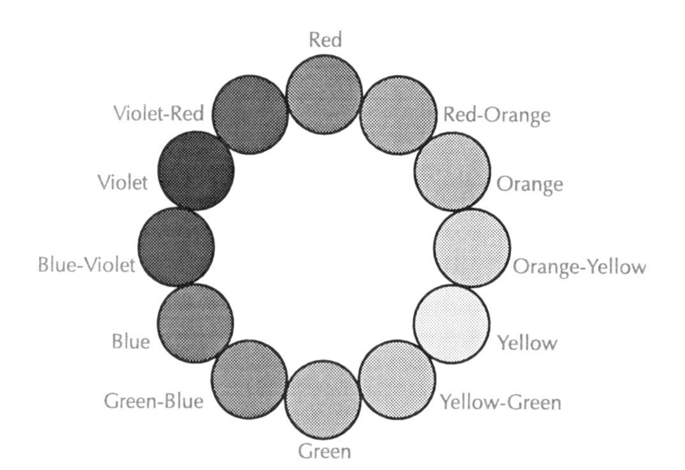

The position of a color on the wheel represents relationships to the other colors. For example, red and green are directly opposite each other and said to be *complementary*. Three adjacent colors such as red, red-orange, and orange, are called *analogous*. Three equally-spaced colors, such as red, blue, and yellow, are called *triads*. Colors are also grouped by "temperature" where reds, oranges, and yellows are called *warm colors*, and blues, greens, and violets are *cool*.

While a full discussion of color theory is beyond the scope of this text, there are certain colors which go well together. Complementary colors like red / green and violet / yellow make effective pairs when you need to draw attention to an area. When printing in three colors, using triads or colors from a single temperature group is useful. Also, when picking colors consider the other colored elements in the publication. For example, a company logo may be primarily red, and cannot be changed. For the rest of the document choose colors which go well with that shade of red. Also consider the effect of the color on your reader. For example, red often signals "Danger" or "Stop"—you would not use a lot of red in a brochure for a retirement home or a relaxing cruise vacation. The library or art stores will have several references for using color. Remember that what colors you use are as important as where and how you use them.

9.11 Inexpensive Color Alternatives

Color printing can be expensive, but there are ways of using inexpensive color effectively. Below are three techniques that can add color to a publication without spending a great deal of money.

Colored and Pre-printed Paper

Every publication is really a two color job when you consider the role that the color of the paper plays in a document's design. Black and white can become black and red, or black and yellow. Paper also comes in a variety of finishes and textures, which adds another dimension to the finished publication. Your printer can help you locate and choose a paper suitable for the publication.

Available from a number of sources are pre-printed papers that already have a four-color design printed on them. These provide a number of options for desktop publishers to produce color documents using only a laser printer, avoiding a large printing bill.

Colored Text

In a single color document the ink does not always have to be black. Depending on the amount and size of the text in your publication a colored ink can be pleasing. This can be combined with colored paper for a number of interesting effects. Try dark blue ink on light blue paper for example, or purple ink on yellow paper. Keep in mind that the text must remain readable for your target audience.

Shades of Grey

The Line and Fill submenus have a number of shades which can be applied to any color, including black. Using shades of grey in lines, fills, and other artwork can give a publication an entirely different feel:

9.12 Tints

The previous section discussed using shades of grey to give a publication a richer look. A shade of a color is called a *tint*, and the different levels of grey are just tints of black. One way to get more use out of a second ink color is to use a variety of tints, created using the Define colors command. Tint is the third color Type listed in the Edit color dialog box, and selecting Tint changes the available options:

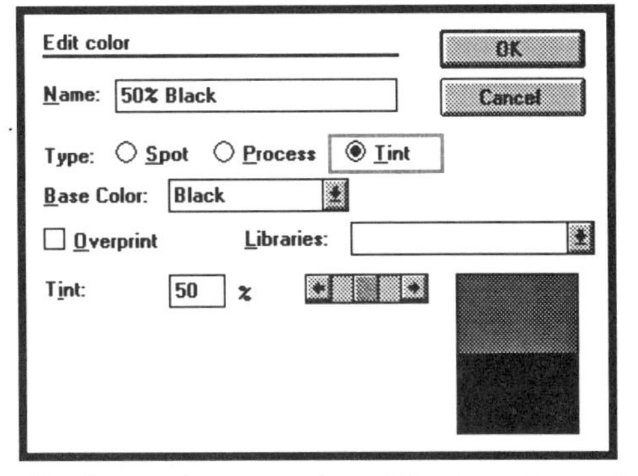

Options change when Tint is selected

As when creating any new color a Name must be supplied. The Base Color is then selected from the list of available colors. (A tint may only be created from a color that already exists in the palette.) The Tint percentage is then specified, either by entering the desired value or using the slider. The color chip to the right shows the new tint in relation to its base color.

After the tint has been created it is listed in the Color palette:

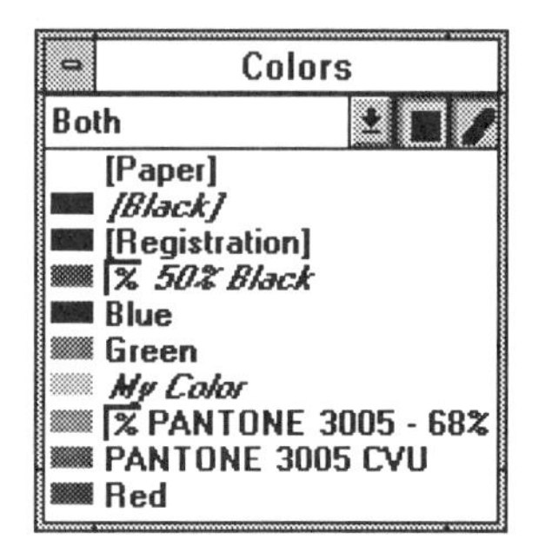

Tints are listed in the color palette

Each tint name is preceded by a percent symbol (%), indicating that it is a tint. When naming tints there are two common conventions which are helpful. The first is to list the base color name followed by the percentage as shown with PANTONE 3005, which keeps the tints listed near the base colors in the palette. The second is to name the color starting with its percentage, as in 50% Black. This has the advantage of keeping the tints together in the palette, but can be irksome if you have many tints with the same percentage. In both cases it is best to use a descriptive name showing the base color, tint percentage, and possibly the application of the color such as "Logo red" or "Page 1 graphic", etc.

You may have noticed in the Color palette above that some color names are italicized (My Color) and others are not. Process colors are italicized, and spot colors are not. Similarly a tint of a process color (50% Black) is italicized while a tint of a process color is not (PANTONE 3005 - 68%).

Practice 5

In this Practice you will create and apply tints. Start PageMaker and open CH9PRACT.PM5 if you have not already done so.

1) CREATE A PROCESS COLOR TINT

a. If not visible, display the Color palette (`Ctrl+K`) and adjust its size and position.
b. Make sure that nothing is selected. From the Element menu, select the Define colors command. The Define colors dialog box is displayed.
c. Select the New button. The Edit color dialog box is shown.
d. Select Tint as the Type. The options in the dialog box change.
e. In the Base Color list, select Black if it is not already listed.

f. Using the slider, create a 50% tint. Note the change in the color chip.
g. Name the color `50% Black`. Select OK to return to the Define colors box, and OK to add the tint to this document's palette. Note that the color name is italicized in the palette indicating that it is a tint of a process color.

2) *FILL A RECTANGLE WITH THE TINT*

a. Draw a 1.5" by 1.5" rectangle at the top-left corner of the document.
b. Fill the rectangle with the 50% Black tint.
c. Copy and Paste the rectangle, placing the copy 0.25 inches to the right of the original.
d. Fill the copy with Black.
e. Select both rectangles and Copy them to the Clipboard.
f. Paste the rectangles, placing the copies 0.25 inches to the right of the first pair:

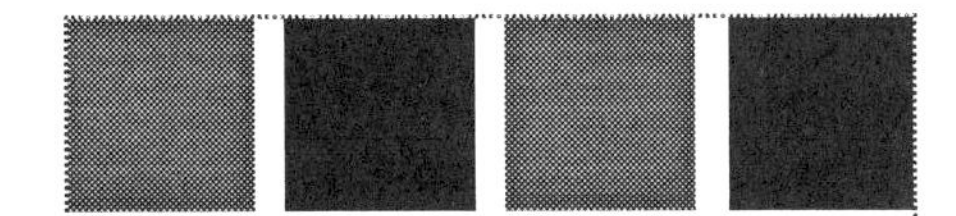

3) *CREATE A SPOT COLOR TINT*

a. Make sure that nothing is selected and execute the Define colors command from the Element menu.
b. In the colors list, highlight PANTONE 3005 CVU and select New.
c. Choose Tint as the Type. PANTONE 3005 is already listed in the Base Color list.
d. In the Tint box type `68` to create a 68% tint.
e. Name the color `PANTONE 3005 - 68%`. Select OK to return to the Define colors box, and OK to add the tint to this document's palette. Because this is a spot color tint, the color name is not italicized in the palette.

4) *COPY AND FILL THE RECTANGLES WITH THE NEW TINT*

a. Select the four rectangles at the top of the document.
b. Copy and Paste the rectangles. Drag the rectangles to the bottom of the document.
c. Color the copied rectangles, alternating PANTONE 3005 and its 68% tint.

5) *PRINT THE PUBLICATION*

a. Save the file.
b. Execute the Print command and select Print. PageMaker prints the publication in shades of grey because Composite is selected.

9.13 Deleting Colors

If you have no more use for a color it may be deleted from the palette using the Remove button on the Define colors dialog box. Before a color is removed PageMaker displays a warning:

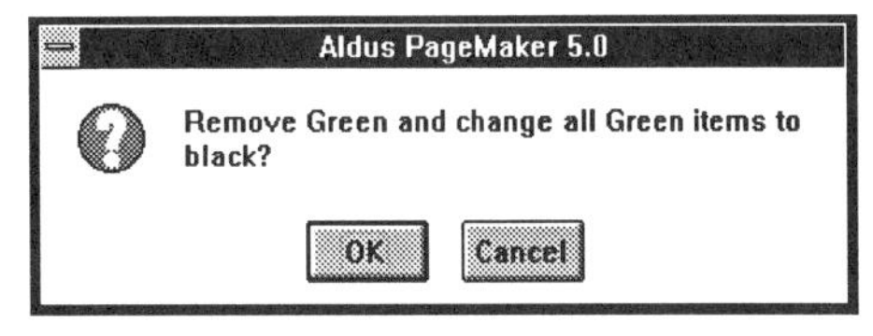

PageMaker warns you before deleting a color

Selecting OK deletes the color and changes any objects of that color to black. If a color is deleted by mistake, immediately selecting Cancel from the Define colors dialog box restores it. Deleting a color from the current publication has no affect on any other publication that also uses that color.

Unfortunately, PageMaker displays the warning message above even when the color being removed is not used in the publication. Before deleting a color you may wish to check that the color is not used in your publication by printing a color separated page of that ink only. If the page is blank it is safe to delete that color.

9.14 Knockout and Overprint

Multi-color printing requires that the paper in a publication receive several layers of ink. This can sometimes cause unwanted effects, such as when a light ink is printed over top of a dark ink. In such a situation the darker ink may "bleed" through, changing the color of the lighter ink. For this reason all objects in PageMaker *knockout* any objects below them—a cut out is made in the object below so the top object prints directly on paper, not on another layer of ink:

Knockout creates white space below the second color

However, a useful technique is to *overprint* layers of ink to produce different colors. For example, overprinting yellow over blue produces a green. This is an inexpensive way to produce three colors (yellow, blue, green) while only paying for two inks (yellow and blue):

Overprinting layers two inks, often creating a third color

Overprinting is controlled using the Overprint option on the Edit color dialog box:

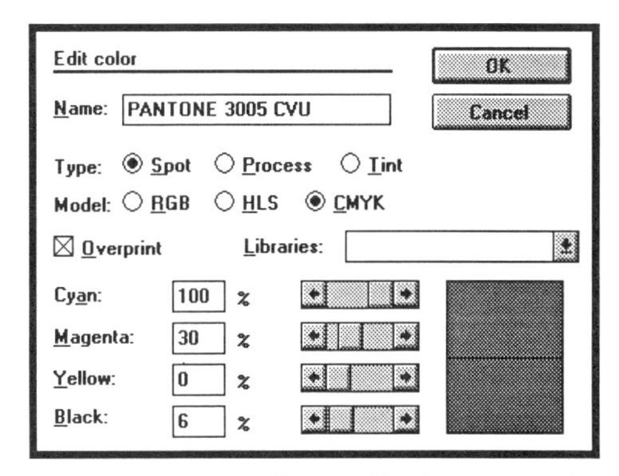

Selecting Overprint affects all objects in this color

All objects in this color will now overprint, including previously created objects.

Practice 6

In this Practice you will delete a color and change a color to overprint. Start PageMaker and open CH9PRACT.PM5 if you have not already done so.

1) DELETE A COLOR

a. If not visible, display the Color palette (`Ctrl+K`) and adjust its size and position. Select the large rectangle in the middle of the page. Its color, as indicated in the palette, is My Color.
b. From the Element menu, select the Define colors command. Highlight My Color in the list if it is not already.
c. Select the Remove button. PageMaker displays a warning.
d. Select OK to remove the color.
e. Select OK to return to the Define colors dialog box. My Color is removed from this document's palette and the rectangle is changed to black.

2) PRINT SEPARATIONS

a. Drag the text block so that it is over the large black rectangle:

(If your text block is covered by the rectangle, select the Send to front command from the Element menu.)

b. From the File menu, execute the Print command.
c. Select the Color button. Select Separations and Print all inks. Note the X's indicating which inks will be printed.
d. Select Options. Under the Markings, select both Printer's marks and Page information.
e. Select Paper. Under Scale, select Reduce to fit.
f. Click on the Print button. PageMaker prints the publication as separations, and you can see how the PANTONE 3005 ink knocks out the Black ink below it.

3) *CHANGE THE COLOR TO OVERPRINT*

a. Make sure that nothing is selected and execute the Define colors command.
b. In the colors list, highlight PANTONE 3005 CVU and select Edit.
c. Change the color to Overprint and select OK twice to return to the publication.
d. Print a copy of the document using the same options as in step 2. The PANTONE 3005 now overprints the Black rectangle.
e. Save and close the file.

9.15 Bitmapped versus Vector Graphics

There are two general types of computer graphics: *bitmapped* (or *raster*) and *vector*. Each has certain benefits and limitations, but knowing when to use each can make a publication look more professional.

Bitmapped or *paint* graphics are based on a grid of dots, like the letters produced by a dot matrix printer (described in Chapter One). The grid frequency is fixed, and cannot be changed in PageMaker. For example, in a certain graphic there may be 150 dots per inch (dpi). Because of this fixed *resolution*, curved or angled lines, especially in text, may appeared jagged. The higher the dpi, the better the quality of the graphic. Bitmap "jaggies" are usually pronounced when the graphic is stretched. Files ending with .TIF, .PCX, and .BMP are bitmapped graphics.

Vector or *draw* graphics are not based on a grid, so their lines stay smoother, even when the graphic is stretched. The files you have placed during the Practices such as CALIFSUN.WMF are vector graphics. Other vector graphic names end in .EPS, .AI, and .CGM.

A stretched bitmap (left) and vector graphic

One way to help avoid some of the roughness when stretching imported bitmap graphics is to use proportional stretching: holding down the `Shift` key while dragging a corner handle.

9

Both forms of graphics have advantages and disadvantages. In addition to stretching better, vector graphics are usually smaller and print faster. However, .EPS graphics can only be printed on a Postscript printer. Some graphics, such as color photographs, can only be produced in bitmap form. In general, if both a bitmap and a vector version of a graphic is available, select the vector version.

9.16 Cropping Graphics

Imported graphics may sometimes contain extra information that you do not wish to appear. If you have the program that originally created the file, such as CorelDraw, you can edit the graphic using that program. If you do not have the graphics program, you can still *crop* the graphic in PageMaker. Cropping means to remove parts of the image to you do not wish to print.

Cropping is accomplished using the Crop tool in the Toolbox. Clicking on a graphic with the Crop tool displays handles. Dragging a handle not only reduces the size of the graphic's frame, but excludes the part of the graphic no longer visible. In other words, anything that the handle is dragged over is removed from the graphic. Cropping in this way does not affect the actual graphic file—its contents are not changed. Only what is displayed and printed by PageMaker is changed.

Cropped and rotated graphics take longer to print than their non-modified version. When at all possible, the cropping and rotating should be done in the original graphics program that created the file, and not in PageMaker.

Practice 7

In this Practice you will stretch a bitmapped and a vector graphic. A graphic will also be cropped. Start PageMaker if you have not already done so.

1) CREATE A NEW FILE

2) IMPORT TWO GRAPHICS

a. From the File menu, select the Place command.
b. Place the file named GR-TEST.TIF near the top left of the page. This is a bitmapped graphic.
c. Place the file named GR-TEST.WMF near the middle left of the page. This is a vector graphic.
d. Zoom in to 200% view and scroll to view each graphic. Both the bitmap and vector versions are similar at this, their natural size.
e. Zoom out.

3) *COPY AND STRETCH THE GRAPHICS*

a. Select both graphics.
b. Execute the Copy command. A copy of both graphics is placed on the Clipboard.
c. Execute the Paste command. Drag the copies to the right, near the 4" horizontal mark. Click to remove the handles.
d. Select the copy of GR-TEST.TIF near the top right of the page. Using the Control palette, increase both the width (W) and height (H) of the graphic to 250%.
e. Select the copy of GR-TEST.WMF near the middle right of the page. Using the Control palette, increase both the Width and Height to 250%.
f. Zoom in to 200% and scroll to view each stretched graphic. Note the differences between the bitmap, which seems rough and jagged, and the vector version, which is smoother.

4) *SAVE AND PRINT*

a. Zoom out and close the Control palette. Make sure that all of the graphics are within the margins of the page.
b. Save the publication using the name GR-TEST.
c. Print a copy of the publication, and note the differences in the four graphics.

5) *CROP A GRAPHIC*

a. Select the Crop tool from the Tool palette.
b. Click on the copy of GR-TEST.WMF near the middle right of the page, selecting it. Handles are shown.
c. Place the tool over a handle. Click and hold down the mouse button. A frame is shown around the graphic as long as the button is held down. Release the mouse.
d. Using the Crop tool, drag the bottom middle handle up slightly, reducing the height of the frame. Release the tool. The graphic is cropped—the material that the frame passed over as it was dragged is no longer visible. Note that this did not stretch the graphic.
e. Continue to crop the bottom and right side of the graphic until it is similar to:

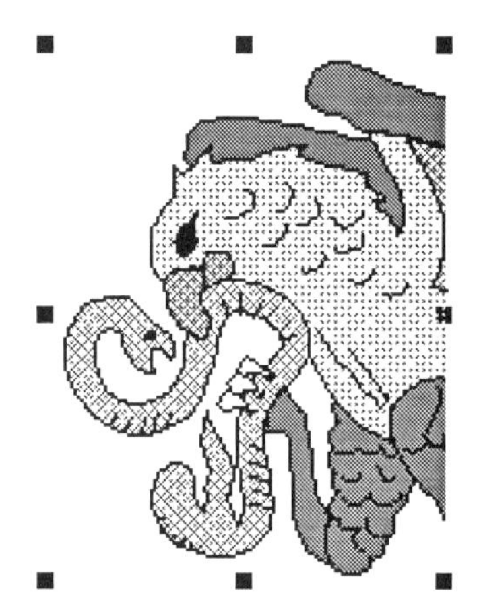

f. Save the file and print a copy.
g. Quit PageMaker and Windows.

9

9.17 Where can you go from here?

Before attempting to produce any serious color work, you should read the Commercial Printing Guide supplied with PageMaker as well as Chapter Eleven in this text. Always confer with your printer early in the design process, and continue your dialog during the production process. Finally, remember that the color shown on the screen is just an approximation of the final printed color. If possible, proof your document on one of the personal color printers (ink jet and dye sublimation) that are now becoming widely available, but remember that those colors may vary from the final printed piece as well.

Chapter Summary

This chapter describes how color can be used in a design and applied in a document. The ability of computer programs to handle complex color with any precision is a fairly new development, and even PageMaker 5 had some problems with color in early releases. Part of the difficulty with creating color publications lies in the different color models used by different output devices. The computer screen uses the RGB (red, green, blue) color model while most printing uses the CMYK (cyan, magenta, yellow, black) model. CMYK printing is also referred to as process color or 4-color printing. Because of the different color models, the colors shown on the screen are only approximations of the printed colors.

Two common production methods are spot color and process (CMYK) color. In spot color a different ink is applied for each color in the document. In process color the four base colors are printed in different layers, combining to create new colors. The splitting of a document into its different colors is called separating, and PageMaker can produce both composite (all colors on a single page) and separated printouts. When printing separations it is a good idea to include both printer's marks (registration marks, color bars, etc.) and page information (page number, color, publication name, etc.).

Color is easiest applied using the Color palette. Colors can be added to the palette using the Define colors command. Added colors can be one of three different types: spot, process, or a tint, which is simply a percentage of a previously defined color. The colors can be specified using different color Models including RGB and four-color process (CMYK), which is the most common.

Color matching systems were developed to ensure that the same color ink would result regardless of how or where a publication is printed. PageMaker supports several major color matching systems including PANTONE, TruMatch, TOYO, and Munsell. Predefined colors can be added to the palette from any of these libraries. Most color matching systems have a printed swatch book of actual ink samples so that you can compare the final printed color to its screen approximation.

Adding color to a print job can be expensive, so this chapter described several ways to get the most use out of color, including using tints and colored papers. Several rules for effective color choice and use were also presented. Overlapping colors either overprint or knockout (leave white space below). This is controlled in the Define colors command. Overprinting often results in a third color, made up of the colors in the two overlapping objects.

This chapter also discussed the differences between bitmapped and vector graphics. Because they are built on a fixed grid, bitmapped graphics can get jagged when stretched. Vector graphics do not have this problem, but some vector graphics will not print on non-Postscript printers. For the most part vector graphics are better than bitmapped, with the exception of color photographs which usually can only be found as a bitmap.

Graphics imported into a PageMaker publication can be cropped (trimmed) using the Crop tool. Dragging a graphic's handle with the Crop tool reduces the graphic on that side. While graphics can be cropped and rotated in PageMaker, it is usually best to perform this type of editing in the program that was used to create the graphic.

Vocabulary

Analogous colors - Three adjacent colors on the color wheel such as red, red-orange, and orange.

Bitmapped - Graphic based on a grid of dots, like the letters produced by a dot matrix printer. Also called a raster or paint graphic.

CMYK - Most common color printing color model: Cyan (an aqua blue), Magenta (a bright purple), Yellow, and blacK. Different colors are created by overlapping layers of semi-transparent inks in each of the four colors. Also called process color.

Color bar - Strip of colors printed in the margin that show if the process (CMYK) colors are being mixed accurately.

Color matching system - Standardized color model system created in order to ensure proper printed color in different situations. PANTONE (PMS) is a popular color matching system.

Color models - Way of describing or defining a color. Each form of output device normally has its own color model.

Color wheel - Arrangement of colors developed for examining the relationships between different colors and families of colors.

Complementary colors - Colors directly opposite each other on the color wheel like red and green.

Cool colors - Colors near the violet end of the spectrum like blues, greens, and purples.

Crop - To trim a graphic with the Crop tool.

9

Crop marks - Printer's marks in the margin at each corner that indicate where to cut (crop) the final page.

Density bar - Gradient printed in the margin that helps the printing press operator determine if enough ink is being used.

DPI - Dots per inch. Often used to describe the resolution of a bitmapped graphic.

Draw graphic - Graphic where objects are not based on a grid, so lines stay smooth even when the graphic is stretched. Also called a vector graphic.

Knockout - When two objects overlap, a cut out is made in the bottom object so the top object prints directly on paper, not on another layer of ink.

Overprint - When two objects overlap, the top object prints directly on top of the bottom. The combined layers of ink for overprinted objects may produce a different color.

Paint graphic - Graphic based on a grid of dots, like the letters produced by a dot matrix printer. Also called bitmapped or raster graphics.

Pixel - Each tiny dot on the computer's screen. Actually composed of three smaller dots: one red, one green, and one blue.

Process color - Form of printing where colors are created by printing overlapping layers of semi-transparent CMYK inks. Also refers to an ink color that is composed of only CMYK components.

Registration - Alignment of the separate plates so that a color document prints properly.

Registration marks - Cross-hair marks printed in the margin that help the printing press operator align the different colored plates.

Resolution - The number of dots per inch (dpi) in a bitmapped graphic.

Reversed - Items set to Paper color, and are printed as white. Often used with text to produce white letters on a solid background.

RGB - Red, Green, and Blue color model useful for defining colors that appear on a computer screen.

Separating / Separations - Splitting the colors in a document into their different plates. Also the different plates themselves.

Spot color - Printing process where each color is applied from a separate plate. Also refers to an ink that is designed for use in spot color printing.

Swatch books - Printed samples of a color matching system's inks.

Tint - A color not printed at 100% density. Greys are tints of the color black.

Triads - Three equally-spaced colors on the color wheel such as red, blue, and yellow.

Vector - Graphic where objects are not based on a grid, so lines stay smooth even when the graphic is stretched. Also called a draw graphic.

Warm colors - Colors near the red end of the spectrum like reds, oranges, and yellows.

Reviews

Sections 9.1 — 9.5

1. a) What is a color model?
   b) What do most types of output devices use different color models?

2. a) What is a pixel?
   b) What color model does a computer monitor use and how is it related to the pixel?

3. What does CMYK stand for?

4. What is four color printing?

5. Why is it important not to rely on the colors shown on the computer's monitor when creating a color publication?

6. a) What is spot color?
b) What is process color?
c) Give some examples of when spot color would be used instead of process color. Of when process color would be used instead of spot color.

7. What does "separating" mean when referring to a color publication?

8. a) How are colors applied to text in PageMaker?
b) How are colors applied to graphics in PageMaker?
c) What two areas in a graphic may color be applied to?

9. What is PageMaker's "Paper" color used for?

10. Explain the process necessary to have PageMaker produce separations.

11. a) What two Print command options are associated with color separations?
b) What does each option produce and how is it helpful?

Sections 9.6 — 9.10

12. What does the Reduce to Fit option do and when would you use it?

13. a) How are new colors created in PageMaker?
b) What are the three types of colors that can be created?

14. a) What is a color matching system and how is one used?
b) Describe how PageMaker can make use of the colors in a color matching system.

15. What design options should you keep in mind when creating a color publication?

16. What alternatives are there to printing full color publications?

Sections 9.11 — 9.17

17. What is a tint and how is one created?

18. a) Describe how to remove a color from a publication's Color palette.
b) What happens to objects in the publication formatted in that color when the color is removed?
c) What happens to objects in other publications formatted in that color when the color is removed?

19. a) What is a knockout?
b) How is a knockout created?

20. a) What does "overprint" mean?
    b) How is overprinting controlled?
    c) What is the primary result of overprinting?

21. a) What is a bitmapped graphic?
    b) What file name extensions are used for bitmapped graphics?
    c) What are two other names for bitmapped graphics?

21. a) What is a vector graphic?
    b) What file name extensions are used for vector graphics?
    c) What is another name for a vector graphic?

22. Describe the advantages and disadvantages of using bitmapped and vector graphics.

23. a) What is cropping?
    b) Describe how to crop a graphic.

24. To avoid costly errors, what should be done when designing a color publication?

Exercises

1. Ivy University needs a color cover for their promotional flyer similar to the following:

a) Create a new publication.

b) Produce the cover shown above. The text is 48-point Times New Roman. The University logo is IULOGO.WMF and the rule is 6 point.

c) Color the type Blue and the rule Red.

d) Save the cover naming it IVYCOV and print a composite copy.

e) Print the color separations, including printer's marks.

f) In reviewing IVYCOV the University public relations department has asked that a green box with a black border be placed around the logo and the logo itself should be Paper colored so that it appears white in the final printing. Make this change so that your new cover appears similar to the one on the next page:

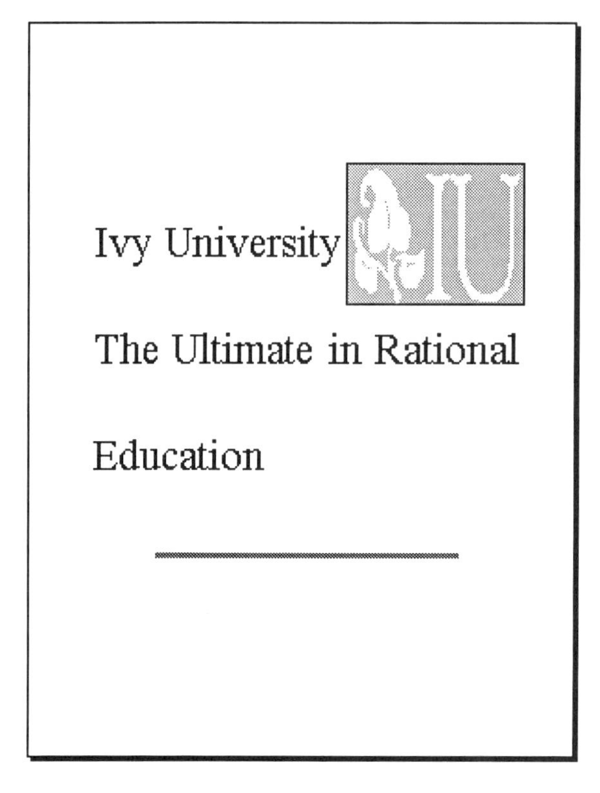

g) Use the Save As command to save the edited cover naming it IVYCOV2 and then print a composite.

2. Using the text, logo, and 6-point rule from Exercise 1, Ivy University's public relation department would like you to create a color cover of your own original design.

    a) Make three thumbnail sketches of the cover indicating fonts, type sizes, colors and other information. Be imaginative and try a variety of formats that are bold and eye-catching.

    b) Select the best sketch, create a new publication, and produce the cover according to your design.

    c) Save the cover naming it IVYCOV3 and then print both a composite copy and all color separations including printer's marks.

3. Ivy University Alumni Day is May 5 this year and the Alumni Association has asked you to produce designs for the T-shirts that will be distributed to the more than 6,000 alumni who are expected to arrive on campus. 8.5" x 11" designs are needed for both the front and back of the shirts. By using margins of 0.5" the shirt design can be maximized. Keeping with tradition the designs should be colorful and display Ivy's logo IULOGO.WMF.

    a) Produce three thumbnail sketches of the shirts front and back indicating fonts, type sizes, colors, etc. Remember the purpose and audience for the shirts which must not be boring or dull! You may want to use tints from the PANTONE Uncoated library and make use of knock outs.

b) Select the best sketches, create a new publication, and produce the front and back of the shirts according to your designs as page 1 and 2 in the file.

c) Save the cover naming it IVYSHIRT and then print both a composite copy and all color separations including printer's marks.

4. In Chapter Eight Exercise 3 you formatted an article titled *The History of Computers*. The article needs a color cover that gives the title, the authors' names (Bruce Presley and William Freitas), and the publisher (Lawrenceville Press, Inc.).

   a) Produce three thumbnail sketches of the cover indicating fonts, type sizes, colors, etc. Describe on paper two new process colors that will be used in printing the cover.

   b) Select the best sketch, create a new publication, and produce the cover. Define the two new colors, assigning them appropriate names.

   c) Save the cover naming it HCCOVER and then print both a composite copy and all color separations including printer's marks.

5. In Chapter Seven Exercise 2 you designed the cover for a CD starring The Sunshines. While happy with the design, the band believes the cover to be dull in just black and white so they have asked you add one color and use one 50% tint of that color.

   a) Open CSROCK, use the Save as command to save it as CSRKTINT and print a copy.

   b) Carefully study the cover and determine how one color could most effectively be added. Mark the printout with the color to be used and where.

   c) Add the color to the Color palette. Create one 50% tint of the color. Color the CD cover as you specified.

   d) Save the edited version of CSRKTINT and print both a composite copy and all color separations including printer's marks.

6. California Sunshine producers of natural fruit juices will sponsor a rock concert featuring The Sunshines to be held on July 4 in Malibu, California. They would like you to design a T-shirt to commemorate the event. The shirt should include their logo and mention their new juice beverage flavor Cherry-Apple. 8.5" x 11" designs are needed for both the front and back of the shirts. By using margins of 0.5" the shirt design can be maximized.

   a) Produce three thumbnail sketches of the shirts front and back indicating fonts, type size, and color. The type of color and number of colors used is up to you, the designer.

   b) Select the best sketches, create a new publication, and produce the shirt designs, using the logo CALIFSUN.WMF.

   c) Save the designs naming the file CSSHIRT and then print both a composite copy and all color separations including printer's marks.

7. The Sunshines are very happy with the T-shirt design you produced in Exercise 6 and now want you to design a poster announcing the concert. The poster will be printed using process colors.

   a) Produce two thumbnail sketches of the poster which will be produced in Tabloid size (11" x 17"). In your sketches, pick up on design elements of your T-shirt so that the shirt and poster share a consistent look.

   b) Select the best sketch, create a new Tabloid size publication, and produce the poster design using the logo CALIFSUN.WMF.

   c) Save the poster naming it CSPOSTER and then print both a composite copy and all color separations including printer's marks. Use the Reduce to fit option to print the Tabloid publication on smaller paper.

Chapter Ten:
Advanced Topics & Tables

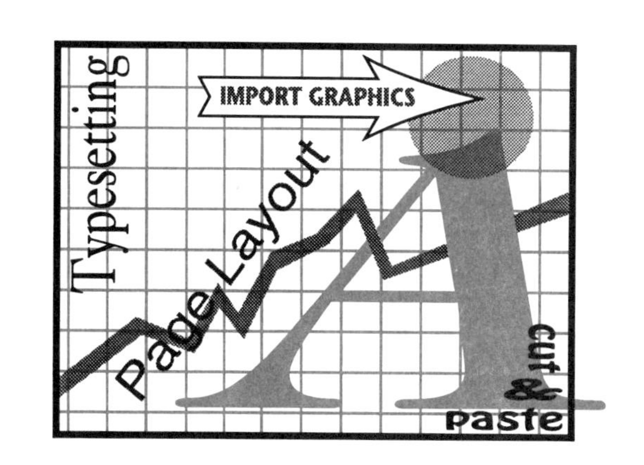

Type - Set width

Small caps

Type - Track

Rules

Type - Hyphenation

Utilities - Aldus Additions

Table Editor

Type - Type style

Element - Borders

Objectives

After completing this chapter you will be able to:

1. Change the width of characters.
2. Apply Small Caps and All Caps to selected text.
3. Adjust tracking for a paragraph.
4. Have PageMaker create rules above and below paragraphs.
5. Control automatic and manual hyphenation.
6. Use special characters to control line and word breaks.
7. Create and modify tables using the Table Editor.
8. Place and size Table Editor tables.
9. Create a drop cap using an Addition.

10

Covered in this chapter are some of PageMaker's advanced commands for formatting and layout. While you will not have a use for all of these commands in every publication, some, such as the ability to create tables, can make your documents look truly professional.

10.1 Setting Character Width

Type
Font
Size
Leading
Set width — Other..., 70%, 80%, 90%, ✓Normal Sh^X, 110%, 120%, 130%
Track
Type style
Type specs... ^T
Paragraph... ^M
Indents/tabs... ^I
Hyphenation... ^H
Alignment
Style
Define styles... ^3

The Set width command from the Type menu horizontally stretches or compresses selected text, increasing or decreasing the character widths by anywhere from 5% to 250%. Widths of 70% to 130% are the most common and these can be found on the command's submenu, with Normal being 100%:

70% The Quick Brown Fox
80% The Quick Brown Fox
90% The Quick Brown Fox
100% The Quick Brown Fox
110% The Quick Brown Fox
120% The Quick Brown Fox
130% The Quick Brown Fox

Set width changes the width of individual characters

The Other command can change the width in amounts of one tenth of 1% (0.1%). Note in the example above that the height of the text has not been changed. Although it may appear that way, this is only an optical illusion caused by changing the width.

In effect, Set width creates a new font with characters that are narrower or wider than the original. This command can be used in a number of ways, primarily increasing width for headlines and special effects, or decreasing it to save space. Width is also available as an option in the Type specs dialog box, and can be made part of a style.

10.2 Small Caps and All Caps

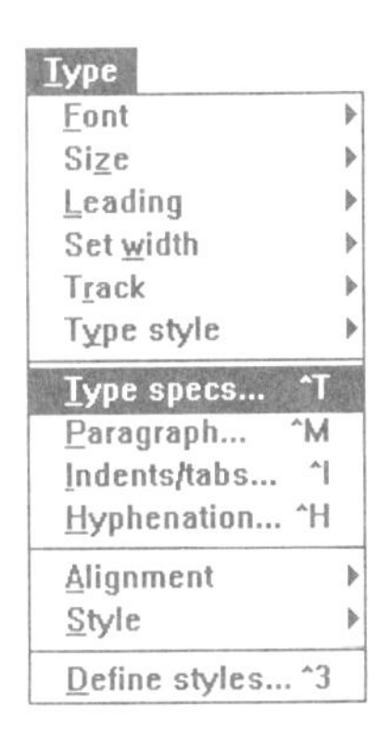

The Type specs command's Case option has two useful options, Small caps and All caps. *Small caps* changes all lowercase letters to their uppercase shape, but in a smaller point size. For example, a lowercase "i" would be changed to an "I", but kept at approximately the same size:

This is Regular text.

THIS IS SMALL CAPS TEXT.

An example of regular and Small caps text

Small caps are often used to give documents an "official" look such as on the letterhead for a legal office. The All caps option changes all lowercase letters to full size capitals. *All caps* is a fix for a typing error when the text should have been entered as all capitals but was not. Case also has a third option, Normal, which is the default, and returns the text to its normal mix of uppercase and lowercase letters.

Practice 1

In this Practice you will open a partially completed publication and apply text formats. The publication is a description sheet for a food preparation product marketed to affluent, health-conscience consumers.

1) START PAGEMAKER AND OPEN CH10PRAC.PM5

a. Open CH10PRAC.PM5. From the Edit menu, execute the Select all command to select all of the elements. There are three unlinked text blocks in this publication. Note the two horizontal guides and the column guides.
b. Click anywhere to remove the selections.

2) FORMAT THE TITLE

a. Zoom in to the top of the publication.
b. Select the Text tool and triple-click on the title, "California Sunshine Juicer."
c. Set the type size to 36 points. Zoom out and look at the title. It is big, but does not seem to get enough attention.
d. Make the title Bold. The title now appears too heavy, so remove the bold.
e. What is needed is a cross between the normal and the bold text. With the title highlighted, execute the Set width command from the Type menu. Select 120% from the submenu. The characters are made wider, and therefore somewhat heavier, but less dark than the bold.

3) FORMAT THE SUBTITLE

a. Zoom in and triple-click on the subtitle which reads "Product Description Sheet."
b. From the Type menu, execute Type specs.

c. Set the Case to All caps and select OK. The text is now shown in all capital letters.
d. Execute the Type specs command and set the Case to Normal. Select OK and the lowercase letters are again shown.
e. Execute Type specs again and set the Case to Small caps. Select OK and the lowercase letters are made smaller versions of the capitals.
f. Save the modified publication. Your titles should be similar to:

California Sunshine Juicer

PRODUCT DESCRIPTION SHEET

10.3 Tracking

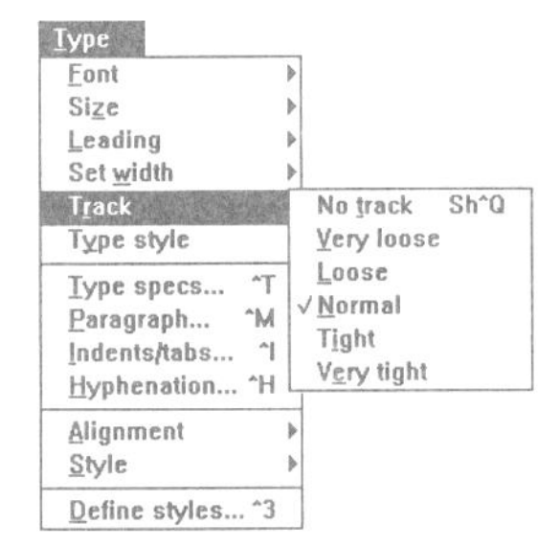

Tracking is the amount of space between words and characters and is an important factor in the readability of text. Increasing the tracking too much leaves disconcerting gaps while not enough tracking can cause the letters to run into one another, making it hard to distinguish individual words.

The Tracking command from the Type menu has six predefined sets of tracking values ranging from Very loose to Very tight. No track (`Shift+Ctrl+Q`) removes any tracking and the letters are displayed as intended by the font's designer:

No Track: The Five Boxing Wizards Jumped.
Very loose: The Five Boxing Wizards Jumped.
Loose: The Five Boxing Wizards Jumped.
Normal: The Five Boxing Wizards Jumped.
Tight: The Five Boxing Wizards Jumped.
Very tight: The Five Boxing Wizards Jumped.

Tracking can affect the way your page appears

Looser tracking is often used to make a block of text "expand" to fill a set amount of space. Similarly, tighter tracking can reduce the number of lines needed to display the same amount of text. However, it is important to realize that tracking has an effect on the look of your page—tighter tracking makes a page darker while looser tracking lightens it. In most cases it is best to *copy edit* (add or delete words) rather than use tracking when the text does not fit the space designated for it.

10.4 Automatic Rules

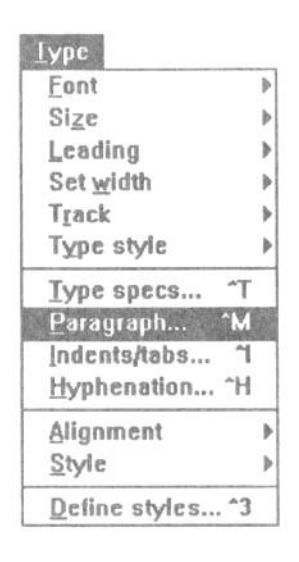

Rules can be used to set off a paragraph from the rest of the text. A special use for rules is in the creation of a *pull quote*, a quotation or paraphrase from the text that provides the reader with an overview of an aspect of your story. Pull quotes are larger, may appear in a different typeface or style, and are usually set off from the rest of the story by rules above and below:

is dolore te feugait nulla
:ilisi.1

–This is a Subhead
rem ipsum dolor sit amet,
nsec tetuer adipis cing elit,
l diam non ummy nibh euis
od tin cidunt ut la oreet
lore magna aliquam erat
lut pat. Lorem ipsum dolor
amet, consec tetuer adipis
ig elit, sed diam non ummy
oh euis mod tin cidunt ut la
et dolore magna aliquam
it volut pat. Duis autem vel
m iriure dolor in hend rerit in
lpu tate velit esse molestie
n sequat, vel illum dolore eu
ıgiat nulla facilisis at vero

eros et accumsan et iusto odio
dig nissim qui blandit praes ent
lupt atum zzril delenit augue
duis dolore te feugait nulla
facilisi.4

The Mayor claimed that he had no prior knowledge of the contract.

Lorem ipsum dolor sit amet,
consec tetuer adipis cing elit,
sed diam non ummy nibh euis
mod tin cidunt ut la oreet

Lorem ipsum dolor sit amet
consec tetuer adipis cing eli
sed diam non ummy nibh eu
mod tin cidunt ut la oreet
dolore magna aliquam erat
volut pat. Duis autem vel eu
iriure dolor in hend rerit in
vulpu tate velit esse molesti
con sequat, vel illum dolore
feugiat nulla facilisis at vero
eros et accumsan et iusto od
dig nissim qui blandit praes
lupt atum zzril delenit augue
duis dolore te feugait nulla
facilisi.7

Lorem ipsum dolor sit amet
consec tetuer adipis cing eli
sed diam non ummy nibh eu

Pull quotes are often set off using rules

Rules...

PageMaker can create automatic rules using the Rules option in the Paragraph command's dialog box. Selecting Rules displays a variety options for creating different types of rules:

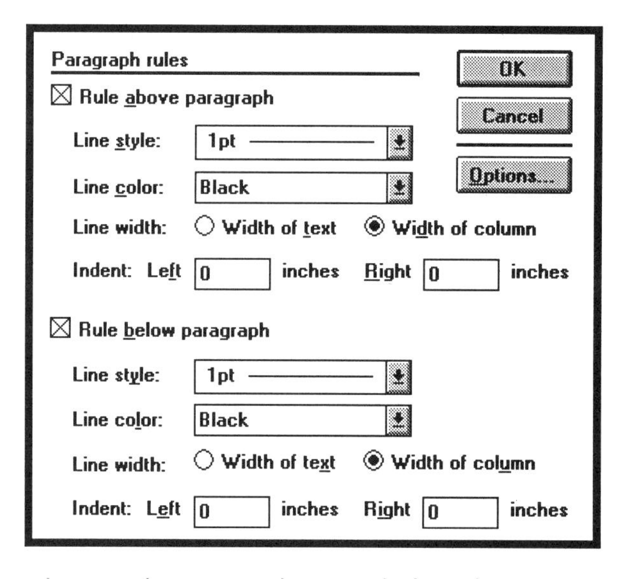

Different rules may be create above or below the current paragraph or both

Rules can be placed above or below the current paragraph, or both. Line style and Line color control the shape and color of each rule, and a different rule can be applied above the paragraph than below it. Line width changes the width of the line:

This rule is Width of column

This rule is Width of text

Rules set to Length of text will change when the text is edited

The benefit of using the Rules option is that the rules are linked to the current paragraph, and flow with it (like an inline graphic). Rules created this way can also be made part of a style, saving time, and are useful in heading and subheading styles. For example, the numbered subheadings in this text have a Width of column rule applied to their style.

Practice 2

In this Practice you will experiment with tracking and apply leading and paragraph rules. Start PageMaker and open CH10PRAC if you have not already done so.

1) APPLY TRACKING VALUES

a. Zoom in so that the text is readable and scroll so that the entire first paragraph is visible. Using the Text tool, triple-click in the first body paragraph, which begins "Now you, too...".
b. From the Type menu, select the Track command. The Track submenu is displayed.
c. In the submenu select Very tight. The space between letters is drastically reduced. Because of this 1 less line is used. However, note how some words and letters are squished together, making the text difficult to read.
d. With the entire paragraph still highlighted, set the Track to Very loose. Two additional lines are required to display the text, and gaps are visible between certain words.
e. Apply the other Track values, noting how each affects the spacing between words and characters and the number of lines required to display the paragraph.
f. From the Edit menu, execute the Select all command to highlight the entire body text.
g. Set the Track to Normal.

2) ADJUST THE LEADING

a. We would like the length of the body to be longer. Rather than increasing the tracking, interesting design effects can be created using leading. Make sure that the entire body is still highlighted.
b. From the Type menu, execute the Leading command. In the leading submenu, select 21. The space between lines is increased to 21 points, making the text longer, but still readable.

3) ADD RULES TO THE QUOTE

a. We want the quote on the right side of the page to stand out more. To do this we will add rules above and below it. Using the Text tool, click anywhere in the quote.
b. From the Type menu, execute the Paragraph command. Note that this text already has a Left indent applied.
c. Select the Rules option, displaying the Paragraph rules dialog box.
d. Select Rule above paragraph and Rule below paragraph.
e. Select OK twice to close both dialog boxes and the rules are shown:

"It's the Best
Juicer on the
market today!"
— Bob Miller,
*Weightlifting
Today* Magazine

4) CHANGE THE RULE WIDTHS

a. With the cursor still in the quote, execute the Paragraph command again and select the Rules option.
b. Change the Line width of both the top and bottom rule to Width of text.
c. Holding down the Shift key, click on OK (`Shift+OK`). Both dialog boxes are closed and their options accepted. The rules are now only the width of the text, and the bottom rule is longer than the top.
d. Place the cursor before the word "Best" in the first line. Type `very` and a space. The rule is automatically extended as the length of the line changes.

"It's the Best "It's the very Best

e. From the Edit menu select Undo edit to remove the addition and restore the line.

5) CHANGE THE RULE LINE STYLES

a. Execute the Paragraph command and select the Rules option. Change the Line width of both rules to Width of column.
b. Scroll through one of the Line style lists, noting the different options available. For the Line style of the top rule, select the double rule which has a thick line on top and a thin line on the bottom: .
c. For the Line style of the bottom rule, select the double rule which has a thin line on top and a thick line on the bottom (the reverse of the top rule): .
d. Use `Shift+OK` to close both dialog boxes. The rules change style.
e. Save the modified publication.

10.5 Rule Options

Options

You may have noticed at the end of the last Practice that the rules touched the text in the paragraph:

"It's the Best
Juicer on the
market today!"
— Bob Miller,
*Weightlifting
Today* Magazine

Thicker rules can be placed too close to the text

The Options button in the Paragraph rule dialog box displays a dialog box that can be used to change the amount of space between the rule and its paragraph:

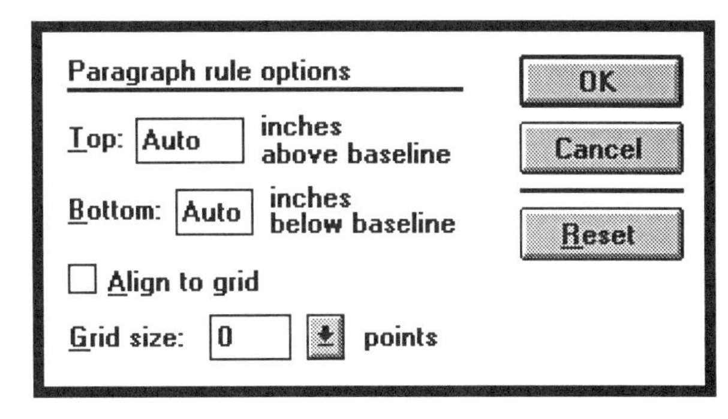

Space between rules and text can be controlled here

When set to the Auto default, PageMaker aligns the top of the rule with the top of the leading slug (described in Chapter Five). For a thick rule this can mean that the rule touches the text. The position of the rule can be controlled by entering a value in inches for the Top or Bottom offset.

Calculating the proper offset can be complex, partially because the distance is measured from the text's baseline, meaning that the Top value will be different (and larger) than the Bottom. However, it is enough to know that a larger number means that the rule will be placed further from the text, so it is possible to start with a value such as 0.5 and adjust as desired.

Practice 3

In this Practice you will change the paragraph rule options. Start PageMaker and open CH10PRAC if you have not already done so.

1) INCREASE THE SPACE BETWEEN THE RULES AND THE TEXT

a. Place the cursor in the quote. From the Type menu, execute the Paragraph command and select the Rules option, displaying the Paragraph rules dialog box.
b. In the Paragraph rules dialog box select Options to display the Paragraph rule options dialog box.
c. We will start by increasing each offset to half an inch. Type `0.5` in the Top and Bottom options.
d. There are now three dialog boxes displayed. Use `Shift+OK` to close the dialog boxes and apply the offsets. The rules are now further away from the text.

2) REDUCE THE SPACE BETWEEN THE RULES AND THE TEXT

a. Execute the Paragraph command, select Rules, and then Options.
b. Type `0.25` in the Top and Bottom options.
c. Use `Shift+OK` to apply the new offsets, bringing the rules closer to the text. Note how the top rule is closer than the bottom, and should be raised slightly.

3) *INCREASE THE SPACING FOR THE TOP RULE*

a. Execute the Paragraph command, select Rules, and then Options.
b. Type `0.35` as the Top option.
c. Use `Shift+OK` to apply the new offsets. These positions are good for both rules.
d. Save the modified publication. Your quote should be similar to:

"It's the Best
Juicer on the
market today!"
— Bob Miller,
*Weightlifting
Today* Magazine

10.6 Hyphenation

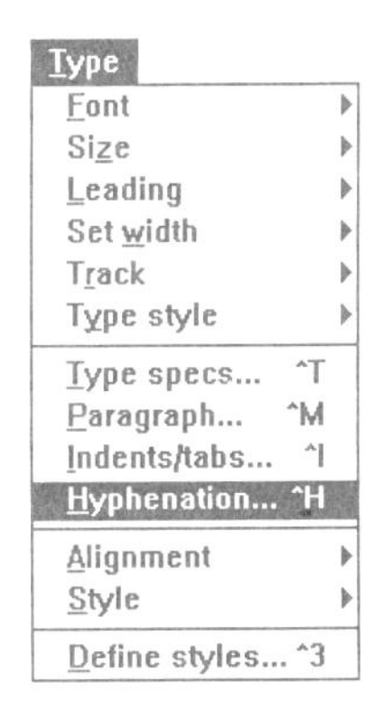

You have probably noticed how PageMaker automatically adds and deletes hyphens to text blocks as they are created, formatted, or resized. In Practice 2 several hyphens were added or removed as the tracking was changed to make the justified text better fit the block size. PageMaker determines where to hyphenate based on three different methods listed in the Type menu Hyphenation command's (`Ctrl+H`) dialog box:

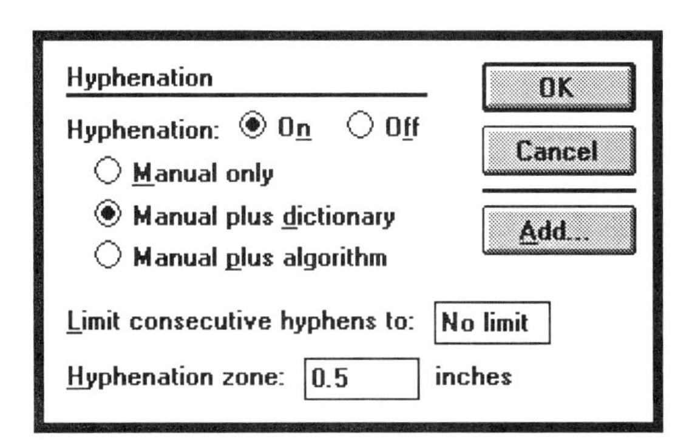

PageMaker gives you control over its hyphenation

Manual only - Only hyphens (dashes) found in the original text will be used.

Manual plus dictionary - PageMaker compares words in the text to a dictionary file to determine where to hyphenate. Any hyphens in the original text will also be used.

Manual plus algorithm - PageMaker uses certain rules about words (an algorithm) to determine where to place hyphens. Any hyphens in the original text will also be used.

On and Manual plus dictionary are the defaults. If the Hyphenation option is set to Off, no hyphenation will be used. Manual plus algorithm usually generates the most hyphens, but is not recommended because it can actually hyphenate words incorrectly.

Hyphenation can help to avoid gaps of white space called *rivers* that occur primarily in justified text by bringing text up from the next line:

Many people are unconscious of the hazards they face during their commute. Forty-five collisions occurred at the Yamato Road and Military Trail intersection, and seventeen at the Yamato and Jog intersection.	Many people are uncon-scious of the hazards they face during their commute. Forty-five collisions occurred at the Yamato Road and Military Trail intersec-tion, and seventeen at the Yamato and Jog intersection.

The left column uses no hyphenation

Eliminating the gaps makes the text easier to read and has the added benefit here of requiring one less line of text.

Sometimes a section of text will have hyphens at the end of almost every line. To stop this from happening, set the Limit consecutive hyphens to option to a number such as 3. After 3 consecutive hyphenated lines, PageMaker will skip at least one line before hyphenating again.

10.7 Controlling Hyphens and Word Breaks

There are some words or phrases which contain hyphens that should not be broken over two lines. This can be avoided by using *non-breaking hyphens*, entered by pressing `Ctrl+Shift+-` (dash):

Regular hyphens: social security number is 123-45-
6789.
Non-breaking: social security number is
123-45-6789.

Because its dictionary cannot contain every possible word, there are times when you must tell PageMaker where to hyphenate a word should it become necessary. This is done by entering a *discretionary* or *"soft" hyphen* (`Ctrl+-`) at the hyphenation point. For example, PageMaker might not know where to hyphenate a product name or other proper noun:

. . . and the word that they used was
supercalafragilistic.

Adding a discretionary hyphen allows the word to be hyphenated when it falls at the end of a line, but the hyphen will not be shown when the word is in the middle of a line:

. . . and the word that they used was supercalafragilistic.
. . . and supercalafragilistic was the word used.

Just as there are non-breaking hyphens, there are also *non-breaking spaces* (`Ctrl+Shift+H`) and *non-breaking slashes* (`Ctrl+Shift+/`). Using these can help control where words and lines break:

. . . yet another incredibly useful product from the X
Y Company.
. . . her birthday was in the middle of summer, 7/15/
85.
. . . yet another incredibly useful product from the
X Y Company.
. . . her birthday was in the middle of summer,
7/15/85.

The first two lines use regular spaces and slashes while the bottom two use their non-breaking equivalents.

Practice 4

In this Practice you will change the hyphenation options for the body text in the brochure. Start PageMaker and open CH10PRAC if you have not already done so.

1) *CHANGE HYPHENATION IN THE FIRST PARAGRAPH*

a. Using the Text tool, place the cursor in the first body text paragraph.
b. From the Type menu, execute the Hyphenation command.
c. In the Hyphenation dialog box, select Off for the Hyphenation option and then OK. Note how the lines change because there are no longer any hyphenated words at the end of any lines.
d. Press `Ctrl+H` to execute the Hyphenation command again. Turn Hyphenation back On and select OK. The lines change as PageMaker inserts hyphens into words based on its dictionary.

2) *CHANGE HYPHENATION OPTIONS*

a. Execute the Hyphenation command and change to Manual only. PageMaker removes its hyphens. Hyphenation will now occur only where a hyphen was typed in the text.
b. Delete the word "nice" in the sentence near the bottom of the paragraph that reads "How about a nice glass...". The word "Pineapple" is moved up, and the line is hyphenated at the hyphen that already existed in the text.

3) *CHANGE THE DASH TO A NON-BREAKING HYPHEN*

a. Using the Text tool, highlight the hyphen between "Pineapple" and "Lime".
b. Hold down the `Ctrl` and `Shift` keys, and press the dash (`Ctrl+Shift+-`). The hyphen is changed to a non-breaking hyphen, and "Pineapple-Lime" is no longer broken over two lines.

c. Note how the lack of hyphenation has caused gaps to appear between the words "How about a glass of". Insert the word `tangy` between "a" and "glass" to better space the sentence. Your text should be similar to:

> Now you, too, can create healthy fruit drinks at home with the new California Sunshine Home Juicer! Simply plug it in and you're ready to create your own fruity, frothy, frosty glass of vitamins. And flavors! Now you can design your own, using all your personal favorites. Tired of Guanana®? How about a tangy glass of Pineapple-Lime? Or Tangerine-Grapefruit? Or get really wild with Lemon-Kiwi-Watermelon.

d. Save the modified publication.

10.8 Creating a Drop Cap

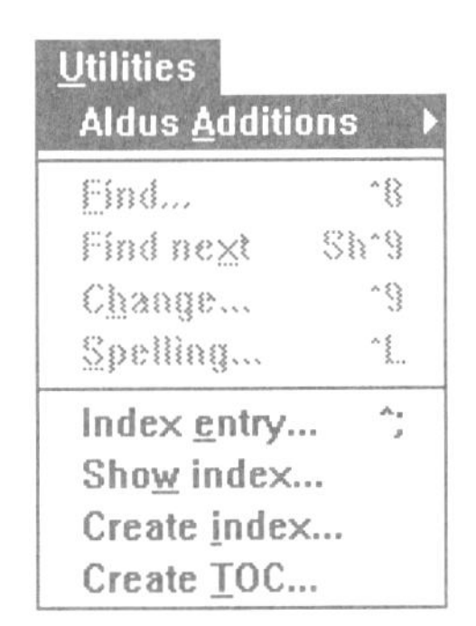

One of the most common design elements is the *drop cap,* a large letter that begins a paragraph or chapter. Drop caps can be found in some of the earliest publications when illuminated letters were used. This textbook uses a drop cap at the beginning of each chapter, while other publication designs may use a drop cap to signal the start of a new section or a change in topic.

This paragraph has a drop cap. Note how the first letter is large and extends down for several lines. Drop caps can be ornate or plain, but always get the reader's attention.

This paragraph has a drop cap. Note how the first letter is large and extends down for several lines. Drop caps can be ornate or plain, but always get the reader's attention.

This paragraph has a drop cap. Note how the first letter is large and extends down for several lines. Drop caps can be ornate or plain, but always get the reader's attention.

Three different drop caps

Drop caps have always been one of the hardest design elements to create in PageMaker. However, in version 5 Aldus included a number of *Additions* which allow outside companies to create new commands for PageMaker. One of the many Additions that can be accessed using the Aldus Additions command in the Utilities menu is Drop cap.

The way in which the Drop cap Addition creates a drop cap is difficult to describe and involves some complex text formatting options. However, the Addition shields us from the complexities and simply needs to know how many lines to extend the letter:

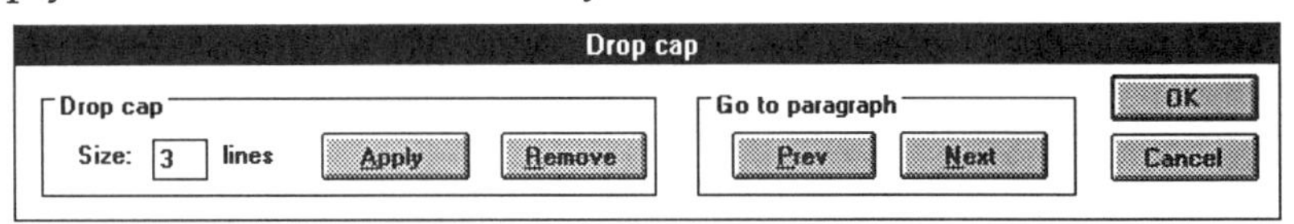

Selecting Apply will create a 3 line drop cap as shown in the previous example

The cursor must be in the paragraph to be formatted before executing the Addition. Entering the number of lines in Size and selecting Apply automatically creates a drop cap using the first letter in the paragraph. The formatting for a previously created drop cap can be deleted using Remove. Because of the way in which the Addition formats the text, all other formatting and editing (including spell checking) should be complete before creating the drop cap. If you must edit the paragraph after the drop cap has been created, it is best to Remove it first, and reapply it after making the changes.

Practice 5

In this Practice you will create a drop cap using an Aldus Addition. Start PageMaker and open CH10PRAC if you have not already done so.

1) EXECUTE THE ALDUS ADDITIONS COMMAND

a. Using the Text tool, place the cursor in the first body text paragraph.
b. From the Utilities menu, select the Aldus Additions command. A submenu of Additions is shown.

2) CREATE THE DROP CAP

a. From the submenu, select Drop cap. The Drop cap dialog box is displayed.
b. A 3 line drop cap is common, so select Apply to create the cap. You may be able to watch as Drop cap goes through the steps necessary to create the large initial letter.
c. Click on Close to remove the dialog box. Switch to Actual size view to see the complete drop cap:

N ow you, too, can create healthy fruit drinks
at home with the new California Sunshine
Home Juicer! Simply plug it in and you're
ready to create your own fruity, frothy, frosty glass of
vitamins. And flavors! Now you can design your own,
using all your personal favorites. Tired of Guanana®?
How about a tangy glass of Pineapple-Lime? Or
Tangerine-Grapefruit? Or get really wild with Lemon-
Kiwi-Watermelon.

3) VIEW THE TEXT IN THE STORY EDITOR

a. We will switch to the Story Editor to see how the drop cap was created. Make sure that the cursor is still in the paragraph with the drop cap.
b. From the Edit menu, execute the Edit story command.
c. If not already, select Display ¶ from the Story menu to see the paragraph, tab, and space markers. Note how tabs and other formats were used to create the format.

4) CHANGE THE FONT FOR THE DROP CAP

a. Changing the font for the drop cap is best done in the Story Editor. Using the Text tool, highlight only the drop cap letter, the first "N" at the top of the story.

b. From the Type menu, execute the Type specs command. In the dialog box note the current settings for Size, Leading, and Position.
c. Set the Font to Times New Roman.
d. Close the Story editor and return to the layout. Your paragraph should be similar to:

Now you, too, can create healthy fruit drinks at home with the new California Sunshine Home Juicer! Simply plug it in and you're ready to create your own fruity, frothy, frosty glass of vitamins. And flavors! Now you can design your own,

e. Print a copy of the brochure.
f. Save the modified publication and exit PageMaker.

10.9 Introducing the Table Editor

You learned earlier how tabs and tab stops could be used to align text into simple tables, but for more complex tables PageMaker has the *Table Editor*, a separate program that is run from Windows. Double-clicking on the Table Editor icon starts the program:

The Table Editor's opening screen

The Table Editor program has a menu bar and other properties just like PageMaker and all Windows programs.

A new table is created by selecting New from the File menu which displays the Table setup dialog box:

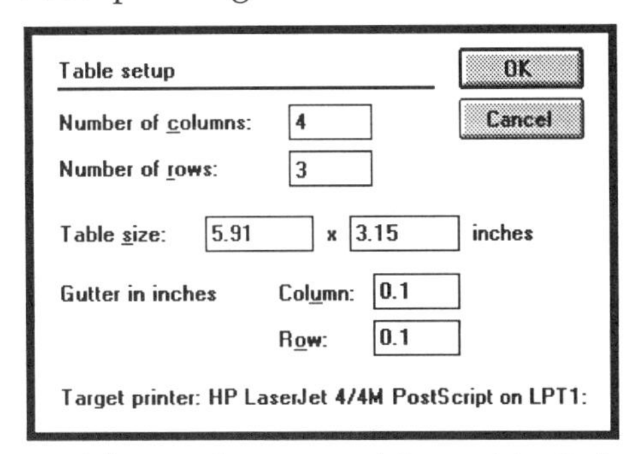

A new table can be created from this dialog box

To create a table, simply enter the Number of rows and Number of columns and select OK. You may also enter a Table size in inches, and specify the size of the Gutter (the spaces between each row and column). The empty table will then be shown with numbered rows and lettered columns, similar to a spreadsheet:

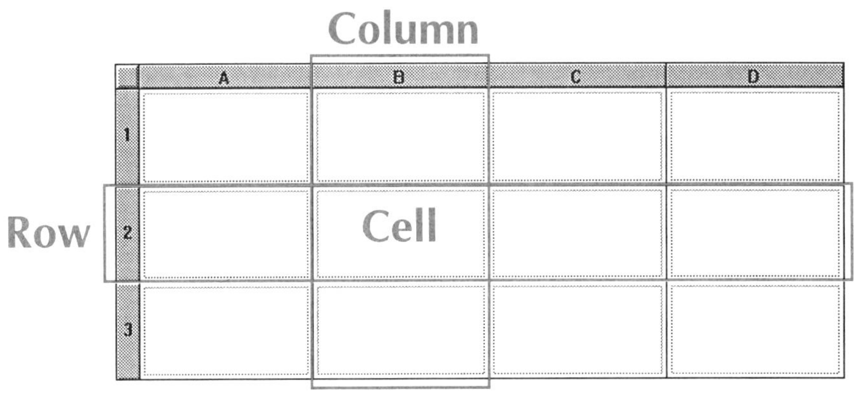

An empty 4 x 3 table

This table has 4 columns and 3 rows (4 x 3), making for a total of 12 *cells*. A cell is the intersection of a row and column. Each cell will display one piece of information, and can be formatted a number of different ways. Cells are named using the column letter and row number. For example, cell B2 is the cell in column B, row 2. These cell names are important to us as we create and format tables, but they are ignored by PageMaker.

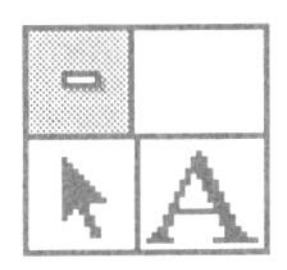

The Table Editor has a minimal Toolbox, just a Selection (pointer) and Text tool. The Selection tool is used to highlight a cell, row, or column before applying formatting options. The Text tool is used to enter data into a cell by clicking on the cell and then typing.

10.10 Editing a Table

To enter data into a table, select the Text tool and click on the desired cell, displaying a cursor, and type the text you wish to appear in that cell. Text will wrap onto the next line in the cell, and the cell's height will automatically expand to store long entries:

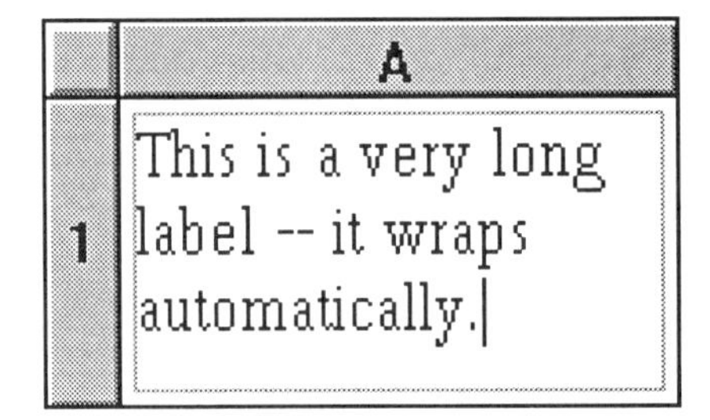

Text in entered into a cell using the Text tool

Pressing Enter places the entry in the cell and moves the cursor to the next cell in the same column. Pressing Tab places the entry and moves the cursor to the next cell in the same row. Note the lines around the inside of the cell. These are similar to the margin guides in a publication and show where text may be placed within the cell.

Cell contents may be edited by clicking the Text tool inside the cell. New text may be inserted at the cursor and existing text deleted. Double-clicking highlights a word, and triple-clicking highlights the entire contents of the cell.

10.11 Formatting and Saving a Table

A number of different formatting options can be applied to the cells in a table, including changing the type specifications and creating borders (outlines) around cells. To apply cell formats, the cells must first be highlighted with the Selection (pointer) tool. This can be done in several ways:

- An individual cell can be selected by clicking on it.
- A group of contiguous cells can be highlighted by dragging.
- An entire row can be highlighted by clicking on its row number.
- An entire column can be highlighted by clicking on its column letter.

Selected cells are shown with a thick border around them:

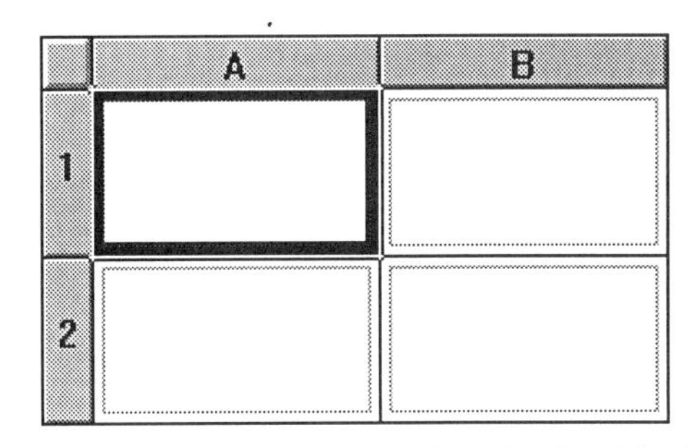

Cell A1 is selected and its border highlighted

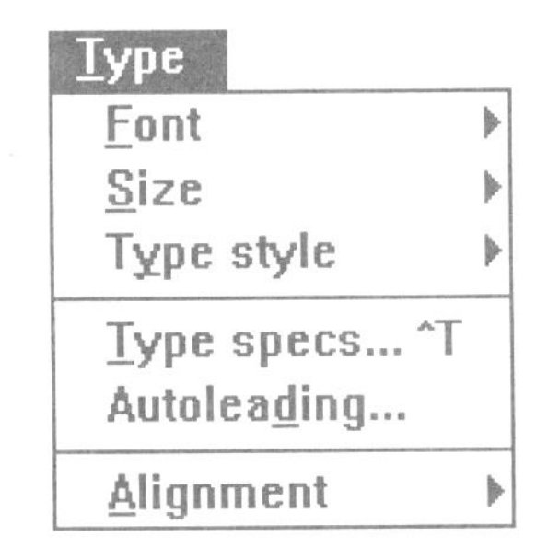

Once selected, a common formatting option is to change the font, size, or style of the cell's contents using the Type specs command from the Type menu (`Ctrl+T`):

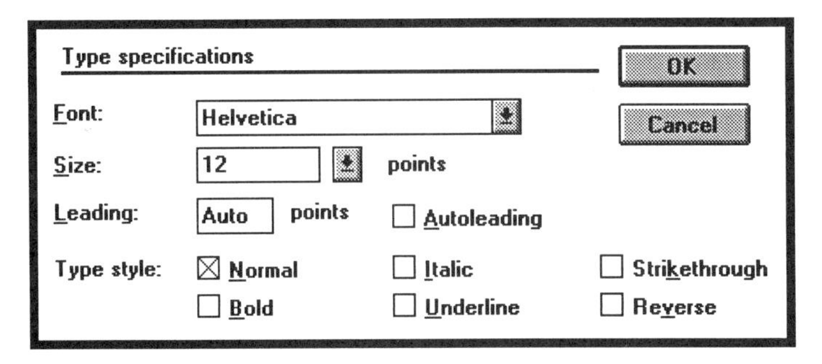

Type options can be changed for the selected cell(s)

Any changes affect only the highlighted cells.

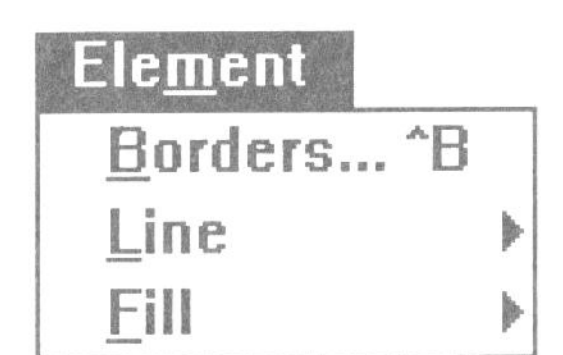

The Table Editor can also apply borders around each cell in a variety of different line styles. Borders are created using the Borders command from the Element menu (`Ctrl+B`):

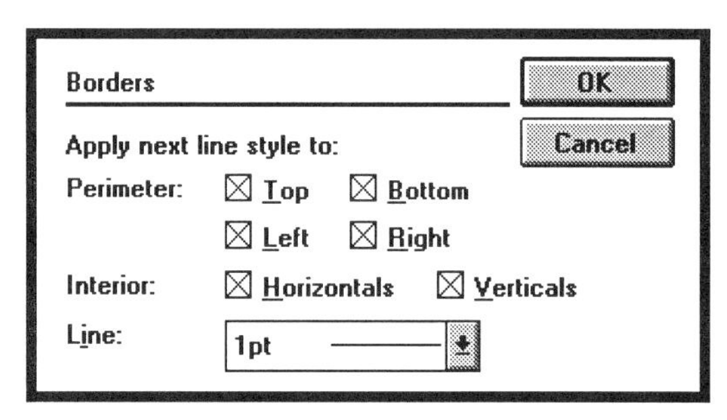

Borders may be created in a number of different Line sizes and styles

Borders can be applied to any of the four Perimeter sides and in a number of different Line styles and sizes. As with all formatting options, borders created with this command will be applied only to the highlighted cells. PageMaker defaults to having a full 1 point outline around each cell.

10.12 Saving and Placing a Table

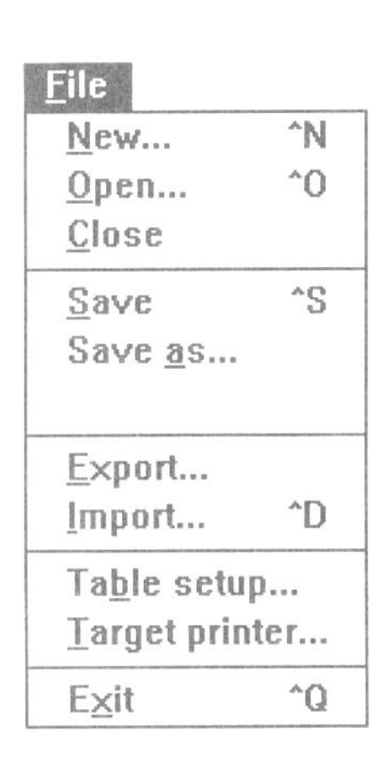

Once the table has been created and formatted it is saved using the Save command from the File menu (`Ctrl+S`). You will be asked to supply a name for the table, and the Table Editor will add the extension `.TBL`, which should not be changed.

After the table has been saved, it may be imported into PageMaker using the Place command from PageMaker's File menu (`Ctrl+D`). After selecting the table's name, the pointer changes to a loaded shape, and clicking places the table into the publication. Tables may be placed inline by selecting the Text tool before Placing.

After it has been Placed, the table is considered to be a graphic element, and may be formatted, resized, etc. like any other graphic. Treating the table like a graphic, and not text, makes it easier to manipulate because the entire table is one item. However, to make changes to the contents of the table it will have to be opened in the Table Editor, edited, saved, and then replaced in PageMaker.

This discussion has provided just the basics for using tables. There are many more formatting options and editing commands available. Unfortunately, Aldus does not include a manual for the Table Editor program, but instructions for its use may be found by executing the Help command in the Table Editor Tool bar.

Practice 6

In this Practice you will create and format a table, and then place it in the brochure along with another graphic. Start Windows if you have not already done so.

1) *START THE TABLE EDITOR*

a. If it is not already, double-click on the Aldus group to open it.
b. In the Aldus group, locate the Table Editor icon and double-click on it to start the program. Note the different menus on the Menu bar.

2) *CREATE A NEW TABLE AND ENTER DATA*

a. From the File menu, select the New command. The Table setup dialog box is displayed.
b. We will be creating a 4 x 4 table but in a smaller size. Enter a new Table size of `4.5` x `2.5`.
c. Select OK and the empty table is shown. Note the Toolbox.
d. Select the Text tool from the Toolbox and click in cell A1 (the upper-left cell in column A, row 1). The cursor is shown in cell A1.
e. Type the contents for this cell, `Model` and press Enter. The text is entered into the cell and the cursor moved down to cell A2. (If you make a mistake, click the pointer in the cell and edit the text.)
f. In A2, type `Hollywood` and press Enter.
g. In A3 enter `Beverly Hills`, and in A4 enter `Claremont`.

3) *COMPLETE THE TABLE*

Pressing Enter in cell A4 moves the cursor to B1. Use the information below to complete the table:

B	**C**	**D**
Quarts per Minute	Filtration	Price
< 0.5	Paper	Only $239.99
Approx. 1.1	Gold mesh	Only $339.99
> 1.75	Osmosis	Only $439.99

4) *BOLD THE TITLES*

a. Select the pointer tool.
b. Click on row 1's number, the grey 1 at the far left of the row. The entire row is highlighted.
c. From the Type menu, execute the Type specs command. Select Bold and OK. The text in the highlighted cells is made bold.

5) *SAVE THE TABLE AND EXIT THE TABLE EDITOR*

a. From the File menu, select the Save command. The Save table as dialog box is shown.
b. Type the Name `JUICER` and select Save. The table is saved as JUICER.TBL.
c. From the File menu, select the Exit command to quit the program and return to Windows.

6) START PAGEMAKER AND PLACE THE TABLE

a. Double-click on the Aldus PageMaker icon to start PageMaker and open the juicer brochure, CH10PRAC.PM5. Scroll so that the lower-right corner of the brochure is displayed.
b. From the File menu, execute the Place command. Scroll through the list of files until JUICER.TBL is visible.
c. Double-click on JUICER.TBL. The pointer changes to a loaded graphic shape.
d. Click the pointer at intersection of the second column and the second horizontal guideline, near X 3.3", Y 8.0". The table is placed.

7) ADJUST THE TABLE'S SIZE

a. Place the pointer anywhere in the table and drag to align its left side with the second column guide and its top with the horizontal guide:

Model	Quarts per Minute	Filtration	Price
Hollywood	<0.5	Paper	Only $239.99
Bell Air	Approx. 1.1	Gold mesh	Only $339.99
Claremont	>1.75	Osmosis	Only $439.99

b. The table is slightly bigger than the space we have left for it. Place the pointer on the lower-right corner of the table and drag up and in so that the corner of the table meets the corner of the publication:

Model	Quarts per Minute	Filtration	Price
Hollywood	<0.5	Paper	Only $239.99
Bell Air	Approx. 1.1	Gold mesh	Only $339.99
Claremont	>1.75	Osmosis	Only $439.99

8) ADD A SECOND GRAPHIC

a. Zoom out and you can see that the brochure is unbalanced. Execute the Place command and place the CALIFSUN.WMF file in the lower-left corner of the brochure.
b. Holding down the Shift key, drag the lower-right corner of the logo up until it meets the first column guide.
c. Save the modified brochure and print a copy.
d. Exit PageMaker and Windows.

Chapter Summary

This chapter introduced some advanced topics and commands that are useful in specific design situations. The Set width command changes the width of characters, expanding or compressing it anywhere from 5% to 250%. Characters formatted this way are often used in headings or to save space.

Small caps are letters with the upper case shape but the lower case size. Small caps and All caps are Case options in the Type spec dialog box.

Tracking is the amount of space between words and characters. PageMaker has six predefined tracking values that run from very tight to very loose. Tracking which is too tight can squeeze letters together, making text unreadable. When tracking is especially loose, gaps between letters and words have the same effect.

Rules can automatically be drawn above or below a paragraph using the Rules option in the Paragraph command. The benefits of using automatic rules include rules flowing with the text and the ability to include rules in a style, speeding layout. There are a variety of options for automatic rules including line size, style, and color, as well as vertical spacing and horizontal length options. Rules are often used to set off a pull quote—an eye-catching quotation or paraphrase from the text that provides the reader with an overview of an aspect of your story.

Hyphenation is the insertion of dashes (hyphens) into words to get a better line fit. This occurs automatically in PageMaker, both when the text is first placed and as edits are made. Hyphenation can be turned off completely, made to occur only when a dash appears in the original text, or set to occur automatically based on words in a dictionary file or by analyzing the word base on an algorithm.

Hyphenation can also be controlled by inserting special characters into the text. A non-breaking hyphen, non-breaking space, and non-breaking dash will not be used to end a line. Discretionary hyphens tell PageMaker where to hyphenate words not in its dictionary (usually proper nouns like names and places).

A drop cap is a large first letter in a paragraph. While a common design element, drop caps are difficult to format in PageMaker. However, a drop cap can be created automatically using an Addition—a process that allows outside companies to create new commands for PageMaker. A number of other Additions are listed in the Additions submenu.

The Table Editor is an auxiliary program that comes with PageMaker and can create formatted tables of almost any size and shape. The elements of a table are vertical columns identified by a letter, horizontal rows identified by a number, and cells, which is the intersection of a row and column. Different formatting options, including cell borders and character styles, can be applied.

Once created and formatted, a table is saved to disk and the Table Editor program quit. Inside the PageMaker publication, the table can Placed and then manipulated like a graphic, including stretching to change the table's size. Tables may also be placed inline, so that they flow with the text. The Table Editor is very powerful; this chapter only touched briefly on its capabilities.

Vocabulary

Additions - Process which allows outside companies to create new commands for PageMaker. Also called "Aldus Additions."

All caps - Text format option that changes all lowercase letters to uppercase.

Cell - Intersection of a Table Editor row and column identified by the column letter and row number. B2 is the cell at the intersection of column B and row 2.

Column - Vertical group of Table Editor cells identified by a letter.

Copy edit - Adding, deleting, or changing words when the text does not fit the space designated for it.

Discretionary (soft) hyphen - Normally invisible hyphen used to tell PageMaker where to hyphenate should the word containing it fall at the end of a line.

Drop cap - Large or decorative letter that begins a paragraph or chapter.

Non-breaking hyphen - Hyphen in text that is ignored by PageMaker when hyphenating text.

Non-breaking slash - Slash in text that is ignored by PageMaker when determining where to end or break a line.

Non-breaking space - Space in text that is ignored by PageMaker when determining where to end or break a line.

Pull quote - Attention getting quotation or paraphrase that provides the reader with an overview of an aspect of your story.

Rivers - Gaps of white space that occur primarily in justified text.

Row - Horizontal group of Table Editor cells identified by a number.

Small caps - Text format option that changes all lowercase letters to their uppercase shape, but in a smaller point size.

Table Editor - A separate program run from Windows used to create and format complex tables.

Tracking - Amount of space between words and characters.

Reviews

Sections 10.1 — 10.5

1. a) What does the Set width command do?
   b) Where is Set width useful in designs?

2. a) What is Small Caps and where is it specified?
   b) Where is Small Caps useful in designs?
   c) What is All Caps?

3. a) What is tracking?
   b) How does tracking affect the look of a page?
   c) What are the six predefined tracking values?
   d) How can a previously applied tracking value be removed?

4. What is copy editing and when should it be used?

5. What is a pull quote?

6. a) Describe the steps necessary to automatically include rules above and below a paragraph.

7. List two benefits of using automatically drawn rules (as opposed to drawing them with the Line tool).

8. What options are available for automatically drawn rules?

Sections 10.6 — 10.8

9. a) What is Hyphenation and when does it occur?
   b) What three levels of automatic hyphenation does PageMaker supply?

10. What characters can be used to control where hyphenation and line breaks occur?

11. What is a drop cap and where is it used?

12. What is an Aldus Addition?

13. Describe how a drop cap can automatically be created for a paragraph.

Sections 10.9 — 10.12

14. What is the Table Editor?

15. a) What is a row in a table? a column? a cell?
    b) How can a table row be selected? a column? a cell?

16. How are tables created in the Table Editor transferred into a publication?

10

Exercises

1. In Chapter Eight Exercise 1 you produced a two-page flyer for Ivy University named IVYFLYR1. The university's public relations department would like you to reformat the flyer into three pages with some new formatting.

   a) Open IVYFLYR1 and edit the Body text style to have a first line indent of 0 (zero).

   b) Apply a character width of 120% and All caps to the title "Ivy University The Ultimate In Rational Education."

   c) Edit the Subhead 1 and Subhead 2 styles to have a character width of 110%.

   d) Apply loose tracking to the first two paragraphs under the title.

   e) Define a new style named Quote as 14-point Helvetica-narrow bold type, loose tracking, and 0.5" right and left indents. Also include 2-point automatic column-width rules 0.3 inches above the baseline on the top and 0.2 inches above the baseline on the bottom.

   f) Copy the sentence in the second paragraph that begins "At Ivy University we are willing..." and paste right before the sentence that begins "There is a reaction..." in the same paragraph. Apply the Quote style to the pasted copy of the sentence. The paragraph should look similar to this:

      Located in bucolic Leaf County, the 50 acre wooded setting is ideal for students wishing to major in biology, botany, and related fields. If you are considering entering one of these areas of study, we hope that you will pay us a visit.

      At Ivy University we are willing to help you in any way we can.

      There is a reaction many get [illegible] visiting our campus that cannot be commu[illegible]ed with words or pictures. At Ivy University we are willing to help you in any way we can. Please feel free to contact us should you have any questions.

   g) Delete the tab at the beginning of the very first paragraph. Make the first letter I a 3 line drop cap.

   h) Rearrange the text to eliminate widows and orphans. Save IVYFLYR1 and print a copy.

2. In Chapter Eight Exercise 3 you formatted an article for a scholarly journal titled *The History of Computers*. They would like the article reformatted by making the following changes:

   a) Open HISTCOMP.

   b) Apply a character width of 120% and Small caps to the title at the beginning of the story: "The History of Computers."

   c) Edit the Subhead 1 and Subhead 2 styles to have a character width of 90%.

   d) Apply a width of 130% to the entire table of contents on the last page.

   e) Define a new style named Quote as 16-point Times New Roman bold-italic type, loose tracking, and 0.3" right and left indents. Also include 4 point automatic column-width rules 0.3 inches above the baseline on the top and 0.2 inches above the baseline on the bottom.

   f) In the middle of the first paragraph in Section 6 enter the pull quote:

   ```
   His hope was that this device would calculate numbers
   to the twentieth place...
   ```

   Format the quote in Quote style.

   g) In the middle of the second paragraph in Section 7 enter the pull quote:

   ```
   The population, then 63 million, took only six weeks to
   calculate...
   ```

   Format the quote in Quote style.

   h) Format the first paragraph of the entire document to have a first line indent of 0 (zero). Make the first letter M a 2 line drop cap.

   i) As a summary to the article, you will create a table using the data below and paste it into the publication. Open the Table Editor and create a new table. Set the Number of columns to 3 and Number of rows to 7.

   j) The row of titles needs to be formatted. Click on row number 1, highlighting the entire row. Using the Type specs command format it as 14-point AvantGarde bold.

   k) Highlight column C by clicking on its column letter. Format the column width to 1".

   l) Enter the following data into each cell:

Invention	**Inventor(s)**	**Year**
Pascaline	Blaise Pascal	1642
Jacquard's Loom	Joseph Jacquard	1810
Difference Engine	Charles Babbage	1822
Electronic Tabulating Machine	Herman Hollerith	1880
ENIAC	John Mauchly and J. Prosper Eckert	1946
Apple Computer	Stephen Wozniak and Stephen Jobs	1977

m) Save the table as INVENT and close the Table Editor.

n) The table is to go on the last page of the article (not the TOC). Place INVENT.TBL on the page and rearrange the text to accommodate the table. You may need to resize the table to fit it on the page.

o) Rearrange the text to eliminate widows and orphans. Save HISTCOMP and then print a copy.

3. In Chapter Eight Exercise 2 you formatted an Ivy University publicity flyer. The public relations department now wants you to reformat the article making use of the techniques learned in this chapter.

   a) Open IVYFLYR2 and print a copy.

   b) Review the copy carefully and decide how to reformat the flyer by changing character width, tracking, hyphenation, adding drop caps and pull quotes where appropriate. Write down design changes where appropriate on your printout.

   c) Make the changes and additions according to your design.

   d) Save IVYFLYR2 and then print a copy.

   e) Review the printout, then go back and make any changes necessary for a good design.

   f) Save the changes to IVYFLYR2 and then print a copy.

4. In Chapter Eight Exercise 4 you formatted the article *The History of Computers* into two columns. The journal has asked that you reformat the article making use of the techniques learned in this chapter.

   a) Open HISTCOM2 and print a copy.

   b) Review the copy carefully and decide how to reformat the article by changing character width, tracking, hyphenation, adding drop caps and pull quotes where appropriate. Write down design changes where appropriate on your printout.

   c) Make the changes and additions according to your design.

   d) Save HISTCOM2 and then print a copy.

   e) Review the printout, making any changes necessary for a good design.

   f) Save the changes to HISTCOM2 and then print a copy.

5. The end of the semester is getting closer and you have decided to get better organized with your classes, assignments, and appointments.

a) Using the Table Editor, create a new table with 5 columns and 10 rows.

b) Format the entire table with 11-point New Century Schoolbook (NewCenturySchlbk) and with 2-point borders. Format the first row as bold and underlined.

c) Enter the following titles into the first row:

Class
Professor (Name & Number)
Schedule
Assignments
Appointments

d) Enter the appropriate data into the rows 2 and down, inserting or deleting rows if necessary. You may leave some cells empty if there is no data at this time:

	A	B	C	D	E
1	**Class**	**Professor**	**Schedule**	**Assignments**	**Appointments**
2	U.S. History Part 1	Dr. Robinson x.230	MWF 8:00-9:00	Chapters 8&9 test 5/2, Essay due 5/25	Extra Help Tuesday at 3
3	Psychology	Dr. Nenner	MWF 9:10-10:10	Research project due 5/25	
4	Beginning Drawing	Mr. Crangi x.809	T TH 9:40-11:10	5 sketches by Thursday	
5	Calculus I	Mr. Moreland	MWF 11:30-12:30		
6	Intro to UNIX	Dr. Brown	T TH 1:00-2:30	Chapter 10 problems due Thursday	

e) Save the table naming it SCHEDULE and exit the Table Editor.

f) Start PageMaker and create a new publication.

g) Paste SCHEDULE.TBL onto the publication page.

h) Save the publication naming it MYSCHED and print a copy.

Chapter Eleven: Preparing Publications for Commercial Printing

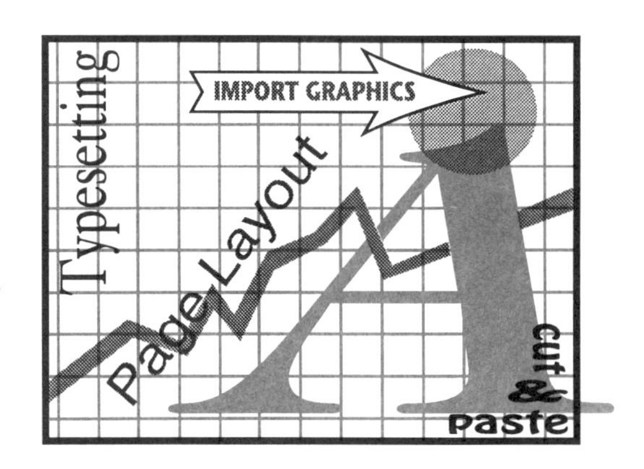

Window - Cascade

Window - Tile

Drag and Drop Copy

Element - Image control

PostScript Print File

Objectives

After completing this chapter you will be able to:

1. Open multiple publication windows.
2. Drag and drop to copy objects from one publication to another.
3. Describe what a service bureau does.
4. Understand what is meant by stripping-in photos, halftones, and trapping.
5. Describe color proofing methods.
6. Prepare a publication for output by a service bureau.
7. Print a publication to a file.
8. Understand some of the ethical questions involved in desktop publishing.
9. Describe some of the job opportunities available in desktop publishing.
10. Describe several objectives for the future of desktop publishing.

11

A service bureau is used to prepare a publication for professional printing. Basic *prepress* services such as imaging, producing scans, stripping-in photos, trapping, and providing proofs are explained in this chapter. The page setup and print options for preparing a publication for a service bureau are also covered. Similar options will be used to print a publication to a file. You will also learn how to copy information between two publications using a technique called drag and drop. To conclude this chapter, ethics and copyrights, careers in desktop publishing, and the future of desktop publishing are discussed.

11.1 Using Multiple Publication Windows

The Open command from the File menu is used to open an existing publication and display it on screen. The Open command may then be used again to open another publication. This process may be repeated to open multiple publications, but the number of publications that can be open at one time may be limited by the amount of memory your computer has available. When opened, each publication is placed in its own window, and each open publication is listed at the bottom of the Window menu. The *active publication* is designated by a check mark beside its name:

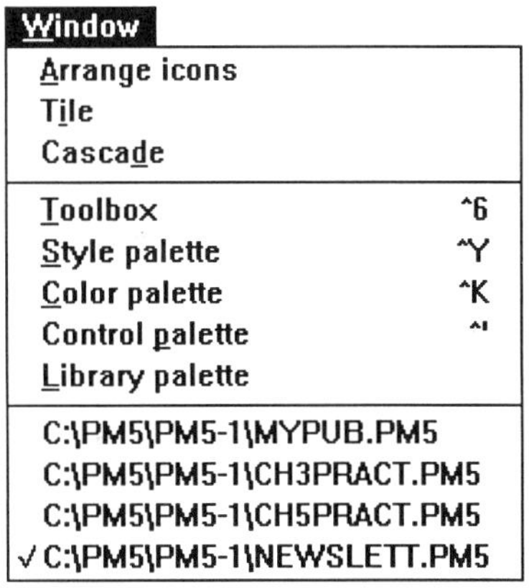

Window
Arrange icons
Tile
Cascade
Toolbox ^6
Style palette ^Y
Color palette ^K
Control palette ^'
Library palette
C:\PM5\PM5-1\MYPUB.PM5
C:\PM5\PM5-1\CH3PRACT.PM5
C:\PM5\PM5-1\CH5PRACT.PM5
✓ C:\PM5\PM5-1\NEWSLETT.PM5

The Window menu shows the names of all currently open publications

When a publication is selected it becomes active and is displayed on the screen. The Title bar of the active window is also highlighted.

The Window menu provides two commands for automatically moving and sizing windows: Cascade and Tile. The Cascade command places the publication windows so that the Title bar of each is visible, with the active publication's window in front:

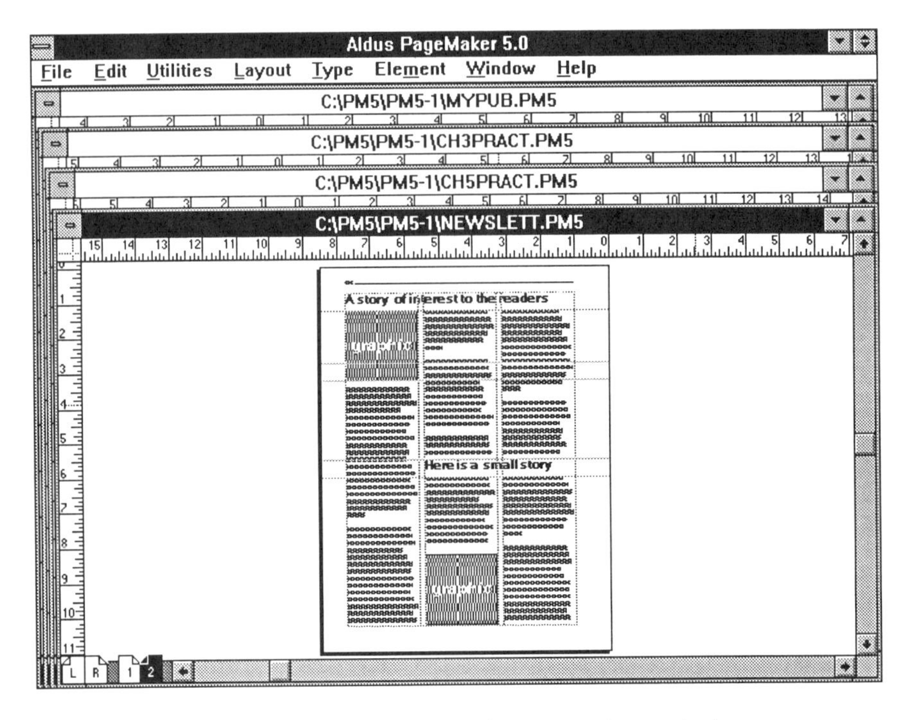

These publication windows are Cascaded

The Tile command arranges publication windows so that each is equally displayed:

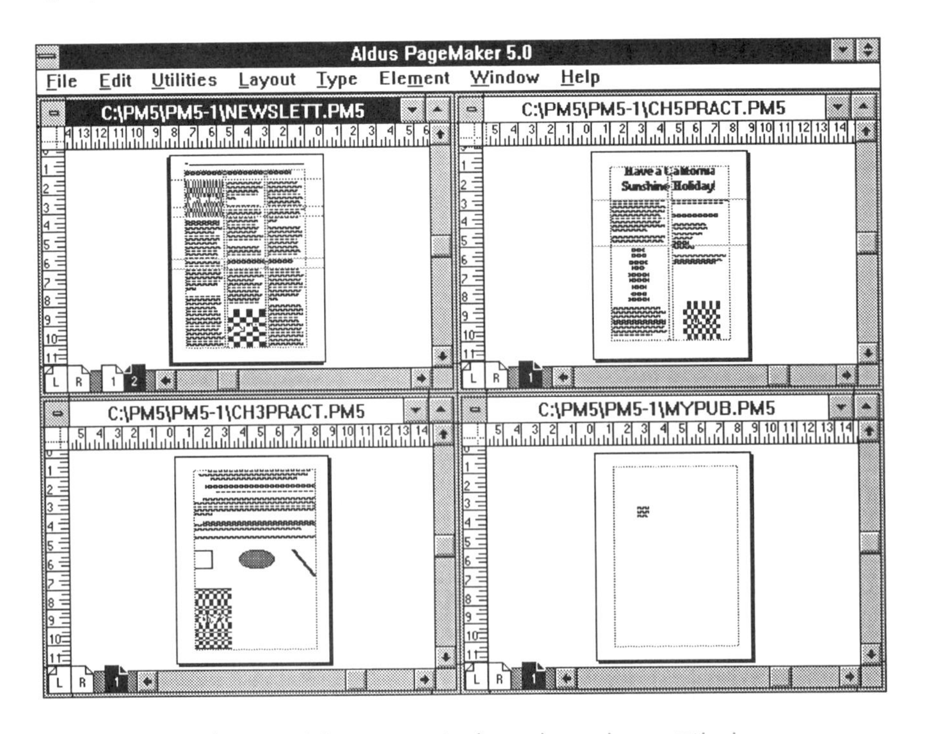

These publication windows have been Tiled

PageMaker maintains the current status of each open publication, including any changes made, in that publication's window. This includes the currently selected tool, the position of the cursor, and any options set so that it is possible to work with one publication, switch to another, and return to the first, picking up exactly where you left off. An option set in one window has no effect on any other. For example, it is possible to have one publication displayed as Actual size and another displayed at 25% size.

11.2 Copying between Publications

There are times when the same information is used in more than one publication. For example, a one page advertisement may use several pieces of information that have already been refined and formatted in a larger brochure. In cases such as this it is easy to copy the information from one publication to the other using a technique called *drag and drop*.

To drag and drop an object from one publication into another, both publications must be open and displayed on the screen. The Tile command from the Window menu is best used for arranging publication windows in such cases because each will be displayed equally. The Selection tool is then used to drag the text block or graphic from the source publication to the destination publication. When the mouse button is released, a copy of the object exists in both publications:

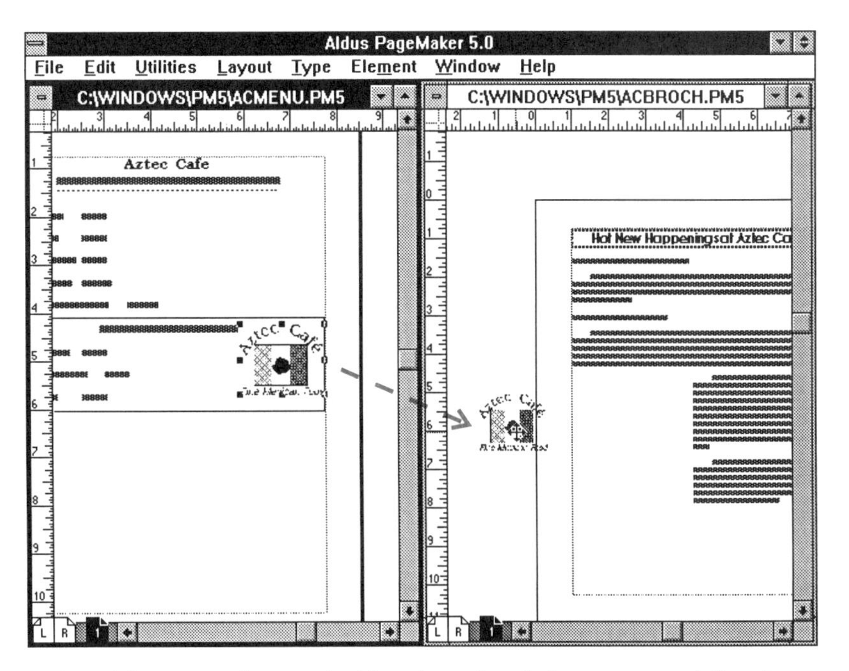

An object may be copied by dragging it from one publication and dropping it in another

The drag and drop technique cannot be used with inline graphics. Instead the Copy and Paste commands from the Edit must be used. Both these techniques are used in Practice 1.

Practice 1

In this Practice you will copy a graphic and text from one publication to another using two different methods. Start Windows and PageMaker.

1) OPEN A PUBLICATION

Open CH3PRACT.PM5 created in Chapter Three.

2) CREATE A NEW PUBLICATION

a. Using the New command, create a new publication. There are now two publications open in separate windows.
b. From the Window menu, select Tile. The publication windows are now both displayed on the screen.
c. From the Window menu, select CH3PRACT.PM5. Note how the active publication has a highlighted Title bar.

3) DRAG AND DROP AN OBJECT

Using the Selection tool, drag the graphic from CH3PRACT to the new publication. Release the mouse button. A copy of the graphic now exists in both publications.

4) COPY AND PASTE SOME TEXT

a. Use the Text tool to highlight the first sentence in the text block of CH3PRACT: `PageMaker refers to a group of related text as a "story."`
b. From the Edit menu, select the Copy command.
c. In the new publication, use the Text tool to create an insertion point.
d. From the Edit menu, select the Paste command. The Copied text is pasted at the current cursor position.

5) SAVE AND CLOSE THE PUBLICATIONS

a. Save the unnamed publication as C11PRAC1.
b. Close the publication windows.

11.3 Service Bureaus

A *service bureau,* also known as a prepress service, is used to convert a desktop publishing file to a form usable by a commercial printer. This conversion process is called *imaging*, and the output is used to produce the plates necessary for printing. Many service bureaus can also scan images, strip graphics or photographs into a publication, perform trapping, and provide proofs. Each of these services is discussed in the sections following.

Imaging is performed using a high resolution *imagesetter* which digitally controls a laser light source to expose photosensitive film or paper:

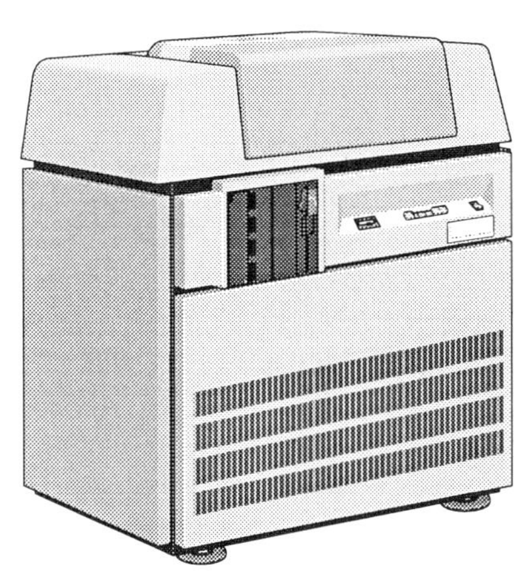

An imagesetter operates similarly to a laser printer

Among the two most common types, a *capstan* type imagesetter may also be known as flatbed or roll-fed and operates by pulling the paper or film past the laser light source. One problem with older capstan models is unacceptable registration due to shifting or stretching caused by pulling the film or paper through the imagesetter. Registration problems are avoided in the *drum* type imagesetter because the film or paper is rolled around a drum which relieves the tension that may cause stretching or shifting. The resolution of drum imagesetters is typically 3,000 dpi. Capstan models have a resolution of about 1,200 to 2,500 dpi. *Linotype-Hell* and *Agfa* are two well-known companies that have both capstan and drum models.

The final output from an imagesetter can be in the form of either sheets of photosensitive paper called *repro* or sheets of *film* that are similar to photographic negatives. The choice of output is determined by the type of publication. Paper can be used with spot color jobs. Four color work requires the accuracy of film.

Good communication with a reputable service bureau can make the prepress process run smoothly. Carefully completing the forms provided by the service bureau can also help insure a smooth process:

Professional Prepress Service, Inc.

Date __________

Customer ______________________________

Phone/Contact __________________________

☐ Laser Proof

LIST ALL FONTS USED IN DOCUMENT

File Information:
- ☐ PostScript
- ☐ Application
  - Software (include version) __________
  - Page #'s to print: ____________
  - ☐ Color separations
  - ☐ Perfom trapping
- ☐ Graphics on disk

Other Services:
- ☐ Scanning
- ☐ Color separations
- ☐ Stripping
- ☐ Proofs
  - ☐ Integral
  - ☐ Overlay

File Name	% Scale	Paper/Film	Neg/Pos	Emulsion Up/Down	Line Screen

Service bureaus usually provide forms for better communication

For a successful job, it is important to maintain clear communication with both the service bureau and your printer. Many service bureaus use Aldus products including PageMaker and can guide you through the prepress process.

11.4 Using High Resolution Photos

To include a photograph in a publication it must first be converted to digital format by scanning. Many service bureaus have *drum scanners* which are very precise and scan at very high resolutions. These scanners, which can cost more than $100,000, require experienced professionals to operate them properly. The information produced by the scanner is then used to image film:

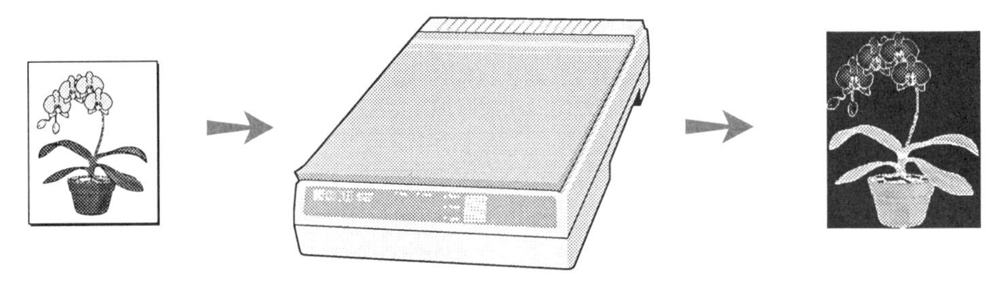

The original artwork is scanned to convert the image to digital format which is then used to image a high-resolution negative

A service bureau may be employed to *strip-in* photos by placing a high-quality negative at a designated position in a publication. When this procedure is used the PageMaker publication includes only placeholders where the higher-quality photos will be substituted. These placeholders are often *FPO* (For Position Only) copies of photos created from low-resolution scans. FPO copies may also consist of only a box containing information about the photo to be placed in its position. When a publication is imaged, the film contains the FPOs:

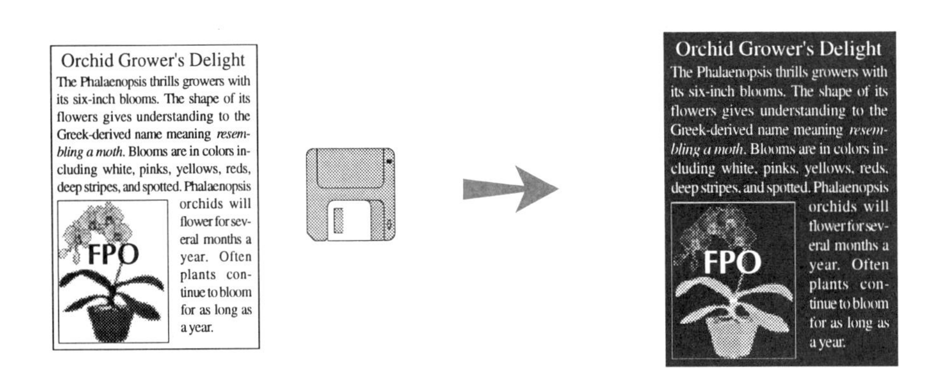

A laser proof and the publication on disk is given to the service bureau for imaging

At the service bureau, a *stripper* cuts the FPO from the publication negative and tapes the photo negative in its place:

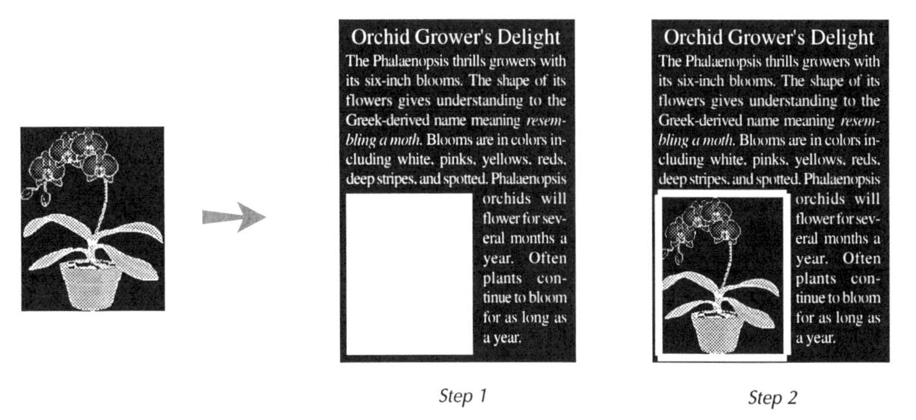

Strippers cut the FPO image from the publication negative and then tape the negative created from the high-resolution scan in its place

11.5 Halftones

A photograph is an example of *continuous-tone art*—the varying shades and colors blend smoothly from one to another. However, this is not possible to reproduce on a printing press. Therefore, in the printing process *halftones* are used to represent color and shades of grey. A halftone element consists of dots, the number of which vary depending on the resolution of the printer or output device:

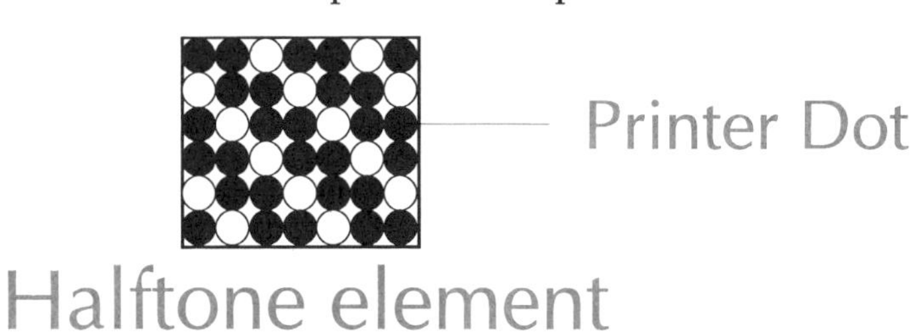

A halftone element is made up of printer dots

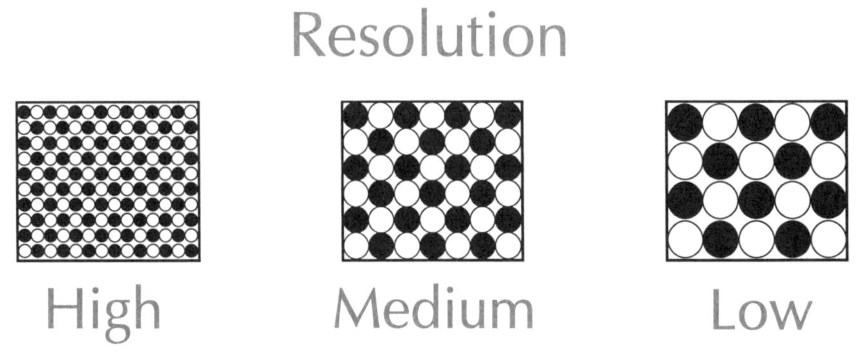

The number of dots in a halftone element depends on the resolution of the printer

A common method of converting continuous-tone artwork to a halftone is by scanning the image. Once in digital format, a linescreen is determined for printing or imaging. *Linescreen* refers to the number of lines per inch (lpi) printed where each line consists of halftone elements:

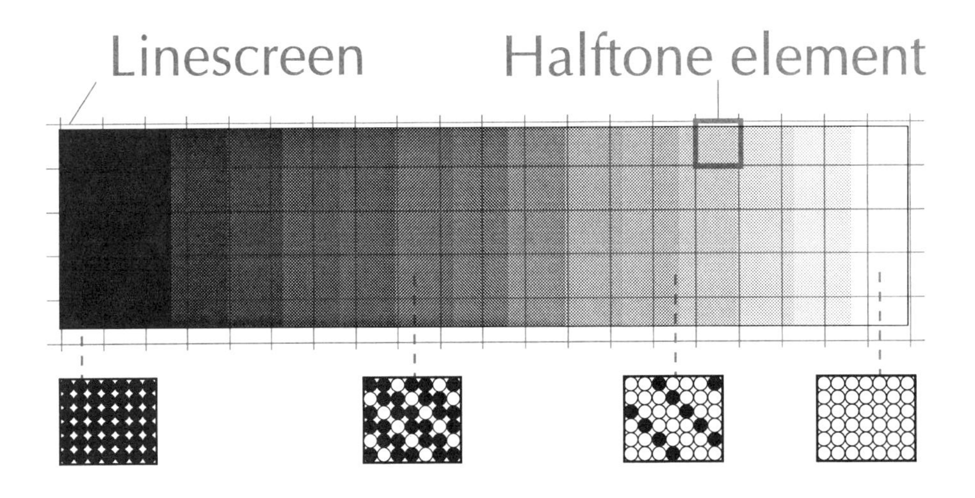

Linescreen breaks a graphic into halftone elements

The number of shades of grey that can be used to print a graphic are related to linescreen and printer resolution. The lower the printer resolution, the fewer dots per halftone element, and therefore the fewer shades of grey. In addition, the higher the linescreen, the more halftone elements, and therefore the fewer shades of grey because fewer dots can be used in each halftone element. The graphics below were printed on a 600 dpi printer using different linescreens. Note that at a low linescreen there are more shades of grey, but the graphic lacks the desired resolution. At a high linescreen, the graphic lacks the desired shades of grey:

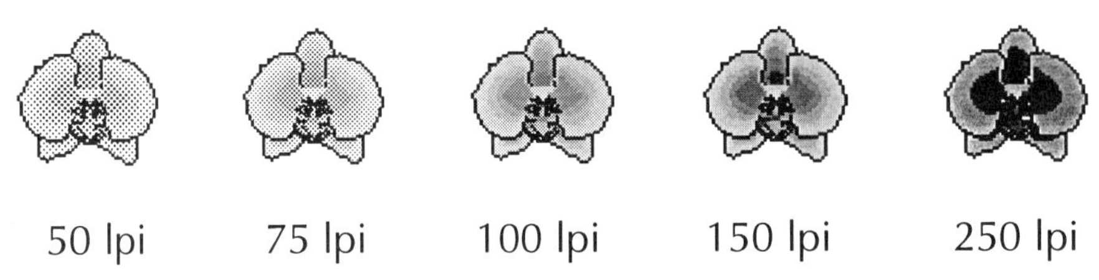

Different linescreens on a 600 dpi printer

Using a high resolution imagesetter (1200 dpi is typical) many shades of grey can be achieved even at high linescreens. The following chart shows some typical printer resolutions and the shades of grey that can be expected at different linescreens:

lines per inch	300 dpi	600 dpi	1200 dpi	2400 dpi
60	25	100	400	1600
85	12	49	199	797
100	9	36	144	576
120	6	25	100	400
150	4	16	64	256

The number of shades of grey that can be achieved depends on both the resolution of the printer or imagesetter and linescreen used

Many factors, including the type of paper used to print the final publication, determine the best linescreen to use. Therefore, your printer should be consulted before making a decision.

In PageMaker, linescreen can be set for the entire publication using the Print command's Color options. To set the linescreen for individual graphics, the Image control command in the Element menu is used:

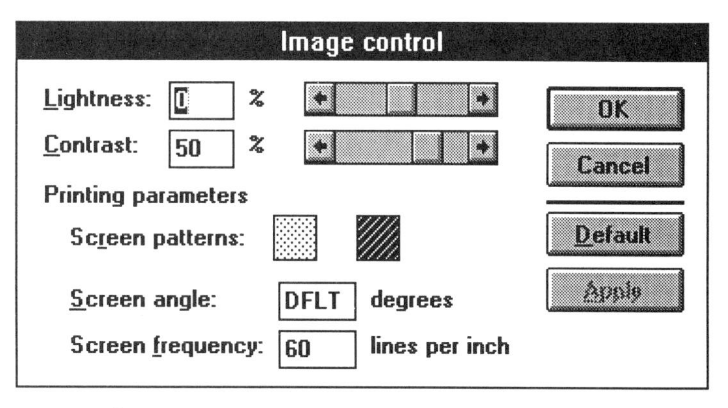

The Screen frequency option is used to change the linescreen of a selected object

Practice 2

In this Practice you will print a graphic using various linescreens. Start Windows and PageMaker if they have not been already.

1) *CREATE A NEW PUBLICATION*

2) *PLACE AND SIZE A GRAPHIC*

a. Place the graphic GR-TEST.TIF just below the top margin guide of the publication. Note the handles indicating the graphic is selected.
b. Use the Control palette to size the graphic so that the Width (W) and Height (H) are 200%.

3) *COPY THE GRAPHIC*

a. From the Edit menu, select the Copy command.
b. From the Edit menu, select Paste. Move the copy below the original.
c. From the Edit menu, select the Paste command. Another copy of the graphic is placed. Move the copy below the other two graphics.
d. Use the Paste command to place a fourth graphic just above the bottom margin guide.

4) *CHANGE THE LINESCREEN OF THE GRAPHICS*

a. Select the graphic at the top by clicking on it.
b. From the Element menu, select the Image control command. A dialog box is displayed.
c. Note the DFLT setting as the Screen frequency option indicating that the default linescreen for that printer will be used. Select Cancel to remove the dialog box and leave the linescreen for that graphic unchanged.
d. Click on the second graphic. Handles are displayed.
e. From the Element menu, select the Image control command.
f. Change the Screen frequency to 50. Select OK.
g. Select the third graphic.
h. Use the Image control command to change the Screen frequency to 125.
i. Change the Screen frequency of the fourth graphic to 275.

5) *PRINT THE PUBLICATION*

a. From the File menu, select the Print command. The Print document dialog box is displayed.
b. Select the Color option to display its dialog box.
c. Note the setting for the Ruling option. This is the default linescreen that will be used to print the top graphic.
d. Select Print. Note the difference in the graphics due to linescreen.

6) *SAVE THE PUBLICATION*

Save the publication as C11PRAC2.PM5.

11.6 Trapping

Trapping is a technique used to compensate for registration problems. One method of trapping involves making an overlying object slightly larger so that it will meet the underlying image even when there is a slight registration problem. For example, no trapping was used in the graphic on the left, but trapping used in the graphic on the right makes the registration problem negligible:

Trapping can reduce the need for tight registration

As you can imagine, trapping can quickly become complex. Many service bureaus have special software such as Aldus TrapWise that may be used to create traps automatically.

11.7 Color Proofs

As you have seen so far, color publications can be complex. Therefore, full-color proofs are usually used to get a good estimate of what the final product will look like before going to press. The service bureau can provide proofs in the form of overlays and integrals using the film from the imagesetter. *Overlays* are created by exposing each separation film onto four layers of colored film-like material (to represent CMYK). These are then hinged together on a piece of paper. This kind of proof offers the advantage of being able to look at the individual color layers. However, overlays may not expose registration problems and colors are only approximate. Overlays may also be referred to by common brand names: *Color-Key* and *CromaCheck.*

Although more expensive than overlays, integrals are the best way to proof color work. *Integrals* are created by replicating each piece of film onto a corresponding pigmented layer (one for each of the CMYK colors) and then laminating the layers together. Integrals are produced at a high resolution with good color accuracy. Registration problems are also revealed. *Matchprint* and *Cromalin* are trade names more commonly used to refer to integrals.

11.8 Preparing Publications for Service Bureaus

Several additional steps must be taken to prepare a publication for prepress work. However, prepress steps should not be taken until the final draft of the publication has been proofed and is exactly as desired. In addition, publications should be fully PostScript compatible since PostScript is the industry standard page description language used by imagesetters and service bureaus. For example, TrueType fonts are not always PostScript compatible and should be avoided. Graphics should be in the TIFF or EPS file format to ensure proper separation. Before preparing a publication for commercial printing, a backup should be made and stored in a safe place.

Once the publication is in its final form, a printout should be obtained from a PostScript laser printer. This serves two purposes. First, if a publication can be printed on the laser printer without generating any PostScript errors, it is likely the imagesetter will not have problems generating the publication. Second, the laser copy will serve as a proof for the service bureau to refer to during production.

The printer and service bureau must be consulted to determine in which form the publication should be output—paper or film. In either case, the information used to control the imagesetter is in the form of a PostScript file (.PS). A PageMaker publication can be converted to this file format by setting options in the Page setup and Print document dialog boxes. The Page setup command is used to define the imagesetter on which the publication will be printed. Available fonts, pre-defined paper sizes, and resolutions depend upon what has been selected for the Compose to printer option. The service bureau can tell you what options should be selected for Page, Compose to printer, and Target printer resolution. The target printer resolution will be greater because of the quality of the imagesetter. The Orientation may also change:

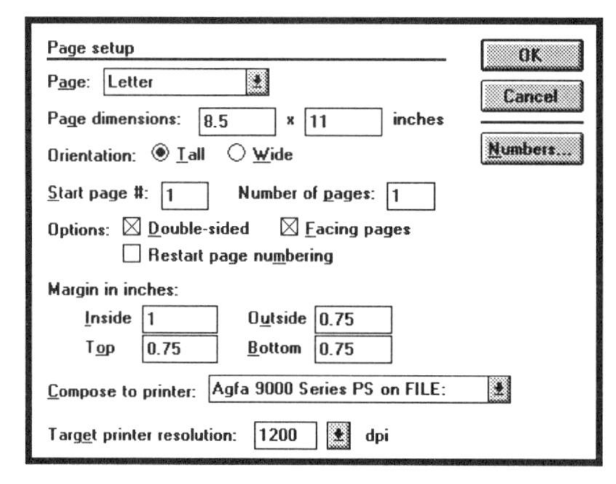

Several options in the Page Setup dialog box will be used when preparing a publication for a service bureau

Several options in the Print document dialog box are set according to specifications from the service bureau and the commercial printer. The Print to option will be set for the imagesetter—the same option used for Compose to printer in the Page setup dialog box. Type is set as specified by the service bureau. Orientation must be the same as that in the Page setup dialog box:

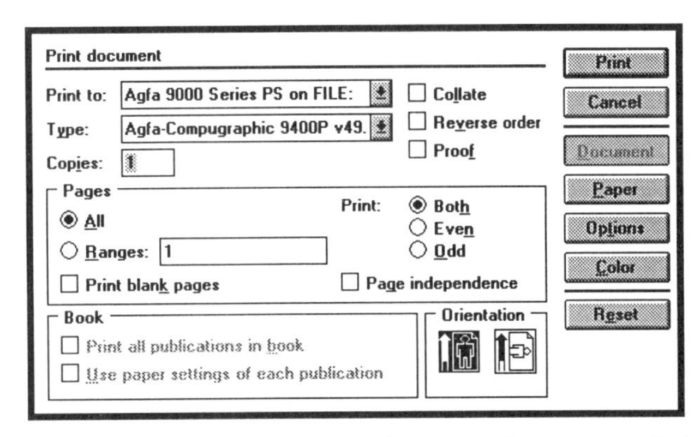

The Print to and Type options in the Print document dialog box will be set for your service bureau's imagesetter

For paper output (spot color work), the Separations option in the Color dialog box is selected. In the Ink list, only process black and any spot colors used in the publication are selected.

In addition to the options set for paper, two other options need to be considered for film. The printer will require film to be printed as "wrong reading" or "right reading", with the film's emulsion-side up or emulsion-side down. These options depend on the type of printing press used and the process used to create the printing plates. To print a publication as wrong-reading with emulsion-side down both the Mirror and Negative options must be selected in the Color dialog box. If only the Mirror option is selected, the publication is printed as right-reading, emulsion-side down. If only the Negative option is selected, the publication is printed as wrong-reading, emulsion-side up. When neither option is selected, the publication is printed as right-reading, emulsion-side up.

In the Options dialog box, Graphics is Normal or Optimized, and Printer's marks and Page information are selected in the Markings box. In the PostScript box, selecting Write PostScript to file displays the default name that will be used for the PostScript file. This file name may be changed by simply clicking in the box and typing. The service bureau may or may not need the Include downloadable fonts option selected depending upon the fonts used in the publication and how many fonts the service bureau has available.

In the Paper dialog box, Size is set as specified by the service bureau. You should expect the page size to increase to accompany printer's marks. Scale should be at 100%. Selecting the Save button saves the application as a PostScript file using the specified options.

When a job is handed off to the service bureau several steps should be taken to ensure a smooth process. In addition to the PostScript file on disk, the service bureau should be made fully aware of every option used in creating the PostScript file including the names of all fonts used in the publication. This may be done by preparing a written list of the settings used in the file. The service bureau probably has its own paperwork it will require to be filled out as well. Depending on the length of the publication, the service bureau will probably want a draft. This could be the laser copy produced prior to creating the PostScript file.

11.9 Proofing Publications

The importance of proofing publications during the development, prepress, and press stages cannot be overemphasized. The type of proofing performed is different, but equally important, at each stage.

Because changes are easiest and least expensive made during the development stage, proofing should be done in several ways throughout this stage. It is always a good idea to spell check each story using PageMaker's Story Editor, even if the text was spell checked in the word processor used to create it. Laser printouts are the best form of proof at this stage. Selecting the Proof option in the Print document dialog box produces a printed document with each graphic replaced by a box with an x in it (☒) of the same size. This kind of proof prints quickly and forces attention to be focused on the text and general layout of the publication. Another printout with the Proof option deselected permits the complete publication, with graphics in context, to be evaluated. For publications that use color, a third printout using the Separations option in the Color dialog box can verify that plates will be produced for each color as expected. The final laser proof at this stage should produce a publication that has the **exact** content and layout desired—spelling errors, misplaced graphics, and poor layout will not be a consideration beyond this stage.

The film or paper produced in the prepress stage is inspected for quality. Are there any blotches or other undesired markings on the film? Do the paper outputs contain any drop-outs or light spots where solid black ink should appear? Be sure that every page was processed. In addition, each page of the publication will have output for every spot color and process color used in the publication. For process color work, integral proofs are recommended because they will be the only way to tell how the final publication will appear.

The printer will use the prepress output to create the plates from which the publication will be printed. *Bluelines* are created from the film that will be used to make the printing press plates, and as the name indicates the publication is blue. Bluelines are inspected for problems with registration, drop-outs, and ink blotches.

Ideally, a press check can then be made during the printing of a publication. When this is done, registration, density, and color can be checked. When this option is unavailable, requesting integral proofs allows a final inspection of the product at a level closest to that of a press inspection. When spot color is used, the printer can provide a sample of the ink on a piece of the paper that will be used in the printing process. This is called a *draw down* and is usually provided at no charge.

11.10 Printing to a File

Publications being prepared for a service bureau should first be proofed using a PostScript laser printer. The laser printer also offers the highest quality output for publications that are not going to be professionally printed. To take advantage of laser printer output even when one is not immediately available, a PageMaker publication may be printed to a file. When this is done, the information normally sent to the printer is stored in a file. This information can then be copied to the appropriate printer using a DOS command to produce the publication.

Printing a publication to a file makes it possible to later print the publication even when PageMaker is not available. To print a publication to a file, both page setup and print options must be set correctly. For example, to create a file that prints a publication on a Hewlett-Packard LaserJet 4M the Page setup command is selected and HP LaserJet 4/4M PostScript is selected as Compose to printer. The Target printer resolution is set to 600. In the Print document dialog box, the Print to option needs to be set to match that in the Page setup dialog box. The Type needs to be set according to the printer used:

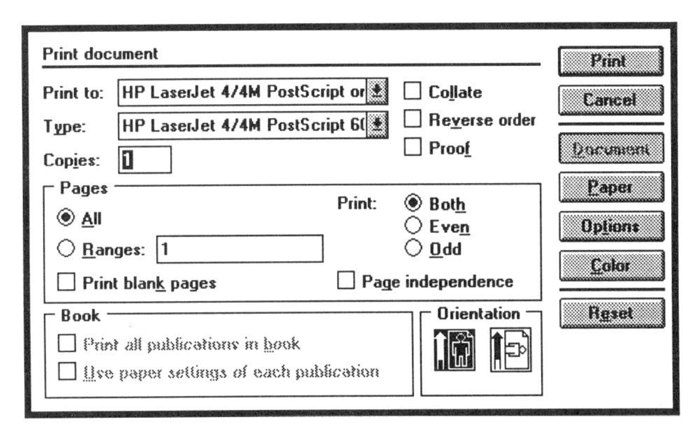

Printer options should match the one selected in the Page setup dialog box

Options

In the Options dialog box, the Write PostScript to file option is selected and a file name entered or the default used. The Include downloadable fonts option also needs to be selected. Clicking on the Save button creates a PostScript file.

Practice 3

In this Practice you will print a publication with graphics and text to a file. The file will then be copied to the printer from DOS as a test. Start PageMaker and open C11PRAC2.PM5 if it is not already.

1) CREATE A POSTSCRIPT FILE

a. From the File menu, select the Page setup command.
b. Be sure your printer is selected as the Compose to printer. Select OK to remove the dialog box.
c. From the File menu, select the Print command.
d. In the Print document dialog box, verify that the Print to and Type options are set for your printer.
e. Select the Options button to display the dialog box.
f. Click on the Write PostScript to file option. Change the file name to `\C11PRAC2.PS` (be sure to include the backslash).
g. If not already selected, click on the Normal option.
h. Select the Save button to create a PostScript file of the publication.

2) PRINT THE PUBLICATION FROM DOS

a. Save and close the publication.
b. Quit PageMaker.
c. Quit Windows. The DOS prompt should now be displayed.
d. Type `CD \` at the prompt and then press Enter to change to the root directory.
e. Type `COPY C11PRAC2.PS LPT1`. The information stored in the PostScript file is sent to the printer. After a few minutes the document printed from PageMaker in Practice 2 is again printed from the PostScript file.

11.11 Ethics and Copyrights

The scanner has made it possible to easily reproduce images electronically. In this form, an image can be included in any number of publications. However, it is not only unethical but also illegal to use someone else's artwork without their permission. It is especially easy to include clip art in a publication because it is already in electronic form, but permission must be granted for the use of this type of artwork as well.

When using information from other publications it is important to acknowledge all sources. The Copyright page is normally within the first pages of a book or publication. Permission may be sought using the information contained on the copyrighted page.

Fonts add variety and a professional look to a publication. Thousands of different fonts are available from software distributors known as font houses. As with other software, it is illegal to obtain or use copies of fonts without paying the manufacturer.

11.12 Careers in DTP

Desktop publishing incorporates both design and computer skills. However, it is good design skills that ultimately produce a successful publication. Knowing how to use the right tools, such as PageMaker, ensures the best possible implementation of a design. A career in DTP should therefore begin with an education that includes design classes as well as computer applications.

An education in desktop publishing could include several months to a few years of study at a design school or art institute. Higher level positions can be gained with an education that includes a Bachelor degree from a college, university, or art institute.

Desktop publishing jobs are available at many different kinds of companies. Work at those companies which do graphic design exclusively could include using PageMaker to create brochures and other advertising pieces. Publishing companies often have their own design division where PageMaker may be used to layout books and other publications. Working in the design division of a service bureau offers exposure to the prepress side of professional printing.

With the power available in a PC and the relatively low cost of PCs and laser printers, it is possible to have a desktop publishing career from home. Almost every business has a need for publishing promotional materials. Smaller companies are especially likely to hire consultants for their promotional needs. Publishing companies may also use consultants to perform layout. Although the home-based career can be rewarding in many ways, there are disadvantages. For example, a consultant must also take care of all the marketing and financial aspects normally handled by other departments in larger companies. The home-based desktop publisher must also usually spend a great deal of time maintaining current customers and acquiring new customers.

11.13 Future of DTP and Multimedia

Currently, most desktop publishing is done in order to produce printed publications. However, there is an ever-increasing trend towards electronic documents including publications on CD-ROM. With the storage capacity of the CD (typically 600 megabytes), it is possible to provide fully formatted, graphic-rich documents that may also include video and sound.

The development of electronic document delivery (EDD) applications such as *Adobe Acrobat* also encourage viewing documents in electronic rather than printed format. *EDD* systems allow documents to be viewed on the computer as originally formatted without needing the application used to create them.

Another area of desktop publishing lies in presentations. Traditional slide shows may now be done using desktop publishing software and a computer to project images onto a screen. This opens the development of presentations to many new areas of layout and design.

Technologies such as computing, communications, and imaging (print and video) are merging so that we will no longer be able to identify one from the other. *Hypermedia* or *multimedia* is an example where graphics, video, and sound are accessible together through a computer. An exciting application of hypermedia is a computerized encyclopedia where the user can access an entry that includes different types of linked information. When accessing an entry on Ludwig von Beethoven the user might be asked if she would like to see a picture of Ludwig, hear a selection from his ninth symphony, or take a tour of his house in Vienna. Hypermedia allows the user to interactively browse through a world of text, sound, and video accessing a very broad array of information. The possible applications of hypermedia are boundless and include computerized repair manuals where the user could, for example, ask for information on an automobile transmission and then access different videos that demonstrate how a certain type of repair is performed. Educational training might include instruction in a foreign language where the student could request to read a word, hear how the word is pronounced, and then ask to see a person holding a conversation that includes the word.

11.14 Where can you go from here?

This chapter has introduced you to some of the prepress services used to produce a professionally printed publication. For more information on service bureaus and how to prepare a PageMaker publication for printing, refer to the Aldus Users Manual and Commercial Printing Guide.

Service bureaus and professional printers are also a source of information. Many provide pamphlets with information about their services, and general information about the prepress and printing processes. Information about newer processes such as creating printing plates directly from digital information, using more than four process colors in the color printing, and the creation of digital color proofs can also be obtained.

Throughout this text, the basics of good design have been emphasized in addition to teaching you PageMaker. To read more about design as it relates to desktop publishing, refer to journals such as *Aldus Magazine*, *Publish*, and *Before and After*. These magazines will often have articles specifically about PageMaker as well.

The Aldus Additions reference manual contains information about the other additions found in the Utilities menu. Like the Drop cap addition, there are many other Additions that perform several actions using a single command, and some of these are specifically geared towards preparing publications for commercial printing.

Chapter Summary

In PageMaker it is possible to have more than one file open at a time, each in its own window. When multiple publication windows are open, objects such as graphics or text blocks may be dragged and dropped between them. The Copy and Paste commands from the Edit menu can be used to copy specific information from a text object and paste it in another publication.

Service bureaus image paper or film using the information contained in a desktop publishing file. The paper or film that has been imaged is used by a commercial printer to produce the plates necessary for printing.

High resolution photos may be included in a publication by scanning. Once in digital format, the photo is imaged to film. Strippers then place the high-resolution negative in the appropriate place of the publication.

Halftones are used to represent color and shades of grey in the printing process. A halftone element is made up of printer dots. The number of printer dots in a halftone element varies depending on the resolution of the printer and the linescreen used.

Trapping is performed to compensate for registration problems and involves making an overlying object slightly larger than the underlying object.

Color proofs are commonly in the form of either overlay or integral proofs. A publication may also be proofed using laser printouts. Bluelines are used to proof the film that will be used to create the printing plates.

A publication may be prepared for a service bureau by creating a PostScript file. Several options in the Page setup and Print document dialog boxes are used to create the PostScript file. The service bureau should be consulted to determine the exact settings.

A PageMaker publication may be printed to a file. The PostScript file can then be copied to a printer from DOS to produce the printed publication.

Although electronic images are easily reproduced, it is unethical and illegal to use artwork without permission. Permission must also be granted to use information from other publications. It is also illegal to make copies of fonts or other software without paying the manufacturer.

Although printed documents are the primary output of desktop publishing, publications on CD are increasing in popularity. Electronic document delivery (EDD) offers a way to display a document on the computer no matter what application was used to create it. Presentations are another area in which desktop publishing may be utilized. Multimedia or hypermedia brings text, graphics, sound, and video together using the computer.

Vocabulary

Active publication - The file currently being worked on. The active publication is indicated by a highlighted Title bar.

Blueline - Proof created from the film that will be used to create the printing plates.

Capstan imagesetter - An imagesetter which operates by pulling paper or film past a laser light source. See also Imagesetter.

Cascade - To arrange open publication windows so that the Title bar of each is visible, but only the active window is not obscured.

Drag and drop - A technique used to copy an object. The mouse is used to drag an object, such as a graphic or text block, from one open publication window to another.

Draw down - A spot color sample placed on the paper to be used in the printing of a publication. Usually provided by the printer at no charge.

Drum imagesetter - An imagesetter which operates by exposing paper or film that has been rolled around a drum to a laser light source. See also Imagesetter.

Drum scanner - A high-resolution scanner used to convert photographs or other artwork to digital format.

EDD - Electronic Document delivery. A system which documents to viewed on the computer without requiring the software used to create them.

Film - One form of output used by an imagesetter.

FPO - For Position Only. Placeholders which will be cut from a publication. Often consisting of low-resolution scans or labeled boxes.

Halftone - Used to represent (simulate) continuous-tone color or shades of grey in the printing process. Consists of groups of printer dots.

Hypermedia - Graphics, video, text, and sound accessed together. Also called multimedia.

Imagesetter - A device which operates similarly to a laser printer by digitally controlled a laser light source to expose photosensitive paper or film. Used to create a high-resolution image of a PageMaker file. See also Capstan imagesetter and Drum imagesetter.

Integral Proof - Pigmented layers corresponding to each piece of film are laminated together to form a color proof. Also called Matchprint and Cromalin.

Linescreen - The number of lines per inch where each line consists of halftone elements.

Overlay proof - A color proof in which each separation film is hinged together. Also called Color-Key and CromaCheck.

PostScript - Industry standard page description language.

Prepress service - See Service bureau.

PS file - PostScript file created using options in the Page setup and Print document dialog boxes.

Repro - Photosensitive paper used in the imaging process.

Service bureau - A company which uses an imagesetter to create a high-resolution image of a desktop publishing file on photosensitive paper or film. See also Prepress service, Imagesetter, Stripping, Trapping, Integral, and Overlay proof.

Stripping - To place a high-resolution at a specified in a document that been imaged to film. Offered by service bureaus.

Tile - To arrange open publication windows so that each is equally visible.

Trapping - A technique in which an overlying object is made slightly larger so that it will meet the underlying object even when registration is off slightly.

Window menu - Lists all the currently open files.

Reviews

Sections 11.1 — 11.2

1. a) What is a publication window?
   b) What steps are required to switch from one window to another window?

2. a) What is meant by cascading windows? How are windows cascaded?
   b) What is meant by tiling windows? How are windows tiled?

3. a) How can an object be copied from one open window to another?
   b) What is this called?

Sections 11.3 — 11.7

4. a) What is the main function of a service bureau?
   b) Name three other services provided by a service bureau.

5. What is an imagesetter used for?

6. What is the difference between a capstan and drum imagesetter?

7. What are the two forms of output from an imagesetter?

8. What is a drum scanner used for?

9. Describe the steps necessary to include a high-resolution photo in a publication.

10. Describe the process used to strip-in photos.

11. What are FPO copies used for?

12. a) What are halftones used for?
    b) What are halftone elements composed of?

13. How are halftones different from continuous-tone art?

14. a) What is meant by linescreen?
    b) How does linescreen affect the way a graphic is printed?

15. Why is trapping performed?

16. Why are color proofs useful?

17. a) What is an overlay proof?
    b) What is an integral proof?
    c) Which kind of proof is better for determining registration problems?

Sections 11.8 — 11.10

18. Describe some of the options that will need to be set when preparing a publication for the service bureau.

19. Why should the final version of a publication be printed on a PostScript laser printer?

20. What are the Mirror and Negative options in the Print document dialog box used for?

21. Why should the service bureau be made fully aware of every option set when handing off a publication?

22. Why is it important to carefully proof during the development stage?

23. a) What are bluelines used for?
    b) What should bluelines be checked for?

24. What is a draw down?

25. How can a publication be printed on a laser printer even when PageMaker is not available on the computer with the laser printer attached?

Sections 11.11 — 11.14

26. Does permission need to be granted for the use of clip art? Why?

27. How can you get permission to reuse information printed in a book or magazine in another publication?

28. a) Name three different kinds of businesses that might employ desktop publishers.
    b) Describe the uses desktop publishing would have in the three companies described in part (a).

29. Name three ways in which desktop publishing could be used other than for printed publications.

30. a) What is EDD?
    b) How is EDD related to desktop publishing?

31. Describe hypermedia.

Appendix A
The Windows Environment

Microsoft Windows, which PageMaker requires in order to run, is a special kind of program known as a *graphical user interface*, or GUI (pronounced "gooey"). When a GUI is running it provides the user with pictures called *icons* that are used to run other programs.

The Windows GUI is appropriately named because related icons are grouped together and placed in their own area of the screen called a *window*. The Program Manager is the main window from which all programs are run and managed. Its properties are the same as those of all windows and include a Control-menu button, zoom buttons, and a Title bar. Most windows also contain a Menu bar and scroll bars:

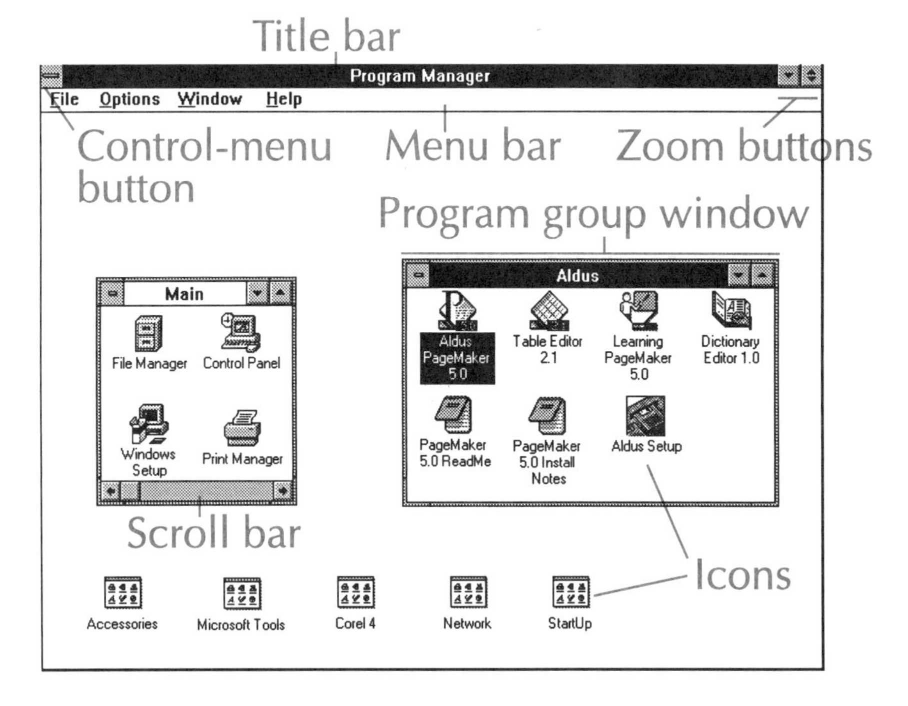

The Program Manager window

Using Windows

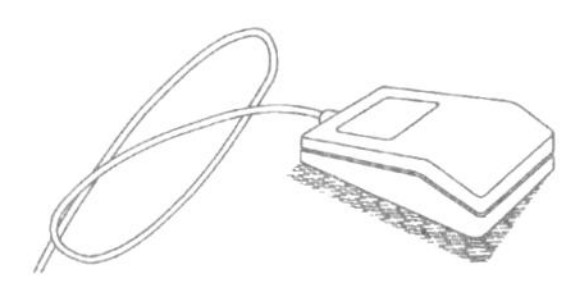

Because Windows is a GUI, a special input device called the *mouse* is usually used with it. When the mouse is in use, an arrow called the mouse pointer is displayed on the screen:

The four actions performed with a mouse are pointing, clicking, double-clicking, and dragging. To *point* to an object the mouse is moved along the top of the table until the mouse pointer is on that object. *Clicking* means to quickly press and then release the left mouse button. *Double-clicking* requires pressing the left mouse button twice in rapid succession. *Dragging* is performed by pressing and holding the left mouse button while moving the mouse.

A window may be moved, sized, scrolled, and closed. *Moving* simply changes a window's location on the screen. *Sizing* changes the amount of information a window can display. When only part of a window's contents is visible, scroll bars are displayed enabling other portions of a window's contents to be viewed by *scrolling*. When a window is *closed*, any program that was running in it is automatically concluded and the window is removed from the screen. The mouse may be used to perform each of these tasks as described below.

A window is moved by dragging on its Title bar which displays a grey outline. When the mouse button is released the window moves to the position of the outline:

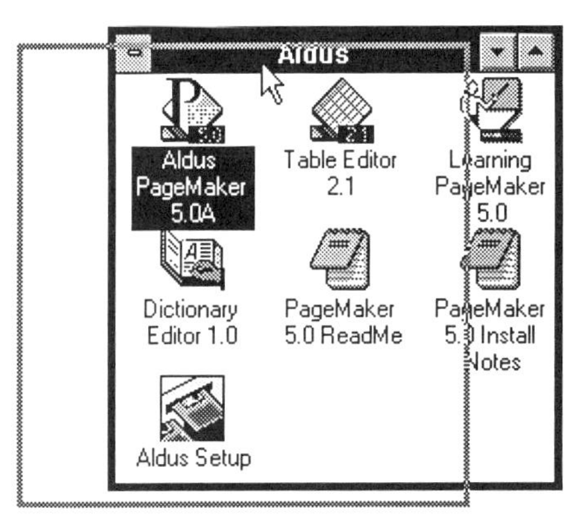

A window may be moved anywhere on the screen

Pointing to the border of a window changes the mouse pointer shape to a double-headed arrow. Dragging when the double-headed arrow is displayed creates a grey outline. When the mouse button is released, the window changes to the size of the outline:

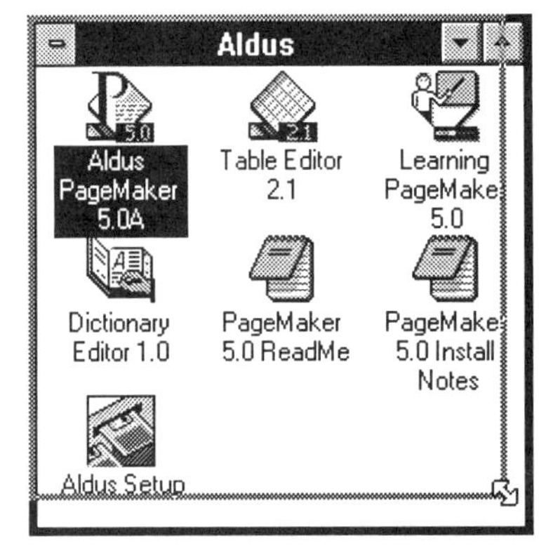

The window will be the size of the grey border when the mouse button is released

The zoom buttons in the upper-right corner consist of a Maximize and a Minimize button which are used for automatic sizing:

Maximize button

Minimize button

Clicking on the *Maximize button* expands the window to the size of the screen. In a maximized window the Maximize button is replaced with a *Restore button* which when clicked returns a window to its original size:

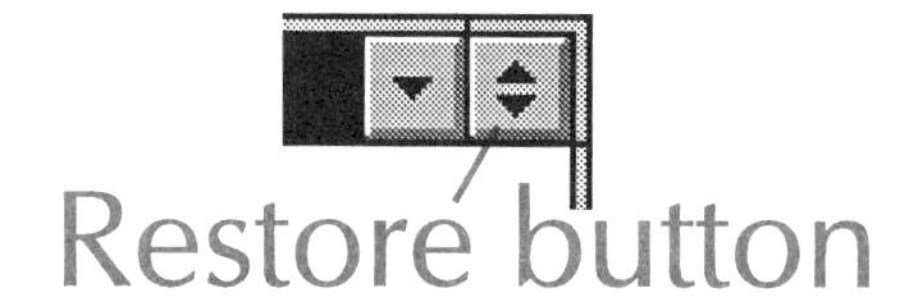

Clicking on the *Minimize button* reduces the window to an icon—a small graphic:

The Aldus group icon

In the graphic above, the minimized window displays its name below the icon. Double-clicking on a minimized window's icon restores it.

When the contents of a window cannot be displayed entirely within its boundaries, scroll bars are displayed. Clicking on the arrow buttons at the top or bottom of the vertical scroll bar scrolls vertically. Similarly, to scroll horizontally through a window's contents, the left and right arrow buttons on the horizontal scroll bar are used:

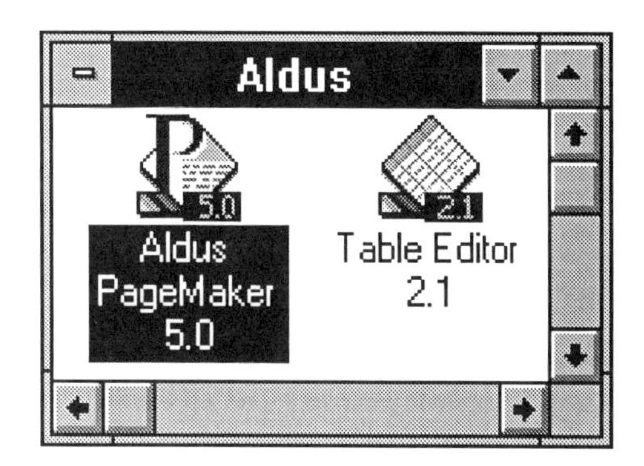

Clicking on the right arrow button displays the icons to the right

A window is closed by double-clicking on its Control-menu button, sometimes called the *Close box*. It is important to understand the difference between a window that has been closed and one that has been minimized. A closed window can no longer be accessed; the application it held is no longer running. However, a minimized window's application is still running. Restoring the minimized window shows the application running within it at the point before the window was reduced to an icon.

A *selected* icon is designated by a highlighted icon label. An icon is selected by pointing to it and then clicking once. Double-clicking on an icon executes the command it represents. For example, double-clicking on the Aldus PageMaker 5.0 icon runs the PageMaker program.

Menus and Dialog boxes

The *menu bar* which runs along the top of a window displays the names of menus. A *menu* is a list of commands and is displayed by clicking on its name. The keyboard may also be used to display a menu by using the `Alt` key in conjunction with the underlined letter in the menu name. For example, pressing and holding the `Alt` key while pressing the `F` key (written as `Alt+F`) displays the File menu:

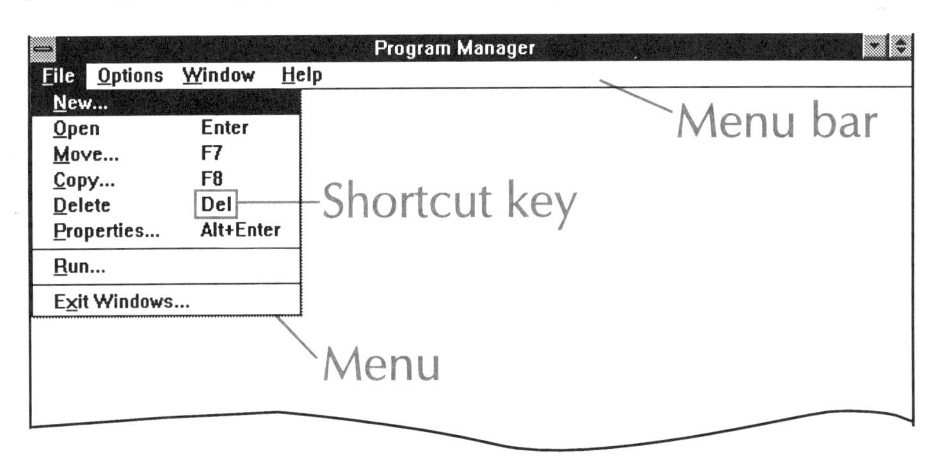

All Windows programs have Menu bars and Menus

New, Run, and Exit Windows are some of the commands listed in this menu. A command may be selected in three ways: clicking on the command with the mouse, highlighting it using arrow keys and pressing Enter, or pressing the underlined letter, for example, `x` for Exit Windows. In the menu above, the New command is selected. Pressing Enter would then execute this command. Frequently used commands have shortcuts which allow the command to be executed without first displaying the menu. Next to the Open command is the word Enter which means that pressing the Enter key will start the application associated with the selected icon.

Clicking once on the Control-menu button in the upper-left corner of the window displays its menu which includes a Restore, Minimize, and Maximize command. The Control menu may also be displayed by pressing `Alt+Spacebar`. Clicking once on a minimized window displays its Control menu. Pressing `Alt+Spacebar` also displays a selected icon's Control menu.

The Help menu is available on every menu bar. This menu has many useful commands that may be used to find information on a particular feature in Windows.

An ellipsis (...) following a menu command indicates that a dialog box will be displayed when the command is executed. A *dialog box* is a group of options from which you may choose. Its purpose is to supply the information Windows or applications running under Windows needs to execute a command. For example, executing the Exit Windows command displays the following dialog box:

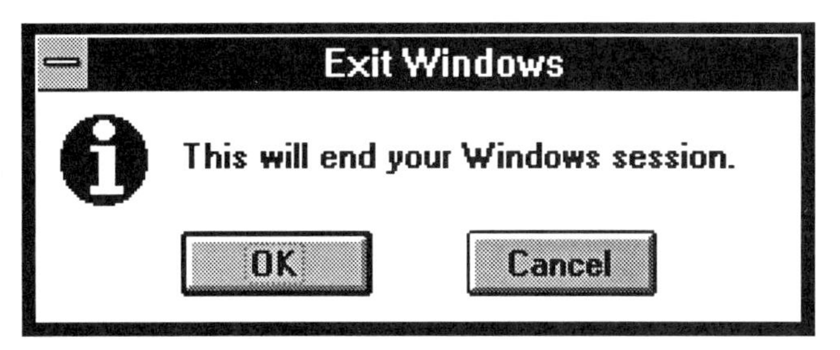

Most dialog boxes have the OK and Cancel options

In the Exit Windows dialog box, OK and Cancel are examples of *buttons*. Clicking on OK quits Windows. Cancel removes the dialog box and does not execute the selected command. The Escape key may also be pressed to Cancel a dialog box.

Other dialog box options are radio buttons, check boxes, lists, and collapsible lists. Examples of each of these options are present in the following dialog box:

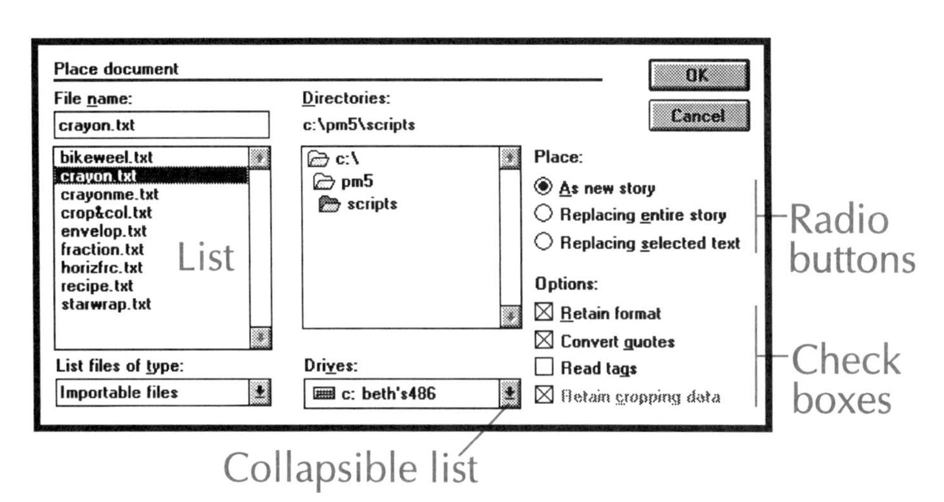

Where *radio buttons* are used to indicate an option, only one can be selected from the group. Any number of *check boxes* may be selected at one time. A *list* is a group of items from which you may choose. Lists are usually scrollable because they may contain more information than can be displayed. Clicking on the triangle in a *collapsible list* displays its contents:

Drives:
c: beth's486
a:
b:

An item in a collapsible list is selected by clicking on it

B

Appendix B
PostScript Character Set & Font Samples

You learned in Chapter Six that in order to choose a dingbat, you need to know what characters are available, and which ASCII code to type. The file CHARSET.PT5 displays all of the available characters for any font in your system. Below are listed the standard characters for most text (i.e., non-dingbat) fonts:

032	*space*	070	F	108	l	146	’	184	¸	222	Þ
033	!	071	G	109	m	147	“	185	¹	223	ß
034	"	072	H	110	n	148	”	186	º	224	à
035	#	073	I	111	o	149	•	187	»	225	á
036	$	074	J	112	p	150	–	188	¼	226	â
037	%	075	K	113	q	151	—	189	½	227	ã
038	&	076	L	114	r	152	˜	190	¾	228	ä
039	'	077	M	115	s	153	™	191	¿	229	å
040	(	078	N	116	t	154	š	192	À	230	æ
041	)	079	O	117	u	155	›	193	Á	231	ç
042	*	080	P	118	v	156	œ	194	Â	232	è
043	+	081	Q	119	w	157	•	195	Ã	233	é
044	,	082	R	120	x	158	•	196	Ä	234	ê
045	-	083	S	121	y	159	Ÿ	197	Å	235	ë
046	.	084	T	122	z	160		198	Æ	236	ì
047	/	085	U	123	{	161	¡	199	Ç	237	í
048	0	086	V	124	|	162	¢	200	È	238	î
049	1	087	W	125	}	163	£	201	É	239	ï
050	2	088	X	126	~	164	¤	202	Ê	240	ð
051	3	089	Y	127	•	165	¥	203	Ë	241	ñ
052	4	090	Z	128	•	166	¦	204	Ì	242	ò
053	5	091	[	129	•	167	§	205	Í	243	ó
054	6	092	\	130	‚	168	¨	206	Î	244	ô
055	7	093	]	131	ƒ	169	©	207	Ï	245	õ
056	8	094	^	132	„	170	ª	208	Ð	246	ö
057	9	095	_	133	…	171	«	209	Ñ	247	÷
058	:	096	`	134	†	172	¬	210	Ò	248	ø
059	;	097	a	135	‡	173	-	211	Ó	249	ù
060	<	098	b	136	ˆ	174	®	212	Ô	250	ú
061	=	099	c	137	‰	175	¯	213	Õ	251	û
062	>	100	d	138	Š	176	°	214	Ö	252	ü
063	?	101	e	139	‹	177	±	215	×	253	ý
064	@	102	f	140	Œ	178	²	216	Ø	254	þ
065	A	103	g	141	•	179	³	217	Ù	255	ÿ
066	B	104	h	142	•	180	´	218	Ú		
067	C	105	i	143	•	181	µ	219	Û		
068	D	106	j	144	•	182	¶	220	Ü		
069	E	107	k	145	‘	183	·	221	Ý		

Characters before 32 are not normally used. Characters showing a bullet (•) are undefined.

Characters without a keyboard equivalent (e.g., £) are called *extended characters* and are entered by first creating an insertion point with the Text tool, then holding down the `Alt` key while typing 0 and the three digit ASCII code on the numeric keypad. The code must be typed on the numeric keypad, not the numbers above the letter keys, and must contain all three digits. For example, placing character number 63 requires holding down the `Alt` key and typing the number `0063` on the numeric keypad (`Alt+0 063`).

Keyboard Shortcuts for Extended Characters

There are keyboard shortcuts for some common extended characters:

•	Bullet	`Ctrl+Shift+8`
®	Registered	`Ctrl+Shift+G`
©	Copyright	`Ctrl+Shift+O`
—	M dash (em dash)	`Ctrl+Shift+=`
–	N dash (en dash)	`Ctrl+=`
‘	Open single quote	`Ctrl+[`
’	Close single quote	`Ctrl+]`
“	Open double quote	`Ctrl+Shift+[`
”	Close double quote	`Ctrl+Shift+]`

The four quotes above are called *typographer's quotes* or *curly quotes*. When you import a document PageMaker automatically changes regular (straight) quotes into their typographer's equivalent. However, when you enter text directly into the publication with the keyboard, you will have to use these keyboard shortcuts.

Standard PostScript Typefaces

PostScript printers come with 35 standard fonts built in. Samples of each of these fonts is given below. (Note that not all faces have bold or italic styles.) Examples of some other font are shown on pages 5-27 and 5-28.

Avant Garde — Normal **Bold** *Italic* ***Bold & Italic*** Under
ABCDEFGHIJKLMNOPQRSTUVWXYZ SMALL CAPS
abcdefghijklmnopqrstuvwxyz 1234567890 @#$%&*?
"Now is the time for all good men and women to come to the aid of the party!" the Boxing Wizard said quietly.

B

Bookman — Normal **Bold** *Italic* ***Bold & Italic*** Under
ABCDEFGHIJKLMNOPQRSTUVWXYZ SMALL CAPS
abcdefghijklmnopqrstuvwxyz 1234567890 @#$%&*?
"Now is the time for all good men and women to come to the aid of the party!" the Boxing Wizard said quietly.

Courier – Normal **Bold** *Italic* ***Bold & Italic*** Under
ABCDEFGHIJKLMNOPQRSTUVWXYZ SMALL CAPS
abcdefghijklmnopqrstuvwxyz 1234567890 @#$%&*?
"Now is the time for all good men and women to come to the aid of the party!" the Boxing Wizard said quietly.

Helvetica — Normal **Bold** *Italic* ***Bold & Italic*** Under
ABCDEFGHIJKLMNOPQRSTUVWXYZ SMALL CAPS
abcdefghijklmnopqrstuvwxyz 1234567890 @#$%&*?
"Now is the time for all good men and women to come to the aid of the party!" the Boxing Wizard said quietly.

Helvetica Narrow — Normal **Bold** *Italic* ***Bold & Italic*** Under
ABCDEFGHIJKLMNOPQRSTUVWXYZ SMALL CAPS
abcdefghijklmnopqrstuvwxyz 1234567890 @#$%&*?
"Now is the time for all good men and women to come to the aid of the party!" the Boxing Wizard said quietly.

New Century Schoolbook — Normal **Bold** *Italic* ***Bold & Italic*** Under
ABCDEFGHIJKLMNOPQRSTUVWXYZ SMALL CAPS
abcdefghijklmnopqrstuvwxyz 1234567890 @#$%&*?
"Now is the time for all good men and women to come to the aid of the party!" the Boxing Wizard said quietly.

Palatino — Normal **Bold** *Italic* ***Bold & Italic*** Under
ABCDEFGHIJKLMNOPQRSTUVWXYZ SMALL CAPS
abcdefghijklmnopqrstuvwxyz 1234567890 @#$%&*?
"Now is the time for all good men and women to come to the aid of the party!" the Boxing Wizard said quietly.

Symbol – Νορμαλ **Βολδ** *Ιταλιχ* ***Βολδ & Ιταλιχ*** Υνδερ
ΑΒΧΔΕΦΓΗΙϑΚΛΜΝΟΠΘΡΣΤΥςΩΞΨΖ ΣΜΑΛΛ ΧΑΠΣ
αβχδεφγηιφκλμνοπθρστυϖωξψζ 1234567890 ≅#∃%&∗?
Νοω ισ τηε τιμε φορ αλλ γοοδ μεν ανδ ωομεν το χομε το τηε αιδ οφ τηε παρτψ! τηε Βοξινγ Ωιζαρδ σαιδ θυιετλψ.

Times (Roman) — Normal **Bold** *Italic* ***Bold & Italic*** Under
ABCDEFGHIJKLMNOPQRSTUVWXYZ SMALL CAPS
abcdefghijklmnopqrstuvwxyz 1234567890 @#$%&*?
"Now is the time for all good men and women to come to the aid of the party!" the Boxing Wizard said quietly.

Zapf Chancery — Normal ***Bold*** *Italic* ***Bold & Italic*** *Under*
ABCDEFGHIJKLMNOPQRSTUVWXYZ SMALL CAPS
abcdefghijklmnopqrstuvwxyz 1234567890 @#$%&?*
"Now is the time for all good men and women to come to the aid of the party!" the Boxing Wizard said quietly.

Zapf Dingbats – ✮❏❐❍✿● ✢●❄ ☆▼✿● ✢✆☆ ✳■❄
✡✢✣✤✥✦✧★☆✪✫✬✭✮✯✰✱✲✳✴✵✶✷✸✹
✿❀❁❂❃❄❅❆❇❈❉❊✱●❍■❏❐❑❒▲▼◆❖◗❘❙
➾➪✓✔✕✖✗✘✙✏ ✠✁✂✆☎✆☛✝
✮❏◗ ❄▲ ▼❄❄ ▼❄❍❄ ❄❏❐ ✿●● ❄❏❏❄ ❍❄■ ✿■❄
◗❏❍❄■ ▼❏ ❄❏❍❄ ▼❏ ▼❄❄ ✿❄❄ ❏❄ ▼❄❄ ❐✿❐▼❙✁
▼❄❄ ✢❏❄■❄ ✱❄❙✿❐❄ ▲✿❄❄ ❏◆❄❄▼●❙✎

In addition, Windows 3.1 supplies several other typefaces:

Arial — Normal **Bold** *Italic* ***Bold & Italic*** Under
ABCDEFGHIJKLMNOPQRSTUVWXYZ SMALL CAPS
abcdefghijklmnopqrstuvwxyz 1234567890 @#$%&*?
"Now is the time for all good men and women to come to the aid of the party!" the Boxing Wizard said quietly.

Times New Roman — Normal **Bold** *Italic* ***Bold & Italic*** Under
ABCDEFGHIJKLMNOPQRSTUVWXYZ SMALL CAPS
abcdefghijklmnopqrstuvwxyz 1234567890 @#$%&*?
"Now is the time for all good men and women to come to the aid of the party!" the Boxing Wizard said quietly.

Wingdings – ☠□❐❍ ✌●♎ ✋♦♋● ✌📖✋ ✞■♎
✌👌👍👎☜☞☝☟✋☺😐☹💣☠⚐🏱✈☼💧❄✞✞✠✠✡☪
♋♌♍♎♏♐♑♒♓🙰🙵●❍■□◻❑❒⬧⧫◆❖⬥⌧⍓⌘
📁📄📄🗐▯⌛⌨🖰✆🕿🗀 ✍✂✍🔔📖✉✍
➑☠□⬥ ♓⬥ ⧫♒♏ ⧫♓❍♏ ♐□❐ ♋●● ♑□□♎
❍♏■ ♋■♎ ⬥□❍♏■ ⧫□ ♍□❍♏ ⧫□ ⧫♒♏
♋♓♎ □♐ ⧫♒♏ ◻♋❐⧫⍓✏➒ ⧫♒♏
✌□⌧♓■♑ ✠♓⌘♋❐♎ ⬥♋♓♎ ❑◆♓♏⧫●⍓✍

For decorative fonts like Symbol, Zapf Dingbats, and WingDings, use the CHARSET.PT5 file to printout a complete character set. Instructions for using CHARSET are included on the Pasteboard of that file.

Index

C

D

E

F

G

H

I

J

K

L

M

N

O

P

R

S

T

I

U

V

W

X

Y

Z